The Politics of
State Feminism

D1715541

The Politics of State Feminism

Innovation in Comparative Research

Dorothy E. McBride
Amy G. Mazur

With contributions by
JONI LOVENDUSKI, JOYCE OUTSHOORN,
BIRGIT SAUER, AND MARILA GUADAGNINI

TEMPLE UNIVERSITY PRESS PHILADELPHIA

Dorothy E. McBride is Professor Emerita of Political Science at Florida Atlantic University.

Amy G. Mazur is a Professor in the Department of Political Science at Washington State University. She received the Midwest Political Science Association Women's Caucus Professional Achievement Award in 2011.

TEMPLE UNIVERSITY PRESS
Philadelphia, Pennsylvania 19122
www.temple.edu/tempress

Copyright © 2010 by Temple University
All rights reserved
Published 2010
Paperback edition published 2012

Library of Congress Cataloging-in-Publication Data

McBride, Dorothy E.
   The politics of state feminism : innovation in comparative research / Dorothy E. McBride and Amy G. Mazur; with contributions by Joni Lovenduski . . . [et al.].
      p. cm.
   Includes bibliographical references and index.
   ISBN 978-1-4399-0207-3 (cloth : alk. paper) — ISBN 978-1-4399-0209-7 (e-book)
   1. Feminism—Political aspects. 2. Women's rights. 3. Women—Government policy. I. Mazur, Amy. II. Lovenduski, Joni. III. Title.
   HQ1236.M375 2010
   305.42—dc22

                                                                    2010010613

ISBN 978-1-4399-0208-0 (paperback : alk. paper)

♾ The paper used in this publication meets the requirements of the American National Standard for Information Sciences—Permanence of Paper for Printed Library Materials, ANSI Z39.48-1992

Printed in the United States of America

2 4 6 8 9 7 5 3 1

To our mothers

Contents

PART IV Conclusion

Methods Appendices

The mixed-methods approach used in this book has produced an array of data analyses, including descriptive statistics, correlations and ordinal regression, QCA truth tables and solutions, and detailed measures of concepts and variables. Although the volume of these materials precluded their inclusion in the published book, they are readily available at http://libarts.wsu.edu/polisci/rngs/ appendices.html under the title *The Politics of State Feminism Methods Appendices*. The materials are organized by chapter. Throughout the book, they are referred to as Web Appendices.

Preface

This volume, *The Politics of State Feminism*, is the culmination of fifteen years of work by more than forty researchers in thirteen countries. The collective odyssey began when a critical mass of researchers working on gender politics and the state became interested in doing a systematic study of government agencies established to address women's status and gender equality. This first scholarly collaboration produced *Comparative State Feminism* in 1995 and then led to the establishment of the Research Network on Gender Politics and the State (RNGS) that same year (http://libarts.wsu.edu/polisci/rngs/). Since then, the network has produced five issue books, a follow-up book to *Comparative State Feminism*, and a comprehensive dataset. *The Politics of State Feminism* uses the RNGS study as a launching pad to show to what extent and why women's policy agencies bring about positive state responses to movement claims that expand women's representation.

This work is the capstone of the RNGS study; however, its focus and approach are broader than RNGS and should be seen as part of a larger scholarly project on state feminism. The central focus of RNGS was the interface between movements and agencies. The network researchers developed a complex analytical approach and model to analyze agencies' influences on women's movement access and policy. Developing a theory of state feminism was not their major goal. Indeed, the RNGS documents and books use the notion of state feminism in a variety of ways: as a term to describe women's policy agencies and as a label to identify the agencies most friendly to the women's movement. It was not until the end of the RNGS study, ironically, that it became clear that state feminism was explicitly about the movement-agency nexus. Thus, this book builds from RNGS work, taking it a step further into systematic empirical theory building across all of the issue areas covered in the project.

The data used in this book come from the qualitative studies of policy debates across thirteen countries published in the five issue books. These cases describe the activities of women's movement actors and women's policy agencies and the results they achieved. The RNGS dataset, available on the RNGS Web site, is also based on those original process-tracing studies. The dataset comprises information on 120 variables for 130 policy debates. In this book, authors have repackaged these original measures into several new datasets appropriate to the specific research questions, propositions, and methods selected for study. In addition, the qualitative studies are the basis for several detailed case studies presented throughout the book.

The Politics of State Feminism uses RNGS's innovative approach, which combines qualitative and quantitative components in its design: in-depth, primary research on cases according to a uniform causal model. Going beyond RNGS, this book sets forth an explicit theoretical framework about state feminism and uses an integrated mixed-methods approach to explore and test the propositions from that framework. These methods are statistical inference, crisp-set Qualitative Comparative Analysis, and causal-mechanism case studies. The goal is to develop an empirically based theory of state feminism.

The idea of bridging the quantitative/qualitative methodological divide, so central to RNGS, has carried over into this capstone study through the rigorous conceptualization of major ideas that compose the theoretical framework. We take a qualitative approach to concept construction, considering the cultural meaning and detailed dimensions before operationalizing core concepts with valid and reliable measures. These concepts, first presented in Chapter 2, derive from in-depth discussions among members in the RNGS project. Throughout the theory-building process, in RNGS and in this capstone endeavor, we have sought to have a dialogue with feminist and non-feminist scholars, taking into consideration the degree to which "mainstream" political science has ignored insights from gender scholarship. Thus, this project is innovative for taking an integrated mixed-methods approach while operationalizing feminist theory and using gender as a significant component of the analysis.

Another innovation of RNGS and of this book is the way countries are considered. From the beginning, a question of research was whether movement and agency relations would follow patterns across specific policy sectors: The universe of policy debates pertained to five different issues—abortion, prostitution, political representation, job training, and priority topics of the 1990s, called "hot issues." By making policy debates rather than countries the units of analysis, the design of the study also provided a way to assess country, versus region, versus sectoral patterns. Readers who are looking for neat country-based analyses of state feminism will therefore be disappointed. In both our treatment of state feminism theory and unpacking state feminism, we compare the policy debates in terms of countries, but also decades, sectors, and regions.

Despite the absence of a country-specific logic to the overall analysis, readers can find information and analysis on all thirteen countries in the study, both systematically and as illustrative examples. The list of 130 debates covered in the book is presented in Table 1.2. Thirty debates are covered in descriptive and theory-building case studies, and eleven women's policy agencies receive detailed treatment as well. For those who want to go directly to the specifics of these cases, consult the index under the name of the country. There are case studies of ten abortion debates, nine prostitution debates, five political representation debates, four job training debates, and two hot-issue debates. These case studies cover policy debates in each of the thirteen countries: France (three), the Netherlands (three), Ireland (one), Germany (four), Finland (one), Canada (two), United States (two), Italy (three), Sweden (three), Austria (four), Great Britain (one), Belgium (two), and Spain (one). Chapter 3 provides an overview of all of the women's policy agencies covered in the debate analyses, again in this same cross-national, cross-temporal, and cross-sectoral logic, with detailed information presented on eleven agencies at the national or sub-national level in Austria, Canada, Finland, Sweden, and the United States. In Chapter 4, we provide an analysis of the record of democratization in each country in the study through an examination of women's movement success and the role of agencies in that success, and in Chapters 7, 9, and 10 analyses of trends within the countries.

The Politics of State Feminism is not about gender, politics, and the state outside of the postindustrial West. Early in the project, RNGS decided to take a mid-range approach, given that the levels of high economic and political development found in the West have produced similar settings for women's movements, feminism, and the policy agencies. Seeking a shared cultural foundation for the research also necessitated excluding countries that had reached similar levels of development with significantly different cultural dynamics. The final theoretical conclusions we make, therefore, apply only to state feminism in the Western World. We leave it to experts of gender politics outside of the West to examine the theory and methods, to put these conclusions to the test, and to determine whether state feminism even makes sense in other cultural, economic, and political settings.

similarity

Given the genesis of the state feminism project and this book's close ties to the RNGS project, we must recognize that without the work of each of the forty-three members of the network, none of this would have been possible. They actively participated at numerous research meetings, where the realities of fieldwork met the exigencies of the design of the project and tough discussions about conceptualization took place. Their names and affiliations can be found on the RNGS Web site, and many of their published chapters are cited throughout the book. These researchers undertook the labor-intensive collection of data in their countries to conduct the process-tracing case studies published in the issue books and used in our presentation of the thirty theory-building case studies in the book. RNGS members also provided additional detailed data to supplement their qualitative case analyses when we turned to converting RNGS findings into a numerical dataset, in some cases five years after the original research had been conducted.

Joni Lovenduski, Joyce Outshoorn, Birgit Sauer, and Marila Guadagnini all played key leadership roles in RNGS and carried their devotion to a new level in planning and executing this book. While Dorothy McBride and Amy Mazur are the co-authors of the book as a whole and also co-conveners of RNGS, the collaborating authors made substantial independent contributions through their chapters. Along the way, they also helped to develop the design of the capstone analysis and the structure of the book at numerous meetings held in Italy, the United States, and France. Their continued engagement in what at times appeared to be an overwhelming and never-ending project was important from the time we began work on the book in 2004 to its final completion in 2009. We want to thank especially Marila Guadagnini at the University of Torino for hosting two planning meetings. Diane Sainsbury contributed to the plan for the book in the early days. Funding for the work done for this book, outside of the grants and institutional support provided for the RNGS project, also helped our team complete the project. The following organizations provided this crucial support: University of Turino, the Regional Council of Piedmont, Sciences Po Paris/CEVIPOF, Birkbeck College, Washington State University, Florida Atlantic University, University of Leiden, and University of Vienna.

We also thank individuals who gave us important help along the way. Benoit Rihoux and Charles Ragin took time to read the whole manuscript to give us feedback on the QCA, and Rosie Campbell was our expert consultant on all things statistical. The three anonymous reviewers at Temple University Press gave us priceless advice to turn a highly technical and methodological book into one that appealed to a broader audience. Season Hoard provided valuable assistance in producing the final manuscript and helped out in the last preparation phase. We greatly appreciate the support of Alex Holzman at Temple University Press, who from the beginning saw this as an important book in social sciences. Emily Taber, Joan Vidal, Clay Cansler, and copy editor Judy Jamison were helpful in the final production stages. Special thanks go to our partners, Curt Lewin and Gene Rosa, who provided us with essential support, home-cooked meals, and jokes—perhaps the most important—throughout the five years we have worked on this project.

Dorothy E. McBride
Tacoma, Washington

Amy G. Mazur
Moscow, Idaho
May 2010

I
Framework and Foundations

This book is divided into four parts. The "Framework and Foundations" section that opens the book is followed by the research results in Part II, "Exploring State Feminism," which assesses theoretical propositions about state feminism, and Part III, "Unpacking State Feminism," where authors consider the implications of state feminism for foundational theories of social movements, political representation, framing, and institutionalism. Part IV, "Conclusion," consists of one chapter that integrates the findings and sets forth a new theory of state feminism.

Part I consists of three chapters that describe the fundamental ideas that have inspired these research endeavors and the methods that researchers used to obtain their results. In addition, it includes a full presentation of the range and variation of women's policy agencies—structures central to the theory of state feminism—over time and across the thirteen countries in the study.

1

The State Feminism Project

The politics of state feminism is at the heart of political processes in postindustrial democracies. Of all of the various social movements of the contemporary era, women's movements have arguably been the most widespread and have endured the longest. One of the responses of political leaders to challenges from women's movement activism over four decades has been to establish institutions specifically designed to deal with demands from women's groups: women's policy agencies, machineries, or offices. The motivation for this project is to learn about the activities of these relatively new agencies and whether they have been allies for women's movements in the state, marginal to power, or merely ineffective symbols. The core question of the work, therefore, turns around the question of *state feminism*—that is, whether, how, and why women's policy agencies have been effective partners for women's movements and their actors in gaining access to state policy-making arenas and influencing policy outcomes. Bringing women's movements into the state is necessarily about representation; therefore, this study of state feminism is ultimately about the process of making democracies more democratic.

This book is the capstone—culminating achievement—of work begun by a small group of scholars that formed the Research Network on Gender Politics and the State (RNGS) in 1995. At that time many were calling for more attention to comparative, especially cross-national, research to assess a wide range of theories. In the discipline of political science broadly speaking, there were debates about methodology, especially how to bring a growing body of case studies to bear on "valid inferences about social and political life" (King, Keohane, and Verba 1994: 1). In this context, RNGS was founded to design and carry out a large-scale study of the effects of the women's movement–women's policy machinery interface in Western postindustrial democracies across five policy sectors from the 1970s to the 2000s. The completion of the study is due to the diligence and commitment of dozens of colleagues who joined RNGS as the project developed. We call this capstone investigation the *state feminism project*, and all of the cases analyzed in this book are *RNGS data*, that is, information collected by network members. Thus, this chapter and those that follow describe the processes and results of in-depth, mixed-methods investigations of the politics of state feminism through the cross-national, cross-sectoral, and longitudinal data collected by RNGS.

We now turn to a presentation of the state feminism framework, its four strands of foundational theory, and the propositions to be explored and unpacked in the rest of the book. After this we discuss the relationship of the state feminism project to RNGS and then provide an overview of the 130 policy debates that are the basis for development of theory. The chapter ends with a detailed presentation of the plan of the book, including summaries of each chapter.[1]

The State Feminism Framework

Research Context

The ideas of state feminism presented here provide an explanatory framework to understand how state-based institutions established to promote women's rights and gender equality—women's policy agencies—can bring about the success of women's movements that originate outside the state in penetrating policy arenas and changing processes of policy formation and representation, substantive policies, culture, and ultimately democracy itself. In order to follow principles of good concept construction, it is important to situate all concepts according to their scholarly use (e.g., Collier and Mahon 1993; Goertz 2006). Conceptualization and operationalization of the components of the state feminist framework should be read and understood in the context of politics of democratic governments in postindustrial societies. Postindustrial democracies are the approximately twenty-three countries that have relatively similar levels of high national wealth, similarly large service, or "post-Fordist" economies, stable nation-states, and well-established traditions of representative democratic institutions and/or the emergence of stable democratic institutions since World War II.[2]

The overarching concept of state feminism as defined in this study must be understood in relation to its use by other scholars. When Helga Hernes coined the term in her 1987 book, she put a name to the idea that governments could pursue feminist aims through policy and also that individuals and actors within the state could promote a "women-friendly" approach to policy and state action.[3] Then, researchers interested in unpacking the state and its actions with regard to women's rights and gender equality identified actors and structures participating in the full range of gender-specific state actions. They used a variety of labels for these structures, such as women's policy machineries, gender equality offices, and women's rights agencies.[4] Australian and Dutch researchers called the actors *femocrats*.[5] With the takeoff in the study of femocrats and women's policy agencies in the 1990s, the notion of state feminism became increasingly associated with these specific structures and actors and less with whether states and government action were generally positively ori-

(handwritten margin note: overall goal)

State Feminism

ented toward feminists and women—although some continued to use the term in that more general sense. For those who take the more specific approach, state feminism has come to have two meanings—to describe the phenomena of women's policy agencies in general and to analyze whether the structures are actually effective in making the state more inclusive of women and their interests.

their definition

In this book we use the concept in its more complex analytical sense: State feminism is the degree to which women's policy agencies forge alliances with women's movements and help them gain access to policy arenas and achieve their policy goals. At the outset, it is important to recognize that there are two types of state feminism in this complex sense: *Movement State Feminism* and *Transformative State Feminism*.[6] In Movement State Feminism, the agencies and the state respond to movement activism by promoting ideas, actors, and demands based on gender consciousness, women's solidarity, and the cause of women. Transformative State Feminism occurs when these ideas, actions, and demands are explicitly feminist—that is, recognize patriarchy and gender-based hierarchy and seek to promote gender equality—thus having the potential to transform gender relations.[7]

Overview of the State Feminism Framework

The state feminism theoretical framework proposes that women's movements are more likely to be successful in achieving favorable state responses when they ally with women's policy agencies. Such alliances occur through agreement on the motivational or strategic frames (i.e., issue definitions and policy goals used by both the agencies and movements) and help women's movement actors achieve procedural access and policies that respond to their goals. The agencies facilitate movement success by gendering issue definitions used by policy actors in ways that coincide with movement frames in policy debates, leading to both access and policy change.[8] Thus, a core assumption of the framework is that if policy actors use a definition of the issue gendered in ways that coincide with movement goals, it will facilitate the entry of women's movement actors into the policy arena and their ideas into policy outcomes.

The patterns of successful agency-movement alliances are the patterns of state feminism. Alliances that achieve specifically feminist goals are cases of Transformative State Feminism; those that achieve movement goals more broadly speaking are Movement State Feminism. Agencies also may form partial alliances or fail completely while women's movements are still successful in achieving their goals. The result is women's movement success but not state feminism. With the accumulation of successful alliances over time, democratic governments become more democratic through increased substantive and descriptive representation of advocates for women, a previously excluded constituency. Explanations for patterns of state feminism are found in combinations of (1) agency resources and structural characteristics, (2) women's movement resources, (3) policy environment characteristics, and (4) elements of left-wing support.

Theoretical and Conceptual Foundations

This state feminism framework integrates several strands of scholarly theory and empirical research: institutionalism, social movements, democratization and representation, and policy conflict and framing. A great expansion of interest in these important areas of social science knowledge in the early 1990s coincided with the development of the RNGS project and inspired members of the network during the crucial early phases. It is impossible here to review all the research in these areas; the discussion is instead an overview, focusing on seminal works that influenced the elaboration of the theoretical framework and the conceptualization of its components. More detailed and current discussions of relevant literature are included in subsequent chapters.

Institutionalism and the State

The 1980s witnessed a "return to the state" in comparative social science (although work such as Nettl 1968 had long been pushing the point).[9] Political scientists produced many essays and case studies trying to sort out the pertinent concepts and variables.[10] The 1985 work that started the debate over the study of the state in comparative politics was *Bringing the State Back In*. In her introduction to the edited volume, Theda Skocpol offered three aspects of state theory that have proved useful in developing comparative state feminist analyses. The first involves how scholars have understood the concept—in other words, their definition of the state. Then as now there is no agreed definition of the concept, and the particular definition used in a study may depend on the cultural orientation of the authors. The second topic—capacity of the state to have an impact through policy on society—allows researchers to question how states fashion distinctive policies, their ability to implement such policies, and the consequences, both intended and unintended. The third topic for organizing state studies suggested by Skocpol is the impact of states on political relationships. This involves the interaction between interest groups and public entities. Even more important, however, is the effect of states on patterns of politics: "the ways in which structures and activities of states unintentionally influence the formation of groups and the political capacities, ideas, and demands of various sectors of society" (Skocpol 1985: 21). Thus, this new way of thinking about the state, in its complex and interactive form, underpins our thinking about how the state-based women's policy agencies interface with the society-based women's movements.

Feminist scholars weighed in as well. Critiques of the welfare state arose from Europe and expanded to both sides of the Atlantic (see, for example, Wilson 1977; Hernes 1987; Sassoon 1987; Gordon 1990). In the 1990s the critiques deepened and widened through the 1994 appearance of *Social Politics*, a journal devoted to international studies of gender, state, and society. Although scholars tended to agree that social policies, which provide income, assistance, and services to workers and families, did little to achieve gender equality or improve the overall status and rights of women, they disagreed on their conceptions of the state. American scholars focused on policies and the policy process only and not on an entity called the state. European feminists took direct aim at the state as a "thing," an actor that embodies the policies that make up the welfare state. Critics of the liberal state are clear in their view of a monolithic authoritarian and hierarchical structure that reinforces patriarchal power structures and maintains women's subordination. As Jean Bethke Elshtain states, "To hope that one might use the state as a vast instrumentality to be turned unambiguously to our good ends and purposes is to be naïve and paradoxically, to find oneself supporting practices that subvert the democratic-egalitarian core of feminism" (1983: 303).

During this period, however, some scholars took a different tack on the question of the state in politics. Calling for a "new institutionalism," they countered the assumption that the "state" is a monolithic entity. James March and Johan Olsen directed attention to the role of state institutions in affecting the political environment. "The bureaucratic agency, the legislative committee, and the appellate court are arenas for contending social forces, but they are also collections of standard operating procedures and structures that define and defend interests. They are political actors in their own right" (1984: 738). This institutional approach was considered new, because it challenged the view popular among political theorists since the 1950s that state institutions are neutral, at the mercy of exogenous social influences, or merely the aggregate expression of rational individual actors. By positing that state institutions other than legislatures may be causal factors in policy and politics, the institutional approach also shifted attention to the links among structures within the state and between state structures and societal groups, such as the link between women's policy agencies and women's movement activists. At the same time it illuminated politics within the state, politics that often offer opportunities for policy advocates.

Some feminist theorists also took issue with the idea of the state as a monolithic patriarchal entity oppressing women. While their colleagues had been writing about the faults of the welfare state and the liberal state, these theorists pointed to thirty years of women's movement activism that had coincided with changes in actual state structures. Many democracies had established agencies officially charged with improving the conditions of women's lives ranging from equal opportunity commissions and councils to departments and ministries for women. Scholars, especially in Australia, looked at these agencies based on the assumption that state action could work to change lives of women for the better.

Whether influenced by postmodernism's obliteration of grand design or sobered by their encounters with the world around them (both explanations were offered), these theorists avoided global definitions of the state. Rosemary Pringle and Sophie Watson (1992) pointed out that while the state was changing from a single sovereign entity to a complex set of institutions and arenas, many feminists had tended to adhere to the older concept. Suzanne Franzway, Diane Court, and Robert W. Connell claimed it would be preferable to conceive of the state as a site of structures and processes that are internally differentiated (1989). They argued, in line with Skocpol's approach to the state, that it is important to recognize that whatever the state means is relative; conceptions vary from culture to culture and may affect the way state agencies intervene in women's lives.

Deconstructing the monolithic state reconstructed the question of its impact on women. Forays into the record of government action led many, including those in the RNGS project, to agree with Drude Dahlerup that we need less theorizing and more studies of the "scope and context of government action and its consequences for the position of women" (1986: 108). Hester Eisenstein (1996) agreed that the question of whether the state has helped or hurt women requires comparative research to assess the impact in a variety of contexts. These ideas cleared the way for a systematic study of state-based agencies assigned with promoting women's status, women's interests, or gender equality.

Social Movements and Women's Movements

To answer the question about whether state institutions have changed the situation for women for the better in postindustrial democracies requires settling on indicators of what "for the better for women" might be. For answers it makes sense to turn to women's movements whose second wave of mobilization beginning in the 1960s swept across all countries, coinciding with and in fact probably responsible for the widespread establishment of women's policy agencies of one kind or another. These movements set forth agendas for women that are the most comprehensive and representative of the elusive concept of "women's interests" in different countries.

The RNGS research design benefited from increased scholarly attention to the outcomes of social movements during the 1990s. Research and theorizing on social movements has largely been within the purview of sociologists stimulated by the rise of labor movements and then civil rights movements in the mid-twentieth century. During the 1960s and 1970s most work focused on trying to understand what led to the rise of these movements, especially those that used unconventional means—protests, strikes, demonstrations—to express their demands. At first, it was usual to look at the grievances and their importance in explaining the rise of movements. This approach was soon followed by propositions that the resources and the movement's ability to mobilize them could better explain the trajectory of social movements (McCarthy and Zald 1977). Others countered by arguing that attention to the "structure of political opportunity" movements encountered was an essential part of explaining their rise and fortunes (Kitschelt 1986). Sidney Tarrow (1989) offered a theory about the cycles of protest as a way of explaining the rise and fall of mass collective action.

Subsequent comparative analyses of social movements continued to devote most attention to understanding the formation and life span of movements (see, for example, McAdam, McCarthy, and Zald 1996; Meyer, Whittier, and Robnett 2002). At the same time a few called for more studies of the outcomes of movements as well.[11] Little had been done on the subject since William Gamson's (1975) research on the impact of U.S. social movement organizations on government. Marco Giugni (1995) reasoned that systematic attention to the effects of movements had been hampered by difficulties in defining and measuring outcomes and in assessing how much a particular outcome could be attributed to actions of the movement organizations. Both Giugni (1998) and Mario Diani (1997) considered that there was too much emphasis on responses of governments through policy and not enough on the internal dynamics of movements and their effect on accumulation of social capital in the larger society.

While Gamson's study may have seemed inadequate to those calling for more attention to movement outcomes, his project offered a scheme for defining and measuring state responses to movement activism that provided a way for the RNGS project to proceed to an empirical investigation of the developing notion of state feminism. Gamson outlined two kinds of government response to movements, what he called "movement success": (1) *procedural*: the recognition and acceptance of movement activists as legitimate representatives of social interests in policy processes, and (2) *substantive*: obtaining new advantages through policy change. From these two categories he fashioned a typology of movement success: complete success (both substantive and procedural), co-optation (procedural success), preemption (policy change), and complete collapse (neither procedural nor policy). Thomas Rochon and Daniel Mazmanian (1993), however, lamented that most scholars studied only policy content change and neglected the procedural or policy process change in the Gamson model. They argued that policy process change may in fact have a much longer-lasting impact than successes—or, more important, failures—in achieving policy outcomes desired by movement activists. To Gamson's typology, Rochon and Mazmanian added cultural change as an important movement outcome, a point further developed by Rochon in *Culture Moves* (1998).

Assuming that the problem of definition and measurement of social movement outcomes could be resolved, the problem of explanation for patterns of outcomes remained. Giugni's (1998) concern about determining causality points to a problem faced in all social science research: It cannot be solved in the absence of ideas about where to seek possible causes. Most studies of movement outcomes look at variants of resource mobilization and political opportunity structure theories of movement development (Giugni 1999; Amenta and Caren 2004). These point toward gathering information about internal movement resources (e.g., leadership, organizations, memberships) and external political structures and processes (e.g., state organization, political parties, legislative processes, media attention, and points of access) that are associated with different patterns of movement success. Along the way, researchers have suggested that public opinion, also called cultural opportunity (Burstein 1979; 1999), and mediation of specific political contexts (Amenta 2006) be added to the mix.

Work on women's movements mirrors the broader social movement literature (Beckwith 2000). Some have used social movement theory to describe and analyze a single movement (Ferree and Hess 2000; Whittier 1995; Buechler 2000; Lovenduski and Randall 1993; Costain 1992; Staggenborg 1991). A few studies have generated comparative propositions about the interaction between the movement and government; especially noteworthy is Banaszak, Beckwith, and Rucht 2003, which examined how changes in democratic states affect movement strategies. For the most part, studies of the outcomes of women's movements are rare, and those that are systematically comparative and cross-national are even rarer. Only a few have focused on assessing and comparing policy successes of women's movements; most use variations of resource mobilization and political opportunity structure theory to explain their findings. Noteworthy are Banaszak 1996, McCammon et al. 2001, Kane 2003, and Soule and King 2006.

A related explanation focuses on a particular combination of movement and political characteristics that could be called left-wing support (e.g., Bashevkin 1998; Beckwith 1985; Weldon 2002b). Left-wing parties and trade unions in many countries have become very close to women's movement actors, incorporating their demands in policy platforms, establishing women's sections, and placing women's movement leaders in top positions. When movement actors are that close to the left wing and the left-wing parties in power, the combination promises to be a recipe for movement procedural and policy access. It follows that governments formed by left-wing political parties close to movements are more likely than other party governments to be sympathetic to women's movement claims and to authorize their women's policy agencies to promote those interests.

Democratization and Representation

What is the significance of women's movement success and state feminism alliances for democratic states? It certainly goes beyond the satisfaction in learning that activism for women outside and inside the state can influence the direction of policy. Elements of democratic theories of representation suggest that state feminism can change democracies themselves by making them more democratic. While the concept of democratization tends to be used in the comparative literature to describe emerging democracies, here we purposefully use the notion to capture the potential for stable democracies to expand group rights and access—arguably an essential part of the democratic process.

Democracies are assessed in terms of the extent to which they achieve inclusion of societal interests, in other words their "representativeness" (Pitkin 1967). Feminist critiques of democracy in postindustrial societies (Pateman 1988; Phillips 1991; Hernes 1987) and nonfeminist critiques (Parenti 1974; Inglehart 1990; Mény 1992; Schattschneider 1960; Bachrach and Baratz 1970;

Edelman 1985) have put into question the extent to which contemporary free-market democracies with their highly developed welfare states are actually democratic. Critics of contemporary postindustrial democracies argue that in reaching high levels of economic wealth these systems have excluded major sectors of society from economic resources and political rights. The question of overcoming barriers to participation has been a long-standing issue for social movements working in postindustrial societies and especially for feminist studies of democracy.

In assessing the degree of representativeness in a democracy, Hanna Pitkin (1967) suggests four types of representation: *authorized*, where a representative is legally empowered to act for another; *descriptive*, where the representative stands for a group by virtue of sharing similar characteristics such as race, gender or ethnicity, or residence; *symbolic*, where a leader stands for national ideas; and *substantive*, where the representative seeks to advance a group's policy preferences and interests. Both descriptive and substantive forms are useful for comparing the extent to which policy processes in democratic regimes include existing societal interests and demands.[12] As feminist theorists like Anne Phillips (1991) point out, postindustrial democracies have been deficient because they fail to represent women's interests and needs adequately, either through direct placement of women in positions of power or indirectly through incorporation of gender perspectives in the policy process. Empirical studies by feminist analysts in Europe and North America also show that the absence of women in positions of power is central to explaining why public policies in many postindustrial democracies are gender-biased and hence discriminate against women (a few examples include Hernes 1987; Lovenduski and Norris 1993; Gelb 1989; Bergqvist et al. 1999). For these analysts, this democratic deficiency can be addressed by making gender more central to the business of government.[13]

The concepts of descriptive and substantive representation coincide with the indicators of movement success suggested by Gamson (1975): Procedural success brings representatives of women's movements into the policy-making processes enhancing descriptive representation. Since women's movements comprise only women,[14] the acceptance of actors from women's movements into policy arenas means increased descriptive representation of women. Policy change institutionalizes women's interests into policy, thus enhancing substantive representation. Taken together, women's movement successes across a range of policies and over time have the potential to overcome some of the exclusion women have suffered in democracies in postindustrial systems and to make those governments more representative and hence more democratic (Weldon 2002a).

Policy Conflict and Framing

Framing theory provides the essential *glue* to connect the elements of the state feminism theoretical framework. It is through framing that movements form alliances with women's policy agencies and that agencies in turn influence policy processes and outcomes, thus securing movement success or failure. The assumption underlying this analysis is a view of policy-making processes in democracies as a series of conflicts over ideas (e.g., Schattschneider 1960; Kingdon 1995; Cobb and Elder 1983; Schneider and Ingram 1993; Muller 1990; Stone 2002; Bacchi 1999). Basic to any conflict is the definition of the problem for policy action—what is wrong and what should be done. At the core of the conflict is a distribution of power. "The *definition of alternatives is the supreme instrument of power* (italics in original); the antagonists can rarely agree on what the issues are because power is involved in the definition. He who determines what politics is about runs the country, because the definition of the alternatives is the choice of conflicts and the choice of conflicts allocates power" (Schattschneider 1960: 66).

In any policy debate, the definition of alternatives used by the decision makers, however it is determined, is the *issue frame* of the debate. Issue frames, once established, determine who has influence and who does not. Furthermore, the frame shapes the outcome. Such frames are likely to vary across policy sectors; this expectation counters more traditional assumptions of country or regional styles of policy making where the assertion is that shared cultural and historical contexts within countries or "families of nations" produce similar political patterns and even policy outcomes and impacts (e.g., Castles 1993, Esping-Andersen 1993; Orloff 2002). Other research has put into question national or regional "policy styles" showing that policy determinants and dynamics can be better understood in the context of a given sector, such as agriculture or employment, within a given country (e.g., Muller 1990; Feick 1992; Baumgartner 1996; Mazur 2002; Htun and Weldon 2010).

Activists in social movements also use frames to mobilize their followers, gain support, counter their opponents, and attract the attention of policy makers. Social movement scholars call these *collective action frames* (Benford and Snow 2000; Snow and Benford 1988; McAdam 1996). These frames are often central to the purpose of the social movement. Robert Benford and David Snow (2000) identify three elements of action frames: (1) *diagnostic*, in which the advocates set forth their grievances and assign blame; (2) *prognostic*, in which the advocates suggest the solution to the grievances and a way to achieve it; and (3) *motivational*, which are aimed to mobilize adherents to action. Framing is a dynamic process in social movements: ideas develop and are reproduced, changed, rejected, challenged, broken apart, and reassembled over the span of movement activism.

Movement activists use strategic framing to seek specific short-term goals. These frames may reflect basic movement ideas only in part or may adapt them in special ways to conform to specific needs. Strategic framing is especially important for movement actors who seek to influence the policy-making process in government. Since the definition of the conflict is the key to power, and issue frames establish winners and losers with respect to policy outcomes, those participants representing social movements seek to convince policy actors to adopt their frame as the dominant issue frame. Women's policy agencies also adopt strategic frames to promote their goals. When these frames match or are compatible with the strategic movement frames, an alliance is formed. Similarly, if agency staff can stand for or work with movement actors to influence policy actors, they succeed in *gendering the issue frame* and the debate.

State Feminism Propositions

The state feminism framework and its foundational literature elaborated above produce eleven propositions that we examine or test as hypotheses in the following chapters using datasets derived from the RNGS project. We offer them along with the rationale for each according to six research questions. The findings reviewed in Chapter 11 address these same questions.

How Important Is State Feminism?

Three propositions link the extent to which women's movements are successful in pressing demands on the state with the extent to which women's policy agencies act on their behalf. The purpose is to get a fix on the significance of agencies to winning favorable state responses for women. First we must determine where and when women's movements have been successful.

- **Proposition 1.** *Women's movement actors have been successful in gaining procedural access and policy change in postindustrial democracies.*

Next, after asserting that women's movement actors have a record of success, the second proposition predicts that agencies will have a record of making alliances with them—in other words, in achieving Movement State Feminism.

- **Proposition 2.** *Women's policy agencies form alliances with women's movement actors to achieve procedural access and policy change in favor of movement goals.*

Positive findings for propositions 1 and 2 lead to testing the extent to which alliances between agencies and movement actors are an important cause of movement success and whether the absence of such alliances leads to failures with the state. If affirmed, proposition 3 is the essential core of a theory of state feminism.

- **Proposition 3.** *Alliances with women's policy agencies are a significant cause of women's movement procedural and policy successes in postindustrial democracies; failure to form alliances accounts for movement failures with respect to policy responses.*

What Conditions Are Favorable for State Feminism and Movement Success?

There are three additional propositions that sort out the probable causes of women's movement success in terms of the state feminism. Each includes one explanation from social movement theory—movement resources, favorable policy environments, or left-wing support—and then posits a place for activities of women's policy agencies in relation to that explanation. There is room to see whether that explanation also has a direct influence on the effectiveness of agency allies inside the state. Thus, each proposition embodies three ideas that are mutually exclusive: first, that the social movement explanation alone leads to success for the women's movement with the state; second, that the women's policy agencies are necessary for movement success in relation to the social movement explanation; and third, that the social movement explanation will increase the likelihood that agencies will be effective movement allies.

- **Proposition 4.** *Women's movements with higher levels of resources (strength, cohesion, degree of interest, activism, and institutionalization) are more likely to achieve success with the state. Activities of women's policy agencies are necessary along with such resources for movement success and in turn are explained by them.*

- **Proposition 5.** *Favorable components of policy environment (issue frame fit, openness of policy arenas, weak countermovement) are more likely than other factors to explain women's movement success with the state. Activities of women's policy agencies are a necessary condition along with the features of the policy environment to achieve movement success and in turn are explained by that environment.*

- **Proposition 6.** *Women's movements are more likely to be successful with the state when there are left-governing majorities and when left-wing parties and unions are ideologically and organizationally very close to women's movement actors. Activities of women's policy agencies are a necessary complement to such left-wing support in achieving women's movement success and in turn are explained by them.*

Does State Feminism Make Democracies More Democratic?

Empirical support for propositions 1, 2, and 3 would confirm the significance of women's policy activities in achieving women's movement success. Findings from propositions 4, 5, and 6 sort out the relative importance of explanations from social movement theory and explanations based on state feminism. Proposition 7 integrates these propositions to focus on levels of success and agency effectiveness in individual countries. The state feminism framework posits that accumulation of movement successes over time signifies greater inclusion and expansion of democracy. The following proposition situates the most effective women's policy agencies as a significant component in the democratization of the postindustrial state within each country as predicted by the state feminism framework:

- **Proposition 7.** *Since the accumulation of complete women's movement successes with the state signals increased democratization within postindustrial countries, the most effective women's policy agencies are important causes of such democratization.*

What Is the Recipe for an Insider Women's Policy Agency?

The first propositions show the place of women's policy agencies as allies of women's movements. The next step is to explain why some agencies are effective while others are either ineffective or uninterested. The literature on agencies predicts that those centrally located agencies that possess more complex structures, policy powers, administrative capacity, and feminist leadership will be more successful. This proposition examines such agency characteristics alongside the explanatory power of favorable policy environments, movement resources, and left-wing support.

- **Proposition 8.** *The structure, leadership, powers, and administrative resources of women's policy agencies affect the success and failure of the agencies as women's movement allies. Agency effectiveness may also be influenced by favorable policy environments, women's movement resources, and left-wing support.*

Is Transformative State Feminism the Same as Movement State Feminism?

Recalling that there are two kinds of state feminism—women's movement and transformative—the next two propositions predict that the patterns of feminist success will be the same as movement success and that explanations of Transformative State Feminism and the most effective agencies will be similar to those found for Movement State Feminism.

- **Proposition 9.** *Feminist movement actors have been successful in gaining transformative procedural access and policy change in postindustrial democracies.*

- **Proposition 10.** *Women's policy agencies form alliances with feminist women's movement actors to achieve procedural access and policy change in favor of transformative feminist movement goals.*

Does State Feminism Vary by Policy Sector, Country, or Region?

The final proposition cuts across all the previous propositions. It springs from the roots of the state feminism framework in policy studies and signifies the central importance of policy sector to the project. The unit of analysis is a single policy debate, and the cases were selected according to five issue areas. At the same time there are no assumptions about country patterns in the framework. On the contrary, the framework is grounded in the assumption that the state is not uniform but instead comprises a variety of arenas. Thus, it is highly unlikely that country patterns or regional groupings will explain differences in movement success or the components of state feminism.

- **Proposition 11.** *Patterns of state feminism, both movement and transformative, will vary by types of policy sectors. Results are unlikely to vary by country or region. Therefore, sector is more important than country as an explanation.*

The State Feminism Project and RNGS: An Overview

The state feminism project in this book has its origins in the research design on women's policy agencies developed by members of RNGS in the context of theoretical discussions of the state, movements, and democracy. The central identity of this research network arises from collaboration among scholars at every step of the research process: to develop a research plan, to agree on methods, to gather data, and to analyze the findings.[15] The plan included concepts, nominal definitions, and empirical indicators for each of the components of the design, and propositions to aid researchers in the preparation of the case analyses as well as guidelines for the selection of debates for each issue area.

The publication of *Designing Social Inquiry* in 1994 had a profound effect on the early years of the project. Like Gary King, Robert Keohane, and Sidney Verba, we wanted to use the comparative method to test hypotheses asserting the significant role of women's policy agencies in promoting women's interests within political systems. To increase the number of cases in a way that would permit the use of statistical as well as qualitative methods required several important decisions. Initially the network looked to women's movements and their activities in policy making in these democracies as the standard for determining whether or not actions of women's policy agencies were in women's interests. Since activists aimed to influence government action through policy-making processes, the network decided to choose *policy debates*, rather than the nation-states, as the units of analysis. Selecting policy debates across several issue areas and over the span of the second-wave women's movements allowed us to examine women's policy agencies across a range of policy patterns and issues.

The design focused on policy debates within nation-states and not activities and influences beyond the state. To be sure, when researchers encountered international issues they were covered. In addition, we asked contributors to gather information about the involvement of women's movement activists with transnational advocacy networks. However, the influence of such networks on national debates did not become part of state feminism theoretical framework investigated in this book.[16]

To study debates, the network selected policy sectors based on four underlying gendered dimensions—that is, aspects that pertain to relations between men and women: Job training represented the work and family dimension, abortion came from questions about reproduction, prostitution came from issues of sexuality, and political representation arose from citizenship rights matters. The fifth area—top national priorities in the late 1990s and early 2000s or "hot issues"—provided an opportunity to examine the influence of women's policy agencies on matters of general significance but without necessarily an underlying gendered dimension.

These choices increased the number of potential observations dramatically; the RNGS data comprise 130 policy debates. They also opened up new avenues for comparative analysis of state feminism in this book. No longer were we limited to cross-country comparisons on one issue at one point in time; now we could ask questions about influences on policy-making processes within countries, across five different policy issues, and over four decades. Thus, using the RNGS sample of policy debates means that investigating state feminism does not assume there are national patterns; whether these patterns exist becomes a central question of research, taken up in each chapter in the book.

The network agreed to study any policy debate from the time a proposal came to the national agenda until it was settled by a government action—either with a decision or a nondecision. The expectation was that researchers would study each policy debate descriptively but as a *case*, not a free-standing *case study*. The difference between these two is important. A case study generally involves the in-depth study of a subject to explore every possible aspect of who, what, where, when, and why (George and Bennett 2005). A case, on the other hand, is a unit of analysis—an observation—where researchers provide descriptive information according to a theoretical model (King, Keohane, and Verba 1994). By using cases, the "*n*"—in quantitative terms the sample size or study population—is increased, while the theoretical framework limits the possible number of variables.

Essential Typologies

At the beginning, the most important conceptual choices in the RNGS design pertained to the measurement of state responses to movement activism and the extent of women's policy agency activities. The network opted to gather information that would permit classification of cases into two typologies (see Table 1.1) and then compare them.[17]

The State Response Typology combines two factors inspired by Gamson (1975): policy content and procedural access.[18] Policy content is measured according to its fit with the claims asserted by women's movement actors during the policy debate. Procedural access means that actors presenting women's movement demands were found among the policy actors in the subsystem at the end of a debate. A policy action that fits women's movement demands and brings them into the policy process is a *Dual Response*. One that achieves neither end is *No Response*. In between, a movement might win either procedural access (*Co-optation*) or policy content (*Preemption*).

The network developed the Alliance Typology to measure the extent to which women's policy agencies form alliances with women's movement actors and intervene successfully on their behalf in policy processes. Using the concept of framing, the network assumed that movement influence would be more likely if the frame of the policy debate was gendered in a way that favored the movement's own frames on the issue. If women's policy agencies could insert these issue definitions and policy goals so that policy actors incorporated them in their own issue frames, they would be very effective allies for movement activists. The typology produces four types of women's policy agencies: *Insider* agencies, which effectively gender debates with women's movements' demands; *Marginal* agencies, which ally with the movement but are not successful in influencing the terms of the debate; *Symbolic* agencies, which take no position on the issue; and non-allies, or *Anti-Movement* agencies, which influence the debates with microframes that do not agree with the views of movement activists.[19]

The Policy Debates in the State Feminism Project

The empirical observations for the analysis of state feminism propositions and the adjacent areas of movements, representation, framing, and institutions in this book are 130 cases of policy debates based on the RNGS design. They pertain to five issues: abortion; job training; political representation; prostitution; and priority, or "hot," issues in the 1990s in thirteen postindustrial democracies.[20] To explore the various state feminism propositions, we select some or all of these debates for analysis, for example, by issue, decade, or outcome. Results from the cases are presented in quantitative form through the description of features or statistical analysis of all of the cases. They are also presented in qualitative form through the search for the combination of factors that lead to women's movement success and full state feminism in the debates and through the detailed discussions of the dynamics of specific cases to identify key causal mechanisms or to illustrate certain phenomena. Chapter 2 includes more detail on how researchers collected data about the debates and how we use the data in a mixed-methods approach. Sometimes, as a result of treating these cases as

TABLE 1.1   ESSENTIAL TYPOLOGIES IN THE RNGS DESIGN

STATE RESPONSE TYPOLOGY		
	Policy Content Coincides with Women's Movement Actors' Microframes	Policy Content Does Not Coincide with Women's Movement Actors' Microframes
Women's movement actors are included in policy subsystem	Dual Response	Co-optation
Women's movement actors are not included in policy subsystem	Preemption	No response
ALLIANCE TYPOLOGY		
	Women's Policy Agency Genders the Issue Frame of the Debate	Women's Policy Agency Does Not Gender the Issue Frame of the Debate
Women's policy agency microframe coincides with women's movement actors' microframes	Insider	Marginal
Women's policy agency microframe does not coincide with women's movement actors' microframes, or it has no microframe	Anti-Movement	Symbolic

units of analysis and in the quantitative reporting of results, it is easy to lose sight of the detail and richness of each case. Thus, it is important to remember that full descriptions of each of the debates have already been published in books on each of the five issues (abortion: McBride Stetson 2001a; job training: Mazur 2001; prostitution: Outshoorn 2004; political representation: Lovenduski et al. 2005; hot issues: Haussman and Sauer 2007).[21] To give readers an introduction and reference point, Table 1.2 lists all debate topics and dates by country and issue area. Throughout the book, readers will find more than thirty of these debates presented in some detail for both descriptive and theory-building purposes; these debates are marked by asterisks in Table 1.2.[22]

Plan of the Book

The aim of the book is to provide readers with a thorough picture of the research processes, analyses, and theoretical importance of the state feminism project and its findings. The next two chapters lay the groundwork for the empirical findings presented in Parts II and III. Chapter 2 describes conceptualization, the mixed-methods approach, and the methodological strategy used in the rest of the book. Chapter 3 configures the women's policy agencies, the central focus of the state feminism framework, in terms of seven different profiles

TABLE 1.2 DEBATES BY ISSUE AND COUNTRY

ABORTION

Austria	Social Democratic Party Proposal to Decriminalize Abortion, 1970–1972 Rejection of People's Initiative to Overturn Legal Abortion, 1975–1978* Legalization of Mifegyne, 1998–1999
Belgium	Ethics Commission Report on Decriminalization of Abortion, 1974–1976 Bill to Suspend Prosecution of Criminal Abortion, 1981–1982 The Abortion Reform Act of 1990, 1986–1990
Canada	Limited Liberalization of Criminal Abortion Law, 1966–1969 Constitutional Court Challenge to Criminalized Abortion, 1988–1989 Bill to Recriminalize Abortion Practices, 1989–1991
France	Reaffirmation of Legal Abortion, 1979* Public Reimbursement of Abortion Expenses, 1981–1983* Sanctions for Anti-Abortion Activism, 1991–1993*
Germany	Legalization of Abortion, 1969–1974* Abortion Compromise after Unification, 1990–1992* Recriminalization of Abortion, 1993–1995*
Great Britain	Lane Committee Investigation of Legal Abortion, 1970–1975 Bill to Limit Abortion under 1967 Act, 1975–1979* Effect of Embryology Act, 1987–1990*
Ireland	Constitutional Amendment to Protect the Unborn, 1983–1985 Right to Travel Abroad for Abortion, 1992 Options for Abortion Policy Reform, 1997–1999
Italy	Legalization of Abortion, 1971–1978 Popular Referendum to Repeal Legal Abortion, 1980–1981 In Vitro Fertilization Policy and Abortion, 1996–1999
The Netherlands	Bill to Liberalize Abortion, 1971–1973* Legalization of Abortion, 1977–1981* Regulations and Services for Abortion, 1981–1984*
Spain	Decriminalization of Abortion, 1983–1985 Administration of Abortion Services, 1986
United States	Constitutional Challenge to Criminal Abortion Laws, 1970–1973 Federal Funding of Abortion Services for Poor Women, 1974–1977 Ban on Partial-Birth Late-Term Abortions, 1995–1998*

HOT ISSUE

Austria	Family Allowance for Child Care, 1999–2001
Belgium	Immigration Reform Bill, 1999–2000*
Canada	Reform of Health Care Funding and Powers to Provinces, 2000–2004
Finland	Rights to Municipal Day Care, 1991–1994
France	35-Hour Work Week, 1997–2000
Germany	Embryonic Stem Cell Research and Abortion, 2000–2002
Great Britain	Reform of House of Lords, 1997–2003
Italy	Constitutional Decentralization, 1997–2001
The Netherlands	Wages and Standards for Home Care Workers, 1997–2001
Spain	Proposal to Restrict Unemployment Benefits, 2002
Sweden	Child Care Services or Family Allowances? 1991–1994
United States	Ending Entitlements for Poor Families, 1992–1996*

TABLE 1.2 *Continued*

JOB TRAINING

Canada	Canadian Jobs Strategy to Combat Unemployment, 1984–1985*
	Reform of Job Training and Unemployment Insurance, 1994–1996*
	British Columbia Expansion of Social Assistance Policy and Youth Job Training, 1994–1996
Finland	Training Programs to Combat Labor Shortages and Unemployment, 1969–1971
	Adult Retraining Programs, 1971–1975
	Training Reform to Address Unemployment, 1977–1987
	Limits on Training for Unemployment, 1992–1993
France	Youth Training and Unemployment, 1978–1980
	Firm-Level Training Programs, 1983–1984
	Employers in Job Training, 1991
	Job Training, Youth, and Retention, 1993
	Training for Long-Term Unemployed, 1993
Ireland	Youth Unemployment, 1981
	Using European Union Funds for Job Training, 1987–1989
	Training for Globalization, 1995–1997*
Italy	Unemployment and Job Training, 1983–1984
	Reorganization of Vocational Education, 1993–1997
Spain	National Training Plan and European Union Funding, 1985
	Creation of General Council for Professional Training, 1985–1986
	Training Program Reform, 1990–1992
United States	Maintaining Employment and Training Services, 1976–1978*
	Devolution of Job Training to the States, 1980–1982
	Federal Funding for Vocational Training, 1989–1990

POLITICAL REPRESENTATION

Austria	Appointing More Women to the Cabinet, 1975–1979
	Overcoming Under-representation of Women in the Civil Service, 1990–1993
	Quotas through Subsidies to Political Parties, 1994–1999
Belgium	Quota for Party Electoral Lists, 1992–1994*
	Quota for Advisory Committees, 1996–1997
	Quota for Federal Government Ministers, 1996–1999
Finland	Reversing Monopoly of Parties over Candidate Nominations, 1972–1975
	Quotas in Decision Making in Leftist Party, (a party debate), 1986–1987
	Quotas in the Equality Act of 1995, 1991–1995*
France	Constitutional Court Challenge of Municipal Election Quotas, 1981–1982*
	Single-Member to Proportional Representation in Parliamentary Elections, 1985–1986*
	Parity Reform in All Public Offices, 1995–2000*
Germany	Quota Rules in Social Democratic Party (a party debate), 1977–1988
	Constitutional Equal Rights Reform and Equal Rights Law, 1989–1994*
	Citizenship for Immigrants' Children, 1998–1999
Great Britain	Reform of QUANGOs, 1979–1981
	Labour Party Quotas for Parliamentary Candidates (a party debate), 1993
	Parliamentary Working Hours, 1997–2002
Italy	Formation of Democratic Party of the Left (a party debate), 1989–1991
	Adding Majority System to Proportional Representation, 1991–1993
	Equal Opportunity Constitutional Amendment, 1999–2003

(continued on next page)

TABLE 1.2 *Continued*

POLITICAL REPRESENTATION *Continued*

The Netherlands	Reform and Reorganization of Social Democratic Party (a party debate), 1966–1977 Overhaul of Equality Policy, 1981–1985 Reform of Corporatist System, 1989–1997
Spain	25% Quota for Socialist Party Parliamentary Candidates (a party debate), 1987–1988 40% Quota for Socialist Party Parliamentary Candidates (a party debate), 1992–1997 Bill for Mandatory Gender Quotas for All Parties, 1998–2003*
Sweden	Responding to Demands for Sex Equality, 1967–1972 Quotas for Appointed Government Positions, 1985–1987 Quotas for Social Democratic Party Lists (a party debate), 1991–1994
United States	Arkansas Debate over Equal Rights Amendment, 1972–1979 Michigan Debate over Term Limits, 1991–1992 Voter Registration at Motor Vehicle Agencies, 1988–1993

PROSTITUTION

Austria	Criminalization of Pimping, 1984* Reform of Criminal Prostitution in Vienna, 1991–1992* Social Insurance to Sex Workers, 1997*
Canada	Frazer Committee Report on Criminalized Prostitution, 1983–1985 Criminalization of Solicitation, 1985 Protecting Children from Prostitution, 1992–1996
Finland	Decriminalization of Prostitution, 1984–1986 Criminalization of Clients, 1993–1998 Ban on Prostitution in Helsinki, 1995–1999
France	Ministerial Study of Prostitution, 1972–1975 Legalizing Brothels, 1989–1990 Penal Code Reform of Soliciting, Pimping, and Trafficking, 1991–1992
Great Britain	Abolition of Imprisonment of Prostitutes, 1979–1983 Criminalization of Kerb Crawling, 1984–1985 Sexual Servitude and Trafficking, 2000–2002
Italy	Protection for Victims of Sex Trafficking, 1996–1999* Criminalization of Clients of Underage Prostitutes, 1998* Social Programs to Prevent Sex Trafficking, 1998–1999*
The Netherlands	Proposal to Repeal Ban on Brothels, 1983–1989 Criminalization of Sex Trafficking, 1989–1993 Legalization and Regulation of Brothels, 1997–2000
Spain	Decriminalization of Prostitution, 1994–1995* Enhancing Criminal Penalties for Trafficking, Pimping and Promoting Underage Prostitution, 1997–1999* Protection for Victims of Sex Trafficking, 1998–2000*
Sweden	Prostitution and Its Impact, 1981–1982* Commission Report on Prostitution and Violence against Women, 1995–1998* Criminalizing the "John," 1997–1999*
United States	Sexual Exploitation of Children, 1976–1978 Federal Sanctions on Child Pornography and Sex Trafficking, 1984–1986 International Trafficking in Women and Children, 1998–2000

*Case studies.

based on administrative characteristics. The chapter includes information on the trends in their capacity and power cross-nationally and from the 1960s to the early 2000s.

Chapters 4 to 6 in Part II analyze the eleven propositions of the state feminism framework presented in this chapter. Chapters 7 to 10 in Part III use RNGS data to unpack the components of the state feminism framework—women's movements, representation, gendering, and institutions—to develop a deeper and broader theoretical understanding. Chapter 11 in Part IV integrates the findings in terms of the theory. We conclude our introduction of the state feminism project in this chapter with a summary of the contents of these chapters.

Part II: "Exploring State Feminism"

"Women's Policy Agencies and Women's Movement Success" (Chapter 4)

The propositions about Movement State Feminism are examined in this chapter: the frequency of movement success and alliances with agencies; the significance of agencies to movement success; the value of Insider agencies to movement success; and the influence of policy sector, countries, and regions. Tabulations show a pattern of complete and partial women's movement success with the state and a decline in failures over time, across countries. Then, we use methods of statistical inference and qualitative analysis to assess the importance of agency allies to women's movement impact on the state in terms of women's movement resources, policy environment characteristics, and left-wing support. A separate qualitative analysis of patterns of Movement State Feminism in all thirteen countries in the study points to how movement activism in the last decades of the twentieth century expanded democratic representation and how important agencies were in that process. Overall, the chapter provides evidence that rejects sweeping generalizations about the drivers of movement success and single-variable explanations for agency activities. The explanations necessarily involve combinations of variables and conditions, as well as a nuanced interpretation of state feminism phenomena.

"Women's Policy Agency Success and Failure: The Search for Explanations" (Chapter 5)

This chapter examines propositions that the characteristics of agencies—form, powers, resources—explain agency success and failure. The influence of such characteristics is related to that of women's movement resources, favorable policy environments, and left-wing support. First, we compare the conditions for effective allies (i.e., Insider agencies) with allies that have little impact on policy debates and outcomes (i.e., Marginal agencies). Then the chapter considers why some agencies fail to take the part of movement actors at all, despite being positioned to do so: These are the Symbolic and Anti-Movement agencies. We find a complex interplay between the composition and support of agencies on the one hand, and the policy environments in which decisions of interest to women's movement actors take place on the other. The feminist nightmare that agencies will work against their movement constituents to further the interest of political leaders is also considered and for the most part put to rest. The chapter offers promising avenues for further research into the drivers of and pathways to agency success and failure.

"What's Feminist about State Feminism?" (Chapter 6)

Part II of the book concludes by asking when and under what circumstances state agencies ally with feminist movement actors to challenge the patriarchal underpinnings of the state itself. To expand the state feminism framework, we offer a definition (and measures of) Transformative State Feminism and apply it to the cases in the study. This definition combines agencies allied with feminist movement actors that are successful in achieving either feminist policy or participation or both. The standard here is high, and only nineteen debates measure up—eleven fully and eight partially. It is interesting that such significant agency-sponsored policy change is found in all countries but one, and in debates on all issues and in every decade. There is little evidence that Transformative State Feminism is becoming more frequent, but we find that such alliances with state actors are often necessary for feminist movements to achieve their goals with the state.

Part III: "Unpacking State Feminism"

"Social Movements and Women's Movements" (Chapter 7)

Joyce Outshoorn shows the cross-national patterns of change in types of women's movement actors, their activities, and their locations since the heyday of the 1970s. She assesses the implications of what she discovers for conventional theories of movement change. The findings confirm that women's movements are not like other social movements, in that their activism often may not be in the form of protest and contentious politics against the state and other authorities. Instead the women's movement actors have adopted a variety of forms and strategies to achieve their goals. In some contexts women's movements may have arisen in the form of autonomous groups and protest activities, but for various reasons actors have moved toward more conventional forms and tactics, eventually forming alliances with parties and governments. At other times in other places the pattern may show a persistence of both autonomous and conventional activities and strategies side by side. Using measures of both activism (measured through protest, policy campaigns, and formation of new organizations) and institutionalization (measured through formal representation in parties, lobbies, and parliament), the chapter compares the patterns of change and the comparative effectiveness of these various forms and strategies in achieving movement goals.

"Political Representation" (Chapter 8)

Many feminist analysts see the substantive and descriptive representation of women as the ultimate form of gendering state institutions. The election to legislatures, the appointment of women to public office as ministers and bureaucrats, the presence of women's policy agencies, and the potential for these women and agencies to promote women-friendly policy outcomes are all an integral part of the complex process of "gendering government" (Chappell 2002b). Ideas about representation are central to state feminism theory; the data allow Joni Lovenduski and Marila Guadagnini to go beyond that theory to examine the dimensions of women's representation and their interconnections. Adapting a framework developed by Karen Celis (2008) to understand analytical approaches to women's representation, they show who has represented women, what policies they promoted, where these policies were put forward and heard, and the relationship among policies, patterns of institutionalization, and more general representation of women. Here the question is whether women's policy agencies should be considered avenues for expanded representation of women, enhancing the substantive and procedural (descriptive) representation of women through women's movement actors or in fact whether they should be considered particular forms of representation on their own.

"Framing and Gendering" (Chapter 9)

Discursive frames, based on taxonomy of general frames, issue frames, and microframes, connect the components of the state feminism theory. Framing also relates more generally to social movement theory and feminist policy analysis. With detailed information on the microframes of women's movement actors for many policy debates, Birgit Sauer traces relationships between strategic frames and broader collective-action frames of women's movements in different countries. Such information also offers insights into the effectiveness of various discursive strategies on a variety of policy proposals. Sauer unpacks the strategic frames to reveal the patterns of different kinds of movement discourse such as equality, difference, and deconstructive frames—those that challenge gender hierarchies. The detailed frame data analyzed in the chapter are key to documenting the use of feminist ideas across issues and countries, and over time. Sauer concludes by examining several assumptions essential to the state feminism framework about the relation of gendering of issue frames in policy debates to the outcomes of those debates with respect to movement descriptive and substantive representation.

"Gendering New Institutionalism" (Chapter 10)

Since the 1980s, scholars' attention to institutions in political life has led to interest in how institutions come about, how they change, and the circumstances of their decline and disappearance. This new institutional literature, however, virtually ignores the question of gendered institutionalism. The state feminism project tells the story of how, why, and to what end women's policy agencies have promoted women's movement actors and ideas within the state in Western postindustrial democracies. Chapter 10 engages this story to build institutional theory and integrate the feminist and gender-blind new institutionalism.

In Chapter 10, authors Amy Mazur and Dorothy McBride place women's policy agencies firmly on the new institutional agenda as a legitimate and important object of analysis; they use data about agency characteristics elaborated in Chapter 3 to put institutional theories of change to the test. The structural analysis over time and across countries assesses the applicability of propositions from historical institutionalism ("constant cause" versus "path-dependent") and from policy-focused theories of "punctuated equilibrium," "agenda setting," and "advocacy coalitions." A second empirical cut on the RNGS data returns to the debate-focused analysis of state feminism to evaluate discursive institutional theories and claims of sectoralization in the performance of women's policy agencies in conjunction with women's movements.

Part IV: "Conclusion"

"The New Politics of State Feminism" (Chapter 11)

The final chapter summarizes and integrates findings from the chapters that explored the propositions of the state feminism framework and the chapters that unpacked its movement, representation, framing, and institutionalist components. Our purpose is to synthesize these complex results into a theory of state feminism in a way that is clear yet incorporates the nuances unearthed in the research. Then we consider the consequences of this new state feminism theory for the foundational theories of institutionalism, social movements, representation, and framing. In wrapping up the impact of the mixed-methods approach in the book, the chapter makes the case against looking for the single variable or the sweeping generalization to explain movement success and state feminism. We argue instead that only through multiple methods can researchers appreciate the elegance and usefulness of ideas of configurational causation and equifinality and the theoretical potential of the search for causal mechanisms in a single case.

2

Concepts and Mixed Methods

This chapter discusses the major tools for assessing propositions from the state feminism framework and its components in postindustrial democracies. Conceptualization is the key step in preparing research propositions for empirical investigation; it is especially important in comparative cross-national and longitudinal studies. Here we focus on five interrelated ideas: women's policy agencies; women's movements; feminism and feminist movements; women's movement change: activism and institutionalization; and frames and framing of policy issues and women's movement ideas. Not only are these central to the theoretical framework, but there have been thus far few instances of successful research definitions of these important topics. The conceptualization described in this chapter, therefore, represents one of the innovative contributions of the state feminism project.

The second part of the chapter presents the mixed-methods approach used to examine the state feminism framework and its components. We describe mixed methods, the rationale for its use in this project, and different patterns of combining qualitative and quantitative analysis. There is a full description of the preparation and content of the RNGS dataset as well as the special datasets that authors have developed from it. Qualitative approaches offered include case-based Qualitative Comparative Analysis and the use of both theory-building and descriptive case studies. A chapter-by-chapter overview of the use of these methods is provided (see Table 2.1), and we end the chapter with a discussion of the limits of the RNGS data used in the mixed-methods investigation.

Conceptualization

Conceptualization is more than offering nominal definitions. This is especially true in the field of comparative politics, where analysts use cross-national studies with an eye toward theory building. It is an intellectual process that explores the history of naming things and ideas, places these names in research contexts, establishes the dimensions of meaning, and sets out the processes for locating empirical observations that stand for the concepts (see, for example, Goertz 2006; Goertz and Mazur 2008; Adcock and Collier 2001). It is a task that is central to scientific inquiry. In comparative cross-national studies, the questions of the validity and reliability of such conceptualization are especially important, as are the dangers of distorting concepts by stretching them beyond their intended application (Sartori 1970; Collier and Mahon 1993).

Women's Policy Agencies

In the beginning of the second-wave women's movement in the 1960s and 1970s, governments took tentative steps toward including issues relating to women by means of institutional forms.[1] In Great Britain, the United States, and Canada, for example, governments established commissions to investigate the status of women and make policy recommendations. In some European countries, such as France and Austria, governments assigned a member of the cabinet to deal with women's movement demands. As the movement gained momentum, some governments established a bureaucratic agency or ministry for a more permanent presence. Offices were set up at all levels of government. In the early 1990s the state-based machineries tended to shift their focus from women as a demographic group to a more complex approach to sex-based inequities (Staudt 1997; Rai 2003b). Some refocused their agencies to gender equality; in other countries the term *women* has remained a part of formal agency titles.

There are three different ways in which agencies can participate in the policy process and state action: (1) through introducing women's status and gender equality in a specific policy area, such as labor or family, across several policy areas; (2) by introducing gender perspectives more broadly to all policy areas that are not explicitly gendered, sometimes called gender mainstreaming; or (3) through formally feminist policies that aim to promote women's rights and strike down gender hierarchies.

Recent research has demonstrated that agencies, especially in European countries, have the potential to play a crucial role in implementing a mainstreaming approach to gender equality (called *cross-sectional mandate* here). This is especially so in training and educating other government actors about the complexities of gender-based disparities and the necessarily transversal response to it. As studies of mainstreaming in the European Union have shown, without an activist agency informed by gender experts, governments can easily circumvent the original intent of gender mainstreaming (e.g., Woodward 2003; Haffner-Burton and Pollock 2009).

Femocrats also play important roles in reaching out to "male and female allies" who are not aware of the intricacies of the policy issue but have the political will to push for a given policy (e.g., Eisenstein 1996). Studies show the pivotal role of femocrats in convincing and cajoling recalcitrant decision makers. Celia Valiente, for example, has pointed to the important "power of persuasion" of Spain's Institute for Women (1995). In a wide range of countries throughout the world, creating agencies that are accountable to groups, yet have enough autonomy within the politico-administrative system, is seen as an important ingredient for achieving effective gender mainstreaming and feminist policy as well (Rai 2003a; Staudt 1997; Weldon 2002a; Malloy 1999). Feminist analyses of the state and public policy have also shown that women's policy agencies and their agents are antidotes to the resistance of established institutions accustomed to reproducing dominant patterns of gender roles and patriarchy in their "logic of appropriateness" (Weldon 2002a and Eisenstein 1996).[2]

The state feminism framework focuses on comparing the activities and effectiveness of women's policy agencies in the policy-making process in postindustrial democracies since the 1960s. Thus, the fairly inclusive definition here seems appropriate: a *women's policy agency* is a structure that meets both of the following criteria: (1) any agency or governmental body formally established by government statute or decree; and (2) any agency or governmental body formally charged with furthering women's status and rights or promoting sex-based equality. The term *women's policy agency*, *office*, or *machinery* applies to state-based agencies, at any level of government (international, national, subnational, or local) or in any type of organ (elected, appointed, administrative, or judicial) that is charged with promoting the advancement of women and/or gender equality. Given the variety of possible locations within the state, the formal role of these agencies can vary a great deal, from studying problems related to their remits and making recommendations, to proposing and adopting policy, to enforcing and implementing laws, and to administrative oversight.

All of these agencies have the potential to speak for women as a group, but they are not part of the women's movement. As Laurel Weldon (2002a: 125) states: "Women's policy agencies are one way of creating state institutions that reflect women's perspectives." In addition, they can present a feminist perspective in the state for any individual or group, man or woman, seeking to advance women's rights and strike down gender-based hierarchies that contribute to inequalities between men and women.

RNGS research uncovered some institutions that act in the policy process as full-fledged policy agencies, but lack the formal governmental directive of establishment. These are called *quasi women's policy agencies*. To act in the policy process as women's policy agencies means that quasi agencies take positions on behalf of women and attempt to influence the outcome of policy debates. Many such offices are in political parties in parliamentary democracies where governing parties dominate policy making. Others may be state structures, without a formal statutory existence, for example, certain women's commissions in legislatures.

In parties, quasi agencies are permanent structures in the party organization, formally charged by the party with promoting women's issues within the party, involved with some aspect of party policy making, and given party funds for a budget and permanent offices. It is the function of the women's organization in the context of party decision-making processes that permits its classification as a quasi women's policy agency. The same party women's organization participating in a debate in the state (parliament, cabinet, commissions) would be classified as a women's movement actor. In cases where the women's party body has a wide membership of women in the party, only the official leadership organization is considered to be a quasi agency; the members may operate separately as women's movement actors in the same debate.

Women's Movements

It is striking that there are many social science studies of social movements in general and, more specifically, women's movements, but little attention to conceptualization. It seems as though scholars have never had occasion to disagree about what these entities are. However, in RNGS, as researchers shared their observations it soon became evident that we could not assume that everyone had the same notion of which entities were women's movements and which were not. While finding agreement may not be important in one or two case studies, failure do so in a project with over 100 observations would seriously undermine its ability to assess state feminism propositions using scientific methods. What women's movements are, what they do, and what they want is central. Following from the framework laid out in Chapter 1, women's movement success—this study's dependent variable or outcome—is measured in terms of the extent to which policy content coincides with women's movement goals and the extent to which women's movement actors are included in the policy-making process. Analysts must evaluate whether women's policy agency positions match up with women's movement demands to determine whether agencies are movement allies. In addition, one of the three series of drivers of state feminism we examine includes women's movement resources.

The conceptualization used here places the idea of a women's movement in the context of the politics of postindustrial democracies between 1970 and the early 2000s—a period selected because it spans the trajectory of what is usually called second-wave movement activism.[3] Movements have two dimensions: *ideas and discourses* women in these societies develop on the basis of their experiences as women, and *collective actors* who present movement ideas in public and social life. This approach separates what cannot be adequately observed (i.e., the formation of women's movement discourse) from what can and has been so observed by many researchers—the actors who present the movement ideas in public and social life. What are studied empirically, then, are the *women's movement actors*—organizations that are inspired by movement thinkers to promote what they see as women's interests. The operational definition of *women's movement discourse* thus identifies women's movement actors.

To observe women's movement actors, researchers looked for actors who use the following elements of women's movement discourse: (1) explicit identity with women as a group, a form of gender consciousness (see Tolleson Rinehart 1992); (2) explicitly gendered language referring to women as distinct from men;[4] and (3) claims to represent women as women in public life. It is possible for many actors to express ideas that fit these criteria. Given the range and activities that have characterized women's movements in postindustrial democracies, the definition also includes a scheme to classify different kinds of actors. It focuses on collective actors that vary according to the dimensions of form, mission, and location. Forms may be informal or formal;[5] missions of organizations may place movement discourse as the top priority or other than a top priority, that is, women's movement organizations or non–women's movement organizations; locations of organization may be free-standing or inside a formal organization. Combining these dimensions produces six types of women's movement actors:

1. *Free-standing informal women's movement organizations.* Examples include demonstrations, consciousness-raising groups, and clubs.
2. *Free-standing formal women's movement organizations.* Examples include lobby organizations and professional organizations.
3. *Informal women's movement organizations inside formal women's movement organizations.* Examples include ad hoc activities such as demonstrations or protests under the banner of formal women's movement organizations.
4. *Formal women's movement organizations inside non–women's movement formal organizations.* Examples include sections of political parties (if not considered a quasi policy agency), women's caucuses in professional organizations, women's studies programs in universities.
5. *Informal organizations inside non–women's movement formal organizations.* Examples include protests inside churches or the military.
6. *Formal organizations inside women's movement formal organizations.* Examples include task forces of women's movement interest groups and local organizations as part of a national advocacy coalition.

In this study, women's policy agencies are treated as conceptually different from women's movement actors. These agencies are formal organizations that may espouse women's movement, even feminist movement, discourse. But their status as formal and official bodies that are part of the state's apparatus distinguish them from other organizations that present such discourse, that is, women's movement actors.[6] Women's movement actors are not official state agencies; in this they share the characteristics of social movement organizations in being, by definition, *non-state* structures. Similarly, individuals who hold positions in women's policy agencies are not women's movement actors. While they may be feminists and may be or have been participants in the women's movement organizations, having a position in a women's policy agency precludes them from being considered part of the women's movement.

Women's movements, like social movements, may adopt a strategy of working within a variety of other state institutions. According to Myra Marx Ferree and Carol Mueller (2007), only when women's movement actors are represented inside institutions with links to organized collective entities, not as independent individuals who happen to use feminist rhetoric, would they be considered women's movement actors. As Ferree and Mueller point out, "When social movements move into institutions, they move not as individuals trying to 'make it' as tokens for the success of their groups, but as organized collective entities that are trying to change the institution's goals, decision-making or modes of operation, whether or not they end up successful, expelled or co-opted" (2007: 587).

Thus, in the data for this project, individuals, such as MPs speaking in parliament or academics writing in the press, are counted as a separate category when classifying women's movement actors, but they are not considered analytically to be separate from the women's movement organizations they represent and are manifestations of collective action.

Given the focus on women's identity that is at the core of the definition, only women are considered to be women's movement actors in this study. While men are not, by definition, a part of the women's movement, they can support women's movement ideas and by doing so assume the role of "male allies." Women acting as women, identifying with each other, and appealing to a constituency of women through a gender-conscious discourse, constitute a form of women's political participation through movement activities. Women's movement actors may engage in a variety of relationships, interacting and organizing collectively as well as participating individually. Taken together in a particular social context (e.g., community, region, institution, nation-state, internationally), these actors and their ideas may be referred to as a women's movement. Moreover, when women's movement actors participate in policy arenas, this is evidence of women's descriptive representation.

Feminism and Feminist Movements

The state feminism theoretical framework places feminism at the center. Yet, this emphasis is not as straightforward as it may appear. The meaning of state feminism has evolved from its origins in the welfare state politics of Scandinavian countries to its current association with women's policy machineries.[7] Until now the concept has not been accompanied by a consistent conceptualization of feminism as a specific set of ideas. Instead, the practice has developed to use the terms women's movement and feminist movement interchangeably. As RNGS researchers contributed their studies of policy debates for the issue books on abortion, job training, political representation, prostitution, and hot issues, the network continued that practice. The need for precise measurement of all the concepts in the theory became evident in the process of transposing the qualitative cases into a quantitative dataset. This forced us to develop a core definition of feminism with special attention to its relation to women's movements.

During the period under study, from the 1960s to early 2000s, the women's movement has become increasingly complex and diverse. Many of the ideas, aspirations, and identities that compose it have become contested among movement thinkers and actors alike. Thus, it is likely that in any policy arena actors could represent a variety of discourses and often do. Some of these discourses may be considered *feminist* and thus are derived from the *feminist movement*. Scholars do not agree on the need to distinguish between the women's movement and the feminist movement. Many use the terms interchangeably (e.g., Chappell 2002a and b; Gelb, 1989, 2003; Kaplan 1992; Katzenstein and Mueller 1987; Mazur 2002; Weldon 2002a). Some writers distinguish the two in terms of their respective aims. For Karen Beckwith, for example (2000, 2005), women's movement aims involve women and women's issues but differ from feminist movements in that they do not necessarily involve challenges to patriarchy. The difference between the women's movement and the feminist movement ultimately relates to differences in the ideas, aspirations, and identities.

The women's movement finds its genesis in *gender consciousness*: "The recognition that one's relation to the political world is at least partly shaped by being female or male. This recognition is followed by identification with others in the 'group' of one's sex, positive affect toward the group, and a feeling of interdependence with the group's fortunes" (Tolleson Rinehart 1992: 32). The varieties of identities, aspirations, ideas, and interpretations of that recognition compose the women's movement. Feminist consciousness is a special kind of gender consciousness. What distinguishes feminist from the more general women's identity and interests is a matter of contention, but it is clear that while all feminists possess gender consciousness, many women with gender consciousness would not be considered, nor consider themselves, feminists. Thus, feminist movements are subcategories of women's movements. All feminist movements are women's movements, but not all women's movement actors express feminist aspirations. A feminist movement is a type of women's movement with a specific feminist discourse.

Feminist movement actors are distinguished by their *feminism*. Like the women's movements, their ideas include identity with women as a group, explicitly gendered language about women, and representation of women as women in public life. In addition, there are specific feminist ideas: first, a view that because there is something wrong with the treatment and status of women, goals must seek to *advance the status of women*; and second, a view that, explicitly or implicitly, *challenges gender hierarchies and forms of women's subordination*.

The adoption of this conceptualization of feminism and feminist movement as a subcategory of the women's movement forced the network to take another look at the state feminism theoretical framework. The framework linked state responses and women's policy agency activities to demands of women's movement actors. Was this adequate for finding the *feminism* in state feminism? With a more precise understanding of feminism, we realized that the concept of state feminism itself must reflect the conceptualization. If feminist movements are a subcategory of women's movements, then state responses that reflect feminist discourses are a subcategory of those that reflect women's movement discourses. Thus, as we discussed in Chapter 1, there are two types of state feminism: Movement State Feminism and Transformative State Feminism.

Women's Movement Change: Activism and Institutionalization

One of the important contributions of constructing the RNGS dataset is that, for the first time, there are measures of change in women's movements for use cross-nationally in postindustrial democracies. In the state feminism framework, degrees of activism and institutionalization are indicators of women's movement resources that may explain successful agency-movement alliances. This advance came about from dissatisfaction with the use of *stage* to conceptualize changes in social movements over time (Tarrow 1983; Rosenfeld and Ward 1996). Research findings from the issue books show no patterns in movement success or the effectiveness of women's policy agencies associated with movement stages, such as emergence, growth, consolidation, or decline and abeyance. The problem is that the use of stage to examine movement change assumes a pattern of growth, consolidation, and decline. However, in many countries the women's movement did not follow such a cyclical pattern. With no such pattern, the concept is not useful.

After another look at the social movement literature, the network built two new concepts that would allow us to map the patterns of change over time more effectively. One measures the results of mobilization of women to movement *activism*, and the other measures the degree of presence of women's movement actors inside social and political institutions, called *institutionalization*. Activism and institutionalization pertain to the women's movement activities in the country as a whole, not just those actors in the policy debates. For that reason, the information is based on a periodization of the debates in the dataset for each country. After assessing the distribution of debates over the time span, we defined periods that cover clusters of debates across issues; there are three or four for each country. Then, country researchers completed new worksheets providing information that became the basis for scales measuring the degree of women's movement activism and institutionalization for each country and period. For the activism measure, these worksheets provide estimates of the frequency of informal networks, protests, local movement communities and cultural centers, formation of new organizations, and policy campaigns. For the institutionalism measure, they estimate the degree of presence of individuals and organizations with links to the women's movement in legislatures, bureaucracies, political parties, unions, interest groups, and academia.[8]

Frames and Framing

The politics of state feminism is expressed in terms of frames, that is, various actors' statements about their views of problems and claims for government action or inaction to handle them. Women's movement actors are identified by the way they frame their demands in a debate. Whether content of government policy responds to women's movement demands is determined by comparing the frames of the women's movement actors to the provisions of the policy outcomes. Women's policy agency allies of women's movements are assessed by comparing the frames of the two groups. The effectiveness of women's policy agencies in policy processes is based on the effect their action has on the dominant issue frame among policy actors. The fit between women's movement actors' frames and policy subsystem actors' frames is one of the important aspects of the policy environment.

Framing is important, not only in the measuring of concepts in the state feminism theoretical framework, but also in the assumptions behind its propositions. With respect to the women's movement actors and the women's policy agencies, the notion of *gendering* the frame of policy debates emerges to question whether or not the women's policy agencies influence the dominant issue frame of the debate by inserting gender in a way that is compatible with women's movement actors' goals. The framework assumes that if women's policy agencies gender the debates in this way, the result will be to bring interests of groups of women into the policy-making arena, opening the door for procedural access as well as policy content, that is, descriptive and substantive representation—a Dual Response. Thus, gendering policy debates is one form of process change, and it provides the basis for a second form of process change: increased participation by women's movement actors in the policy-making process (Schattschneider 1960; Kingdon 1995; Cobb and Elder 1983; Schneider and Ingram 1993; Muller 1990).

This approach to framing arises from a view of the policy-making process in democratic systems as a conflict of ideas, focusing on issues and the modes of defining problems. We study arguments among policy actors over the meaning of problems that deserve attention and what should be done about them. This study assumes that the struggle over the definition of public policy is at the center of the political forces in democracies. Society-based groups and state actors line up around the definition of policy issues in a certain light that often reflects their own positions and aims. The term *framing* captures the way in which actors define policy issues in terms of problems and policy goals.

From the literature we developed a hierarchy of policy definitions at three levels: general frames, issue frames, and microframes. At the *general frames* level, the definitions of policy problems and the actors that are involved occur in the national or even extranational arenas; these dynamics affect action and policy content on a wide range of policy issues (e.g., Jenson 1989). An *issue frame* is the definition of meaning of a specific policy area (e.g., employment, health, or environment) used by actors in a policy subsystem dealing with that issue. Change in an issue frame may or may not affect the larger general frame. The notion of issue frames reflects comparative public policy scholarship that finds that there are no national patterns of policy formation, but that policy formation trends occur within different policy areas (Hayward 1992; Heclo 1978; Feick 1992; Van Waarden 1992).

The third level of framing occurs at the *micro* level, that of individuals or organizations, both inside and outside of the state. In other words, any actors within the policy arena, bureaucratic agencies, political parties, interest groups, etc., can seek to bring their microframes into a specific policy debate. Studies of social movements frequently characterize modes of defining problems as frames that they refer to as structures of organized meanings (Snow and Benford 1992; Gamson and Meyer 1996). This scholarship on *social movement framing* discusses how specific organizations or actors might have a position on a certain issue that they seek to insert into the issue frame to change policy content. A *microframe* is composed of an issue definition and policy goals that specific actors use to influence the issue frame. It may form the core identity of the group in question or be a strategic move that departs from core identities to achieve a policy outcome. Both women's movement actors and women's policy agencies develop microframes.

A Mixed-Methods Approach to State Feminism

Writings on mixed-methods research typically begin by placing this approach in the context of a decades-old debate between advocates of quantitative approaches in social science and their critics who favor qualitative approaches (e.g., Tashakkori and Creswell 2007; Burke and Onwegbuzie 2004; Bennett 2007). Mixed methods (also called multiple or multi-methods) appeared as a means of bridging this quantitative-qualitative divide by combining the two. In introducing their new journal on the subject, editors Abbas Tashakkori and John W. Creswell's definition is typical: "We have broadly defined mixed methods here as research in which the investigator collects and analyzes data, integrates the findings and draws inferences using both qualitative and quantitative approaches or methods in a single study or program of inquiry" (2007: 4).

Adopting a mixed-methods plan, however, is not simply mechanically combining quantitative and qualitative data (e.g., do a survey and do a case study, and voila! mixed methods). It is necessary to consider that any method is part of a larger mode of thought, often called a methodological paradigm or culture. In the case of the debates in social science, especially in political science and comparative politics, the perspectives that give rise to quantitative methods on the one hand and qualitative methods on the other involve quite different world views and loyalties (Mahoney and Goertz 2006).[9] Thus, it appears that mixing methods requires mixing cultures; at the least, one has to appreciate the strengths and weaknesses of both.

Pragmatism—a tendency to choose methodologies that will best answer research questions—is recommended for scholars using mixed methods to achieve their research objectives; pragmatism necessarily implies methodological pluralism. As Creswell (2003: 12) asserts, "Thus, for the mixed methods researcher, pragmatism opens the door to multiple methods, different world-views, and different assumptions, as well as to different forms of data collection and analysis in the mixed methods study." This perspective fits the research presented in this book—exploring the state feminism theoretical framework and its implications for other theories pertaining to politics in postindustrial democracies. Pragmatism does not mean that we abandon our commitment to contribute to knowledge based on rigorous and systematic analysis of valid and reliable empirical observations. It means that we, as researchers and authors, recognize that there is more than one way to reach that goal.

The purpose of the state feminism project is to understand how and to what extent state-based institutions established to promote women's rights and gender equality—women's policy agencies—can bring about the success of women's movements, originating outside the state, in penetrating policy arenas, changing processes, substantive policies and culture, even democracy itself. To achieve this goal, we presented several propositions in Chapter 1; each points toward a particular method or methods.

Typical of much research, some propositions take the form of hypotheses, for example: *Alliances with women's policy agencies are a significant cause of women's movement procedural and policy successes in postindustrial democracies; failure to form alliances accounts for movement failures with respect to policy responses.* If this statement is considered a hypothesis, it directs researchers toward data amenable to techniques of statistical-causal inference to test the impact of women's policy agencies' activities and alliances with women's movement actors while controlling for other possible drivers of procedural and policy successes.

Another proposition suggests a different direction: *Women's movements are more likely to be successful with the state when there are left-governing majorities and when left-wing parties and unions are ideologically and organizationally very close to women's movement actors. Activities of agencies complement such left-wing alliances in achieving women's movement success and in turn are explained by them.* Here, the idea is that understanding what determines women's movement success as well as the place of women's policy agencies in that success involves looking for combinations or configurations of conditions. Rather than isolating independent causes, the approach here is to trace the determinants of particular outcomes—an approach that lends itself to more qualitatively based methods.

Finally, consider this proposition: *Women's policy agencies form alliances with women's movement actors to achieve procedural access and policy change in favor of movement goals.* It is fairly straightforward to find many empirical examples that support this proposition. However, such observations alone do not show how these alliances actually work to achieve such outcomes. So, some questions call for more in-depth examination of particular cases to trace the processes that bring about the outcomes the researchers have observed.

Thus, for exploring state feminism propositions, using several methods is more suitable than relying on a single method. Being open to using those techniques that work with respect to different research questions and propositions gives us the chance to more fully explore the validity of the state feminism framework in Chapters 4 to 6. Similarly, for those researchers assessing the significance of state feminism findings for social movement, representation, framing and institutionalism theories, in Chapters 7 to 10, the pragmatic perspective expands choices about research questions, goals, and means.

Recent work on mixed methods strives to provide guidelines to researchers to help them make the most of this pragmatic approach.[10] Evan Leiberman (2005), for example, provides a visual map showing how to nest qualitative case studies inside an overall quantitative approach. Creswell (2003) offers taxonomies of ways to combine methods in a single project. Researchers can follow quantitative and qualitative methods sequentially or concurrently for the purposes of triangulation, explanation, or exploration.

For the study of state feminism propositions in Part II, we adopt a concurrent integration strategy (Creswell 2003). As described below, all the data is from one source collected and developed by the RNGS network, and the analysis is concurrent. We use three methods—descriptive statistics and statistical inference, specifically correlations and ordinal regression; causal configurations through crisp-set Qualitative Comparative Analysis (csQCA), a type of Configurational Comparative Method; and causal mechanisms through case studies— to cross-validate and corroborate the findings. By assessing the contributions of each method to these findings, we engage in what is sometimes called *triangulation*.[11] Rather than testing the methods against each other, however, our goal is to *integrate* the findings from each method to contribute to the validation of the state feminism framework.

In examining the foundational underpinnings of state feminism propositions in Part III of the book, the authors also use different methods to explore the implications of the empirical observations for propositions found in these theories. For the most part, they opt for a more *sequential mixed-methods* approach, using different datasets and tools to explore or explain discrete questions rather than a formal integrated approach. We maintain that this use of mixed methods, which Andrew Bennett (2007) calls "one of the most exciting and promising developments in a field that has for far too long been defined by isolated methodological communities dining at separate tables," constitutes an important innovation in comparative politics research. Similarly, Peter A. Hall argues, "The field of comparative politics is one of the liveliest sites for methodological debate in the discipline. That, in turn has encouraged reflection about how conclusions are to be drawn about the political world, which ultimately strengthens the discipline" (2004: 4).

Methods Used in This Book

The research propositions and questions of the state feminism project lend themselves to a mixed-methods approach. This section describes the different techniques and the data sources used for each method: hypothesis testing and the quantitative dataset; causal configurations and the csQCA datasets; and causal mechanisms-description in detailed case studies. Each of the datasets is derived from the same source: completion of comprehensive worksheets by RNGS researchers on 130 policy debates that were covered in the issue books.[12]

Quantitative Datasets and Analyses

The RNGS Dataset

The process that produced the RNGS quantitative dataset began with a thorough revision of conceptualization to set forth nominal definitions, operational definitions, and measurement instructions for all concepts in the state feminism framework.[13] The resulting codebook contains separate sections on twenty-eight concepts, including policy response, procedural response, gendering issue frame, policy subsystem structure, and cohesion among women's movement actors. In turn, one to ten variables that measure dimensions of each concept are presented along with operational definitions and explicit measures and codes found in the dataset. Most of the variables are measured quantitatively, but some are in the form of descriptions—for example, the microframes of women's movement actors or the issue frame at the beginning of the debate—and they are found for each case in the Text Appendices (RNGS 2007b). These appendices also contain other information about the debates, such as the way the issue came to the agenda. The codebook provides the coding instructions for 120 different variables.

Working from the comprehensive worksheets and the appendices, the main authors of this text (McBride and Mazur) coded all cases on all the variables. The approach was to assign values for a set of variables separately, compare the codes, and settle any disagreements by further investigation. The quantitative-variable measures in the dataset are nominal, ordinal, and interval. This mixture is the result of a conscious decision to "unpack" the concepts to find their components and provide the basic information for scholars to adapt the data to a variety of theoretical interests, not just the state feminism theoretical framework. For example, in measuring the participation of women's movement actors in the policy subsystem, there are four variables: (1) women's movement actors' participation in the subsystem at the beginning of the debate (yes or no); (2) degree of presence of women's movement actors at the beginning of the debate (percent); (3) women's movement actors' participation in the subsystem at the end of the debate (yes or no); (4) degree of presence of women's movement actors at the end of the debate (percent). For measuring the gendering of the issue frame, there are eleven nominal variables that provide information on the frame at the beginning and end of the debate as well as whether it was gendered and how the frame changed during the course of the debate.

New Datasets

Because the concepts are stripped down to the component variables in the RNGS dataset, it is possible to use these components to form new constructs not in the original project. In addition, the Text Appendices provide a wealth of information available for additional coding (RNGS 2007b). This has allowed us to use subsets of the full dataset or to develop datasets appropriate to various research propositions and methods. New datasets from the RNGS data on policy debates were developed for nearly all of the chapters in the book. Here we identify these new datasets; they are discussed in more detail in each chapter and included in Table 2.1, which summarizes the methods used in each chapter.

For Chapters 3 and 10, the Women's Policy Agency dataset includes the fifty-seven national-level agencies, ten quasi agencies, and six subnational-level agencies that were active in the RNGS policy debates. For Chapter 6, the Transformative State Feminism dataset contains recodings of the 108 national-level debates on the measure developed for the chapter. The Women's Movement Actor dataset, developed by Outshoorn for Chapter 7, comprises information about 354 different movement actors that took positions in the 130 debates. Lovenduski and Guadagnini also used women's movement actors as the unit of analysis in their Women's Movement Actor Location dataset including 217 different cases. And for Chapter 9, Sauer created a new dataset of Women's Movement Actors' Frames with 1,002 frames, from which she analyzed 512 observations of the issue definition portion of the microframes. Sauer's dataset also includes information on policy goals in microframes of women's movement actors in 130 debates.

Quantitative Analysis: Using Description and Statistics

The quantitative datasets provide a precise and reliable way to examine the propositions developed from the various theories examined in this book. For example, for the assessment of state feminism propositions, one of the important questions is to determine whether women's policy agencies are more important than other factors, such as movement resources, favorable policy environments, or left-wing support, in explaining state responses to women's movement actors, and then assess their influence compared to women's policy agencies activity. The assumptions behind this type of analysis are that notions of cause are based on the association between variables, that other variables that might explain the dependent variable must be controlled, and that the observed associations must be beyond chance to be accepted.

The quantitative datasets allow researchers to use a variety of descriptive and inference statistics to answer research questions. Through frequencies it is possible to map the range of characteristics of women's policy agencies, state actions, women's movement characteristics and activities, and features of the policy environment for debates. Cross-tabulations suggest possible bivariate associations for examining findings by issue, country, and over time. Researchers can test hypotheses relating to state feminism and other theories using bivariate correlations and ordinal regression. These datasets have proved to be a fruitful resource for developing composite measures that are offered in several of the chapters, such as administrative capacity of agencies in Chapter 3, degree of women's policy agency activity in Chapters 4 and 5, Transformational State Feminism in Chapter 6, whether women's movement actors are institutionalized or not in Chapter 7, the activities of women legislators in Chapter 8, and the type of frames used by women's movement actors in Chapter 9.

Qualitative Comparative Analysis

Despite the promise of quantitative methods, for researchers who explored in depth a variety of policy debates for the issue books and worksheets, statistical inference seems to overlook the complexity of the politics of state feminism. In addition, there are not enough cases in the dataset to permit the use of statistical methods in subsets, such as all debates in one issue or one country. Although the separate-issue books published between 2001 and 2007 retain complexity of the cases and permit analysis of debates in separate groups, there were problems of comparability from one book to the next, limiting what one could say that would assess the state feminism propositions overall. Qualitative Comparative Analysis, one of the Configurational Comparative Methods (Rihoux and Ragin 2008), offered another approach (Ragin 1987 and 2008).[14]

Not based on principles of statistical control and multivariate analysis, QCA retains the assumptions of qualitative case studies: Each case or observation, such as a policy debate, is also a composite of conditions associated with an outcome of interest. Several scholars have used the approach to study social movement successes and failures (e.g., Amenta et al. 1992; Giugni and Sakura 2007). Their work shows that QCA allows researchers to explore and compare the cases across issues and over time while maintaining some of their complexity. It also lends itself to our interests in understanding the ways women's movements have been successful with the state and also the ways they have failed.

QCA assumes there may be more than one pattern of conditions that result in a particular outcome, that is, *equifinality*. By looking at all the ways that the sets of conditions meet with possible outcomes, QCA describes and analyzes them as *configurations*. In approaching a study, the researcher assumes that all possible configurations of causal conditions are possible and the job is to map them and relate this mapping to the outcome that the researcher is trying to explain. This exercise expands the descriptive approach used in single historical "thick" case studies to a mathematical analysis of a large number of cases. Charles Ragin and Benoît Rihoux (2004: 4) clarify that this is close to the idea of explicit connections. "An especially useful feature of QCA is its capacity for analyzing complex causation, defined as a situation where a given outcome may follow from several different combinations of causal conditions—different causal 'paths.'" It is a search for "decisive recipes" in achieving a particular outcome. Even more ambitious, QCA analysts use the method to determine which configurations or conditions are *necessary* or *sufficient* or both. This promise is intriguing for this project, because our goal is to determine whether a case can be made for *state feminism*, which we define as women's policy agencies playing some sort of causal—necessary and/or sufficient—role in women's movement success.

We have opted for csQCA that uses measures of the presence (1) or absence (0) of an outcome of interest or any condition that may be part of a causal configuration as opposed to multi-value QCA or fuzzy sets QCA.[15] It is left to the researchers to select, based on theoretical and case knowledge, the particular combinations of conditions that may lead to the outcome. Here we call such proposed configurations *models*. Thus, it is necessary to produce a series of datasets that measure for each case the presence or absence of all conditions in the models as well as the presence or absence of each outcome of interest. The first step is to complete descriptive tables including each case; only cases that are complete for all conditions are included. The information for these tables comes from the debate worksheets and is checked for accuracy and reliability against the measures in the dataset. The entire coding procedure is informed by our deep knowledge of the cases themselves. Then, csQCA uses formal techniques of Boolean algebra based on the dichotomous measures to map out the configurations found in the observed cases and the causal results, if any.

Theory-building and Descriptive Case Studies

Statistical analysis and csQCA are useful for assessing the validity of state feminism propositions, as well as for providing insights into other theories, and the findings across several research questions are presented in Part II of the book. At the same time, there are questions left unanswered by these approaches. The cross-tabulations may show tendencies and patterns of characteristics of different women's policy agencies' activities, for example, but no statistical associations; does this mean that these characteristics are not important? There may be correlations found that are not explained by the theoretical propositions. There are exceptional cases where women's movements have achieved success despite unfavorable conditions, according to theory. Sometimes csQCA shows no causal patterns among the conditions in the study. We have also found that particular conditions are important for some issues and not in others, and in some countries and not others.

To help find answers to the puzzles produced by csQCA and statistical analysis, we turn to the third method in this mixed-methods study: case studies that trace the trajectory of individual policy debates to find mechanisms of causation, the paths that connect one variable to another—in other words, case studies used for *theory building*. Finding such causal mechanisms through process tracing can also unearth variables and conditions not included among the codified variables in the datasets or in the csQCA models. They can thus suggest amendments to theoretical propositions and research questions. *Descriptive* case studies can also add an important dimension to the more aggregate findings through the illustration of the workings of women's policy agencies and their leaders within political processes. All information in the case studies is from the debate worksheets, the Text Appendices, and the narratives in the issue books.

Methods and Datasets by Chapter

Table 2.1 presents the methods and datasets used for analysis in each chapter. While all of the chapters use the large-N datasets descriptively through presenting frequencies, cross-tabulations, and bivariate correlations, only Chapters 4, 5, and 8 undertake multivariate analyses based on statistical inference, that is, Ordinal Regression. We use csQCA in the chapters in Part II of the book based on three different datasets. Theory-building and descriptive case studies of debates are an important component of the analysis of the state feminism framework in all of Part II and in Part III, "Unpacking State Feminism," in Chapters 8 to 10. Some of the case studies are on a single debate and others compare the dynamics of two or three debates. Chapter 3 includes descriptive case studies of quasi women's policy agencies and subnational agencies that supplement the aggregate analysis of the fifty-three national-level women's policy agencies.

Strategies for Integration of Methods and Findings

Sometimes there are conflicting guidelines in the emerging literature on mixed-methods research about how to treat the results of different methods in the same study. Some, especially those immersed in the debate between quantitative and qualitative cultures and approaches, insist that the goal of mixed methods is primarily to compare the methods themselves to see which one leads to the "better" result. Quantitative analysts often use qualitative case studies to improve their regression analyses. Others suggest that quantitative methods overcome the weaknesses in the qualitative ones. In this project, the goal of using more than one method is to gather a more complete understanding of the theory and politics of state feminism.

We have, thus, adopted the following strategies to integrate the findings:

- Clearly state the findings of each method in terms of the research questions.
- Group the findings of each method to assess what they mean together: do they complement each other or compete with each other? Is there a convergence of knowledge, or are there separate findings for each method?
- Assess the implications of findings for state feminism theory in the chapters that examine state feminism propositions and the conclusion to the book itself.

The discussion in Part IV, Chapter 11, reviews to what degree this mixed-methods approach has enhanced the study of state feminism. We hope it contributes to continuing efforts to institutionalize mixed-methods research more generally.

TABLE 2.1   SUMMARY OF METHODS AND DATA SOURCES BY CHAPTER

Chapter	Topics	Method 1: Quantitative	Method 2: csQCA	Method 3: Case Studies
3	Profiles of agencies; characteristics analyzed over time and by country	Frequencies; cross-tabulations. Women's Policy Agency dataset, N = 73	None	Eleven descriptive case studies
4	State feminism theory: explaining state response and the influence of Insider agencies: Movement State Feminism	Frequencies; cross-tabulations; correlations; Ordinal Regression. National state debates from RNGS dataset, N = 114	Issue-based and country-based crisp-set datasets of national state debates with full and quasi agencies, N = 108	Four theory-building case studies
5	State feminism theory: explaining agency successes and failures	Cross-tabulations; Ordinal Regression. National state debates with full women's policy agencies from RNGS dataset, N = 104	Issue-based crisp-set datasets of national state debates with full and quasi agencies, N = 108	Six theory-building case studies
6	State feminism theory: assessing Transformative State Feminism	Frequencies; cross-tabulations. National state debates with full and quasi agencies from RNGS dataset with added feminist variables, N = 108	Issue-based crisp-set datasets with measures of Transformative State Feminism, N = 108	Four theory-building case studies
7	Social movement theory	Frequencies; cross-tabulations; correlations. Women's Movement Actor dataset, N = 354. All debates with movement actors from RNGS dataset, N = 129	None	None
8	Theories of representation	Frequencies; cross-tabulations; correlations; Ordinal Regression. Women's Movement Actor location dataset, N = 217. All debates with movement actors from RNGS dataset, N = 129	None	Three theory-building case studies

TABLE 2.1 *Continued*

Chapter	Topics	Method 1: Quantitative	Method 2: csQCA	Method 3: Case Studies
9	Framing/gendering theory	Frequencies; cross-tabulations; correlations. Women's Movement Actor frame dataset, $N = 1002$. All debates with movement actors from RNGS dataset, $N = 129$	None	Eight descriptive case studies
10	Gendering new institutional theories	Frequencies; cross-tabulations. Women's Policy Agency dataset, $N = 73$. All debates with agencies from RNGS dataset, $N = 124$. National state and party debates with agencies from RNGS dataset with added feminist variables, $N = 117$	None	One theory-building case study

Boundaries of the RNGS Data

Following the methods outlined here, researchers have provided rich descriptive information about 130 debates in thirteen countries across five issue areas over more than three decades. This empirical foundation is at the core of all the datasets and data analysis used in the book to explore the state feminism framework and its components. However, before launching into the results of that exploration, it is important to take a moment to recognize the boundaries of the RNGS data with respect to their representativeness and the application of any generalizations to larger populations.

Three key decisions determined the range and span of the study. The first was the decision to study postindustrial democracies. To be sure, the women's policy agencies, women's movements, and the processes related to state feminism may have occurred in countries with other types of political and economic forms. From the beginning, however, the group decided to focus only on the countries of the world with similar political, economic, and cultural profiles, a most-similar-systems comparative strategy. It will be left to experts from regions outside of the West to determine whether the framework and findings are applicable to other countries.

The second decision involved the sample of policy issues. We selected one topic for each of four gendered dimensions of policy—reproduction policy;

work and family policy; sexuality policy; and citizens' rights policy—plus one topic of national priority, the hot issue. This allowed for adequate exploration of differences across issues; however, there are other debates that are also possible venues for these studies.[16]

The third decision provided a procedure and criteria to researchers on how to select policy debates for each issue area within each country in the study in a way that would enhance their representativeness. The procedure was first to locate the institutions in the political system of the country that made the most important and binding decisions about the issue. Such policy subsystems may vary over time and could be at subnational or party arenas. Next, the task was to construct the universe of policy debates that had come up in these subsystems since the 1960s and took place when a women's policy agency was in existence. From this list of debates, the selection of three debates to study was to adhere to the following criteria of representativeness: (1) *decisional system importance* when more than one subsystem is involved in making policy in the area; (2) *life cycle* of deliberations on the issue over the 1970s to 2000s; and (3) *issue area salience*, that is, the importance of the debate to overall policy on the issue. Researchers could face conflicts among the procedures and criteria. Sometimes the most important decisions about abortion—for example, initial legalization and implementation—took place in the 1970s, before the establishment of any women's policy agencies. At other times, all the salient decisions took place in one decade, thus limiting coverage of all decades in the study. Although most of the researchers were able to fulfill all the criteria in selecting their debates, there were exceptions so that not all debates have a women's policy agency, for example, and there is an uneven distribution across decades.

The RNGS network intended to recruit researchers to study debates on all five issues in all the countries of Western Europe as well as Canada and the United States. For a variety of reasons, we were not able to secure that complete coverage.[17] Only slightly more than half of postindustrial democracies are represented here. Box 2.1 shows the distribution of issues by country. The most comprehensive coverage pertains to the hot issue, for which there are debates in all countries except Ireland. Abortion, prostitution, and political representation have debates in ten or eleven countries, while there are job training debates in seven of the thirteen countries in the study.

Whereas the issues of abortion, job training, political representation, prostitution, and national priorities provide a comprehensive span of gender dimensions, there are many issues in those dimensions that could not be included.[18] Although the policy debates were selected according to rigorous guidelines to represent fully the most important debates over three decades, not all issues are covered in all countries, nor is there an even distribution of the debates across decades. Thus, any generalizations from the analysis of these data must be tempered by these limits of representativeness. At the same time, the rich range of cases that we do have provides a solid basis for the nuanced and "modest" generalizations found in the book (Rihoux and Ragin 2008).[19]

Box 2.1 RNGS Debate Coverage by Country and Sector

All Five Issue Areas

France

Italy

Spain

United States

Four Areas

Austria: abortion, political representation, prostitution, hot issue

Canada: abortion job training, prostitution, hot issue

Finland: job training, political representation, prostitution, hot issue

Great Britain: abortion, political representation, prostitution, hot issue

Netherlands: abortion, political representation, prostitution, hot issue

Three Areas

Belgium: abortion, political representation, hot issue

Germany: abortion, political representation, hot issue

Sweden: political representation, prostitution, hot issue

Two Areas

Ireland: abortion, job training

3

Mapping Women's Policy Agencies

Women's policy agencies sit at the intersection between movement and government. As such, they are the primary focus of state feminism. The agencies studied in this book are those that RNGS researchers found to be in a position to participate in policy debates across the five issues covered in the original study—abortion, job training, political representation, prostitution, and hot issues. In tracing the trajectories of debates, information was gathered not only about whether agencies ally with women's movement actors and participate in policy arenas, but also about their form, mandate, powers, and resources. This chapter maps out these characteristics across time, country, and region using seventy-three women's policy agencies presented in Box 3.1. Clearly, there is no single blueprint for these machineries.

In the RNGS dataset there are one or more agencies in 124 of the 130 policy debates. Fewer agencies are studied in this chapter, because we have eliminated the duplications that researchers found when looking at several debates over just a few years in a country. At the same time some agencies lasted such a long time that their budgets and leadership changed from one period to the next. We repeat those agencies found to span two decades, (e.g., 1978–1985); one version of the agency is included for each decade (e.g. 1970s and 1980s). Based on these criteria, the agencies studied in this chapter include fifty-seven national-level agencies, ten quasi agencies, and six subnational offices.

We use the information on the following agency characteristics, collected for the RNGS study, to understand the structural capabilities of all seventy-three offices.

> *Type:* Is the agency a ministry, an administrative office, a commission in the political executive, a judicial body, an advisory council, a legislative council or section of a political party, or something else?
>
> *Appointment of agency head:* Is the appointment of the agency head a political appointment, a bureaucratic appointment, lay panel appointment, or a combination of all three?

Box 3.1 Women's Policy Agencies Analyzed in Chapter 3

Austria

1984 Women's State Secretary
1998 Ministry of Women's Affairs
2002 Unit for Women's Affairs
1979 Women's Section of Social Democratic Party
1991 Vienna Councilor for Women's Affairs

Belgium

1975, 1981 Consultative Commission for the Status of Women
1987 State Secretary for the Environment and Social Emancipation
1993 Minister of Equal Opportunities
2000 Minister for Labour and Equality of Opportunity

Canada

1969 Royal Commission on the Status of Women
1985, 1994 Status of Women Canada
1984 Canadian Advisory Council on the Status of Women
2002 Women's Health Bureau
1995 Ministry of Women's Equality–British Columbia

Finland

1969 Temporary Committee on the Status of Women
1973, 1986, 1993 Council for Equality
1979 Working Group
1996 Helsinki Equality Board

France

1975 Deputy Ministry of the Feminine Condition
1980 Women's Work Committee
1980 Delegate Minister for the Status of Women and the Family
1984 Ministry of the Rights of Woman
1990 Deputy Ministry of Women's Rights
1991 Deputy Ministry of Women's Rights and Daily Life
1991 Deputy Ministry of Women's Rights
1993 Women's Rights Service
1995 Observatory for Parity
1999 Deputy Minister of Women's Rights and Job Training

(continued on next page)

Box 3.1   *Continued*

Germany

1991 Ministry for Women and Youth
1995 Ministry for Family, Women, and Youth
2001 Ministry for Family Affairs, Senior Citizens, Women, and Youth
1984 Working Group of Social Democratic Women

Great Britain

1971, 1990 Women's National Commission
1981 Equal Opportunities Commission
2000 Women and Equality Unit
1990 Labour Shadow Ministry of Women's Rights
1993 Women's Committee of the National Executive Council
    of the Labour Party

Ireland

1981 Equal Employment Agency
1986 Minister of Women's Affairs
1992 Joint Oireachtas Committee on Justice, Equality, Defense,
    and Women's Rights
2002 Department of Equality and Law Reform

Italy

1984 National Committee for Equal Opportunities, Ministry of Labor
1996, 2002 Ministry for Equal Opportunities
1996 National Commission for Equal Opportunity between Men and Women
1991 National Commission for Women's Emancipation and Liberation
    (Communist Party)

The Netherlands

1983, 1997 Department for Coordination of Equality Policy
1976 Women's Contact (Social Democratic Party)

Spain

1984, 1991, 2002 Women's Institute
1987, 1997 Socialist Party Women's Secretariat

Box 3.1 *Continued*

Sweden

1981 Equal Opportunities Ombudsman
1985, 1996 Minister of Gender Equality
1993 Social Democratic Women's Section

United States

1974 Secretary's Advisory Committee on the Rights and Responsibilities of Women
1977 National Commission for the Observance of International Women's Year
1975, 1980 Women's Bureau of the Department of Labor
1996 White House Office of Women's Initiatives and Outreach
1999 The President's Inter-Agency Council
1994 Congressional Caucus on Women's Issues
1971 Governor's Commission on the Status of Women
1984 State Sex Equity Coordinators
1992 Michigan Women's Commission

Policy orientation/mission: Is the formal and informal policy orientation of the agency single-issue, multi-issue, or cross-sectional?

Proximity to decision-making power: Is the agency close to, moderately close to, or distant from decision-making power within its institutional setting?

Policy-making powers: What policy making responsibility does the agency have: propose policies, review and recommend, enforce laws, or some combination of these?

Leadership: Has the head of the agency ever belonged to a women's movement or feminist movement organization?

Administrative resources: How many of the following administrative resources does the agency have: staff, administrative divisions, field offices, a separate budget, subsidies for women's groups, and research resources? What is the level of these resources? How many staff members, divisions, field offices? How large are budgets for subsidies and research?

The type of agency, type of appointment, policy-making orientation, policy-making capacity, and administrative resources pertain to the autonomy and authority of agencies. Two dimensions show ties to women's movements—whether the agency head has women's movement–feminist movement experience, and whether and how much agencies subsidize women's groups, a category of administrative resources.[1] When compared across agencies, these characteristics form several composites or profiles, the subject of the first section of this chapter. Next, in order to go beyond a static snapshot, we examine the characteristics of the national-level agencies over time across all of the countries in the study.[2] The chapter concludes with an assessment of the extent to which there are country or regional patterns in the structural characteristics of the national-level agencies.

Profiles of Women's Policy Agencies

In comparing characteristics through cross-tabulations, we find that the central distinguishing feature of a women's policy agency is its type, that is, the basic institutional form.[3] Autonomy, authority, and ties to women's movements vary according to whether agencies are ministries, administrative offices, executive commissions, advisory councils, or party sections. Among the national-level agencies, there are six different institutional types. However, most (84 percent) belong to one of only three types: nineteen (33 percent) are ministries; seventeen (30 percent) are administrative offices; and twelve (21 percent) are executive commissions. Of the remaining nine national-level agencies, seven are advisory councils; there is one judicial body—an ombudsman—and one legislative committee, included in the "one-of-a-kind" category. In addition, there are nine party sections that have similar characteristics, while for the six subnational offices diversity in structural features is the norm. These are trends and not rigid typologies, however, since individual agencies may not share all the characteristics of others in its type. Nevertheless, based on the type of institutional structure to which a women's policy agency is assigned, a great deal can be known about the other characteristics. The profile of each type is described here: ministries, administrative offices, executive commissions, advisory councils, and party sections. Given their low numbers, subnational and one-of-a-kind agencies require separate descriptions that follow the profiles.

Ministries

If the "women's portfolio" is assigned to a ministry—whether the Ministry of Women's Affairs in Austria, the Ministry for Equal Opportunities in Italy, or the Ministry for Women and Youth in Germany—it will be placed close to the center of policy-making power in the executive and will have power to propose policies to the executive as well as to review and make recommendations on a wide range of issues. Some ministries may be given a cross-sectional remit similar to gender mainstreaming. All ministers are politically appointed, and three times out of five, the job goes to a women's movement activist, but not all of these have feminist experience. One third of ministries have enforcement powers. Ministries tend to be well resourced; they all have permanent staff, and most have some organizational capacity with separate divisions and budgets.

However, only a minority (one third) have field offices. Around two thirds of ministries have research budgets and award subsidies to women's groups. Generally, the potential strength of ministries for promoting women's movement goals is likely to be found in their proximity to the central power and their policy-making powers.

Administrative Offices

A standard institutional form for women's policy agencies is an office established more or less permanently within the bureaucracy of the state, typically in a ministry. Such offices, like the Women's Institute in Spain, the Department for Coordination of Equality Policy in the Netherlands, and the Women's Bureau of the Department of Labor in the United States, for the most part have great staying power and participated in two or more debates in the RNGS study. Most of these offices are assigned a wide range of issues pertaining to women's status, but 30 percent are single-issue in nature, such as the U.S. Women's Bureau.

Unlike the ministries, administrative offices are not close to central power and do not have policy proposal powers. Their role is to review and recommend to the heads of departments where they are placed; at the same time about half have law-enforcing powers, which ministries typically do not have. Although they tend to be located away from the political executive, most of the leaders are politically appointed, and a slim majority have women's movement experience. At the same time, these administrative offices are the least likely to have leaders with feminist experience (only 25 percent). Like ministries, they have several types of administrative resources, but these are a bit more complex with more separate divisions, separate budgets, subsidies for women's groups, and research budgets. Only 30 percent have field offices, but this is the highest proportion of all the types of agencies. It is the placement of these offices inside the state bureaucracy that may provide the greatest help to women's movement actors seeking to penetrate closed policy arenas.

Executive Commissions

Sometimes top political executives assign the gender equality portfolio to a specialized commission within the executive branch. Commissions such as the Council for Equality in Finland, the National Committee for Equal Opportunity between Men and Women in Italy, and the Consultative Commission for the Status of Women in Belgium, are usually close to the centers of power and expected to review and make recommendations on policy proposals made by others. Only about a third have policy proposal powers, and none enforces laws. The leader is always politically appointed. Over the course of this study, there is a high likelihood that the agency leader has experience in a women's movement organization. In fact, unlike the ministries or administrative offices, a majority of the heads of commissions have feminist experience as well.

What commissions gain in proximity and leadership, they tend to lose in administrative capacity and resources. Most have some staff, but much smaller than the other agencies. About half have separate budgets, only one has any divisions at all, and not one has field offices or budgets for subsidies or research. The membership of these commissions varies, but they are likely to be composed of party leaders, government officials, and representatives of constituency organizations. Despite the lack of administrative resources, feminist leaders of commissions may be able to help women's movement actors bring their views to the center of high-level policy preparation.

Advisory Councils

Advisory councils are set up to provide consultation for policy leaders in ministries or the executive with people and organizations from outside government. Some turn out to be permanent, such as the Council for Equality in Finland, while others, such as the U.S. Secretary's Advisory Committee on Rights and Responsibilities of Women, disappear quickly. Like executive commissions, these are political appointments and focus on a multi-issue agenda. Their role is simply to review and recommend policy proposals coming from others, with no proposal or enforcement powers of their own. They tend to be close to the centers of power, where they function in an advisory capacity but are generally low on resources. They may have a small staff, a separate budget, and leaders with women's movement experience. However, they do not have separate divisions, field offices, subsidies for women's groups, or research staff. Placement in the institutional hierarchy is the key to the usefulness of advisory councils to women's movement actors.

Party Sections: Quasi Women's Policy Agencies

Examining quasi women's policy agencies places the analytical focus at the margins of the state, given that by definition these agencies do not have the same level of formality as state agencies and are often located outside of formal state policy-making arenas. All but one of the quasi agencies appearing in the policy debates were in left-wing political parties that held central policy-making functions. These permanent structures in the party organization are formally charged by the party with promoting women's issues and are involved with some aspect of policy making. The party quasi agencies in Austria and the Netherlands were active in the 1970s; in Spain, Germany, and in Great Britain they were in the 1980s; and in Italy, Spain, Sweden, and Great Britain they were active in the 1990s. There are no party quasi women's policy agencies found in debates studied in Belgium, Finland, France, Canada, Ireland, or the United States. Most of the party agencies participated in political representation debates; the exceptions are in Austria, where the Women's Section of the Social Democratic Party was also influential in abortion debates in the 1970s, and in Great Britain where a Labour Party Shadow Minister of Women's Rights was important in abortion debates in the late1980s.[4]

Party women's policy agencies, here and more generally speaking, tend to have two roles: to organize women, often in auxiliary groups, like the women's sections of the Austrian and Swedish parties, presented in Box 3.2, or Women's Contact (Social Democratic Party) in the Netherlands; and to represent women's interests at the policy-making level of the party in congresses and/or executive councils. The two roles can be carried out by women's sections, but some parties create a smaller women's commission or group to participate in decision making, usually in the executive council of the party, such as the Working Group of Social Democratic Women in Germany, the National Commission for Women's Emancipation and Liberation in the Communist Party in Italy, the Socialist Party Women's Secretariat in Spain, and the Women's Committee of the National Executive Council of the Labour Party in Great Britain. In countries where parties set up shadow governments, the women's shadow minister can also have a policy-making role within the party, as in the case of the Labour Party Shadow Minister of Women's Rights in Great Britain, along with the party's steering committee for women.

The nine party quasi women's policy agencies reflect the frequently partisan and less institutionalized setting of the parties; the heads are appointed following logic of the political configurations of the particular party, or government in power, or by the members of the commission itself evenly split between the two, but not by any administrative logic. Given their focus on women's issues, all agencies have multi-issue, but not systematically cross-sectional, policy orientations. The policy-making capacities are also quite similar. Five of the nine are close to decision-making centers of power, while only two are distant. Five party agencies have the power to propose policies to top party leadership—one of the most authoritative instruments for a full-fledged agency. Of these five, four also have the power to recommend; the remaining three have no policy-making power. None of the party agencies have any implementation power. Similarly, they have quite low levels of administrative capacity, all but one have no or just one resource, usually staff. Although six of the nine party structures have staffs, they are relatively small, ranging from one to twenty-five members. None has separate divisions, separate budgets, or subsidies for women's groups. The Women's Section of the Social Democratic Party in Austria, discussed in more detail in Box 3.2, is the only quasi women's policy agency to have offices at the subnational level—nine in all.

All agency leaders, except those in Women's Contact in the Social Democratic Party in the Netherlands and the Working Group of Social Democratic Women in Germany, had some sort of women's movement experience, and almost all of these, except one leader in Italy, had been active in feminist movement activities either inside or outside of the party. In Great Britain, Claire Short and Jo Richardson, the heads of the two party quasi agencies, were Labour MPs with strong records of promoting feminist positions on legisla-

---

Box 3.2 Successful Party Agencies

Women's Section of the Austrian Social Democratic Party

Women have long had a separate organization within the Austrian Social Democratic Party, for years a major governing party. The party statute establishes the Social Democratic women's organization as one of several affiliated organizations (other examples include the youth and senior citizens groups). There are women representatives and groups at the local, regional, and national levels. The women's section holds annual conferences (*Bundesfrauenkonferenz*) at the national level and passes resolutions forwarded to the party's national conferences, where they have direct representation. The national Women's Conference is a forum to articulate concerns and press demands directed at the party elite. The chairwoman of the women's organization is co-opted in the party's highest decision-making body (RNGS 2007b: 28; Köpl 2005). Because of the central role of the Social Democratic Party in governing coalitions over the years, the party decisions often have nearly the same effect as state decisions. The conflicts are hammered out in the party, and the leaders put them into law through their dominance in the Parliament. Thus, the Women's Section has had a direct line to influence government policy and was active in state policy in the 1970s when there were no state agencies.

Social Democratic Women's Section in Sweden

The organization of the Social Democratic Women's Section is patterned after the party organization. The highest decision-making body is the section's congress, which adopts major policy guidelines and programs and elects its officers—the president, governing board, executive committee, and major administrative officer. At the local level, women's clubs are affiliated with the local party organization—*arbetarekommun*—and this is also the case for the district level, which is the parliamentary constituency organization. At the national level, the president of the Swedish Women's Section has had the right to attend and to speak, but not vote, at the party congress and the party governing board (RNGS 2007b: 613; Sainsbury 2005). Since Sweden has active women's policy agencies, it is likely that the influence of the Social Democratic Women's Section is limited to making policy inside the party itself. At the same time, because the party decisions about quotas in this large majority party were so important for representation of women, these party decisions, influenced by the section, had a large impact on the opportunities for women to gain power.

---

tion in the House of Commons and in their constituencies. Herta Firnberg, head of the Women's Section of the Social Democratic Party in Austria, had been a member of the women's section since the 1930s and had been involved with women's organizations outside of the party in the 1950s and 1960s. Livia Turco, the head of the National Commission for Women's Emancipation and Liberation in the Italian Communist Party, also was an activist on women's issues throughout her career. Similarly, Matilde Fernandez, before becoming head of the Socialist Party Women's Secretariat in Spain, had been a leading socialist feminist in trade union and left-wing circles.

Women's Policy Agencies at the Subnational Level

Researchers interested in state feminism have paid little systematic attention to the highly complex and diversified subnational level of the state—regional, provincial, cantonal, municipal, and the like.[5] Agencies have proliferated in many countries. For example, the West German government set up offices for women (*Frauenbeauftragte*) in the Länder and some municipalities as early as the 1970s (Ferree 1995). In France, in addition to the 119 field offices of the national women's policy agencies at the departmental and regional levels and more than 80 information centers for women's rights also administered by the central administration at regional and departmental levels, women's rights positions have been established by both regional and city governments. It is difficult to know for sure how many state bodies exist outside of the field offices in France, since there has never been a systematic survey of them. The Women's Rights Service did conduct an informal survey of departmental delegates at the end of the 1990s and found nine city women's commissions. As the French case shows, autonomous municipal-level agencies created by subnational governments can exist alongside field offices of national-level offices whether or not the country has a federal distribution of power.

Researchers working on RNGS, using the criteria for selecting debates, studied five debates at subnational levels. Subnational femocrats were active as well in one of the national debates. All of these subnational agencies are in federal systems, except for Finland, and four are situated in state or provincial governments, with three of these in the United States. Their appearance in the debates is connected with particular issues. In Austria and Finland, the municipality is an important arena for policy debates on prostitution, since Vienna and Helsinki are highly urbanized cities where prostitution has been relatively widespread. In Canada, provincial governments have important roles in job training policy, with British Columbia being a particularly important player in the 1980s. In the United States, policy issues of political representation are often left to the state governments; women's policy agencies in Arkansas and Michigan are included here. State-level sex equity coordinators, required by federal statute but placed in state governments, are here as a group, given their role in the national-level debate around the Vocational Training and Worker Productivity Act of 1990.

Thus, we have six discrete cases of subnational offices in three countries at the municipal and state or provincial level. They appeared in three decades and include a range of types of agencies—three commissions, two ministries, and one administrative office. It is interesting to note that in terms of the success rate of these subnational offices, only the Canadian agency presented women's movement demands and introduced a gender frame in a subnational policy debate. The U.S. sex equity coordinators were influential through their representations at congressional hearings. We now present the structural profiles of each of the subnational agencies included in the RNGS study to shed more light on these under-studied agencies.

Arkansas Governor's Commission on the Status of Women (1971). Appointed by the state's governor and located in that office, this agency had a multi-issue orientation, according to its annual report in 1971, "examining the role of women in Arkansas and finding ways by which women might become fuller participants in our State's economic, political and social institutions." Its policy capacity was limited to making recommendations to the governor, and it had minimal administrative resources, with a tiny budget of $5,000 funded from the governor's emergency fund and a part-time executive secretary. The chair was a political appointee by the governor. From 1971 to 1975, Diane Kincaid (later, Blair), a feminist political science professor, headed the commission, followed in 1976 to 1978 by Harryette Dorchester, a long-time "fellow traveler" of the feminist movement (RNGS 2007b: 677; Parry 2005).

State Sex Equity Coordinators (1989–1990). Appointed by the state departments of education in the United States, the sex equity coordinator positions were established to oversee the implementation of the gender equality provisions of the federal Vocational Education Act. These state-level bureaucrats were thus far from decision-making power, with a single-issue policy orientation; their mandate "was to administer programs for single parents and homemakers and sex equity, including gathering data, assessing programs, developing recommendations for information and outreach, providing technical assistance and advice, and assisting administrators, instructors and counselors to increase the access of women to vocational education, especially nontraditional occupations"(McBride Stetson 2001b: 288). While the coordinators had no staff, divisions, field offices, or subsidies for women's groups, the Federal Vocational Education Administration required states to allot at least $60,000 from their federal grants for each coordinator. The background of coordinators across the fifty states of course varied, but as one analyst indicated, a number of coordinators had been movement activists before appointment, and many had strong links to the National Coalition for Women and Girls in Education (RNGS 2007b: 669–670).

Vienna Councilor for Women's Affairs (1991). Appointed by the mayor of Vienna and as one of the Viennese government ministers, the *Stadtratin* or councilor was quite close to decision-making power at the municipal level, with powers to recommend, propose, and enforce policy. The minister focused on a number of women's issues including equal opportunity, employment, violence against women, and, beginning in the late 1980s, prostitution. With four full-time staff members, a small separate budget, and some subsidies for women's groups, the number of resources was quite high, although at relatively low levels of support. Ingrid Smekjkal, the councilor starting in 1991, had no prior experience in any women's or feminist groups (RNGS 2007b: 46; Sauer 2004).

Michigan Women's Commission (1991–1993). The commission was composed of fifteen members appointed for three-year terms by the governor and approved by the Senate. Directors of the state departments of civil service, education, labor, and social service were ex officio members. Created in 1968, it moved from the governor's office to the more distant Department of Civil Rights in 1991. According to its executive order, the commission "shall study and review the status of women; direct attention to the problems confronting wives, mothers, homemakers, and workers; recommend methods of overcoming discrimination in employment, civil rights, and political rights; promote methods for enabling women to develop skills, continue their education, or be retrained; make surveys and appoint committees, and secure recognition for women's accomplishments and contributions to the State" (RNGS 2007b: 681). With no separate divisions, field offices, subsidies for women's groups, or specific research staff, a general staff of three, and a budget of $300,000, it has quite low levels of overall administrative capacity in comparison to national counterparts but the highest budget compared with its subnational counterparts. Patricia Thomas, the chair from 1991 and 1993, had no prior experience in women's movement groups (Parry 2005).

British Columbia Ministry of Women's Equality (1991). The Ministry was one of the executive departments in the government of the Canadian province of British Columbia. The New Democratic Party established the Ministry in 1991 to have a multi-issue orientation including violence against women, as well as legal issues such as family law, child care, and support for women's centers. The Ministry provided policy advice to the rest of the provincial government, implemented women's programs, and funded women's groups for specific purposes. Among all the subnational agencies, the British Columbia ministry has the highest level of administrative capacity, similar to the top 10 percent of all women's policy agencies. Its staff of 277 is the highest number of staff for *any* women's policy agency in the study. There were four separate divisions, six regional offices, and a budget amounting to .001 percent of British Columbia's total operating budget. While it devoted 10 percent of its own budget to subsidies to women's groups, it had no research staff. Penny Priddy, the Minister of Women's Equality from 1991 to 1996, was involved with Surrey Women for Action before becoming minister. During the mid-1990s the Ministry developed and then revised the Gender Lens. The Gender Lens was a policy analysis tool designed to assist analysts across government departments to attend to the gender implications of policies at all stages of their development and to encourage them to facilitate input from diverse groups of women. Ministry staff conducted training sessions in its use (Teghtsoonian and Grace 2001; RNGS 2007b: 133).

Helsinki Equality Board (1996). As a consultative body attached to Helsinki's City Council, the Equality Board's major roles were to gather background information on gender equality matters, to cooperate with other municipal bodies in the promotion of gender equality, and to monitor the implementation of gender equality in the municipality. The City Council selected members to represent its partisan composition, and the Equality Board elected the chair. It focused on sex equality issues across many different areas. With only one secretary and no other administrative resources, it has the lowest level of administrative capacity of all of the subnational agencies and is similar to offices at the national level with the low levels of resources. Reflecting the partisan logic of the appointment, the chair was a man from the National Coalition Party with no background in women's movement activity (Holli 2004; RNGS 2007b: 205).

One-of-a-Kind Agencies

These agencies do not fit into the composites discussed earlier. The following descriptions complete the entire range of agencies that appeared in the policy debates.

Equality Ombudsman in Sweden (1981). The Equal Opportunity Act of 1980 created an ombudsman position to enforce its prohibitions of discrimination in the workplace. Ombudsman positions are characteristic of Sweden's institutional structure. In principle, they are advocates for citizens against state action. The Equality Ombudsman was empowered to bring lawsuits against companies on behalf of workers' claims of illegal sex discrimination. However, in the early 1980s, when it appeared in the RNGS study, its mandate was severely limited to the small number of workers not part of collective bargaining contracts. From its position inside the Ministry of Industry, it had the opportunity to weigh in on policy proposals up for consideration but remained primarily a judicial office. There was a small staff of five and a small budget to match. There were other women's policy offices in Sweden that typically responded to women's movement claims. However, in the debate on the regulation of public pornography the ombudsman represented women's movement claims, whereas the other agencies did not (RNGS 2007b: 617; Svanström 2004).

Joint Oireachtas Committee on Justice, Equality, Defense, and Women's Rights in Ireland (1992). In the absence of a permanent committee system, the Irish Parliament establishes all-party committees with special assignments. These are created at the beginning of each new Parliament and disbanded at the end. There have been four such committees assigned to promote women's rights, and the 1992 committee was in a position to participate in a debate on abortion studied here. The committee investigated issues and presented reports and recommendations to ministries and the national cabinet. It could also propose legislation. It served as a forum for women's movement actors to make representations and present demands and grievances. Other than a small budget for research, the committee had no staff, budget, or organizational resources. Its potential as a women's movement ally was based on its location inside the Parliament and its all-party membership (RNGS 2007b: 399; Mahon 2004).

Congressional Caucus on Women's Issues in the United States of America (1994–1996). The Congressional Caucus on Women's Issues was the only quasi women's policy agency not located in a party. The caucus was organized in the late 1970s to establish a direct link between women's movement organizations and women members of the House of Representatives and the Senate. All women in the Congress, both Democrats and Republicans, were members, and they worked to develop and support legislation that promoted the status of women. They received some funds from the Congress to assemble a support staff to advance their agenda. In the 1990s, when the caucus was active in the welfare debate studied in the RNGS project, there were two leaders, one from each party, and both had long experience promoting women's rights in Congress and their parties. As more women were elected (a slow process to be sure) and time passed, several of the members had leadership positions on committees from which they could develop policy and participate in debates. Working closely with women's movement actors, the Congressional Caucus on Women's Issues was in a position to provide that link that is usually reserved for more formal women's policy agencies (RNGS 2007b: 655; McBride 2007).

Women's Policy Agencies across the Decades

Women's policy machineries are relatively recent arrivals on the political scene in Western democracies—for most countries beginning in the early 1970s—and they have links to the ebb and flow of women's rights politics and women's movements themselves. Thus, it is of great interest to compare their characteristics over time, here across nearly four decades.[6] To what degree have agencies become permanent fixtures within their states through increased decision-making power, administrative resources, and links to women's movement groups? In fact, there has been growth in both power and resources of the national state agencies that appear in debates. From the 1970s to the early 2000s, an increasing proportion of the agencies were ministries, a form that we have seen has powers of both policy proposal and of review and recommendation. The agencies became closer to the decision-making centers of power and enjoyed higher overall administrative capacity as measured by the number of different resources they possessed. In the later years of this time span, the degree of financial support had grown; more agencies had full-time staff and separate budgets with more subsidies to women's groups and research activities. Of the fifty-seven agencies compared in this section, fourteen were in the 1970s, seventeen in the 1980s, twenty in the 1990s, and six in the 2000s.

Structures and Powers

The most notable change in type since the 1970s pertains to the steady increase in ministries from 21 percent of all agencies in the 1970s to 50 percent in the 1990s through 2000s. Administrative offices seemed to be popular in the 1980s, when over 40 percent took this form, but declined again to 27 percent in the 1990s through 2000s. The executive commission was the most frequent form in the 1970s, making up 50 percent, but has dropped dramatically since, to only 15 percent (three) in the 1990s and none in the early 2000s. The number of agencies taking the form of advisory councils remained relatively constant at two (14 percent) in the 1970s, three (18 percent) in the 1980s, and two (10 percent) in the 1990s. The trend is also toward greater proximity; in the 1970s, half the agencies were close to centers of decision-making power, while in the 1990s to 2000 the rate was 62 percent. Similarly there was a downward trend in the number and proportion of offices that were found in distant locations.

The proportion of agencies with powers to propose policy and to review and recommend has also increased steadily over the decades; in the 1990s through 2000s, 100 percent of the agencies had review and recommend power and 62 percent had proposal powers. Few agencies had enforcement powers in any decade; the highest proportion was in the 1980s (seven of seventeen, or 41 percent). That number remained constant and declined as a proportion of all agencies. This pattern continues the trend toward more permanence from the 1970s to the early 2000s.

There was only a slight change in the policy orientations of the agencies studied. Although single-issue offices declined and cross-sectional agencies increased slightly, a multi-issue orientation remained the most frequent type of policy orientation across all of the decades, with a rise in the period from the 1990s to the early 2000s. Reflecting the trend toward gender mainstreaming in the 1990s in Europe, four of the six cross-sectional offices were active in the 1990s and in 2000, and all of them were in European Union member states— Finland, Germany, Italy, and the Netherlands. However, the agencies in Finland and the Netherlands took on cross-sectional goals in the 1980s, preceding the European Union gender mainstreaming directives in the 1990s. Thus, there was not a major shift toward cross-sectional agencies taking part during these debates, either in the European Union member states, where one might expect gender mainstreaming agencies, or in other countries in the 1990s and in 2000.

Leadership

For many, leadership is a key factor in determining the general direction and approach of a given agency. Researchers and activists alike claim that heads of agencies from women's movement groups have the potential to be more sympathetic to and proactive with respect to women's movement demands and actors and hence more likely to bring women's movement voices and perspectives into the state arena (e.g., Eisenstein 1996; Outshoorn 1994). Leadership type is determined by examining whether the agency head was previously active in women's movement organizations or feminist organizations before the appointment. The data show that a majority (thirty-seven or 65 percent) of women's policy agencies have had leaders with women's movement experience, with more than half of these (twenty-one) in feminist groups. Overall, however, only 37 percent had experiences with action that specifically targets gender-based hierarchies and the advancement of women's rights. There was a decline in the proportion of agencies whose leaders had movement experience, with a high of 78 percent in the 1970s to only 54 percent in the 1990s through 2000s. There was an even sharper decline in feminist leadership, with only 27 percent of agencies in that category in the 1990s, down from 50 percent in the 1970s.

Administrative Resources

The distribution of agencies in this study according to the number of administrative resources across the six levels—staff, divisions, field offices, separate budgets, subsidies, and research—shows a tendency toward more capacity. Of the fifty-five agencies for which we have data, twice as many—20 or 35 percent—have higher numbers of resources (five and six), compared to those with few resources (none and one)—10 or 17.5 percent. Nearly half (twenty-five or 45.5 percent) of all offices have mid-level scores (two to four). Over time there has been a steady increase in the proportion of agencies with more staff, offices, budgets, and the like. In the 1990s, only two of twenty agencies had no resources and only seven had fewer than three kinds of support. Of all agencies in the 1990s to 2000s, nearly 70 percent had between four and six types. It is interesting to note that all of the agencies in a position to participate in any of the debates in the early 2000s tended toward the high end of the distribution.

The presence of a full-time staff seems to be the rule; overall only 10.5 percent or six of all fifty-seven agencies had no staff, and half of these were in the 1970s. Since then, 95 percent have had staff. In general, the offices tend to have had small numbers of personnel, half with fewer than 20 and only 25 percent with more than 100. Some offices had no employees: the Consultative Commission for the Status of Women in Belgium in the 1970s and 1980s; the Working Group in Finland in the 1970s; the Joint Oireachtas Committee on Justice, Equality, Defense, and Women's Rights in Ireland in the 1990s; and in the United States the Secretary's Advisory Committee on the Rights and Responsibilities of Women in the 1970s and the President's Inter-Agency Council in the 1990s. The proportion of agencies with a large number of full-time employees remained stable until the 1990s, when almost 40 percent had more than 100 full-time employees.

Looking at the development of budgets over time, the proportion of the fifty-seven machineries that had separate budgets increased from the 1970s to the 1980s—from 69 percent to 80 percent—and remained stable through the early 2000s. None of the six offices in the early 2000s was without its own budget line. There was a steady increase in the proportion of offices that provided subsidies to groups over time as well, from only 15 percent in the 1970s to 38 percent in the 1980s, and 65 percent in the 1990s through the 2000s. Five of the six agencies active in the early 2000s provided subsidies. Those agencies that offered such subsidies tended to devote an increasing share of their budgets to this support into the 1990s through the 2000s. In the 1970s and 1980s, only 20 percent assigned more than 25 percent of their budgets to women's movement groups. By the 1990s, it was over 40 percent. Resources for research also increased across the three decades. In the 1970s, only 23 percent of agencies had a separate budget item for research; that figure grew to 56 percent in the 1980s and 69 percent in the 1990s through the early 2000s. The proportion of budgets for research tended to be low throughout the period, however; a majority provided less than 6 percent of available funds for research staff and activities.

Country and Regional Patterns

A theme throughout this book is to report any variations in the data by country and region. In this chapter, this means assessing whether the characteristics and trajectories of agencies since the 1970s are the same within countries or regional groupings.[7] Generally, we found that there are no "national styles" of women's policy machineries, although there are patterns.

Structure, Powers, and Leadership

For some countries, such as Germany and France, we can say that the ministry is typical. In Germany all of the agencies that had an opportunity to participate in the seven debates on abortion, political representation, and the hot issue were ministries. Seven of ten agencies in France were ministries, along with one advisory council, one commission, and one administrative office. Other countries show various combinations of agencies. In Sweden, Belgium, and Ireland there are two or three ministries along with other types of agencies. Austria has one ministry and two administrative offices. There are no ministries found in the United States, Canada, the Netherlands, Spain, or Finland. Machineries in Canada and the United States disperse among all forms except ministries, whereas the Netherlands and Spain specialize in the administrative office. The commission form dominates in Finland.

The proximity of agencies to central decision-making power tends to follow type, and countries with more ministries show greater proximity, while those with administrative offices are less close. Similarities in Sweden and Finland show a possible regional trend: All agencies are close or moderately close to power despite having various forms. There are no other regional groups: Germanic-Benelux, southern European, and Anglo American countries show no common patterns. There does not seem to be any division between member and nonmember states of the European Union either.

With respect to policy-making powers, a given agency such as Ireland's Department of Equality and Law Reform (in 2002) may have had all three: policy proposal, review and recommend, and policy enforcement. The norm, however, is for agencies to have no more than one or two powers. Nearly half of all offices had policy-proposing power, although no agencies in Canada and Spain had this power; 91 percent of agencies found in all countries had the power to review and recommend. Less than a third, 28 percent, had the power to implement and enforce; no offices in Austria, Belgium, Canada, Finland, Germany, and the Netherlands had implementation powers. But once again, no clear regional patterns emerge from this overview. There is little variation across countries in the extent to which agency leaders have women's movement or feminist experience. Such leaders appear in all countries with the exception of Germany, where none of the ministers had feminist movement experience.

Administrative Resources

To get a sense of whether some countries consistently provide greater administrative and budget support to their agencies than others, we classified them in terms of the aggregate capacity of their agencies.[8] By combining information on the number of resources present with a summary of the size of these resources, as measured by staff, divisions, field offices, budgets, subsidies, and research in agencies by country, we found four categories.

At the highest level, only in Germany and Spain were agencies in debates endowed with both a large number of resources and consistently high levels of support. The German agencies were all ministries, usually promoting family matters as well as women's issues. Spain's Women's Institute, which was the only agency found in the studies of debates, is an administrative office that over the course of our study enjoyed not only relatively high staff and budget levels but also a complex organizational structure. A second pattern appears in studies of the agencies in Austria, Canada, Great Britain, and Sweden. We found that machineries in these countries typically had a large number of resources, but there is no consistent pattern of level of staff, budget, or complexity. In Canada, for example, some agencies had subsidies and some did not. The third group of countries includes France, Ireland, the United States, and the Netherlands, where at least one agency was very well endowed, such as the Women's Bureau of the Department of Labor in the United States or the Department of Equality and Law Reform in Ireland, but most of the rest of the country's agencies had fewer resources. The uneven support in France is related to change over time. The ministries that appeared in the 1980s and 1990s had strong capacity. However, there were agencies from the early days with few resources. A fourth pattern of moderate numbers of resources with mixed levels applies only to Belgium, where the agencies range from commissions to ministries. Finally, Italy and Finland show the least administrative support. In both countries, women's policy agencies include typically executive commissions, such as the Council for Equality in Finland and the National Committee for Equal Opportunities

(Ministry of Labor) in Italy. Italy did have the Ministry for Equal Opportunities which, unlike counterparts in other countries, had a tiny staff.

Conclusion

This mapping exercise has produced both aggregate and in-depth comparisons of the characteristics and presence of women's policy machineries in thirteen Western postindustrial democracies since the 1970s. All agencies studied had the potential to be active in one or more of the debates studied on abortion, job training, prostitution, political representation, and hot issues. Most of these agencies were in the national governments and one of three types: ministries, administrative offices, or executive commissions. Each of these types is associated with a pattern of proximity, powers, and administrative capacity. At the same time, agencies can appear in other forms, including advisory councils, legislative committees, and judicial officers such as the Equality Ombudsman.

Policy debates in this study that affected women's movement interests sometimes occurred in arenas other than national state institutions. In the federal systems of the United States and Canada, some debates in political representation and job training were at the level of constituent governments—states or provinces. In Austria and Finland, major prostitution debates played out at municipal arenas. Thus, we found some agencies active at these regional and local levels. In parliamentary systems, where parties are especially important to policy leadership, some debates attracted the attention of party women's agencies, what we call quasi women's policy agencies. These were always found in left-wing parties and, other than debates on abortion in Austria in the 1970s, were concerned with debates over political representation.

Although researchers in the RNGS project brought a range of agencies into play, the examination of state feminism theory in the next chapters focuses primarily on the national state agencies and their role (exceptions will be noted). Ever more of these state agencies have become permanent players over time. While the trajectory of increased presence is clear, there is not a consistent pattern of structural attributes by country or region. It is possible, however, to group countries with similar machineries together. But the ability to generalize is limited by the fact that the agencies examined here do not constitute a complete set in any country.

These trends toward permanence must be tempered with the recognition of the limits of the changes: Staffs remained generally small; budgets were a tiny proportion of overall government spending; many offices had no budgets for women's groups or staff for research; and agencies with very low levels of administrative capacity were still quite numerous in the 1990s through early 2000s. In addition, there was a decline in the proportion of agency heads with movement and feminist experience.

The patterns of structural change in national-level offices do not follow either a country or regional logic for the most part, despite the inclination of many researchers to expect national differences. The absence in the analysis of virtually *any* regional patterns of characteristics also flies in the face of arguments claiming that trends in general political dynamics and feminist politics vary according to groups of countries—for example, liberal, corporate, or social democratic. In fact, there were only two instances where countries from a similar region shared the same characteristics not found in other countries: Offices in Finland and Sweden tended to be moderately close or close to the centers of power despite being different types (executive commissions versus ministries and a judicial body), and all party quasi women's policy agencies were found only in parliamentary systems in Western Europe.

To sum up, there was an increasing presence from the 1970s to the early 2000s of women's policy agencies according to this study of the Western postindustrial democracies. Given uneven patterns, we must temper any claims that such agencies will continue to increase in numbers, power, or influence, or remain important actors in the politico-administrative systems. At the same time, there is a certain resilience over time that suggests women's policy machineries are likely to be a lasting presence in most governments. With this picture of the diversity and range of women's policy agencies, we now turn to a systematic analysis of their impact on promoting women and their interests in policy debates to achieve state feminism.

II

Exploring State Feminism

The exploration of the politics of state feminism involves three investigations. The first, which we undertake in Chapter 4, is to establish the importance of women's policy agencies, in relation to other key influences, to the success of women's movement actors in gaining access to policy arenas and favorable policies—Movement State Feminism. The second investigation, covered in Chapter 5, is to find the factors that explain why some agencies are effective while others fail to respond to women's movement goals, with a particular focus on the characteristics of the agencies. And the third, in Chapter 6, is to conduct an initial assessment of the extent to which women's policy agencies act as allies to feminist movement actors and achieve Transformative State Feminism. The plan of each chapter centers on the examination of the central propositions from the framework of state feminism, presented in Chapter 1.

4

Women's Policy Agencies and Women's Movement Success

The goal of this chapter turns out to be the most ambitious in our exploration of state feminism, in that it examines eight of the eleven propositions presented in Chapter 1, and the most complicated, in that it seeks to understand the place of women's policy agency activities *in relation to* other possible explanations for women's movement success. In addition, like the rest of the book, the analysis looks at variations across issues, over time, and across countries. Understanding the relationships among movement actors, agencies, policy environments, and state responses as they play out in policy debates on five issues in thirteen countries makes for diverse and complex subject matter. There are, therefore, no simple results. We group our original propositions into four categories of inquiry, presented in the next section. We examine each category in the rest of the chapter. As promised in Chapter 1, there are both quantitative and qualitative analyses of the RNGS policy debate data, with the goal of integrating the findings.[1]

Propositions and Methods of Analysis

Frequency of Success and Agency Alliances

There are two propositions that establish the degree of women's movement success and agency activities: (1) Women's movement actors have been successful in gaining procedural access and policy change in Western postindustrial democracies; and (2) women's policy agencies have the potential to form alliances with women's movement actors, through presenting movement actor demands in policy debates *and* gendering the frame of those debates. Agencies that ally with women's movements in this fashion are Insiders. We use frequency distributions, cross-tabulations, and descriptive statistics in this section to show the patterns by issue and over time that characterize women's movement success and the links between that success and alliances between movements and agencies.

Significance of Agency Alliances

Positive findings for the propositions about the frequency of successes and alliances lead to the essential core of state feminism—that is, the proposition that Insider agency alliances with women's movements are a significant cause of women's movement procedural and policy successes in Western postindustrial democracies. It follows that failure of the agencies to form full alliances with movement actors accounts for movement failures with respect to policy responses. To determine the significance of agency activity, we use statistical inference, specifically Ordinal Regression.

Value of Agency Alliances, Dual Response, and Democratization

After establishing the significance of agencies in the study, we consider the place of agency activity in relation to other explanations for women's movement success with the state. Inspired by social movement theory, propositions examine the influence of women's movement resources, favorable policy environments, and support of left-wing parties and governments on movement success. For each of these, there is a key state feminism proposition that asserts that the presence of agencies that ally with women's movement actors, Insiders, adds to the explanatory power of movement resources, favorable policy environments, and left-wing support. Since the accumulation of complete women's movement successes with the state signals increased democratization in Western postindustrial countries, we investigate whether the most supportive agencies are important causes of such democratization within each country. Given that the propositions point to configurations of influences on movement success, csQCA is an appropriate method along with case studies of causal mechanisms. The case studies assess the value of agencies generally and their contribution to democratization.[2]

The Importance of Policy Sectors

This final section looks at all the findings—frequency of movement successes, significance of women's policy agencies in movement success, and the relative value of movement-agency alliances, according to issues, countries, and regional groups. The proposition suggests that these results will vary by types of policy sectors, but rarely by country or region. Cross-tabulations, csQCA, and case studies of causal mechanisms are methods that suit this analysis of debates by policy sector, country, and region.

Datasets and Measures

Before assessing the propositions, it is important to review the data to be used in the mixed-methods analyses. The RNGS research design established the unit of analysis as a policy debate on one of five issues: abortion, job training, political representation, prostitution, and priority issues of the late 1990s and early 2000s, called "hot issues." From the 130 cases collected by researchers, we selected 114 policy debates to examine propositions about frequency of successes and alliances. These are the policy debates that took place in national-level arenas with (108) or without (6) the existence of state or quasi women's policy agencies.[3] To examine propositions about the significance and value of agencies, we used only the 108 national debates with agencies.

Women's movement success or impact in a debate is determined using the State Response Typology described in Chapter 1. To recap: Complete movement success, called Dual Response, finds women's movement actors achieving both *procedural access* (i.e., inclusion as participants in the policy process) and *policy goals* (i.e., inclusion of demands in policy outcomes), an outcome that increases both descriptive and substantive representation. At the same time, complete failure or No Response is found when movement actors reach neither procedural access nor policy substance. It is possible for women's movement actors to achieve *either* substantive (Preemption) *or* descriptive representation (Co-optation) in a policy debate.

To compare agency activity or alliances we use two measures. First, the Alliance Typology classifies women's policy agency activities into four types. The classification is based on whether agencies adopt the positions on debate issues that coincide with those of women's movement actors and bring considerations of gender into policy debates in a meaningful way (in other words, whether agencies gender the frame of the debate). Insider agencies do both; Symbolic agencies do neither; Marginal agencies present women's movement actors' demands without gendering the frame of the debate. Offices that gender debate frames without advancing the women's movement position are Anti-Movement agencies. The second measure, Agency Activity, used in the Ordinal Regression analysis, ranks the degree of agency activity and alliance from none or opposing movement goals to active and effective, an ordinal scale.[4]

Women's Movement Success and Agency Alliances: Frequencies

The patterns of women's movement impact are found in Figure 4.1.[5] They show that in 50 percent of the 114 debates, women's movement actors achieved complete success in the form of *Dual Responses*. In contrast, in just 17 percent of the debates, women's movement actors found *No Response*—that is, were met with complete failure to penetrate the policy process). The greatest complete success rates occurred in hot issue debates (75 percent), followed by debates on issues of abortion (61 percent) and political representation (55 percent), with the lowest in prostitution (37 percent) and job training (32 percent) debates. Job training debates showed the greatest failure rate (50 percent), as well as accounting for more than 58 percent of all the No Response cases.

Partial representation occurs when women's movement actors achieve either Co-optation (inclusion in the policy subsystem) or Preemption (policy content

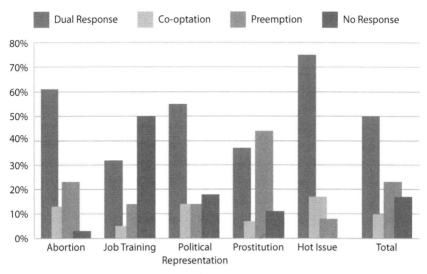

Figure 4.1   Women's movement impact by issue.

congruent with their goals). Of these, a higher percentage gained only a positive policy response (23 percent), whereas 11 percent gained only procedural access. Taking the issues into account, twelve or 44 percent of the twenty-seven Preemption cases are in the prostitution debates, although prostitution debates are just 24 percent of all debates. Co-optation is slightly more likely to be found in the abortion debates than on other issues, accounting for 33 percent of all Co-optation cases, although they compose just 27 percent of all debates.

There is a variation in success rates over time shown in Figure 4.2. In sorting the cases according to the decade when the debate ended, the overall trend from the 1970s through the early 2000s is toward higher rates of complete success for the movements and a decline in the rate of complete failures to 0 percent in the latest period. There is no clear pattern in the incidence of Co-optation or Preemption, although in comparing the ratio of these two, both the 1970s and the 1990s see an increase in policy responses that include women's movement demands, while cases where women's movement actors participated with no policy response remained at similar low levels.

We next turn to the activity of women's policy agencies and the alliances they formed with women's movement actors. Figure 4.3 shows the issue patterns. Offices were most effective in the political representation debates and least effective in the hot issue debates. Features of these debates could explain the variation here. Many of the political representation debates were about increasing women's representation, therefore justifying the more active involvement of the agencies. The hot issue cases, on the contrary, were rarely seen as relating to gender matters, and most agencies did not take a position on them. Job training had the highest incidence of Marginal agencies, where offices

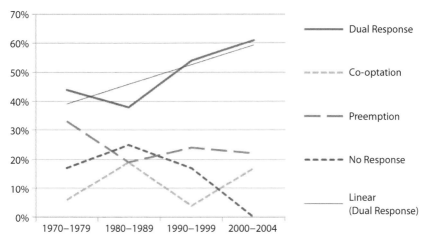

Figure 4.2 Women's movement impact by decade.

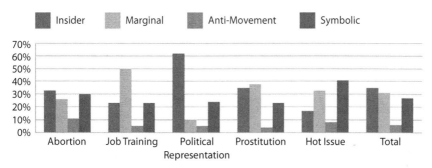

Figure 4.3 Women's policy agency activity by issue.

backed women's movement demands in official policy discussions without successfully gendering the issue frames. This tendency may reflect the special difficulty women's policy agencies face in confronting issue frames pertaining to work and education. Thus, whereas women's policy agencies responded to the women's movement actors in adopting supportive microframes, they were twice as likely to face obstacles in penetrating the job training issue frames of the policy makers.

Figure 4.4 shows the pattern of agency alliances for 108 debates with agencies by decade. In the 1970s, half the agencies took up women's movement actors' demands but were not able to bring any influence to bear on the outcome. The rate of effectiveness increased sharply through the 1980s and 1990s. And although the debates in the 2000s were mostly hot issue debates where the topics were often far removed from the interests of agencies charged with promoting the status of women, the distribution of types of agency activity is quite close to the pattern of all agencies taken together.[6]

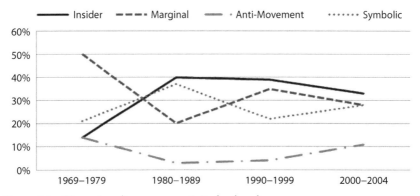

Figure 4.4 Women's policy agency activity by decade.

Overall, the rate of Insiders activity is lower than the rate of movement success; thus, women's movement actors can achieve success without forming such alliances with the agencies. Of the fifty-five cases of Dual Response, twenty-six or 46 percent also had Insiders active and achieved Movement State Feminism. But this pattern varied greatly by issue. In political representation debates, 82 percent of the Dual Responses also involved Insider agencies while 62 percent of prostitution successes occurred with Insiders. Much lower rates of Insider–Dual Response are found in job training (43 percent), abortion (33 percent), and hot-issue debates (22 percent). Thus, although women's movement actors saw their highest rates of success with the state in the 1990s and 2000s hot issue debates (75 percent Dual Response), they were the least likely to credit an alliance with women's policy agencies for that success.

These frequency distributions show that women's movement actors have been successful in gaining either procedural access or policy content in the majority of cases, with only 17 percent failures. A majority of agencies have formed alliances with actors, but only 35 percent have been effective as Insiders in policy debates. About half of movement successes coincide with these Insider alliances. There is considerable variation across the issues and a general pattern of more women's success over time. We now turn to assessing the significance of women's policy agency activity in explaining women's movement impact.

Significance of Movement Agency Alliances: Ordinal Regression

The goal of this section is to test the proposition that alliances with women's policy agencies are a significant cause of women's movement success in entering the policy arena and getting their claims included in policy outcomes.[7] To determine significance, we use Ordinal Regression, a form of statistical inference, to investigate the association between the variable Agency Activity (on behalf of women's movement actors) while controlling for other possible explanations of success. The control variables are ordinal indicators from the RNGS dataset of Women's Movement Resources, Favorable Policy Environments, and Left Support.[8] For Women's Movement Resources, the variables are women's movement change: activism or institutionalization; priority of issue to the movement as a whole; and cohesiveness of women's movement actors in the debate. The Favorable Policy Environment variables are openness of subsystem structure; issue frame fit; and countermovement strength. To indicate Left Support, the variables are organizational closeness of the women's movement to left-wing parties and trade unions; ideological closeness of women's movement to left-wing parties and unions; and governing majority—Left, Center, or Right. The dependent variable is the ordinal measure of State Response to women's movement actors.[9]

We use the technique PLUM (Polytomous Universal Model in SPSS), an ordered probit procedure (Norušis 2007). PLUM provides estimates of the changes in the ordinal categories of the dependent variable—State Response—on the basis of changes in each of the categories of independent variables and the statistical significance of these estimates. The resulting model is called a proportional odds or logit model and permits the calculation of $EXP(\beta)$, which is the ratio of odds for changes in the dependent variable—State Response—for each category of each independent variable. The program also gives probabilities of goodness of fit and the strength of association.[10]

We found first a significant bivariate correlation between Agency Activity and State Response—Spearman's rho of .279 ($p < .003$). Then, we ran the three separate models to test the state feminism proposition about the key role of Agency Activity in women's movement success in relation to Women's Movement Resources, Favorable Policy Environment, and Left Support clusters of variables. The results show that for all models the variable Agency Activity has an independent effect on State Response. Significant parameter estimates indicate that where Agency Activity is lower—where policy agencies do anything less than gendering the policy debate and presenting positions in the debate that match the women's movement—it is also less likely that there will be an improvement in policy change and procedural access.[11] From the three models, therefore, we can conclude that the more women's policy agencies are successful in gendering debates and supporting women's movement actor goals in debates, the more likely that movement actors will be successful in gaining positive state responses.

The analysis also shows the significant effects of two independent variables other than Agency Activity. With respect to the Favorable Policy Environment, the degree to which the subsystem is more open rather than closed affects the likelihood of state response to women's movement actors. In the Women's Movement Resources model, the priority of the issue—whether or not it is among the top five goals on the women's movement national agenda—is also a significant factor in state response.

The PLUM technique not only shows the independent effects of variables on State Response, it also helps us to assess the direction and strength of the effect of each of the significant findings. Which has the stronger effect—agency activity, subsystem openness, or priority of the issue to the movement? Tables 4.1 and 4.2 show the parameter estimates of significant variables in each model and the exponential ratio or EXP(β) by categories of each variable.

The last column of each table lists the exponential ratio—EXP(β)—for each level of the significant predictor; this figure gives an indication of the relative strength of the categories in relation to the reference category. An EXP(β) less than 1.0 indicates a negative effect; an EXP(β) more than 1.0 indicates a positive effect. For example, in the Favorable Policy Environment model (Table 4.1), cases in the category *Agency genders debate with compatible microframe* are .084 times less likely to achieve greater state response than the reference category *Agency genders debate with matching microframe*. Women's policy

TABLE 4.1   STRENGTH OF AGENCY ACTIVITY AND SUBSYSTEM STRUCTURE VARIABLES

Independent Variable Measures	DEPENDENT VARIABLE: STATE RESPONSE	
	Parameter Estimate	EXP(β)
Agency—no activity	−3.449*	.032
Agency—movement compatible microframe	−1.620	.197
Agency—movement matching microframe	−3.435*	.032
Agency—genders debate with compatible microframe	−2.474*	.084
Agency—genders debate with matching microframe	Reference category	N/A
Subsystem structure—open or moderately open	3.026*	20.61
Subsystem structure—moderately closed	2.451*	11.6
Subsystem structure—closed	Reference category	N/A

*$p < .01$

TABLE 4.2   STRENGTH OF AGENCY ACTIVITY AND PRIORITY VARIABLES

Independent Variable Measures	DEPENDENT VARIABLE: STATE RESPONSE	
	Parameter Estimate	EXP(β)
Agency—no activity	−3.353*	.034
Agency—movement compatible microframe	−1.733**	.176
Agency—movement matching microframe	−3.309*	.036
Agency—genders debate with compatible microframe	−3.055**	.042
Agency—genders debate with matching microframe	Reference category	N/A
Priority: issue not on agenda	−1.452**	.234
Priority: issue on agenda	Reference category	N/A

*$p < .001$
**$p < .10$

agencies with no activity are .032 times less likely than cases in the reference category to achieve state response. With respect to the subsystem structure variable, cases where the *Subsystem structure is open or moderately open* are 20.61 times more likely to achieve higher state response than cases in the reference category *Subsystem structure closed*. Thus, these figures show that if the subsystem structure is more open than it is closed, there is a greater likelihood of positive state response than when cases move along the values of the women's policy agency activity variable.

Similarly, in the Women's Movement Resource model, cases where the issue is not a priority for the women's movement actors as a whole are less likely to achieve positive state responses, odds that are slightly stronger than the odds in categories of the women's policy agencies variable.[12] These results show that while agency activity is a significant predictor of positive state response for women's movement actors, the odds are higher that subsystem structure and movement priority will promote a successful state response. Finally, no measures of closeness to the Left or Left in power have a significant effect on state response; in that model, only women's policy agency activity increases the odds of success for women's movement actors.

The results of using methods of statistical inference, specifically regression tests of three ordinal models, support the proposition that the activity of women's policy agencies has a significant effect on the chances of positive state responses to women's movement actors. At the same time, they show the need to understand agency activism in the context of characteristics of the policy environment and the women's movement as a whole, specifically openness of the subsystem structure and priority of the issue to the women's movement.

The Value of Agency Alliances across the Issues: Crisp-Set Qualitative Comparative Analysis

The results of the Ordinal Regression pertain to the effect of the independent variables separately on women's movement outcomes. That is, Agency Activity is an important factor in movement success *along with* an open subsystem and issues given a higher priority by the women's movement. These findings suggest that a combination of conditions and not the role of a single factor is important in understanding movement outcomes. Therefore, to learn more about the value of alliances in conjunction with other influences, we require a different method, one that will allow assessment of the configurations or combinations of factors in explaining movement success. This section uses csQCA and case studies of causal mechanisms to investigate the set of propositions that predict that higher resourced movements, policy environments with more favorable components, and Left support for movements are more likely to explain movement success (Dual Response) when considered in combination with effective agencies (Insiders).

The Logic of csQCA

Crisp-set Qualitative Comparative Analysis[13] is a method designed to help researchers dig into a group of complex case studies and uncover any combinations of conditions that may be called *causal*.[14] The assumption behind this analysis is that an outcome, such as women's movement success, depends on a variety of conditions working together; this is called *multiple conjunctural causation*. In addition, the approach assumes *equifinality*, a situation in which different sets of conditions may lead to the same outcome (Rihoux and Ragin 2008: 8). To illustrate, we may find that women's movements achieve Dual Responses from the state under conditions where the policy subsystem is open and the women's movement actors are close to the left-wing parties, a form of conjunctural causation. At the same time, we could find that another set of conditions also leads to Dual Response, that is, where the policy subsystem is closed and there is a weak countermovement, a result demonstrating equifinality.

We want to discover whether there is any regularity in the combinations of conditions that lead to women's movement success. Such combinations are called *solutions* or *consistent* paths[15] to achieve the outcome of Dual Response. That is, each combination always achieves Dual Response, but there may one or more other combinations that reach the same outcome among the entire group of cases studied. However, even if we find such consistencies we cannot come to the conclusion that such patterns are *causal* unless these patterns lead only to the presence of Dual Response and not to other outcomes—that is, not to Preemption, Co-optation, or No Response. By producing truth tables that line up the presence and absence of conditions of interest in terms of the outcomes, csQCA shows which patterns always produce Dual Responses, which patterns never produce Dual Responses and which patterns are contradictory—that is, they sometimes produce Dual Responses and sometimes the other outcomes.

Truth tables have much detail, especially in studies whose the cases are as complex as this one, and there are many different consistent paths to outcomes of interest.[16] This is where a csQCA program is useful because, by means of techniques of Boolean algebra, it simplifies the many combinations and removes those conditions whose presence or absence does not affect the outcome in a particular configuration.[17] It is also possible, in some instances, to show the importance of a particular condition in connection with the outcome of interest. This feature makes this method especially appropriate for the exploration of state feminism propositions, because we are interested in the effect of Insider alliances between women's movement actors and women's policy agencies in relation to characteristics of movement activism and the policy environment. The csQCA program can show whether any condition is either necessary or sufficient, or both, for achieving Dual Response.[18] If the condition is necessary, then every solution or path would include that condition. If it is sufficient, then the presence of Insider agencies alone, for example, could bring about Dual Response, but there would be other paths to the same outcome.

Conditions and csQCA Protocol

The goal is to use csQCA to assess how the presence of effective women's policy agencies (INSIDER) combines with Women's Movement Resources and/or Favorable Policy Environment and/or Left Support conditions to explain movement success with the state as defined by DUAL_RESPONSE. (Note that presenting a condition in all uppercase letters signifies its presence; all lowercase indicates the absence of that condition.) The movement conditions are *high levels of movement activism or institutionalization* (ACTIVE_WM); where the issue at hand is a *high priority for the movement as a whole* (PRIORITY); where movement actors in the debate are unified or *cohesive in their claims* (COHESIVE).[19] The policy environment conditions are the presence of a policy subsystem that is *not closed* but moderately closed or even open (SUBSYSTEM_ OPENNESS); the *absence of a strong countermovement* (WEAKCOUNTER); and where the movement claims are *compatible with or match* the dominant issue frame of the debate, referred to as issue frame fit (FIT). The Left Support conditions include whether the women's movement actors are ideologically and organizationally *very close to the Left* (IDEOL; ORGL) and whether or not the left-wing parties are in the governing majority (LEFT).

In order to discover the combinations of conditions that lead to women's movement success and assess the importance of Insiders, we examined various combinations of these conditions. First we focused on conditions of movement, policy environment, or left-wing support only. Then we examined each combination by adding the state feminism condition: the presence of Insiders.[20]

All the QCA in this book uses crisp sets: The conditions and outcomes are measured in dichotomies—1 for present and 0 for absent. As discussed earlier, csQCA involves preparing truth tables that link various combinations of the presence or absence of conditions in each typology to the Dual Response outcome and the combinations associated with the absence of this outcome as well. Often truth tables show contradictory configurations of conditions, that is, the same set of conditions leads to Dual Response and the absence of Dual Response. The csQCA program removes all cases covered by these contradictions from the analysis, and any solutions about the conditions for success apply only to the remaining cases. We studied the contradictions carefully to determine the usefulness of the solutions in relation to our data and if we could resolve these contradictions. In the end, only those truth tables with no more than one contradictory configuration covering up to three cases are included in the analysis; sometimes the contradictory configurations have brought us back to the cases to understand the findings. It is important to remember that csQCA is a process of exploration and discovery *within* a number of cases that will permit "modest generalizations" (Rihoux and Ragin 2008). It requires researchers to return again and again to the content of the cases in the analysis.

The problem of *limited diversity* in comparative studies hampers the ability of researchers to make even modest generalizations. Few are able to include substantive cases that represent all the possible combinations of conditions;

this is especially true when one examines more than two or three conditions with respect to an outcome. The cases that are "not there" are considered hypothetical. Findings that apply only to the observed cases provide limited theoretical value, because it is impossible to generalize beyond them. Looming is the likelihood that the next study will find other cases that negate the reported results.

To deal with the problem of limited diversity, the csQCA method can produce two kinds of solutions. One applies only to the conditions of the observed cases in a particular study, and not to hypothetical cases with other combinations of conditions that may exist but that researchers have not yet observed. Such findings usually show great equifinality; that is, there are many different combinations of conditions that produce the same result, and each of the combinations applies to only a few cases, even just one or two. The second method includes *logical remainders*, that is, hypothetical cases with combinations of conditions that can be logically included, along with the observed cases, in the Boolean computation.[21] By thus extending the range and diversity, this second type of solution applies to cases beyond those in the study and has more theoretical value.[22] Where possible, we opted to include the logical remainders; in reporting we indicate whether they are complex (without remainders) or parsimonious (with remainders).

Causal Paths to Dual Response:
The Place of Insider Agencies

Following the protocol outlined here, we examined various combinations of the Women's Movement, Favorable Policy Environment, and Left Support conditions with and without the presence of Insider agencies looking for solutions that explained Dual Response in the 108 national state debates with women's policy agencies by issue (abortion, 27 debates; job training, 22 debates; political representation, 21 debates; prostitution, 26 debates; and hot issue, 12 debates) and by decades: 1970s, 1980s, 1990s, and 2000s. Because of the excessive number of contradictory configurations, there were no solutions for the cases grouped by decades. With respect to the cases according to issues, there were too many contradictory configurations and thus no possible solutions for any combination of conditions without the presence of an Insider agency as one of the conditions. Thus, propositions that either a high level of women's movement resources, favorable components of policy environment, or left-wing support alone explains women's movement complete success with the state are not supported across the issues.

There is some support for the second part of these propositions about the relative importance of Insiders: that effective women's policy agencies combine with movement and policy environment conditions to explain the outcome of Dual Response. When the presence of an Insider agency was included in the combination of conditions, we discovered solutions meeting the criterion of no more than one contradiction covering three cases, indicating causal configurations in job training debates and hot issue debates. Next, we take a closer look to explore the relative importance of Insiders in explaining women's success in first job training and then the hot issue area.

Job Training

Women's movement actors face many difficulties in achieving success in job training debates. In this study, they prevail in only seven of twenty-two debates, or 32 percent, the lowest rate of all the issues. There is also a low incidence of Insider agencies, only five or 22 percent. Movement State Feminism—Insiders coupled with Dual Response—occurs in only three instances: the Canadian Jobs Strategy debate in 1984–1985; the debate in the United States over federal aid for vocational education, the so-called Perkins Act of 1990; and the deliberation over training with respect to globalization in Ireland in 1995–1997.

Despite these relatively low numbers, the analysis reveals a great deal about the way Insider agencies work with women's movement actors in different policy environments. These findings are based on applying a specific model or combination that includes the following conditions: a set of women's movement actors who agree 100 percent on their demands for job training; a policy subsystem that shows some openness to outside actors; matching or compatible fit between the microframes of the women's movement actors and the issue frames of the policy actors; and the presence of an Insider women's policy agency.[23]

When applied to the job training debates, the results document the great importance of subsystem openness and issue frame fit (these findings include logical remainders and are generally applicable to job training debates). The combination of these two conditions explains Dual Response in five of the seven cases for a coverage of .71.[24] In csQCA notation this path is: SUBSYSTEM_OPENNESS * FIT → DUAL_RESPONSE. It means that the presence of these two conditions is sufficient for women's movement success whether or not the women's movement actors present a cohesive front or there is an Insider agency present. This solution covers two job training debates in the United States: the 1978 policy extending job training in the Comprehensive Employment and Training Act (CETA) and the passage of the Job Training Partnership Act in 1982. It also pertains to the struggles in Finland (1969–1971) and Italy (1983–1984) over efforts to reduce unemployment. None of these debates had an Insider agency. However, the solution also covers the Canadian Jobs Strategy debate of 1984–1985 where an Insider agency was present. This is an example of the minimizing of causal conditions performed by csQCA. Since all of the cases covered by this solution have both open subsystems and issue frame fit in the environment, the differences in cohesiveness and Insider presence do not make any difference to the outcome. These findings also show the great importance of the subsystem and whether the frame of the issue matches the frames of the women's movement actors in the debate; women's movement actors do not need Insider agencies if these two conditions are present.

What happens if these favorable conditions are not present in job training debates? The analysis shows that under those circumstances, Insider agencies can make the difference. In the second solution using the model, when the policy subsystem is closed, agencies backed by a cohesive cohort of women's movement actors bring success. The csQCA notation is: subsystem_openness * COHESIVE * INSIDER → DUAL_RESPONSE.

Although this path covers only two of the seven cases of Dual Response (for a coverage proportion of .29), it does point to a role for women's movement actor–women's policy agency alliances in job training debates in two cases of Insiders out of five in the job training group of cases: vocational education debates of 1990 in the United States and the Retraining and Globalization controversy in Ireland in 1994–1995. The consistency of Insider influence is thus relatively low, at .40.[25]

Hot Issue

Of the twelve hot-issue debates, nine achieve Dual Response and only two of these have an Insider agency. Looking at groups of conditions, we find that these Insiders are successful when they work with actors from women's movements that are both organizationally and ideologically very close to the left-wing parties and trade unions.[26] Being organizationally "very close to the Left" means that the parties and unions have separate sections for women and include them in overall leadership positions. Ideologically, "very close" means that the parties and unions incorporate women's movement frames in their platforms and support the positions the actors take in the particular hot-issue debate. In the cases in this study, these conditions combine with an effective Insider agency to produce the result, but it has a low coverage of .22.[27] The csQCA notation for this sufficient path is: ORGL * IDEOL * INSIDER → DUAL_RESPONSE.

For these cases, the composition of the government did not matter to the outcome. In Italy, a 1997–2001 debate on the constitutional reform of the state occurred when the Left was in power, and in Sweden, a 1991–1994 debate over child care allowances faced a Center-Right government. The closeness of the women's movement actors to the Left in Sweden provided important resources for success given the strength of these parties even when they are in opposition. This configuration covers the only cases with Insider agencies, for a consistency of 1.00. In other words, there were not many cases of Insider alliances in the hot-issue debates of the 1990s, but when agencies allied with women's movement actors close to the Left, the success rate was 100 percent.

For the other five hot-issue debates, in Austria, Canada, Finland, United States, and Spain, the path to success seems counterintuitive: the left-wing parties and unions were ideologically very close to the women's movement as a whole, but the Left was not in power and the women's policy agencies were not Insiders. The csQCA notation for this path is: IDEOL * left * insider → DUAL_RESPONSE, and the coverage is .56. These debates were Family Allowance for Child Care (1999–2001) in Austria; Health Care Reform (2000–2004) in Canada; Rights to Municipal Day Care (1991–1994) in Finland; Proposal to Restrict Unemployment Benefits in Spain (2002–2003); and Ending Entitlements for Poor Families (1992–1996) in the United States.[28]

Looking more deeply into these cases, we can see how this configuration of conditions leads to outcomes that coincide with, if not always meet fully, women's movement actors' demands. The outcomes of the Austrian, Canadian, Finnish, and U.S. debates were compromises between Left and Center-Right representatives in legislatures. In Austria, Canada, and Finland, the absence of Insider agencies (the agencies are Marginal or Symbolic) is related to the absence of Left governing parties. This meant that carrying the torch for the movement demands fell to members of Parliament. The women's movement demands were advanced by women MPs from the left-wing parties who were able to forge compromises with other politicians, often women MPs from Center parties, and obtain favorable policy outcomes. In the U.S. case, feminist Republican and Democratic members of the Congressional Caucus for Women's Issues promoted women's movement demands. With a right-wing majority, the Republican women, especially, held some power on the committees and were able to include these demands in the final policy.

In all of these cases, the left-wing parties and unions adopted women's movement and feminist movement demands and were valuable allies in the deliberation in the legislatures and with the governing parties. The importance of this closeness is especially evident in the case of Spain. In the debate over unemployment reform, the right-wing government launched a proposal that was anathema to the left-wing parties and unions. The women activists on the issue were from the very unions that protested the government's plan with demonstrations and strikes, leading the prime minister to withdraw the reform and leave unemployment policy unchanged, an outcome fully supported by women's movement actors.

What is of note so far is how the presence or absence of left-wing governments in the hot-issue debates seems to be irrelevant to success. They can help in individual cases; however, as we have seen, women's movement actors through their connections with MPs, and parties and unions of the Left are able to gain at least some positive state response when the Right rules and silences their women's agencies.[29] We now turn to the three cases of Dual Response where the Left was in power that we have not yet examined.

The csQCA of hot-issue debates yielded one contradictory configuration. The combination of women's movement organizational and ideological closeness to left-wing parties while the left-wing parties are in power but the absence of an Insider produced Dual Response in two cases, but Not Dual Response (Co-optation, in fact) in a third case. The csQCA notation is: ORGL * IDEOL * LEFT * insider → DUAL_RESPONSE/dual_response.

Two of these cases, the Nationality Law debate in Belgium in 1999 and 2000, and the controversy over biotechnology genetics in Germany, achieved a Dual Response for the women's movement. That path fits the idea that support by left-wing parties and governments can produce success for women's movements. However, a third debate over the reform of the British House of Lords in 1997–2003 ended in Co-optation. In this case, the women's policy agency was effective, but not in support of the movement; it is an Anti-Movement agency. The Minister for Women in the Labour Government wielded great influence over the debate but actually opposed the proposal to establish quotas for women in an elected upper body, a goal backed by 100 percent of all women's movement advocates.[30]

Summary: The Value of Insiders

Finding explanations for Dual Response using the configurational method csQCA clearly depends on the issue. For some issues—abortion, prostitution, and political representation—there are no consistent configurations of features of Women's Movements, Policy Environments, Left Support, or Agency Activity that lead to successful outcomes. Instead, many specific combinations of these conditions produce both Dual Response and Not Dual Response—that is, they are contradictory. We can conclude that for debates on these issues, paths to success are best understood on a case-by-case basis, which permits taking a deeper look into the place of agencies—Insiders and Non-Insiders—along with other conditions. The results in job training and hot-issue cases are remarkable, therefore, because they produce paths that consistently lead to Dual Response outcomes only. As such, they reveal important clues to the way conditions combine and the place of Insider agencies in relation to them.

We have discovered that Insiders are neither a necessary nor sufficient condition for Dual Responses from the state. For job training debates, movement actors that confront more open subsystems and compatible or matching issue frame fit will find success, regardless of what the agencies do. However, if they do not find such favorable policy environments—when the subsystem is closed—movement actors who are 100 percent in agreement on their policy demands find that Insider agencies can overcome this obstacle and reach success. An unfriendly policy environment is important, but not fatal, to movement goals if Insider agencies exist. With respect to hot-issue debates, there was a role for Insiders in two debates, but most of the time actors found other allies to promote their goals regardless of the government in power.

Left-wing parties and unions are important to movements in hot-issue debates, but it is not necessary that they hold the governing majority on issues such as these. Most cases involve compromises between right-wing and left-wing members of the legislature, and the connections between the left-wing parties and movement actors are crucial. In fact, ideological closeness to the left-wing parties and unions is a necessary condition—always in combination with other conditions and found in all solutions—for movements to be successful in gaining favorable policy input and outcomes. These findings clarify the importance of the Left to women's movements; it is not a matter of seeking left-wing governments but one of maintaining ties between movement actors and the left-wing parties and unions that operate inside the policy arenas.

State Feminism and Democratization: A Country-Based Analysis

Another way to get an idea of the value of Insiders in achieving women's movement policy success is to look at the patterns of movement successes over time within each country in the study.[31] The democratization proposition defines the accumulation of successes as a pattern of substantive and descriptive representation of women's movement actors over time and hence asserts that Insider agencies may be an important cause of such democratic expansion. In this section, we examine the patterns of movement successes by country and the relative value of Insiders to those outcomes in relation to other factors, using, where possible, csQCA as well as case studies of causal mechanisms. We have grouped the countries into three categories of women's movement policy success rates in the debates studied: high, moderate, and low. This categorization allows us to better identify trends in the accumulation of representation over time, the role of agency activity in that representation and other possible causes within countries. This country-based analysis also allows us to see if countries with similar levels of women's movement success display similar combinations of conditions in terms of Movement Resources, Favorable Policy Environment, Left Support and Agency Activity.[32]

High Movement Success: Sweden, United States, Canada, Austria, Italy

Sweden

There are six cases of state debates covering three issues studied in Sweden; all achieved Dual Response for the women's movement actors, an impressive 100 percent record showing a steady democratization. What we see in Sweden illustrates the effects of Insider alliances.[33] The debates range from the successful campaign to establish the first women's policy agency (1967–1972) through prostitution and political representation debates in the 1980s and 1990s. There was no agency in the first debate; of the rest, Insider agencies led to women's movement representation or success in all but one. Since the 1970s, there have been two agencies—the Minister for Gender Equality and the Equality Ombudsman. Although they can work together, it is often that one will support the women's movement actors' microframes while the other either takes no position or disagrees with the movement goals. Thus, women's movement actors have always had one or the other to take up their case in a debate.

Furthermore, we see that the left-wing parties and unions have been very close to the women's movement actors, especially after the 1970s. Many of the women's movement actors were members of Parliament, benefiting from the rapid increase in women's representation, especially in the left-wing parties. They were not always able to expect that the governing majority would be left-wing as well, however. There were Insiders and Dual Responses in two of the six debates when the Left was not in power. The debates attracted the interest of a variety of women's movement actors, including standalone organizations, women's movement actors in the parties and unions, and members of Parliament. The Ombudsman and the Minister for Gender Equality have both been Insider allies to the movement. The exception—when the women's policy agencies took a marginal role—proves the rule. The women's movement actors in Parliament were ahead of the agency on that issue—the proposal for a violence against women act in 1995–1998—and had already gendered the debate before the minister had a chance to intervene.

United States

Like Sweden, the United States has a very high rate of women's movement success—eight of eleven debates—from the early 1970s through 2000, and in all decades and all five issue areas. Over these decades, the rate of Dual Response increases showing the accumulation of substantive and descriptive representation in national arenas. Exceptions were the 1970s debate over the Hyde Amendment to limit funding for abortions for poor women; there the women's movement actors were among the policy actors involved with the debate, but the outcome was Co-optation. In two prostitution debates—both on trafficking of children—the outcomes were Preemption, although the congressional decision makers did not define the issues as pertinent to gender.

Women's movement actors have achieved success in the United States, but this record is not due to Insiders. Of eight successes, there were only two with Insider agencies. Instead, among the other successes, three agencies were Marginal, one Symbolic, and one debate had no agency at all. Despite the fairly large number of Dual Response cases, csQCA revealed no causal paths because many configurations produced contradictory results. The conditions for movement success in the United States vary greatly; none of the social movement or state feminism theories studied here is useful in finding the paths.

Austria

In six national state debates covering abortion, prostitution, political representation, and the hot issue from 1972 to 2001, there are four movement successes, all in the 1990s. The women's policy agencies for the most part remained Symbolic or Marginal, with two exceptions, and one of these—a 1990s debate on expanding women's representation—found the only Insider in the three debates that yielded a Dual Response. The sufficient paths to increased substantive and descriptive representation in Austria are not due to Insider agencies. Rather, it is the relation of the women's movement to the left-wing parties and unions that made the difference.

Austrian women's movement activists achieved success when a left-wing government representing parties and trade unions organizationally and ideologically very close to the women's movement as a whole held the governing majority. The csQCA solution is: ORGL * IDEOL * LEFT → DUAL_RESPONSE.

This occurred in three of the four cases of Dual Response: two political representation debates, one on representation of women in the civil service (1990–1993) and another on subsidies to political parties (1994–1999); and the 1998–1999 controversy over legalizing mifegyne, the "abortion pill." The presence or absence of an Insider agency did not matter; in fact, for these three debates there were one Marginal, one Insider, and one Symbolic agency. When the logical remainders are included, however, the solution is simplified to one necessary and sufficient cause of movement success in these and the hot-issue debate on family allowances as well: left-wing parties' organizations very close to women's movement actors or ORGL → DUAL_RESPONSE.

Italy

Features of the women's movement actors appear to be the key to determining success in gaining descriptive and substantive representation in Italy. All five issues are covered in Italy, with seven of eleven outcomes achieving Dual Response. The pattern of accumulation of substantive and descriptive representation has been steady, from full success in the abortion debates of the late 1970s and early 1980s, all the way to the last political representation debate in 2003. Women's policy agencies were not established until the1980s, but they have been Insiders in two political representation debates, the hot issue and one prostitution debate. Yet, csQCA evidence shows that the presence of Insiders—only two in the seven successes—does not have much to do with the overall expansion of substantive and procedural response in Italy. Instead, the Women's Movement Resource components explain the great majority of the successes.

Crisp-set QCA with logical remainders found a causal path that explains six of the seven successful cases or .86 coverage. The path has just one condition that is sufficient and nearly necessary: 100 percent agreement of the women's movement actors. The csQCA notation is: COHESIVE → DUAL_RESPONSE.[34] It does not matter whether there is an Insider agency. Four of these debates occurred in the late 1990s: protections for victims of trafficking; maintaining legal abortion in the context of a debate on in vitro fertilization; a constitutional amendment allowing affirmative action to promote equal opportunities in the access to public offices and elective posts; and providing for gender equality in constitutional reform of regional governments. It also pertained to the first abortion debate in the 1970s that initially legalized abortion and the first job training debate to reduce unemployment in the 1980s.

Canada

In Canada, movement actors also have known considerable success, but the pattern of accumulated representation is different from Austria or Italy. The debates covered all the issues except political representation ranging from the mid-1960s to 2004; however, there were no debates in the 1970s. Unlike Austria, where successes grouped in the 1990s, the Canadian women's movement has gained complete success with the state six times (of nine total debates), from the first abortion debate that ended in 1969, through the 1980s, 1990s, and early 2000s. At least one women's policy agency has formed an alliance with movement actors and achieved Dual Response in prostitution, job training, and abortion debates.

The fit between women's movement actors' frames and the frames of other policy actors in the arena at the beginning of the debate is sufficient to achieve Dual Response in four debates, a coverage of .67 (logical remainders included).[35] The solution explains successes in all three abortion debates leading to decriminalization, as well as in the job training debate that gendered the Canadian Jobs Strategy and provided programs for women in 1984–1985. In two of the four cases there was an Insider agency, but when the four cases are considered together, Insider presence or absence, along with priority and cohesiveness, do not matter so long as issue frame fit is present.

There is one case where the presence of an Insider agency was crucial to representation in the absence of priority interest or cohesion among movement actors and where issue frame fit was threatening. In 1984, women's movement actors sought to influence a pending report on the criminalization of prostitution when a conservative majority controlled the government and Parliament, and the movement actors were not strong on the issue. In this case, the Insider agency assured a Dual Response to the movement. As we have seen before, when women's movement conditions are favorable for women's movement success on a series of debates in a country, Insiders do not matter to the outcome. When those favorable conditions are not present, however, the Insider can come to the rescue.

Moderate Movement Success: Belgium, Ireland, Finland, and Great Britain

Belgium

In Belgium, there were seven debates on three issues that characterize the patterns of women's movement representation within the state. All successes occurred in the 1990s. The three abortion debates followed the fortunes of the long campaign for abortion law reform in Belgium. The women's movement actors were divided on the issue, with conservative women opposed to changes in the law. The first debate in the 1970s ended in Preemption, only because the lack of action suited some of the movement actors. It was not until the enactment of abortion reform in 1990 that a majority of the women's movement actors agreed and achieved Dual Response. In the debates that took place in the 1990s—two on political representation issues and one on the hot issue of immigration reform—movement actors enjoyed complete success.

There were women's policy agencies in place through all the debates, but they took an interest in only two of them. It was striking that throughout the contentious debates on abortion, the agencies—the Consultative Commission for the Status of Women and later the State Secretary for Social Emancipation—remained silent, although there was nothing in their remits that prevented these agencies from developing a position on the issue. The division among move-ment actors could be to blame. In the 1990s, the Ministry for Labor and Equal-ity of Opportunity was an Insider in two political representation debates but slipped into the Symbolic mode for debates about quota for federal ministers and the immigration reform. When the agencies were Insiders, women's move-ment actors achieved success; still, there were other routes to Dual Response for the movement when the agencies remained silent. In the Belgian debates, there were no consistent patterns of causal conditions for these routes found through csQCA.

Ireland

We have information about debates in Ireland on two issues: abortion and job training. While the women's movement actors achieved success in two abortion debates, the women's policy agencies remained Symbolic. The one instance of state feminism is in a job training debate, as the following case study of causal mechanisms shows. As an exception, this case provides clues into, but not gen-eralizations about, the conditions for women's movement success and represen-tation in Ireland.

Case Study: Training for Globalization in Ireland, 1995–1997

The outcome took the form of a white paper on training and retraining, a major government plan to respond to the influences of changes in the global economy and Ireland's shifting place. The Irish economy had grown rapidly in the 1970s and 1980s, and job training programs had expanded along with economic development policy. Yet the issue frames and the policies remained ungendered, by default (Good 2001). The Department of Equality and Law Reform ended this situation by bringing gender and women's status in the work force to the center of the debate frame. As a result, the 1997 white paper marked a dramatic shift in framing and policy content for women. Gender equality in job training became one of major stated goals of the new policy, along with plans to devote funds to training and retraining of women explicitly.

The department did not act alone, and it is useful to trace the process leading up to this result. In 1993 the Commission on the Status of Women, a body representing women's movement organizations, reported a comprehen-sive agenda for improving the status of women in the work force, including a major component on job training. In 1994 a left-wing coalition won the gov-erning majority and in 1995 created a new women's policy agency, the Depart-ment of Equality and Law Reform, with Cabinet membership and a sweeping mandate to monitor gender equality in Irish policy. The White Paper on Social Partners appeared in 1996 and included commitments for equality in training and openings for participation by organizations such as the National Wom-en's Council of Ireland. Finally, throughout the 1990s, the European Union policies on job training and gender equality became increasingly important to the Irish government, which received substantial subsidies for promoting development.

Despite this favorable environment, when the job training debate came to the agenda in 1995, the issue frame used by policy makers remained ungendered. It was not until the Department for Equality and Law Reform intervened to bring in the agenda and perspective developed by the Commission on the Status of Women that the debate frame changed, justifying the participation of women's movement actors as social partners and leading to the favorable policy outcome. The conditions that explain the Dual Response in this debate include: Left in power; cohesive women's movement actors; corporatist subsystem structure that included women's movement actors;[36] international influence of the European Union; and an Insider agency. The Insider was necessary to the outcome but was not sufficient without the other components. It was able to overcome the closed subsystem and the lack of priority importance of the issue of job training to the movement as a whole.

Finland

In Finland, women's movements achieved full success, Dual Response, in five of nine debates. Although there was one Dual Response in the first debate (1969–1971), it was not until the 1980s that the state regularly responded to movement actors by giving them both procedural access and policies that coincided with their goals. These occurred in debates on all issues except abortion, which was not studied in Finland. The only failure in the later period was the fourth job training debate in 1992–1993.

A configuration including the presence of Insider agencies explains two of the five successes in Finland: the proposal to decriminalize prostitution in 1984–1986 and the debate over gender quotas in 1991–1995. This solution, which includes logical remainders, shows that the movement actors who agree 100 percent on their policy goals benefit from an Insider ally, whether or not there is a compatible issue frame fit or a more open policy subsystem. The csQCA notation is: COHESIVE * INSIDER → DUAL_RESPONSE, and has coverage of .40.[37] Consistency for the Insider condition is .75. For four cases of Dual Response—proposals to decriminalize prostitution (1984–1986); whether to extend criminal penalties to sex clients (1993–1998); strategies to combat labor shortages and unemployment through training (1969–1971); and the hot-issue debate on rights to municipal daycare (1991–1994)—the analysis reveals that one policy environment condition is sufficient: a policy subsystem that is not closed, or SUBSYSTEM_OPENNESS → DUAL_RESPONSE. This condition has a consistency of 1.0. That means that in Finland, when the policy subsystem is not closed, women's movement actors always achieve success.

Great Britain

While women's movement activists in Great Britain found success in the abortion debates in the 1970s, it was not until the 1990s that there was an accumulation of substantive and descriptive representation resulting in a rate similar to that of Finland. The debates cover all issues except job training. Despite a high consistency of Insider–Dual Response connections (1.0),[38] when using logical remainders the csQCA simplified the results to produce one condition that is both necessary and sufficient to Dual Response for women's movement actors: a policy subsystem that is not closed, but rather open, or moderately open. The csQCA notation is: SUBSYSTEM_OPENNESS → DUAL_RESPONSE. This solution covers all three abortion debates, as well as two debates that occurred in the early 2000s: questions of trafficking and reform of the House of Commons. There is a coverage proportion of 1.0 and consistency of 1.0—the definition of a necessary and sufficient condition, and the first and only case of this in our study. Movement actors can prevail with or without issue frame fit, 100 percent agreement, or Insider agencies if they can get access to Parliament or policy commissions. When the subsystem is closed, they fail to gain complete success in any of the debates.

Low Movement Success: Germany, France, the Netherlands, and Spain

Germany

The six state debates in Germany cover abortion, political representation, and the hot issue. Of these, two were successful for women's movements. Here we describe the only one with an Insider agency (in the other debate the agency was Symbolic). Looking at the causal mechanisms in the following case study shows how important an Insider agency can be in a country where movement successes are not frequent.

Case Study: Constitutional Equal Rights Reform
and Equal Rights Law, 1989–1994

The unification treaty of 1990 in Germany between the former Federal Republic and the former Democratic Republic specified the need for enhanced measures for gender equality in the expanded Basic Law or constitution (Kamenitsa and Geissel 2005). Many women in the former Democratic Republic were concerned that they would lose legal and economic status, because women in the former Federal Republic had lower status. The Bundestag, the legislative lower house, reported in 1991 that women held only 7.2 percent of positions on government commissions and advisory boards. Thus, the question of finding ways to increase this admittedly tiny representation was the subject of the Second Federal Equal Rights Law debated in the early 1990s.

In this case, the issue frame was gendered from the beginning in the sense that the purpose of any action would be to enhance the participation of women in government. There was disagreement, however, about the reasons for their status and over what to do about it. Women's movement actors, especially those in the political parties and in Parliament, agreed that there were deep social patterns that discriminated, especially with respect to work and family roles. They wanted a major constitutional reform and some kind of compensation or affirmative action to bring women in quickly. Others—especially leaders of the governing parties, the Christian Democratic Union (CDU) and the Free Democratic Party (FDP)—suggested that removing discrimination and treating everyone equally would be sufficient and worried that the so-called compensation would discriminate against men.

The Minister for Women and Family, Angela Merkel, went against the leaders of her own party (CDU) to advocate strongly for the women's movement actors' position. She influenced the issue frame, so that at the end the debate was about patterns of discrimination and the need for strong constitutional action. She also brought out the underlying causes of discrimination and advocated measures to help both men and women combine work and family. She pushed strongly for compensatory action.

The policy outcome addressed only one part of the movement actors–agency demands: a constitutional revision stating that women and men deserve equality and that the state is committed to removing disadvantages and promoting equal rights. However, the legislature did not enact any compensatory policies such as affirmative action or quotas for women in government positions. Nevertheless, the constitutional change was a victory, and movement actors were central to the debate in the legislature. With the opposition of the CDU leadership to any significant change, it is unlikely that even this result would have occurred without the strong and effective advocacy of an Insider women's policy agency.

In considering the causal mechanisms that led to this Dual Response, Lynn Kamenitsa and Brigitte Geissel (2005) point out that since this debate was of less interest to the CDU than the two very controversial abortion debates occurring simultaneously, it left more room for the agency to act against the strict party line. In those abortion debates, it is true that Merkel took the position of an Anti-Movement agency introducing gender into the frame of the debate without supporting the women's movement. The conditions that explain the Dual Response in the debate over the Federal Equal Rights Law include: unification treaty provisions; cohesive movement actors; supportive movement actors in Parliament from all parties; competing abortion debates; and an Insider agency.

France

Although there were only three successes in France and a low level of accumulation of substantive and descriptive representation, the debates show the importance of Insiders, particularly since debates were covered in all five issue areas in the study. csQCA, including logical remainders, found that a more open policy subsystem along with an Insider agency are sufficient for the success of movement actors in abortion, prostitution, and political representation debates. The notation is: SUBSYSTEM_OPENNESS * INSIDER → DUAL_RESPONSE and has a coverage of 1.0. The consistency of Insider–Dual Response is .75 or three of four cases with Insiders. Although this solution is compelling, when we look more closely at the cases, we see that it may underestimate the necessary role of Insider activism in France. To illustrate, we trace the process by which a women's policy agency intervened on behalf of the women's movement activists to achieve success in both procedural access and policy content.

Case Study: Public Reimbursement
of Abortion Expenses, 1981–1983

The debate involved the question of public funding of abortion services (Robinson 2001). Abortion in the first ten weeks of pregnancy had been legalized fully in 1979. In 1981, the Socialist Party won control of the presidency and both houses of Parliament. The party had become a fertile ground for feminist activists and in 1981 was very close to the women's movement organizationally and ideologically. President François Mitterrand put a strong agency—the Ministry of Woman's Rights—in place, led by an experienced socialist feminist, Yvette Roudy. One of the agency's first acts was to launch a campaign for government reimbursement of abortion costs. This plan was fully in line with demands of the women's movement organizations that had been instrumental in winning legal abortion. Minister Roudy advocated a microframe to replace the pronatalist approach dominant in previous policy debates, including the one that legalized abortion. She claimed that abortion funding was a matter of women's rights and class—equity and justice for women. In the legislature, the issue was fully gendered, making for easy entrance of feminist women deputies into the debate.

Roudy encountered opposition to her plan from within her own party, the Cabinet, the Senate, and the National Assembly. The opponents maintained that they did not want to see abortion become ordinary, which would be the result of ordinary public funding. If there was going to be reimbursement, they argued, let it come from a special fund set up for that purpose. Roudy stuck to her microframe of equity and justice, and at first considered whether abortion was ordinary or extraordinary was the wrong frame. Women's movement activists rallied to the minister's proposal through public discussions and street protests. These activities occurred even though the general women's movement was at a low level of both activism and institutionalization. Minister Roudy took advantage of this resource and fully consulted the women's movement organizations, bringing them into the policy-making process. This helped her to overcome the opposition she faced in the government and the party. She also agreed to add the notion of ordinary vs. extraordinary procedure to the agency's microframe.

It is safe to say that without the activities of the Minister for Woman's Rights, the movement actors would not have achieved either their policy or their procedural goals. The minister brought them into the policy subsystem and developed the policy of reimbursement from the general budget (not a special fund), thus signaling that abortion was officially an ordinary medical matter. Furthermore, the notion that abortion policy is a matter of women's rights and equality has remained the dominant issue frame in all subsequent debates on abortion. What no agency has been able to do since, with one exception (a prostitution debate in 1989–1990), is to secure procedural access for movement actors. The explanation for the success in 1983 is the activities of the Minister of Woman's Rights and her agency.

The Netherlands

The only women's movement complete success out of nine state debates in the Netherlands was in the final abortion debate in the 1980s. Here, we examine in more detail the conditions for this one success to gain insight about democratization in the Netherlands.

Case Study: Regulations and Services for Abortion, 1981–1984

As is usual in Dutch politics, a coalition Cabinet was in place with the Christian Democrats and Liberal Party in charge. Parliament had just legalized abortion in 1981 after a debate that framed the issue as a women's rights question, especially the right to control the abortion decision. The statute required the Cabinet to issue administrative rules, and Christian Democratic opponents of the abortion law saw another chance to limit the reform. They aggressively moved to redefine abortion as a special medical procedure to be handled by experts, not women, and to limit access to the procedure.

There were two women's policy offices that stepped in to counter this move: the Department for Coordination of Emancipation Policy and the Emancipation Council. The Department was a bureaucratic agency in the Ministry of Social Affairs; its political head was a junior minister who took part in Cabinet deliberations. She was resolute in countering the Christian Democrats' strategy, maintained abortion was a women's decision, and threatened to resign if abortion funding was not included in the policy. Like her French counterpart, she also agreed to the idea that abortion was a normal procedure and that women were normal patients. The overall frame that the decision to have an abortion was a woman's alone remained dominant among policy makers.

While the junior minister, supported by the Department staff, was successful in maintaining the favorable issue frame in the debate and a favorable policy outcome, the Emancipation Council brought women's movement actors into the policy process. The early 1980s was a time of high activism in the Dutch women's movement. The council reflected the growing institutionalization of movement actors. It was a corporate-style body that included a few representatives of the women's movement. Because the council worked closely with the department on the issue, the women's movement actors gained access to the policy subsystem. The movement resources were fairly strong; movement actors were 100 percent cohesive on the goals, and the issue was a high movement priority. The policy environment was not friendly to movements, however, and without the two women's policy agencies the movement actors would not have achieved this success. One can conclude that the Insider agencies were helped in making their presentations by political leaders' awareness of the movement's strength at the time.

The agencies could not maintain their record; although studies of subsequent debates found three cases where the Department acted as an Insider, in one the outcome was Co-optation or procedural access only, and in two the outcome was Preemption or policy content only. In this third abortion debate, the policy subsystem worked to the advantage of the policy agencies, because the subsystem included only the Cabinet and the bureaucracy. Most of the other debates took place in Parliament, where the Department had less influence. In later debates as well, the Emancipation Council was limited or disappeared altogether, making it difficult for movement actors to gain access to policy venues in the corporate system (Outshoorn 2001).

Spain

The debates in Spain date from the mid-1980s through 2002. These debates covered all five issues, but there were only two cases of Dual Response in state debates, and they show no accumulation of successes that would mean a significant expansion of descriptive and substantive representation. There is no case of a state women's policy agency acting as an Insider and gaining a Dual Response. Thus, state feminism has not developed in Spain's young democracy, at least within the national-level state. The analysis of the party-level debates in Chapter 10 provides a more promising picture for movement-agency success.

Country Democratization

As indicated by the proportion and patterns of women's movement successes in policy debates, democratization varies, as does the usefulness of women's policy offices as allies. Insider agencies tend to be less important for movement actors in countries with higher rates of overall success. Among the five most successful countries, Insiders matter in only two. Sweden's formula mixes the presence of Insiders with support from leftist parties and unions. In Canada, Insider offices act as a backup when the sufficient condition—issue frame fit—is not present. In the remaining countries, successes are due to left-wing support (Austria), women's movement cohesion (Italy), or a variety of paths (United States), but not women's policy agencies.

Insiders play a backup role in three of the four countries with moderate proportions of movement success. In Finland, a more open subsystem is sufficient to success, but when there is an Insider agency and a cohesive movement, the subsystem does not matter. Subsystem is key in British debates as well, where csQCA found that it is both necessary and sufficient. However, there are also sufficient paths in the observed debates that include Insiders. In Ireland, a case study shows that an Insider agency is necessary but not sufficient for one of three Dual Responses. In Belgium, like the United States, movement actors can achieve success with or without Insiders.

Tracing causal mechanisms reveals the crucial role of Insider agencies in three of the four countries with low rates of Dual Responses. In France and the Netherlands, only with Insiders did movement actors reach success; in Germany, an agency took credit for one of the two cases of Dual Response. In Spain, Insider agencies had not yet opened the policy-making process within the nation-level state to greater substantive and descriptive representation for the Spanish movement.

The Importance of Policy Sector

Policy sector dynamics are prominent in the analyses of the state feminism propositions. Whether the debate is in the area of abortion, job training, political representation, prostitution, or the hot issue will affect the degree of movement success and the likelihood of forming effective alliances with women's policy offices. Qualitative analysis explains outcomes by issues, specifically the finding that Insiders act as a backup in job training debates and the particular significance of left-wing support in understanding debates on hot issues.

Country differences appear in the patterns of democratization as well as the value of Insiders to women's movement successes over time. There are, however, no regional dynamics in these results. Countries do not group together according to any of the typical regional classifications in the extent to which movement actors have opened up the policy processes. Among the English-speaking liberal states, the United States and Canada are in the high-success category, Great Britain and Ireland in the moderate category. Similarly, Social Democratic and Nordic Sweden and Finland are in different categories. We find the Southern European Catholic countries divided as well: Italy ranks among the countries with the highest successes, while France and Spain are in the lowest. Finally, the corporatist group of Germany, the Netherlands, and Belgium are split, with Belgium among the moderate successes, and Germany and the Netherlands among the lowest successes.

Conclusion

This chapter has examined four categories of propositions derived from the state feminism framework: frequencies of women's movement success and alliances with women's policy offices; the significance of activities of offices in achieving success with the state; the value of Insider agencies in achieving state responses and democratization; and the importance of policy sectors.

Based on the analysis, we can say that women's movement actors have been very successful from the 1960s to the 2000s in gaining positive responses from the states and have found, more often than not, agencies amenable to forming alliances to support their demands. About half of such alliances are successful in reframing the policy debates to include movement perspectives. The more active the agencies are, from no activity through full gendering with matching microframes, the more likely the state responses will be positive to the movement goals. Priority of the issue to the women's movement and openness of the policy subsystem also explain state response.

The value of Insider agencies, except in specific cases, is neither necessary nor sufficient for movement success; instead, they are a backup to bring success in the absence of usually favorable conditions. At the same time, they must be taken into account. Using qualitative methods, we found no configurations of Women's Movement Resources, Favorable Policy Environment, or Left Support that explain outcomes without considering the presence or absence of an Insider agency.

The analysis of hot-issue debates, both through csQCA and a look at specific cases, provided a nuanced perspective on propositions about the explanatory power of the Left Support factors—that is, the argument that women's movements that are close to the leftist parties are more successful when the leftist party forms the government. It is the movement actors' alliances with the leftist parties and unions and their representatives in policy arenas that are important whether or not the Left is in power.

The section on democratization investigated the value of Insider agencies in the thirteen countries in the study, in the context of the pattern of accumulation of Dual Responses over time. We found that Insider agencies function as backup allies when usually favorable conditions are not present—a finding similar to the results of the csQCA analysis by issue. The value of Insiders increases for countries with the lowest rates of Dual Responses. Patterns of women's movement successes and state feminism vary by policy sector. Country patterns are evident in looking at accumulation of Dual Responses and state feminist outcomes over time. There is no evidence, however, of regional groupings in the results.

Ordinal Regression, csQCA, and causal-mechanisms methods applied to the propositions examined in this chapter show the need to incorporate state feminism theory into the current social movement theories for explaining women's movement success. With respect to studying other social movements, it means that along with movement resources and political contexts, researchers should look at state agencies as potential allies of movement actors.

The results demonstrate that using methods that are most appropriate to investigating particular propositions from state feminism theory provides an integrated set of findings. The lesson here is that the assumption of complexity as represented by equifinality and in-depth case studies must be incorporated into research plans along with hypothesis-testing approaches. In the final analysis, a mixed-methods approach has allowed us to assess the activities of movements and agencies and their significance, as well as to identify women's policy agencies when they are crucial players in women's movement success and where they make Western postindustrial democracies more democratic. At the same time, it has produced evidence of the importance of open subsystems, overall movement interest in debate topics, and support from left-wing parties and unions to women's movement success with the state.

5

Women's Policy Agency Success and Failure

The Search for Explanations

The activity of women's policy machineries is a significant influence on state responses to women's movement demands; at the same time, the most effective agencies—Insiders—are not necessary to achieve complete success. Instead, Insiders tend to be a backup when women's movement actors do not have the necessary resources, favorable policy environments, or support from left-wing parties and unions to achieve complete success with the state. Weak women's movements and unfavorable policy environments are the norm in countries with the lowest level of women's movement success. Insider agencies in those countries have been important in bringing about the few successes women's movements have enjoyed. In a majority of the debates, however, agencies were not Insiders. They either adopted the movement goals but failed to change the frame of the debate—Marginal allies—or they did nothing at all—Symbolics. A few even worked against movement actor goals—Anti-Movement agencies. Why are some agencies effective allies and others ineffective? Why do some offices refuse to form alliances with women's movement actors? Answering these questions necessarily involves a systematic search for explanations of agency success and failure, to which we now turn in this chapter.

The proposition that agency characteristics—structure, leadership, powers, and administrative capacity—are most likely to affect the success or failure of state offices as women's movement allies is at the core of the analysis here. At the same time, the state feminism framework goes beyond the machineries themselves to look at the influence of women's movement resources, of characteristics of the policy environment, and of support from the left wing. Thus, this chapter examines agency characteristics alongside the explanatory power of the same sets of conditions that were important in understanding women's movement success in Chapter 4.

We continue to use an integrated mixed-methods approach in the analysis of the full-fledged women's policy agencies in 104 national debates.[1] First, Ordinal Regression helps to determine if any agency, movement, policy environment, or Left support variables affect degrees of agency activity. Next, using csQCA and case studies of causal mechanisms, we look for configurations of characteristics that distinguish fully Insider agencies from Marginal ones. In the last part of the chapter, the darker side of state feminism is explored—both those agencies that did nothing to help women's movement actors (Symbolics) and the few that acted against their goals (Anti-Movement agencies).

Ideas about Agency Success and Failure

Ever since the United Nations declared women's policy machineries to be the main engines for achieving equality for women, observers have considered the conditions that are conducive to reach that goal. A host of factors have been suggested: structure and capacity of the agencies, characteristics of women's movements, state-society relations, state configurations, regime type, gender regimes, political will, and cultural factors. While analysts have used the tools of comparative analysis to determine the relative importance of factors through single-nation case studies as well as through comparisons of agencies in several countries or in groups of countries—both within regions and across regions—there is no definitive answer to questions about which determinants produce successful agencies. This section reviews what we know from previous research in relation to the cluster of Agency Characteristics as well as features of Movement Resources, Favorable Policy Environment, and Left Support used in this study.

Women's Policy Agency Characteristics

Studies suggest that certain administrative profiles produce more successful outcomes in a given national context. Weldon's (2002b: 132) discussion of "effectiveness and accountability" shows agency independence, resources, formalized channels of access, and an ability to act across all policy areas to be important attributes for effectiveness. Similarly, Jonathan Malloy (1999, 2003), in his research on women's policy agencies in Australia, points to agency autonomy, relations with groups, and resources as important factors. Findings of *Comparative State Feminism* (McBride Stetson and Mazur 1995a) and other studies (e.g., Squires and Wickham-Jones 2002) identify both administrative resources and a cross-sectional agency approach as important. Research on femocrats in Australia and the Netherlands shows that agency leadership, particularly with respect to any ties to the women's movement and its feminist leanings, affects agency activities (Outshoorn 1994; Eisenstein 1996; Chappell 2002a; Sawer 1990). Shirin Rai (2003b) identifies critical features of machineries: location, clarity of mandates, links with movement groups, resources, and accountability. Using measures from the RNGS dataset, we assess here the impact of *agency proximity*, *administrative capacity*, and *leadership* as well as *type of agency and formal powers to make policy proposals* on agency success and failure.

Women's Movement Characteristics

As discussed in Chapter 1, a rich literature on social movements, women's movements, and feminism in Western postindustrial democracies indicates that the strength, structure, and position of the women's movement is a decisive ingredient in the ability of women's movements to influence policy outcomes (e.g., Banaszak, Beckwith and Rucht 2003; Costain 1992; Katzenstein and Mueller 1987; Threlfall 1996). Studies of women's policy machineries also point to the importance of strong and autonomous women's groups prepared to work with state actors in explaining the ability of agencies to make and implement feminist policies that go beyond symbolic gestures (Weldon 2002b; Malloy 1999, 2003; McBride Stetson and Mazur 1995a). For example, a comparative analysis of the formation of feminist policy in Western democracies shows that women's policy offices, in tandem with women's movements, are key players in many cases (Mazur 2002). In this chapter, we assess the effect of Women's Movement Resources, with the same measures used in Chapter 4 (*movement activism* and *institutionalization, issue priority*, and the *cohesiveness of women's movement positions* in the debates), on agency effectiveness.

Policy Environment

Feminist and nonfeminist studies of public policy show the context for policy making—that is, the policy environment—to be an important factor in determining policy processes and outcomes. Although actions of women's policy agencies are a part of state action, few actually look at how these policy processes relate to agency activities and effectiveness. Instead, scholars have named conditions that explain larger institutional features, such as types of state-society relations (e.g., Keeler 1987), the design of government (e.g., Lijphart 1999), veto points (e.g., Stephens and Huber 2001), political opportunity structure (e.g., Tarrow 1998; Kriesi et al. 1995), and types of gender welfare regimes (e.g., Sainsbury 2008). Much of this literature focuses on explanations at the national level of a given country, while comparative-policy scholars increasingly argue that policy dynamics tend to vary within countries across policy sectors (e.g., Baumgartner 1996; Van Waarden 1992; Feick 1992; Mazur 2002). We examine three Policy Environment variables—*structure of the policy subsystem, issue frame fit to women's movement actor demands*, and *presence of a weak countermovement*. These pertain to the policy arena of each debate within its issue area, not at the overall national level.

Left Support

Research on feminist policy formation and women's movements has identified the importance of parties, trade unions, and governing majorities that espouse left-wing ideologies focused on social justice and equality as important potential partners for women's movement actors (e.g., Beckwith 1985; Stephens and

Huber 2001; O'Connor 1999; Norris 1987). At the same time, many feminist scholars question the degree to which left-wing actors and governments actually defend women's movement interests. Comparative studies have shown that in certain policy areas the presence of a left-wing government is often not a crucial factor in feminist policy outcomes (Mazur 2002; Elman 1996; Kittilson 2008; Weldon 2002b). Others point out the hostility of the male-dominated culture of left-wing trade unions to feminist approaches as an obstacle to women's movement success and women-friendly policy (Gelb 1989).

Studies of women's policy agencies have only begun to identify the link between left-wing organization and ideology and agency effectiveness (e.g., Malloy 1999). The precursor to the RNGS study, *Comparative State Feminism*, found that the more effective national machineries in Norway, Denmark, Australia, and the Netherlands were established under social democratic governments that placed gender issues high on their agendas (McBride Stetson and Mazur 1995a: 288). In this chapter, the potential for Left support for women's movement actors is assessed through three different concepts: *women's movement organizational closeness to the Left, women's movement ideological closeness to the Left*, and the *presence of a left-wing governing majority*.[2] The question here, therefore, is whether the movement closeness to the parties and trade unions of the Left and the presence of left-wing governments are key factors in agency effectiveness.

Explaining Agency Successes

Looking for Answers through Ordinal Regression

Based on these possible drivers of agency effectiveness, we adapted appropriate variables in the RNGS dataset to assess their strength in explaining agency activity, using the ordinal measure presented in Chapter 4 as the dependent variable.[3] The propositions about the effects of the four clusters of conditions on agency performance are addressed in four models, running each as a separate Ordinal Regression.[4] Only one variable—issue frame fit in the Policy Environment model—shows an independent significant effect on the degree of women's movement agency activity.[5] This variable measures the fit between the women's movement actors' microframes and the frame of policy subsystem—the issue frame—at the beginning of the debate. Controlling for subsystem openness and countermovement, as cases move from those where the issue frame was threatening to movement actors' demands toward those where the frame was compatible and matching, the greater the likelihood that the agency will become more active on behalf of the movement. The reference category is Matching Fit. The EXP(β) values for each of the other categories are: Threatening, .284; Incompatible, .278; Compatible, .169. Thus, if the issue frame fit is threatening, an increase women's policy agency effectiveness is .284 times less likely than if the issue frame fit is matching. Other than this finding, statistical analysis yields no results that explain the effectiveness of women's policy offices. What is most striking at this point is that none of the characteristics of agencies have an independent effect on the likelihood that agencies would be more active on behalf of women's movement actors.

Comparing Insiders and Marginal Allies: What Makes the Difference?

Thirty-five percent of the agencies studied in this chapter gendered policy debates with movement actors' goals and ideas (i.e., Insiders). Another 30 percent are Marginal; they adopted microframes that matched or were compatible with movement actors' goals and ideas but did not gender the issue frame of the debates. In this section, we look at these sixty-nine national agencies (thirty-six Insider, thirty-three Marginal) to try to explain why some agency allies were able to gender policy debates and become Insiders, while others remained Marginal to the policy process.

We concentrate on agency attributes and how they may combine with the features of the three other explanatory clusters under study to affect whether agencies are Insiders or Marginal allies. We begin by comparing the effective and ineffective agencies in terms of agency characteristics.[6] Insider agencies, in contrast to Marginal agencies, tend to

- be ministries and not advisory councils
- have more indicators of administrative capacity
- be closer to centers of power in their institutional settings with the power to propose as opposed to review or enforce policy
- be slightly less likely to have leaders with women's movement actor or feminist experience before taking office

These frequencies support the findings of other studies showing that successful agencies tend to have higher levels of administrative capacity. At the same time, they do not tell how important these administrative resources are in relation to women's movement resources and political opportunity factors in explaining the effectiveness of women's policy agencies in policy making. We now turn to csQCA to uncover which combinations of factors may explain agency effectiveness.

Crisp-Set Qualitative Comparative Analysis

The search for explanations of agency effectiveness (Insiders vs. Marginals) across the issues yields causal configurations only for the political representation debates. Examining these, we develop a model by combining conditions with a consistency of .90 or higher in configurations with high levels of coverage of the political representation cases (more than 50 percent). The result is a new model that includes Agency Characteristics, Movement Resources, and Left Support to reveal a causal configuration covering a majority of the Insider outcomes and fits expectations. Political representation debates, in contrast to other issues, are fertile ground for agencies with ministerial status and proposal powers that operate in the context of a women's movement with very close organizational ties to the leftist parties and unions, and where the issue at hand was a top priority. The csQCA notation is: MINISTRY * PROPOSAL_POWER * ORGL * PRIORITY → INSIDER. This configuration, produced without including logical remainders, explains the effectiveness of agencies in seven of the thirteen Insider cases for a coverage of .53. One of these is in Austria, where the Ministry of Women's Affairs in 1990–1993 promoted the women's movement position in the debate over equal treatment of women and men in the civil service, in accord with the policies of its left-wing government. Similarly, in Great Britain and Sweden, women's movement closeness to the Left occurred, along with the presence of Insider ministries in left-wing governments, the classic Left Support configuration. In Great Britain, the debate involved parliamentary working hours and adjusting them to permit more involvement by women as MPs, promoted strongly by the Minister for Women. In Sweden, the Minister of Gender Equality in the 1980s was effective in gaining quotas for women in appointed government positions.

We might expect that Insiders in the other four cases were part of left-wing governments as well, but this is not the case; Left majority is not part of a sufficient path to Insider in political representation debates. In Belgium, the Minister of Equal Opportunities not only gendered the issue frame of the two quota debates in the 1990s but successfully brought the issue to the agenda of Parliament. Its position was fully supported by both the Center-Right and Center-Left governments (always including Christian Democrats). Similarly, in Italy, the Minister for Equal Opportunity successfully launched an amendment to the constitution that made it possible to adopt quotas within the electoral legislation even though the government shifted from Left to Right. Finally, in the 1989–1994 debate over a Federal Equal Rights law in the newly united German Federal Republic, the Ministry for Women and Youth in the right-wing government allied with the women's movement and successfully amended the constitution to promote the status of women.

There are six cases of Insider agencies not explained by this solution, and they demonstrate several configurations among types, administrative conditions, and women's movement characteristics. In three, the agencies are councils or commissions. In the parity debate in France (1995–2000), for example, the temporary *Observatoire de la Parité* had a special mandate to gender the debate and to represent movement actors on the issue. In 1991–1993, Italy did not yet have a Ministry for Equal Opportunity. At the same time, its National Commission for Equal Opportunity was a close advisor of the prime minister, a perch that enhanced its effectiveness. Similarly, in Finland, when the Council for Equality promoted the gender quotas in a new Equality Act, it benefited from proposal power as well as an alliance between the movement and the left-wing government.

The two debates in the Netherlands involved an administrative office, the Department for Coordination of Equality Policy. As is pointed out in Chapter 3, administrative offices are likely to have high levels of capacity. With resources and proposal powers, the department was an effective Insider in both debates: women's representation in an Equality Plan in 1981–1985 and reform of corporatist system in 1989–1997. Whether the movement was close to the Left or the issue was a high priority did not make a difference in these debates.

In Spain, we find a well-resourced agency, the Women's Institute, and a right-wing government. Although the office is defined as an Insider, it turns out that the microframe it promoted coincided with only a minority of movement actors—the women MPs in the governing party—who favored soft measures to bring more women into political party candidacies rather than the mandatory quotas promoted by the women's movement and the Left.

There were only two cases of Marginal agencies in this set of political representation debates, and looking at the causal paths to that outcome reinforces the findings with respect to Insiders. Neither agency was a ministry, and neither had a high capacity; in addition, the policy issue was not a high priority for the movement during the debate. Both debates were early in the sequence for the country. In Finland in 1972–1975, the Council for Equality promoted attention to women in a new electoral law, but for the most part the women's movement actors were indifferent; thus, despite its proposal powers, the council was unable to gender the debate. In Great Britain, a debate over QUANGOs (Quasi Non-Governmental Organizations) was framed as an efficiency matter, and although the Equal Opportunities Commission protested that it might adversely affect women, the agency was so far from power that it had no effect. Similarly, only one MP was concerned about gender effects.

We ran the model on the political representation debates including the logical remainders, combinations of conditions that were not observed, and found two conditions, each of which is sufficient to bring about the outcome of Insider in the political representation debates: high degree of administrative capacity or priority of the issue. The csQCA solution is: CAPACITY + PRIORITY → INSIDER. Each has a 1.0 consistency; whenever there is high capacity or high priority, there will be an Insider agency in political representation debates. Of these, the priority of the issue pertains to twelve of thirteen Insider cases, or .92 coverage. For capacity, the coverage is nine of thirteen, or .69. Priority, a Movement Resource indicator, explains more cases than the agency administrative resources condition and is closer to being a necessary condition. For Marginal outcomes, the path is the absence of capacity *and* the absence of priority. The solution is: CAPACITY * PRIORITY → MARGINAL. Because the solutions are produced with logical remainders, these findings apply beyond the observations in this study.

Case Studies: Causal Mechanisms for Agency Success

The following two case studies are intended to explore further the relationship between agency resources and contexts in determining the success of agency alliances. We have selected these cases because they were exceptions to expectations of the state feminism framework. The first looks at a single agency with few resources in Finland that participated in nine different policy debates with varying success and its triumph in a debate over quotas in the 1990s. The second compares activities of agencies with similar characteristics but different outcomes in job training debates in Canada and the United States.

Quotas in Equality Act in Finland, 1991–1995. Since the 1970s, the Council for Equality, an executive commission, has been the primary women's policy office in Finland. Located in a national ministry, it is only moderately close to the centers of power in the Cabinet, and, as a commission, has little staff and a tiny budget; moreover, its members represent different parties. While typically adopting perspectives that match those of women's movement actors, the council has a mixed record of success. In the 1970s, it was Marginal in debates on job training and political representation. In the 1980s, the council began to be more influential, becoming an Insider in prostitution debates and the following political representation debate in the 1990s. Overall, its Insider activities coincided with a Dual Response in three of the nine debates.

There is a long tradition of gender equality in Finland that has frequently translated into little support for "women's rights," an idea that was seen to single out a group for special treatment (Holli and Kantola 2005). Thus, when the question of quotas for women's representation in public bodies came to the national agenda in the early 1990s, it seemed to counter the basic paradigm that had shaped equality policy for decades. Within that perspective, the Finnish Parliament had the highest percentage of women of any country in Europe (39 percent). At the same time, the Equality Act of 1987 prepared the ground for a shift in conventional thinking with a paragraph generally referring to balancing the gendered composition of public, nonelected state organizations. This was the stimulus for a debate about establishing gender quotas to improve representation of women on commissions and other public bodies.

There was little disagreement among the policy actors about two things: Women were under-represented, and their numbers in the referenced organizations should increase. The debate was about the means. On the one hand, women's movement actors and leftist parties saw the problem as structural; in the absence of quotas, nothing would change, and qualified women would be overlooked. Norway had recently adopted quotas, and these advocates pointed to that example. The employers and rightist parties, on the other hand, considered quotas too drastic and unfair to individual rights; they suggested that education and attitude change would lead to an increase in the number of women serving on the public bodies.

The Equality Act gave the Council for Equality and the Equality Ombudsman, a judicial officer also in the Ministry of Social Affairs, responsibility for equality policy, and initially (early 1991) both agencies supported the idea of quotas. Changes in personnel in these agencies affected what happened next. First, a new ombudsman came on the scene with close ties to business interests and began to work against the adoption of quotas, becoming an Anti-Movement agency. The Council for Equality members were divided on the issue and provided information to the minister and Cabinet but did not become active. This agency was on its way to becoming a Symbolic presence in the debate. In 1992, however, a new chair came to the council and gave it a more active role, and beginning in 1994 the agency supported quotas. The chair, also a member of a centrist party in Parliament, worked to assemble a majority for quotas in both the council and in Parliament despite the official opposition of the ruling Center-Right coalition. She was helped by the fact that nearly all the women MPs, both right-wing and left-wing, supported the quota proposal.

What are the mechanisms that led the Council for Equality to become an effective women's movement ally in this case, despite its weak resources and the presence of a right-wing government? First of all, the institutional context was favorable; that is, the council had formal policy responsibilities for overseeing the question of gender equality within the Ministry of Social Affairs. Second, the most active women's movement actors on the issue were the women in Parliament of left- and right-wing parties, and the leader of the council was one of them. Thus, although institutionally not close to the center of national power, the agency was networked to the policy makers. The chair had no previous women's movement experience, but she took a leadership role by forming a consensus in the council in favor of quotas and then forging the same in Parliament. The different perspectives of the two agency leaders—the pro-quota head of the council and the anti-quota head of the Equality Ombudsman—explain the different outcomes of their activities. In looking at the effectiveness of the Council for Equality in Finland as an ally of women's movement actors, it is evident that the issue and the agency's institutional location are very important.

Comparing this case with the simultaneous hot-issue debate over municipal daycare (Aalto and Holli 2007), we see how the combination of the statutory responsibility, the council's agenda, and its leadership came together to bring the agency to an Insider outcome on the question of quotas. In the hot-issue debate, on the other hand, there was a different configuration: The issue was low on the council's agenda, the members did not take a strong position, and although the same leader who promoted quotas also promoted the women's movement position on the daycare issue in Parliament, she did not do so as a representative of the council, and thus the council could not be credited with the successful outcome.

Job Training in Canada and the United States: Same Conditions, Different Outcomes. In the course of running various groups of conditions in csQCA, we found a configuration that leads to different outcomes in these job training debates.[7] Both agencies had high capacity but no feminist leadership; the women's movement actors were institutionalized into formal structures such as parties, interest groups, and the bureaucracy, and the actors placed the job training issue as a high priority, despite not having complete agreement about how to frame the issue to improve women's place in the job training policy. Yet, the Status of Women Canada was an effective ally by contributing to gendering the debate and, finally, gaining a Dual Response from the state, whereas the U.S. Women's Bureau remained marginal to the debate despite its strong support for women's movement goals (Teghtsoonian and Grace 2001; McBride Stetson 2001b).

There are other similarities between these two debates. First of all, both involved adjustments to job training statutes already in place. In Canada, the 1985 debate revolved around the Canadian Jobs Strategy to implement a National Training Act of 1982. In the United States, the issue was the 1978 reauthorization of the CETA program initially enacted in 1974. Second, the movement actors' frames were essentially the same. In Canada, activists complained about the low rate of women's participation in job training for jobs that could break old sex stereotypes. Women were relegated to programs that trained them for traditional women's jobs. They demanded the government develop new programs that would give women skills for well-paying, stable jobs and launched a systematic campaign to promote women's participation in these training programs.

In the United States, the CETA provisions were designed to help the disadvantaged groups acquire training and jobs. Movement actors pointed out that women were the main clientele of the program, but that policy makers did not recognize that fact. Activists focused on sex stereotyping in education, fought discrimination in job training programs, promoted special training to qualify women for nontraditional jobs, and defined the problem of displaced homemakers who needed help to recover from the effects of taking time from careers for raising children.

The agencies had many parallels as well. Both were administrative bureaus with relatively large staffs and separate budgets. They were located in the offices of members of the national Cabinets—the Minister Responsible for the Status of Women in Canada and the Secretary of Labor in the United States. Both were actively interested in the question of women's employment equality generally and job training especially, and both had close ties with women's movement actors campaigning on those issues. In Canada, there was another women's policy agency that brought women's movement representatives into the debate: the Canadian Advisory Committee on the Status of Women. There was a parallel lay panel in the U.S. Department of Labor as well: the Citizens' Advisory Committee on the Status of Women.

What explains the differences in the effectiveness of these women's movement allies? In tracing the causal mechanisms for the outcomes in both cases, there are three factors that stand out. First, is the type of decision required to change the job training policy. Canada's Job Strategy was an executive policy implementing a parliamentary statute; it did not require further legislative action. (It is somewhat unexpected that this was on the initiative of a Conservative government, but that government's main motivation was to save money. At the same time, it was a Democratic executive and Congress making policy in the United States). In the United States, the decision was the reauthorization of an act of Congress through the legislative process. Second, because of the nature of the decision, the policy subsystems were different, and thus, these two agencies differed in relation to the policy subsystems that made the final policy. The Status of Women Canada had access to Cabinet-level deliberations through the Minister Responsible for the Status of Women, although it was not itself at that level. The U.S. Women's Bureau needed permission from the Secretary of Labor to enter the congressional policy subsystem by bringing testimony to hearings. The secretary sent the director of another Labor Department agency, the Employment and Training Bureau.

Finally, there is a difference traced to the way gender issues had been treated in job training policy discussions before these policy debates—in other words a path dependency. In Canada, the debate was gendered at the beginning; the job training issue had incorporated gender equity objectives in the 1970s in response to another women's policy agency. Thus, because it was a gendered issue, the agency was justified in weighing in on any subsequent job training debate. In the United States, the job training issue was not gendered at all; instead, it was framed as a matter of help to the disadvantaged, a category that was associated more with racial minorities and the disabled than with women. The challenge in the U.S. debate in 1978 was to gender job training debates for the first time. The Women's Bureau was not seen as an administrative expert on job training or the disadvantaged, so the Secretary of Labor did not turn to this agency (although the director was later able to get a ruling to review all policy of the department for possible impact on women). It was only after movement actors influenced Congress in the reauthorization of the CETA program that women's interests became explicit. It did not last long, however. In 1982, with the consideration of the Job Training Partnership Act, the frame of the issue was de-gendered, while the Women's Bureau, under a right-wing director, was a Symbolic player. In Canada, on the other hand, Status Women Canada remained involved and influential in job training debates into the 1990s.

The Findings So Far

Thus far, we have used three methods to examine the reasons for agency effectiveness in influencing policy debates on behalf of women's movement actors. Ordinal Regression results are limited. With the exception of issue frame fit with women's movement microframes, none of the measures of Agency Characteristics, Women's Movement Resources, Favorable Policy Environment, or Left Support has an independent effect on women' agency activity. These results suggest that scholars need to go beyond statistical inference to unravel the mystery of effective state feminist agencies. At the same time, the Ordinal Regression estimates reinforce results from the process tracing in case studies throughout this chapter. The issue frame at the beginning of the debate, defined by the regular policy actors in that arena and its fit with women's movement actors' frames, can explain both whether women's policy agencies take up the questions raised by women's movement actors as well as their success or failure in gendering the debate.

Using csQCA to explain the differences between effective movement allies (Insiders) in comparison with ineffective allies (Marginals) resulted in a causal configuration of conditions covering most political representation debates. It shows the importance of agency type (ministry) and capacity combined with the priority of equality in political representation to the women's movement generally in leading agency allies to influence debate frames.

Causal mechanisms found in three case studies point to the significance of agency leadership in combination with institutional location in relation to subsystem structures and the path dependency of debate frames. These results suggest looking at specific connections between formal responsibilities of agencies and the type of decision and subsystem—whether executive or parliamentary—in determining agency effectiveness. Thus, one must consider more than just the openness of subsystem structures and the proximity of agencies to central power by investigating the institutional relation of an agency to particular kinds of arenas where policies are made. Path dependency influences deserve attention as well, a study that is probably most effectively done through the causal-mechanisms approach.

Explaining Agency Failures

Now we turn to agencies that fail to ally with movements. There are twenty-nine (27 percent of all debates with women's policy agencies) Symbolic agencies and seven (6 percent) Anti-Movement agencies. Both counter expectations that women's policy offices tend to ally with, and on behalf of, women's movement actors. When agencies are Symbolic, the structures do nothing: They take no position on the issue, express no microframe, and do not work to have influence in the debate. The agencies exist and are situated so they can take part, and thus have the potential to become active in policy discussions, but they are of no help to women's movement activists. Anti-Movement agencies take a position—they have a microframe—but it is incompatible or threatening to the goals of the movement actors. In some cases, the Anti-Movement agencies are successful in gendering the debates, but in a way that conflicts with the movement goals; in others, the agencies have no effect on the policy debate.

It remains to apply csQCA and case study methods to discover what factors account for the failure of agencies to assist women's movements in their engagements with the state. The only way to find out why these agencies did nothing is to compare them with those that did something. The goal of this part of the chapter is to compare the characteristics and contexts of the Symbolics with the agency allies (Insiders and Marginals). After a look at cross-tabulations comparing agency characteristics of allies, Symbolics, and Anti-Movement agencies, the results of csQCA show paths to Symbolic outcomes for debates on prostitution and the hot issues. Then the puzzle of Symbolic agencies is further explored by searching for causal mechanisms in the three Italian prostitution cases. This section ends with an analysis of the darkest side of state feminism—six cases of Anti-Movement agencies.

Characteristics of Failed Agencies

The cross-tabulations show that the two types of failed agencies have less in common with each other that they have with the allies. In comparing administrative resources, Symbolics and allies have similar administrative capacity, defined as the number of organizational and budget attributes.[8] With respect to proximity, Symbolics tend to be a bit more distant from the center of power in their institutional setting than the allies. Anti-Movement agencies, on the other hand, are in even closer proximity than agency allies. Symbolics are less likely to have policy proposal powers than Anti-Movement offices or agency allies. Symbolic agencies are more likely to have leaders with women's movement as well as feminist experience. The Anti-Movement offices, in contrast, are less likely to have feminist leadership (two out of seven).

Paths to Symbolic Failure: csQCA

To explore the causes of Symbolic outcomes, we apply combinations of the same four clusters of characteristics used in looking for paths to Insider rather than Marginal outcomes in the first part of the chapter. The expectation is that whereas administrative resources may be important conditions in separating effective allies from marginal ones in some issues, Symbolic outcomes are likely to result from less resourced agencies. If Symbolic agencies have high organizational capacity, then particular agency conditions would combine with other characteristics to explain the failures as a women's movement ally.

The csQCA found both types of results. The first type applies to agencies in prostitution debates. A model combining the absence of indicators of agency strength produced two causal combinations for Symbolics.[9] Including logical remainders, the solution that covers the most cases combines low capacity and the absence of feminist leadership with proximity to centers of power to produce a Symbolic outcome. The csQCA notation is: capacity * PROXIMITY * feml → SYMBOLIC_AGENCY, with a coverage of .60. One is the French Deputy Ministry of the Feminine Condition's role in a debate on prostitution in the early 1970s. Deputy Minister Françoise Giroud considered prostitution to be a man's problem and not part of her mandate to promote the status of women. French women's movement activists failed to convince her and other policy makers to adopt their definition that prostitution was an abuse by patriarchy. The other agency activity explained by this configuration involves Great Britain's Women's National Commission in debates during 1979–1983 and 1984–1985. British feminists active on the issue argued that prostitution should be defined as sex work and be decriminalized, but the commission refused to take up these demands. Both the French and British agencies were tiny but positioned at the Cabinet level. Their leaders were in a position to have some influence, but they had little experience with or sympathy for feminist views on the prostitution issue. The other solution for agencies in prostitution combines the administrative office and its usual high capacity with a lack of proposal power to explain the Symbolic outcome, with a coverage of .20. The csQCA notation is: ADM_OFFICE * CAPACITY * proposal_power → SYMBOLIC_AGENCY.

The second type of result explains Symbolic offices in hot-issue debates. The findings go against the expectation that lack of agency resources or conditions of women's movement weakness explain the failures. Some of the most well-endowed agencies pushed by strong movement actors remained Symbolic. We found a configuration that covers a proportion of .60 of the Symbolic outcomes: presence of high capacity and feminist leadership combined with high movement institutionalization levels and cohesiveness. Extending the analysis to remainders along with the observed hot-issue debates clarifies that the presence or absence of the movement characteristics did not matter and focuses on the combination of higher capacity and feminist leadership. In csQCA notation this is: CAPACITY * FEML → SYMBOLIC_AGENCY.

Thus, for these priority issues in the 1990s, the combination of high resources and feminist leadership was sufficient to produce a non-ally for movements in the hot-issue debates. This path describes agency inaction in the child care–family policy debate in Austria, immigration reform in Belgium, and the controversy over wages for home care in the Netherlands. The other path with .40 coverage (two cases) combines a high level of agency resources with a low level of women's movement institutionalization; for these debates, the weakness of the overall movement is part of a sufficient path. It applies to the biotechnology debate in Germany and the issue of reform of the unemployment insurance system in Spain.[10]

The analysis of agencies in abortion, job training, and political representation debates produced no consistent causal combinations for outcomes of interest in understanding agency failures. Thus, while the tentative results described here may begin to uncover the complexities that determine how agencies remain Symbolic rather than becoming women's movement allies, they also point to the need to delve into some cases to understand more fully the way conditions interact with agency activities in these debates.

Looking Deeper for Causal Mechanisms That Produce Failure

In this section, we explore case studies of some debates in the search for explanations of agency failures. The first discussion focuses on agencies in Italy, where in three prostitution debates the same offices were present and the characteristics were identical, yet there were three different outcomes. Then we look at the Anti-Movement agencies on a case-by-case basis, a task that produces further explanations for agencies' opposition to their movement constituents.

Italy Prostitution Debates in the 1990s:
One Agency, Three Outcomes

The Ministry for Equal Opportunities in Italy was involved in three prostitution debates between 1996 and 1999; in each it played a different role. In the first, it was Marginal, in the second Symbolic, and in the third Insider (Danna 2004). The agency had exactly the same characteristics in each: a ministry with low capacity, small staff, and little budget, yet close to central power, with the authority to propose policy and with the same feminist leader. We now compare these different outcomes across the three debates to gain further insight into the determinants of agency-movement alliances.

Since the 1950s, debates about prostitution in Italy have been about the abolitionist law of 1958 that closed the brothels, permitted women to engage in prostitution without regulation, but prohibited trafficking, aiding, or abetting prostitution for financial gain and even without. Aspects of the debate have long been gendered, with the idea that prostitution is the result of male exploitation of women. Thus, when, at the beginning of the 1990s, the European Union Commission recommended member states adopt new regulations against trafficking of women, the debate focused on the situation of foreign women in Italy who were at the mercy of both traffickers and the police. In 1996, the Minister for Equal Opportunities proposed the idea of a protection permit for women who were trafficked; however, the debate was already gendered when the minister made the proposal. In fact, the frame was feminist, mostly as a result of the influence of a nongovernmental organization named Irene. The Minister for Equal Opportunities did not gender the debate, and its position was compatible with the women's movement actors' frame, but not feminist. The minister saw prostitution as a women's issue and moved to help the victims. From her office's institutional location as a member of the Cabinet with proposal power, the Minister for Equal Opportunities joined with the feminist Minister for Social Affairs and the Minister of Internal Affairs to push the proposal successfully. Our Alliance Typology classifies the office as Marginal, because the minister did not gender the policy debate; yet because the debate was already gendered, she took the lead in promoting the proposal that eventually became law in 1999.

While deliberations on the protection proposal were taking place, the United Nations stepped in to encourage member states to take action for minors caught up in trafficking. Some mayors in Italy started to arrest the male clients of underage prostitutes. The idea of a national law that criminalized clients of the young began to take shape. Although blaming the clients had become common discourse among some feminists, other women's movement actors opposed blanket criminalization but offered no other proposal. At the national level, the question was framed in terms of ending child prostitution; it was linked to campaigns against pedophilia and provoked little opposition generally. With no pressure from the women's movement and an issue frame that did not mention

women, the Minister for Equal Opportunities took no position on the issue—
a Symbolic agency.

Another prostitution debate in 1998 occupied the minister, one that was
also related to the trafficking question. It stemmed from concern about the
increase in trafficking and prostitution in Italian cities and the harms, especially to health, that could result. The minister proposed an initiative to reduce
the harm; she pushed to fund projects for education and intervention to reduce
health hazards. The minister framed her proposal as a way to give female victims of male violence self-determination, eliminating forced prostitution.
She took charge of the issue and gendered the debate; Parliament held hearings where she promoted her initiative and gave access for women's movement
actors, among others, to the subsystem. Not only was the minister an Insider
in the debate, she was directly responsible for achieving a Dual Response to the
women's movement on the issue.

What caused the differences in the agency activities and effectiveness in the
three debates? The explanation lies in the variations in the confluence of three
factors: the initial frame of the debate, the mobilization of the women's movement actors around the issue, and the interests and concerns of the Minister
for Equal Opportunities. When the debate was already gendered at the time it
came to the national agenda, as in the first debate, the agency had nothing to
add. Since the minister was interested in the issue, she worked within the existing framework, which was already supportive of the goals of the movement
actors. When the debate over child prostitution was completely ungendered, as
in the second and third debates, the minister had a choice to intervene. In the
absence of pressure from the movement actors, she did not. She did intervene
actively and successfully in the debate on protection grants. In the latter case,
there were many movement activists who cared about the health and civil rights
of prostitutes, and the minister responded by promoting a policy that shifted
the terms of the debate and changed the policy.

The Darkest Side of State Feminism:
Cases of Six Anti-Movement Agencies

There are seven debates in which the agency worked actively against the goals
of the movement in the debate; in one of these, there were no active movement
organizations.[11] That leaves six to study: three on abortion, and one each on
political representation, prostitution, and the hot issue. There were two cases in
France, two in Germany, and one each for Great Britain and the United States.
This is the darkest side of state feminism—the threat that women's policy offices will use their position inside the state to defeat women's movement activists. Critics of agencies have long suspected that this could come about, because
political leaders may use the agencies for their own purposes or as a way of
co-opting women in politics to follow party goals (Everett 1998; Naples 1998;
Sawer 1990).[12] There were some feminist analysts concerned that the agencies would respond to antifeminist women and push the agendas of right-wing

women by claiming that they represent women's interests. Instead of doing individual detailed case studies, this section describes the terms of each debate, the outcomes, and the agency activities, and then shows the common features in Table 5.1.

The 1975 law that legalized abortion in France in the first ten weeks of pregnancy was up for reconfirmation four years later (Robinson 2001). Women's movement actors were consistent and cohesive in framing the abortion issue as a matter of women's rights: the right to choose to give life or not. They used language of self-determination and demanded complete decriminalization, not just reconfirmation. The Delegate Minister for the Status of Women and the Family, Monique Pelletier, disagreed with this frame. She supported the reconfirmation but argued that women should be mothers and explicitly promoted pronatalism. Pelletier opposed abortion but justified reconfirmation of the 1975 law, because it had reduced illegal and unsafe abortions. She was more comfortable discussing ways of preventing abortion than anything about women's self-determination.

The conflict between the movement actors and machinery was similar in German abortion debates fifteen years later (Kamenitsa 2001). Unification of East and West Germany had brought abortion reform to the agenda during 1990–1992, and the German women's movement activists, especially those from the East, like their French counterparts, demanded decriminalization of abortion based on woman's right to self-determination and to make decisions about her own reproduction. The Minister for the Family, Women and Youth, Angela Merkel, did agree that abortion was a women's issue, but not a right. She admitted that the issue pertained to women especially because they bear children, yet maintained there was a need to balance women's interests against those of the fetus. Merkel favored a law that legalized abortions under certain conditions, not the periodic law the women's movement actors and the Socialist Party advocated and that the Parliament enacted.

When the Federal Constitutional Court nullified that law, the issue was back on the agenda in 1993. Movement actors again campaigned for decriminalization and women's self-determination. The court set guidelines that would require counseling for an abortion to be legal. Movement actors in the debate wanted that counseling to be unbiased instead of pro-life pressure not to abort. The agency leadership changed during the debate. While Merkel continued to admit that abortion affected women and it was ultimately their decision, she did strongly advocate pro-life counseling and a conditional law. Her successor, Claudia Nolte, was even more anti-movement. She brought her pro-life views and experience to the job and focused on fetal rights, pro-life counseling, and continued criminalization of abortion policy. This position was threatening to the women's movement actors' ideas in the debate.

The three cases discussed so far took place under governments dominated by right-wing parties. However, the other three cases occurred under left-wing governments. Most surprising is the debate over proportional representation in France in 1985 (Baudino 2005). The Socialist majority, worried they were going to lose in the next election, proposed to change the electoral system to proportional representation to ease the blow. Women's movement activists argued that such a change should include a quota to increase women's very low representation in the French Parliament. Most of the supporters of the bill said that proportional representation on its own would benefit women and "other minorities." Minister of Woman's Rights, Yvette Roudy, the self-proclaimed socialist feminist who was an Insider in other debates, supported the reform in the name of women but favored a gender-neutral approach. She ignored demands of women's movement actors and did nothing to change the issue frame to advance women.

Democrat President Bill Clinton brought the issue of sex trafficking to the national agenda in the United States, urging Congress to stiffen penalties and protect the victims (McBride Stetson 2004). Movement actors were delighted and promoted a frame that defined sex trafficking as a form of slavery and all prostitution as sex exploitation. They wanted the law to have a special focus on all women and girls brought to the United States for sex and not just so-called forced prostitution. They did not want sex trafficking to be lumped in with other forms of trafficked labor. The women's policy machinery—the President's Inter-Agency Council—thought differently about trafficking. They defined trafficking in gender-neutral terms as an economic issue. They argued that sex trafficking should be treated the same as other forms of coerced labor. The women's movement actors tried to change minds at the council, but they had to form an alliance with more conservative members of the Congress who considered sex trafficking as especially awful, but for moral rather than feminist reasons.

Finally, the British Labour Government under Tony Blair campaigned on the promise to reform the House of Lords and appointed the Wakeham Commission, a study group, to advance proposals for its new form and composition (Lovenduski 2007b). Women's movement actors saw an opportunity to press their demands for increased representation of women in the reformed body. Many favored an elected body with a quota for women. Those who participated in the Wakeham Commission deliberations and mentioned women's representation did so to justify having an appointed House and not to improve the status of women. They tended to lump women together with other underrepresented groups. The Minister for Women, Baroness Jay, a member of the Cabinet, took a position for her agency, the Women's Equality Unit. Contrary to the movement actors' approach, she argued that recruitment by appointment alone would secure a fair presence for women, and these views were incorporated into the Wakeham report.

As Table 5.1 indicates, all of the leaders of the women's policy offices in these debates were ministers of one sort or another and members of the governing executive bodies. Some had previous experience in the women's movement, and some did not. In each case the agency head voiced a microframe that favored her boss and not her constituency among women's movement actors. These cases tell us that the heads of highly placed well-resourced agencies, as all of these were—even vocal feminists like Roudy—can become caught up in their

TABLE 5.1 SUMMARY OF ANTI-MOVEMENT AGENCIES

Debate	Agency Head	Governing Coalition	Movement Experience	Policy Position
France				
Abortion, 1979	Monique Pelletier, Delegate Minister for Status of Women and the Family	Center/Right	Pelletier founded *Dialogues des femmes*, a small Center group for women focused on political representation	Pelletier took her position from the perspective of the parties in her government
Germany				
Abortion, 1990–1992	Angela Merkel, Minister for Women and Youth	Center/Right (CDU/FDP)	None	It was a moderate position, trying to find a way to reach legal, but limited, abortion as favored by her party, the CDU
Abortion, 1993–1995	Claudia Nolte, Minister for Women, Family and Youth	Center/Right (CDU/FDP)	None, but active in the right-to-life movement	Nolte represented the Catholic strain in her party, the CDU
France				
Political representation, 1985–1986	Yvette Roudy, Minister of Woman's Rights	Left (Socialist Party)	Key figure in the Socialist Party's women's section; socialist feminist	To protect the Socialist Party and improve its chances at the next election
United States				
Prostitution, 1998–2000	Madeleine Albright, Chair of the President's Interagency Council	Left (Democrat)	None	Followed the Department of State's wish not to take a position on prostitution as exploitation when allies such as the Netherlands and Germany were decriminalizing it
Great Britain				
Hot issue: House of Lords Reform, 1997–2003	Baroness Jay, Minister for Women	Left (Labour Party)	None	Her loyalties were to the prime minister, and she described herself as nonfeminist

responsibilities to their political connections in government and not respond to women's movement demands. However, we have also seen cases where these highly placed ministers have been Insiders that worked to bring about Dual Responses; for example, Roudy in the debate over reimbursement of abortion expenses in 1982 and Merkel over the Federal Equal Rights Law, both discussed in Chapter 4.

Conclusion

In this chapter we assess general propositions that women's policy agency characteristics affect their success or failure and that Favorable Policy Environments, Women's Movement Resources, and Left Support may also be important. We found only limited evidence that, as the literature suggests, agency administrative capacity, with open channels of access, and policy proposal power are significant in determining successful alliances. Configurations of Agency Characteristics and Women's Movement Resources explained Insider agencies in political representation debates but not other issues, a sectoral result. Similarly, two pathways to ineffective agencies show some evidence that the absence of one or more administrative characteristics may explain inaction in prostitution debates but not in the hot-issue debates.

We offer three propositions to amend and enhance the state feminism framework with respect to the potential of agencies as movement allies.

First, the designs, remits, and support for agencies must be considered in relation to the various arenas where policies are made. How adequate are the resources to the subsystems of interest to women's movement actors? For example, when the subsystem is closed to outside participation, an agency "inside" the system has potential as an effective ally, regardless of the number of staff or the size of the budget. We have found effective agencies inside the bureaucracy as well as the Cabinet.

Second, the specific context of the policy arena is also a key to determining the importance of agency leaders with feminist experience. For example, activism of such leaders is likely to be related to the way a particular debate is initially framed. Agencies tend to be more effective in gendering policy debates in line with movement goals when the issue frame at the beginning of the debate is in opposition to those goals. A feminist leader, especially in a well-situated ministry, can thus become an important ally. If the debate is already gendered in a way that is compatible with movement goals, on the other hand, there may be no need for the feminist leaders of an office to intervene. The number of agency resources would not matter in such circumstances. Another example pertains to the influence of top government positions on the stances of feminist agency heads. We have seen that feminist leaders of Anti-Movement offices can have many resources and proximity to power, yet oppose movement goals following the position of their political bosses. We can conclude that feminist leaders of well-resourced agencies take such conditions as issue frame and political executive demands into account in deciding whether to become allies, oppose the movement, or just sit out the debate altogether.

Finally, studies of agency success and failure should incorporate aspects of path dependency in the mix. There are two conditions or variables that might incorporate the impact of previous actions on debates being studied. First, the statistical analysis and the tracing of causal mechanisms found that issue frame fit is often a key ingredient of agency success. Case studies show that the issue frame at the beginning of a new debate may be carried over from previous debates. Although this study looks at the agencies in discrete segments of time covering individual debates on a single issue, we realize that agency activity occurs in the context of previous policy decisions, the agency's own record pertaining to those decisions, and its attention to many other policy matters.

Another indicator of path dependency pertains to women's movement actors. Each agency has a record of relationships with movement actors whose interests and activism may vary as policy debates come and go. For example, in conducting csQCA, we found that ministries with higher capacity are Insiders in political representation debates only if the issue of equity is a priority for movement actors. Another example involves the Minister for Equal Opportunities in Italy: The minister had a different record on two prostitution debates based on the interest of the movement activists in the particular aspect of the issue being considered.

We conclude with a word about the results of a mixed-methods approach in understanding agency successes and failures. This chapter shows that it is premature to expect that this approach will yield firm results. Although the literature suggested some variables that might explain agency effectiveness, we have found it is not just a matter of showing statistical associations between broad measures of administrative capacity or agency leadership and effectiveness. Similarly, using csQCA to cast a wide net searching for possible causal configurations produces more contradictions than anything else. The third approach—the exploration of the causal mechanisms for agency outcomes in the debates—has the best potential to solve puzzles of agency success and failure by refining research questions.

The results of exploring policy debates in this chapter illustrate the limits of using the same conditions to explain agency activities as those used to explain movement success. On the basis of these studies, we suggest a reworking of some of these conditions and their application to understanding agencies using csQCA in future research:

- Instead of women's movement actor cohesiveness, specify the presence or absence of agreement among women legislators for movement goals.[13]
- In addition to gathering information about the experience of an agency head in the women's or feminist movement, include leader initiatives on a particular debate issue.

- Although issue frame fit proves to be important in explaining agency activities, a refinement would consider the presence or absence of a gendered issue frame at the beginning of the debate in relation to all kinds of outcomes.
- An open subsystem proves to be important in understanding movement success for some issues; to understand agency effectiveness, however, a measure of agency powers within the subsystem is likely to have a more direct explanatory effect.

6

What's Feminist
about State Feminism?

In examining the politics of state feminism through comparative analysis, we have found that Insider agencies can be a key component for women's movements to achieve positive state responses to their demands. Going further, we have investigated the agencies themselves to see why some are more effective than others, and have determined conditions and configurations that may produce these important Insider actors. In this chapter, we complete our exploration of state feminism by questioning to what extent these Insiders are allies on the part of women's movement actors who seek explicitly feminist action. In other words, what *is* feminist about state feminism?

Feminism is an ideology that has its origins in women's movement discourse.[1] What distinguishes feminism from the more general beliefs about women's identity and interests expressed in women's movement discourse is a matter of contention. What is clear is that while all feminists express gender consciousness, many women with gender consciousness would not be considered, nor would they consider themselves, feminists. In other words, just because something is "about women," it is not necessarily feminist. Similarly, when the state establishes an agency for women or advances the claims of women's movements, this does not mean that the agency is necessarily feminist.

How can we reconcile this conceptualization of feminism and state action with the state feminism concept that has been the focus of this book? Central to solving this contradiction is the distinction elaborated in Chapter 1 between Movement State Feminism and Transformative State Feminism. Overall, state feminism pertains to activities of women's policy agencies as allies of women's movement actors and their effectiveness in bringing about state responses that give these actors access to policy subsystems and policies that are matching or compatible with the women's movement's own definitions and policy goals. Policy outcomes, based on their frames and content, vary in the degree to which they conform to ideas of feminism (i.e., their potential to change gender hierarchies and improve the status of women). Similarly, both women's movement actors and feminist movement actors may gain procedural access.

To assess whether state feminism is actually feminist—and, hence whether Transformative State Feminism occurs—we adapt here the basic state feminism propositions pertaining to the frequency of successes and agency alliances and to the significance and value of alliances to movement success. The first task is to make the case for studying the question of Transformative State Feminism and present the central measures of the components. Next, we report on the frequency of feminist successes with the state and the incidence of Feminist Insiders among the women's policy agencies. To assess the value of agencies in achieving transformative feminist outcomes, we use descriptive statistics, csQCA, and case studies. We investigate the influence of the clusters of explanatory conditions used throughout this analysis: Women's Movement Resources, Favorable Policy Environment, and Left Support. Given the underdeveloped nature of the notion of Transformative State Feminism, our main goal here is to revise and expand state feminism propositions to set an agenda for future research.

Making the Case for Transformative State Feminism

The Concept

Although analysts have used state feminism to identify a wide range of political phenomena, none until now has specified the meaning of the "feminist" part of state feminism. In the 1980s, when Scandinavian scholars found that Nordic welfare states promoted a women-friendly approach through policy, structure, and women inside and outside of the state, they called it state feminism (e.g., Hernes 1987; Siim 1991). In the 1990s, Australians and others focused on the individuals, called femocrats, who worked in "feminist" bureaucracy and women's policy agencies (e.g., Eisenstein 1996; Outshoorn 1994). Across this wide range of applications, most scholars have treated the feminist part of the concept interchangeably with women and women's interests. Virtually none of the scholarship on state feminism has considered to what extent state action pertaining to women relates to or can be identified with the ideology of feminism. This is consistent with much of the comparative scholarship on women's movements, gender, and the state.[2] Scholars often use the notion of feminism without defining it and treat it as a synonym for women's movements and women's activism. A handful of analysts assert that women's movements are not all feminist and provide working definitions of feminism (e.g., Beckwith 2000; Ferree and Mueller 2007; Ferree 2006).

The case for distinguishing between agency–movement actor alliances that achieve movement goals and those that achieve feminist goals is in many ways the same as that for differentiating between women's movements and feminist movements. Given the extent to which scholars use the terms feminism and feminist without being precise about their distinguishing features, it appears that many assume there is agreement on what those attributes are. This approach, however, limits comparative research, because the concept of feminism is sometimes hotly contested among movement thinkers and actors alike. We learned in the course of our research that one cannot assume that what an observer considers to be feminist in one country will be the same as what another observer labels feminist in another country. In fact, many who promote women's equality reject being labeled feminist. Furthermore, with the growing political participation of women throughout the world, it is increasingly likely that women's movement actors will seek to promote ideas that no one would agree are feminist.[3] For comparative research, the problem is exacerbated by the resentment of some activists in the global South against what they see as a hegemonic effort by Western activists to promote Western feminism that neglects local women's own perspectives of their situations and what to do about them (Tripp 2006). Efforts at conceptualization can be further complicated by the political status of feminism in various research contexts and the strong beliefs held by both researchers and activists about what is "true" feminism.[4]

Nevertheless, as Mazur (2002) argues, there is some agreement among those scholars who do provide definitions of feminism, feminist movements, and women's movements in Western postindustrial democracies: Women's movement aims involve women and women's issues, while feminist movements involve specific challenges to patriarchy and the subordination of women (Beckwith 2000, 2005; Ferree and Mueller 2007; Ferree 2006). The difference between the women's movement and the feminist movement ultimately relates to differences in the ideas, aspirations, and identities presented by collective actors.

Thus far, we have argued that to take on the question of Transformative State Feminist action, as opposed to Movement State Feminism, requires being precise about the meaning of feminism. Such conceptual precision places gender firmly at the center of analysis. The promotion of explicitly feminist goals entails necessarily addressing gender-biased hierarchies that contribute to sex-based inequities across all spheres. Examining Transformative State Feminism, therefore, becomes an exercise in determining when women's movement actors present feminist frames in policy debates (and thus become feminist actors), and, in turn, whether women's policy agencies gender policy discussions in a way that conforms to feminist ideas promoted by these feminists—essentially becoming Feminist Insiders. It then involves determining when the Feminist Insiders influence the state to insert feminist ideas into policy content and to accept feminist actors in the policy subsystems, yielding Feminist Dual Response.

At the foundation of such framing and gendering is a discourse that identifies the cause of women's subordination to men in gender hierarchies and provides policy solutions to overcome it. As Dahlerup first pointed out in 1986, the very essence of women's policy agencies is to "institutionalize gender conflict" (p. 17)—in other words, to bring the feminist challenge to gender inequity into the state. Moreover, women's policy agencies that promote feminist goals are an institutional counterbalance to the gender-biased, patriarchal features of the state. Instead of functioning as a tool for furthering the masculinist state, they are a potential means to bring it to an end; thus, introducing feminist ideas and actors into the state is necessarily a transformative process.

The Measure of Transformative State Feminism

There are two dimensions of Transformative State Feminism to be examined: feminist actions of women's policy offices—whether or not they support feminist ideas and gender debates with feminist ideas—and state responses to the feminist women's movement actors through the adoption of feminist policy outcomes and feminist actor participation in the debates. To measure these dimensions, we gathered information on four indicators for each policy debate and combined them to form a measure of the degree of Transformative State Feminism:

1. Was there matching fit between agency microframes on the debate issue and feminist microframes of movement actors—yes or no?
2. Did the agency gender the policy debate with a feminist microframe—yes or no?
3. Did the policy content at the end of the debate match the feminist microframes of movement actors—yes or no?
4. Did the movement actors expressing feminist microframes become part of the policy subsystem at the end of the debate—yes or no?

For each indicator, coders decided whether the microframes expressed by women's movement actors contained feminist ideas.[5] They looked for shorthand terms often used by actors in public debate to refer to feminist ideas, issue definitions, and policy goals, with no explicit mention of the term feminist. Such phrases as "overcoming conditions of women's poverty, exploitation, mistreatment, and inequality," and advocacy of goals like equality, equity, emancipation, choice, and autonomy represent feminist ideas of improving the status of women in relation to men and challenging the foundation of gender hierarchy.

Using this classification, coders were able to answer the four questions for each debate. Based on score rankings, each policy debate with an agency was assigned a value from 0 to 6 (see Table 6.1). Although cases can be arrayed along the full range of values, only values of 5 and 6 show Transformative State Feminism—that is, complete involvement of women's policy agencies in feminist responses to the movement and influences in the policy processes with at least one feminist outcome. Values of 0 and 1 show the absence of any feminist activities by agencies, although cases measured as having values of 1 show some state activity in response to movement actors' feminist ideas. The analysis in this chapter is based on a dataset of 108 cases that includes all the national state debates with full-fledged agencies or quasi agencies. The anomalies of the dataset with very high numbers of Transformative State Feminism failure (0–1 on the scale) and very low numbers of success (5–6) prohibit its use for multivariate statistical analysis.

Patterns of Transformative State Feminism: Dynamics and Determinants

This section begins with a review of the patterns of Transformative State Feminism in general across issues and countries and over time. We then present the results of the investigations in terms of factors that may explain these feminist outcomes in three parts. First, we examine the characteristics of cases of successful Transformative State Feminism with other debates in the study. Second, there is a search for those factors that explain why some cases reach complete feminist success while others find partial success. The last section takes a closer look at the differences between Feminist Insiders and other Insider agencies.

Describing Patterns in Transformative State Feminism

There were plenty of feminist perspectives offered during the debates.[6] At least one women's movement actor advanced a feminist microframe in eighty-five (79 percent) of the debates. Yet they achieved feminist state action—Dual Response—in only twenty-one (19 percent). In another twenty-nine cases (27 percent), feminist actors achieved procedural access, and in seven (6 percent), they achieved only policy success. Let's look at the activities of the women's policy agencies to see if we can fill in the gaps between feminist activities and the state response.

Nearly half of the women's policy agencies also adopted feminist goals (forty-eight or 44 percent), but not all matched the frames of movement actors in the debate; there were fourteen debates where the agency took a more feminist position than the movement actors. Still, in thirty-three debates, there was an alliance between the agency and the feminist movement actors: The feminist microframes matched. Yet, even with these strong alliances, nearly half of these agencies were unable to gender the issue frame of the debate in a feminist direction, leaving only nineteen Feminist Insiders constituting 18 percent of the cases. In every case where there is a Feminist Insider agency, there is a complete or partial feminist state response. However, without Feminist Insiders, feminist actors were able to gain Feminist Dual Response in ten debates, Feminist Preemption (where there was a feminist policy response but no feminist movement actor participation) in four debates, and Feminist Co-optation in twenty-four debates (participation with no policy response).

TABLE 6.1   DISTRIBUTION OF CASES ON TRANSFORMATIVE
           STATE FEMINISM MEASURE

Ranking	Women's Movement Policy Agency Feminist Frames Match (Indicator 1)	Women's Policy Agency Gendered Feminist Issue Frame (Indicator 2)	Policy Content Feminist (Indicator 3)	Feminist Women's Movement Actors Participated (Indicator 4)	Number and Percentage of National State Debates	
6	Yes	Yes	Yes	Yes	11	(10.2%)
5	Yes	Yes	Yes/No*	Yes/No*	8	(7.3%)
4	Yes	No	Yes	Yes	3	(2.8%)
3	Yes	No	Yes/No*	Yes/No*	1	(1%)
2	Yes	Yes	No	No	0	(0%)
1	No	No	Yes/No*	Yes/No*	35	(32%)
0	No	No	No	No	50	(46%)
					108	(100%)

* Yes in at least one of these categories.

Another way to look at the relation between Feminist Insiders and feminist state response is provided in Table 6.1, which shows the distribution of cases according to the Transformative State Feminism measure described above. Eleven cases that scored 6 are complete Transformative State Feminism, combining Feminist Insiders with Feminist Dual Response.[7] Partial Transformative State Feminism scored 5 and comprises eight cases where Feminist Insiders achieved either procedural (5) success or policy content (3).

There are only four cases that fall between these two ends of the measure. One of these scored 3: a prostitution debate in Canada in 1985. Here it was found that the agency allied with feminist movement actors in seeking to decriminalize prostitution, but it was hobbled by its association with a Conservative Party government that refused to adopt this position. Thus, although the feminist actors were able to testify during parliamentary negotiations, neither they nor the agency were effective in changing the frame of debate or the policy outcome in their favor.

Three debates scored 4; that is, the agency's microframes matched the feminist microframes of movement actors, and the actors received a complete feminist state response. But the agencies were not Insiders but Marginals. Two of these were abortion debates in the United States and in Canada. In both, the policy subsystem was the supreme court, an arena where the agencies did not have access to affect the terms of debate. In part, we can credit the influence of the women's movement actors themselves for the feminist policy outcomes. In the third case, a prostitution debate in Sweden during the 1990s, the Minister of Gender Equality took a feminist position but did not participate in the debate until the issue frame had been gendered in a feminist way by party women in Parliament.

To examine the patterns across issues, across decades, and over time, the following discussion compares the distribution of cases scoring 6 (complete Transformative State Feminism) and those scoring 5 (partial Transformative State Feminism) against the cases scoring 1 (absent agency involvement but feminist outcomes) and those scoring 0 (neither feminist agency nor state response). Across the issues there is little variation in Transformative State Feminism, and no strong patterns developed over time.[8] Between 17 and 19 percent of debates were complete or partial transformative alliances for all issues except job training, where the rate was 14 percent. The debates in the 1970s, 1980s, and 2000s were similar. The 1990s had a higher ratio of feminist outcomes at 21 percent. The 2000s were the least successful.

Looking at the cases that received the highest scores, 6 and 5 (see Table 6.2), we see that all countries except Spain have agencies capable of Transformative State Feminism, but there is no country that has 100 percent feminist success. Complete or partial Transformative State Feminism successes were found in Austria (three), France (three), Canada (two), Finland (two), Sweden (two), Belgium (one), Germany (one), Great Britain (one), Ireland (one), Italy (one), the Netherlands (one), and the United States (one). Even so, some countries had a more successful rate than others, ranging from 50 percent for the Austrian debates to 10 percent for the United States. Some of these variations can be explained by differences in the mix of debates studied in each country. Job training debates tended to be less successful with respect to Transformative State Feminism, and Ireland, France, and Finland had a large proportion of these debates, while Austria and Sweden had none. At the same time, some of the other low-scoring countries, such as Great Britain and the Netherlands, also had no job training debates. Spain, with debates on all five issues, had no debates that achieved Transformative State Feminism.

Comparing Most Successful with Least Successful

We compared the features of agencies, movement resources, policy environments, and Left support for the transformative (scores of 6 or 5) cases with the least successful (scores of 0 or 1) in national state debates.[9] In the successful cases, the women's policy offices tend to be ministries in close proximity to power centers and led by individuals with experience in feminist organizations. The women's movement was more likely to be institutionalized, place the debate issue as a high priority, and be very close ideologically to the Left, although somewhat less close organizationally than the unsuccessful cases. These actors participate in policy subsystems that are less closed and where there is a matching issue frame fit between women's movement actors' frames and the issue frame of the policy subsystem. There was little difference in the following characteristics between the Transformative State Feminism successes and failures: administrative capacity of women's policy agencies, strength of countermovements, level of women's movement activism, number of feminist actors, and governing majority.

Characteristics of Complete and Partial Transformative State Feminism Successes

We next look a bit more deeply into the nineteen cases of Transformative State Feminism—the eleven fully successful cases and the eight partially successful cases. These are listed by country and issue in Table 6.2. Specifically, what makes the two groups of cases different? In terms of the Transformative State Feminism measure, the agencies in the partial cases are just as active in promoting the feminist goals and gendering the policy debates in feminist frames. However, the partially successful offices and their allies achieve *either* feminist policy content *or* feminist participation, but not both.

In comparing the two sets of cases with respect to the four types of characteristics, we identify frequencies of characteristics that distinguish the complete successes from the partial ones. The policy environment was distinctly more favorable in the complete cases: The policy subsystem tended to be more open, with an issue frame compatible or matching the women's movement actors' microframes. The government majority was more likely to be left-wing. In this context, women's policy agencies tended to be closer to the center of power, to have policy proposal powers, and perhaps especially importantly, to have leaders with experience in feminist movement organizations. Finally, the women's movement overall tended to have a higher degree of activism in the completely successful cases.

Having found these distinctive qualities of the eleven cases of complete Transformative State Feminism in comparison to the eight partial ones, the next step is to explore which are the most important factors and how they combine to produce successful feminist outcomes as compared with partial ones. To answer this question, we have submitted various combinations of these conditions in the state debates to csQCA.[10] Including logical remainders, we find three configurations that lead to complete transformative success. The path that covers the most cases brings characteristics of Feminist Insider agencies to the fore: The combination of close proximity to centers of power and feminist leadership produced complete feminist success in five of the eleven cases, for a coverage of .45. The csQCA notation is: PROXIMITY * FEML → COMPLETE_FEMINIST_SUCCESS. If these two conditions are present, the successful outcome is not affected by whether the Left is in power or there is issue frame fit.

Does a leftist government play any role in achieving complete feminist success? The second and third paths reveal a partial tradeoff between government in power and issue frame fit. Fit combines with government not from the left wing, thus centrist or right-wing government, to explain complete success. This combination covers three cases for a coverage of .27. The

TABLE 6.2 COMPLETE AND PARTIAL CASES OF TRANSFORMATIVE STATE FEMINISM

Outcome	Country	Issue	Policy Content
Complete	Austria	Political representation	Addressing the under-representation of women in the civil service in 1990–1993
Complete	Canada	Abortion	Bill to return regulation of abortion practices to the criminal code in 1989–1991
Complete	Canada	Job training	Development of Canadian Jobs Strategy to combat unemployment in 1984–1985
Complete	Finland	Prostitution	Proposals to decriminalize prostitution and related activities in 1984–1986
Complete	France	Abortion	Reimbursement for nontherapeutic abortions by state in 1981–1983
Complete	France	Political representation	Proposals to require parity in all public offices in 1995–2000
Complete	France	Prostitution	Controversy over proposal to reopen state brothels through regulated prostitution in 1989–1990
Complete	Ireland	Job training	Responding to globalization with enhanced human resource development in 1995–1997
Complete	Italy	Hot issue	Decentralization of the Italian state in 1997–2001
Complete	Sweden	Prostitution	Criminalizing the "john" in 1997–1999
Complete	United States	Job training	Federal funding for vocational training in 1989–1990
Partial/ procedural	Belgium	Political representation	Efforts to establish a gender quota for party electoral lists in 1992–1994
Partial/ procedural	Finland	Prostitution	Criminalization of clients, 1993–1998
Partial/ procedural	Germany	Political representation	Changing Basic Law for equality of rights and Equal Rights Law in 1989–1994
Partial/ procedural	Great Britain	Abortion	Embryology act and effect on abortion in 1987–1990
Partial/ procedural	Sweden	Hot issue	Child care services or family allowances in 1991–1994
Partial/ content	Austria	Abortion	People's Initiative to overturn legal abortion in 1975–1978 ultimately rejected
Partial/ content	Austria	Prostitution	Extending social insurance to sex workers in 1997
Partial/ content	The Netherlands	Abortion	Establishment of regulations and services for abortion in 1981–1984

third path indicates that in two cases (.18 coverage), a left-wing government can help a Feminist Insider overcome a lack of compatible fit between micro-frames of women's movement actors and those of policy makers. The csQCA notation for these second and third solutions is: left * FIT + LEFT * fit → COMPLETE_FEMINIST_SUCCESS.

To what extent are the conditions of agency proximity, feminist leadership, issue frame fit, and left-wing governments part of sufficient paths to complete success? The measure of consistency answers that question: All four conditions have consistent proportions over .70 (proximity, .72; feminist leadership, .70; issue frame fit, .75; left-wing government, .72); that means that in 70 to 75 percent of the cases where one or another of these conditions is present, the outcome is complete feminist success. However, when logical remainders are included in the analysis, left-wing government is often irrelevant when other conditions are present.

These findings are reinforced by seeing the configurations that led to partial success. Two solutions explain this outcome, and together they include the absence of both issue frame fit and agency proximity. In csQCA notation, these are: left * fit + LEFT *prox → PARTIAL_FEMINIST_SUCCESS. The first solution provides a coverage of .63 of the cases and suggests that without favorable issue frames in a centrist or right-wing government, feminist actors and Feminist Insider agencies have difficulty achieving complete feminist outcomes. For the rest of the cases of partial success, the absence of agency proximity couples with leftist governments to limit success. Presence or absence of feminist leadership is not part of these consistent paths.

Comparing the paths to complete transformative success to those paths to partial success suggests the combinations of conditions that make the difference between cases where Feminist Insiders go all the way to feminist procedural and policy outcomes, and those cases in which either procedural or policy goals of feminist actors are achieved. The evidence points first to the agencies, their location, and their leadership. Second, issue frame fit, an indicator of Favorable Policy Environment, distinguishes between the two groups. Less clear is the place of governing majorities. The presence of a leftist government is found in configurations for both complete and partial outcomes. The coverage for each of these configurations is quite small, only two cases.

Feminist Insiders Compared to Other Insiders

All of the cases of complete and partial transformative feminist success include Insider agencies along with measures of feminist policy and participatory responses by the state. However, there are an equal number of Insiders that did not take feminist positions or achieve any feminist responses from the state. Table 6.3 shows the distribution by issue. What is striking about this table is the low percentage of political representation debates with Feminist Insiders (21 percent) in relation to their proportion of all debates (34 percent); a majority of the Insiders in these debates are not feminist. One reason is likely to be the

TABLE 6.3   FEMINIST INSIDERS AND OTHER INSIDERS BY ISSUE

Issue	Feminist Insiders	Other Insiders	Total
Abortion	5	4	9
	26%	21%	24%
Job training	3	2	5
	16%	11%	13%
Political representation	4	9	13
	21%	47%	34%
Prostitution	5	4	9
	26%	21%	24%
Hot issue	2	0	2
	11%	0%	5%
Total	19	19	38
	100%	100%	100%

framing on the issue: Sauer, in Chapter 9, shows that in political representation debates, women's movement actors developed a strategic frame that emphasized women's difference rather than equality.

What distinguishes debates with Feminist Insiders from other Insider agencies? To suggest some answers to that question, we considered the features of the policy environment, the women's movement characteristics, Left support, and the women's policy agencies, and compared frequencies between the Feminist Insiders and other Insiders in the national state debates. The resulting composite is based on differences of 20 percent or more.[11]

The agencies that performed as Feminist Insiders tended to be ministries rather than administrative offices, were situated very close to the centers of power, and had leaders with experience in feminist organizations. Feminist Insiders benefited from a high degree of cohesion among the women's movement actors presenting their policy goals to the agencies for action, and these demands were compatible or matching with the dominant issue frame in more than 60 percent of the debates.

Agencies that were Insiders effective for the women's movement but not feminist goals tended to be administrative offices rather than ministries and not very close to power. They had policy proposal powers and administrative capacity similar to those of the Feminist Insiders, but more than 60 percent of these agencies had leaders with no experience as feminist actors. There were identical proportions of feminist actors promoting their goals, but in a majority of these cases the actors had less than 100 percent agreement on a single microframe. More telling, the issue frame of the policy subsystem at the beginning of the debate tended overwhelmingly to be threatening or mixed with respect to the microframes of women's movement actors.[12]

There were minimal or no differences between the Feminist Insiders and other Insiders with respect to administrative capacity; number of feminist women's movement actors; level of movement activism or institutionalization; organizational or ideological closeness of the Left to the women's movement;

priority of the issue (on the agenda or not); governing majority—Right, Center, Left; openness of the subsystem structure; or strength of the countermovements.

The Search for Causal Mechanisms in Case Studies

Case studies help us understand the nuances in the relationships among conditions during debates and the outcomes. First, we look at an outstanding success in Sweden that documents the importance of a Feminist Insider and support of the Left to the outcome. Then, we compare two partial successes with Feminist Insiders that were quasi agencies, which show the significance of the policy subsystem and relations of women's movement actors to it in explaining the outcomes. The section concludes with a comparison of gender quota debates in Belgium and Spain to see what may make the difference between Feminist Insiders and Insiders that are not feminist.

The Debate in Sweden over Criminalizing the "John," 1997–1999

The question of what to do about prostitution had long been on the national agenda when the bill to penalize clients (also known as "johns") for purchasing sexual services was introduced in 1997 (Svanström 2004). The idea of focusing on the johns was only one of many proposals that had been circulating without the development of agreement on any one approach. Action was delayed in the early 1990s as the parties argued about the composition of a commission to study the issue.

Finally, in 1997, the Minister of Gender Equality, Ulrica Messing, a member of the Social Democratic Cabinet, made the proposal part of the Violence Against Women Act presented to Parliament. The minister's view of the matter matched that of all movement actors active in the debate: They agreed that prostitution was a system of oppression of women and that the solution was to protect prostitutes from criminal action and decrease demand by criminalizing the clients. Through this policy, the law would promote greater gender equality. The bill split the parties in Parliament: Greens, Social Democrats, the Centre Party, and the women in the Liberal Party supported it; the Christian Democrats, Conservatives, and male Liberals opposed it. Leading the way in the debate in Parliament were the women MPs in the parties who presented this feminist position on prostitution. The bill passed by a large majority (the Christian Democrats abstained) and went into effect in early 1999.

The subsystem where this debate took place was the Cabinet and Parliament; the feminist success for the women's movement actors was due in large part to the fact that both the movement actors and the agency were inside that subsystem from the beginning and that the subsystem was dominated by a Left majority that was in close agreement ideologically with the women's movement actors on the subject. The larger context was closely connected: The women's movement was highly integrated into mainstream government, party, and union institutions, rating the highest score, a 10, on the institutionalization scale.[13] The issue was a top movement priority, and the actors had 100 percent agreement on their feminist position. The left-wing political parties took formal stands in favor of the proposal. The Minister for Gender Equality was a member of the Cabinet and in charge of the legislation. Messing was a young leader, barely 30 years old, and had held the post briefly. She actively promoted the feminist position on this issue. She was supported by a staff of around thirty, an advisory Gender Equality Council, and several regional agencies.

Quasi Agencies in State Debates on Abortion in Austria and Great Britain

There are two cases where party-level agencies were Feminist Insiders in national state debates on abortion: the Rejection of People's Initiative to Overturn Legal Abortion in Austria (1975–1978) and the Effect of the Embryology Act on Abortion in Great Britain (1987–1990). They are similar in that both involved efforts by anti-abortion activists to overcome laws permitting women to obtain legal abortion. The quasi agencies, the Austrian Socialist Party Women's Section and British Labour Party Shadow Minister for Women—in the absence of action by state agencies—were instrumental in maintaining a feminist framing of the abortion policy within the parliaments. Yet, they had different outcomes. In Austria, the feminists achieved policy success in the final decision but not participation in the policy subsystem (i.e., Feminist Preemption), and in Great Britain, the outcome was the reverse, participation but not a feminist policy result (i.e., Feminist Co-optation).

Case Study: The Rejection of People's Initiative to Overturn Legal Abortion in Austria, 1975–1978

The Austrian debate took place in the mid-1970s, right after Parliament legalized abortion without restriction in the first trimester of pregnancy (Köpl 2001). The anti-abortion forces launched a campaign for a People's Initiative, whereby at least 100,000 citizens can submit a bill to Parliament through petition. Their goal was to recriminalize abortion and amend the constitution to protect human life. They did not succeed in this effort, and the credit goes, in large part, to the Women's Section of the Austrian Social Democratic Party. Because it is not a state agency, it has the status of a quasi agency. In this debate, however, its place in the Social Democratic Party was significant. The women's section framed the abortion issue as a matter of women's emancipation and self-determination. And, although the Social Democratic Party agreed on legalization, its frame focused more on class justice and less on women's rights. The women's section influenced the party leaders and members of Parliament, who in turn rejected the People's Initiative, achieving a feminist success for the women's movement actors.

The activists in the women's movement were outside the policy subsystem, however. Although the movement had a relatively low level of mobilization overall in these early days, autonomous organizations used street action to protest the anti-abortion forces. While the women's section and the women's movement actors had matching microframes in the debate, the autonomous groups pushed to use the abortion issue to put the entire male-dominated system in question. The movement actors were successful in turning back the People's Initiative because of the following: The Social Democratic Party had so many seats that they were effectively the ruling party; the women's section promoted a feminist view of the abortion issue and functioned as a quasi agency through its influence on the Social Democratic members of Parliament; the initial issue frame of the debate among policy actors included feminist ideas; what the quasi women's policy agency did was to ensure that the feminist perspective prevailed and took precedence over the frame that focused on the rights of the unborn. The policy subsystem was closed to outside groups such as the autonomous activists, denying them procedural response. The quasi agency was influential *inside* the subsystem, guaranteeing feminist policy success.

Case Study: Effect of the Embryology Act on Abortion in Great Britain, 1987–1990

The British debate took place nearly twenty years after the adoption of the Abortion Reform Act of 1967, which legalized abortion throughout pregnancy (McBride Stetson 2001c). Anti-abortion activists had tried to push back the reform through introducing private member bills in the House of Commons. After battles in the 1970s, most of these bills went nowhere until the Conservative government allowed some time to debate a proposal to set a gestational time limit for legal abortion. This idea cropped up in 1987 through a bill to place the limit at 18 weeks of pregnancy, after which abortion would be prohibited; there was a lively debate on the subject, but the House of Commons ran out of time before taking a vote. The main goal of the abortion opponents was to reframe the debate about abortion to focus on the rights and condition of the fetus, and to downplay or remove attention to women's choice.

The state women's policy agencies—the Women's National Commission and the Equal Opportunities Council—were Symbolic on the whole question of abortion; however, there was an office in the Labour Party called the Shadow Minister for Women, and its leader, Jo Richardson, was a member of Parliament. She and other women MPs joined in a strong coalition with women's movement actors outside Parliament called the Pro-Choice Alliance and turned the tables on the opponents by shifting the subject toward a liberalization of the 1967 law. Thus, feminist movement actors were fully inside the policy subsystem during the entire debate. However, their proposal never came to a vote; instead, as part of the Human Fertilisation and Embryology Act of 1990, the House voted to place the upper limit for abortion at twenty-four weeks. The vote was taken without party discipline, other than that the Conservative Party controlled the proceedings, forming a moderately closed policy subsystem.

The movement actors were able to sustain a feminist issue frame in Parliament on the abortion issue and beat back the efforts to de-gender the question in favor of fetal rights. They tended to oppose any limit on abortion, so the outcome did not fit with their goals; yet they were pleased that the final language of the law included several exceptions. Yet, this outcome was not a feminist one. The shadow minister helped with the framing, but since it was part of the opposition party it could not, unlike its counterpart in Austria, have an influence on policy proposals. At the same time, the framing success was consequential, because the initial approach to the issue during the debate was heavily focused on fetal rights and threatening not only to feminists but to women's movement frames more generally.

Quota Debates in Belgium and Spain in the 1990s

Two debates on gender quotas in Belgium and Spain suggest the importance of political parties and their women's movement actors in determining whether an Insider agency will be feminist or not. These debates took place in the 1990s as a wave of activity relating to the question of equal representation for women in decision-making swept through European countries. In both cases, the debates involved proposals to enact sex quotas for electoral lists in parliamentary elections. The women's policy offices were in governments run by right-wing parties and gendered the debate with frames that were compatible with movement actors' frames on the issue. In Belgium, however, the agency was a Feminist Insider in the debate leading to the Act Promoting Balanced Representation of Men and Women on Lists of Electoral Candidates (1991–1994); whereas in Spain, the agency opposed the Bill on Mandatory Quota of 40% Women on Election Lists during 1998–2003 and contributed to its defeat. What accounts for this difference?

The answer lies in the differences in the governing parties and the context of the proposals for quotas. In Belgium, the Center-Right Christian Democrats held the dominant power in the central government, and they introduced the bill to establish quotas (Meier 2005). The need to increase women's representation had been on the national agenda since the 1970s and was promoted by movement actors across the political spectrum. In 1991, the governing Council of Ministers introduced a two-thirds quota limit (no list could have more than two thirds of the candidates of one sex). The Minister of Equal Opportunities—a Cabinet-level official who also was Minister of Labor and Security—promoted the bill and defended it among the ministers, in Parliament, and in the press. Minister Miet Smet argued that quotas were necessary to fight systematic discrimination against women in politics. The microframe she advocated fit nicely with that of feminist movement actors, recognizing and criticizing underlying gender power relations in politics, and she successfully brought this idea into the parliamentary debate. The feminists, however, sought equal representation, and Smet had to accept her government's two-thirds to one-third proposal. Thus, the outcome did not match the feminists' goals. Still, the Belgian government did approve a policy that required parties to adopt quotas to improve women's representation (Meier 2005).

Spain, too, was governed by a Center-Right party when it considered the quota bill; the Popular Party and its supporters opposed quotas as a solution to the under-representation of women (Valiente 2005). The quota bill came, in fact, not from the Cabinet, but from the Socialist Party, which had adopted an internal quota for its own candidates some years before. The Socialist feminists were inspired by the parity movement to advocate equal sharing of power for all parties and saw quotas as the only way to overcome male discrimination. In this they agreed with their Belgian counterparts. However, there were some movement activists, based in the Popular Party, who favored "soft" measures to increase women's representation, such as training and educational programs. They feared that quotas would bring unqualified people to power and were not fair. The women's policy agency, the Women's Institute within the Ministry for Labor and Security, promoted microframes that reflected views of the Popular Party's women's organizations and the ruling party. The institute's Equality Plan, which was published during the debate, included a defense of the "soft" measures approach and was influential in shoring up the Popular Party's opposition to the quota bill. Parliament defeated the proposal in 2003.

What explains the fact that the Belgian Minister of Equal Opportunities was a feminist Insider while Spain's Women's Institute was an Insider that opposed feminist ideas and goals? There are two important factors. First, both offices had to conform to the wishes of the party that appointed them; however, in Belgium the Christian Democrats favored quotas, while the Popular Party in Spain opposed them. Also, the women's organizations within these two parties favored the party's view. Thus, both agencies adopted microframes that coincided with the positions of these actors in the party to become Insiders. The fact that the Belgian Christian Democrats women took a feminist position allowed the Minister of Equal Opportunities to be a feminist actor inside the state on their behalf. Second, the political environment in Belgium is more supportive of the idea of quotas in general than that in Spain. On one hand, given its ethnic makeup and political history, citizens there are more favorable to descriptive representation according to ethnic identity and language. It is not a great leap to extend the idea to sex when the evidence showed under-representation of women. Spain, on the other hand, does not have this tradition. Identity politics is not favored by the centrist and right-wing parties, who are more influenced by liberal notions of individual rights and fair competition.

Conclusion

Comparative politics research does not just answer questions, it provokes new ones. We see evolution in the meaning of concepts like state feminism as scholars have adapted them through their empirical studies, including this one. The state feminism propositions examined in Chapters 4 and 5 are grounded in the research and discussions of the concept of state feminism taking place in the

1990s and early 2000s. At the same time, underlying the trajectory of the project is another story of continued examination and rethinking of the central concepts of the project in light of the empirical findings as they unfold. This chapter uses what we have learned to launch a new way of thinking about the responses of governments to women's movement activism. As such, the analysis here is a next step in the evolution of state feminism theory.

The goal has been to introduce the concept of Transformative State Feminism, map out its incidence in national policy arenas, and develop propositions to explain patterns found in the cases. When a rigorous definition of feminism was applied, we found that whereas half (fifty-seven) of the debates studied in Chapter 4 were Dual Response, there were only nineteen cases of Feminist Dual Response, just 33 percent of all Dual Responses and 18 percent of all debates. About half of the Insiders effectively promoted microframes that matched the frames of feminist movement actors in debates (eighteen of thirty-eight, or 47 percent). On one hand, whereas 46 percent of the cases of Dual Response involved Insiders, 77 percent of Feminist Dual Responses were facilitated by Feminist Insider agencies. On the other hand, of the forty-four cases of partial feminist state response, only eight, or 18 percent, involved Feminist Insiders. Feminist movement actors may reach partial feminist outcomes in their efforts to influence policy debates without the aid of Feminist Insiders; however, to go all the way may depend on finding feminist agency allies inside the state. There were nineteen cases of Transformative State Feminism, where Feminist Insiders helped feminist movement actors to achieve feminist outcomes, either complete or partial, from the state. There were no cases where Feminist Insiders were involved that did not achieve some feminist state response (a score of 2 on the Transformative State Feminism measure). These findings show that women's policy agencies have the potential to be effective in countering patriarchal ideas and processes in Western postindustrial democracies and to "institutionalize gender conflict" in the way that Dahlerup highlighted nearly twenty-five years ago. Until the early 2000s, however, such cases were isolated—one or two per country—and Transformative State Feminism had not yet turned into a trend. There are few differences among the issue sectors, although political representation debates show a slightly lower rate of Transformative State Feminism than the other issues.

In the comparisons across the different levels of Transformative State Feminism, three characteristics of the policy agencies and the policy environment appeared. Agencies in debates with more feminist outcomes—Feminist cases versus other cases, complete Transformative State Feminism versus partial outcomes, and Feminist Insiders versus other Insiders—are more likely to be in close proximity to central power and have feminist leadership. The importance of these conditions is reinforced by csQCA results comparing complete and partial successes among Feminist Insiders. In addition, the issue frame fit at the beginning of the debate—that is, the movement actors' microframes and the issue frame—tend to be matching or compatible. There is little that can be said for certain about the effect of particular parties in the governing majority and how they help or hurt feminist activists and agencies. Both successes and failures are found under Left majorities as well as Center-Right and Right majorities. In a small number of cases, left-wing governments can overcome the absence of a fit between the positions of movement activists and the frame of the dominant policy arena.

For each comparison, other factors are important. A higher frequency of ministries among the cases of Feminist Insiders stands out. The importance of the feminist perspective of agency leadership and 100 percent agreement between the positions of movement actors, or cohesiveness, distinguishes the Feminist Insider agencies from other Insiders and the complete Transformative State Feminism cases from partial.

Exploration of the causal mechanisms in cases of feminist success and failure suggest other conditions that may drive Transformative State Feminism. For example, in some cases, quasi agencies, quite different from the more typical Feminist Insider ministries at the center of power, can be very effective in reaching feminist success. In the cases of successful Transformative State Feminism explored in depth, both full and quasi agencies were able to overcome the effect of a closed policy arena by being located inside that arena; in all these cases, the policy subsystem was based on the parliament being closely controlled by political parties. Another factor that is important in this scenario is the ideological and organizational closeness of the women's movement to the Left parties and unions, whose MPs are reliable supporters in the legislative process. Finally, the comparison of the Belgian and Spanish debates over gender quotas shows that a Center-Right government can support feminist proposal, and, if they do, can pave the way for Feminist Insiders to gain Feminist Dual Responses from the state.

As promised, we close this chapter with a set of propositions to consider in the development of a theory of state feminism that includes Transformative State Feminism—propositions that benefit from a mixed-methods approach. Although statistical inference methods were not possible, the results of cross-tabulations, csQCA, and case studies of causal mechanisms are consistent and provide an integrated basis for these propositions.

- Feminist movement actors are able to gain some feminist response from the state without the help of Feminist Insider agencies, but Feminist Insiders increase the chances of Feminist Dual Response.
- Agencies, usually ministries, headed by leaders with feminist experience, holding policy proposal powers and close proximity to the centers of power are more likely to be effective allies for feminist women's movement actors than agencies with other characteristics.
- Transformative State Feminism is more likely to be the outcome when the positions of the movement actors are matching or compatible with the dominant frame of the debate.

Finally, there are two other sets of conditions that may lead to Transformative State Feminism, even in the absence of these favorable agency and policy context characteristics.

- Even when the policy subsystem is closed, and the issue frame fit is mixed or threatening to feminist actors, supportive agencies inside the policy subsystem can successfully promote feminist goals to achieve Feminist Dual Responses.
- Second, movement actors that are very close ideologically to the Left parties and unions can take advantage of the positions of the full or quasi agencies in parliamentary debates if the Left is in power or if the Center-Right parties in power support feminist proposals.

III

Unpacking State Feminism

The chapters in Part III take the study of state feminism beyond the testing and exploration of propositions to deepen and broaden the implications of the framework for theories of social movements, representation, framing, and institutionalism. The authors develop new datasets to investigate what RNGS policy debates have to contribute to major scholarly issues and questions. Each chapter enhances the development of state feminism theory as presented in Part IV, "Conclusion."

7

Social Movements and Women's Movements

Joyce Outshoorn

There is by now a substantial amount of literature on women's movements in postindustrial democracies, mainly descriptive and historical case studies focusing on the women's movement in a particular country.[1] There are fewer studies taking a cross-national comparative approach, some of which also cover other postindustrial political systems (e.g., Dahlerup 1986; Katzenstein and Mueller 1987; Kaplan 1992; Nelson and Chowdhury 1994; Threlfall 1996; Lycklama, Wieringa, and Vargas 1998; Banaszak, Beckwith, and Rucht 2003). None of these, however, has used a strict common framework, allowing for a systematic overall in-depth comparison. In the comparative social movement literature, the women's movement has been absent in most of the cross-comparative studies as well (e.g., Kriesi et al. 1995; Kriesi 1996; Rucht 1996, 2003). But increasingly, edited volumes on social movements are incorporating chapters on women's movements (Imig and Tarrow 2001; Davis et al. 2005; Snow, Soule, and Kriesi 2007). Many of the social movement studies that provide an overview of the field or focus on developing theory have used the secondary literature on the women's movement to support the more general points addressed (Tarrow 1994, 1998, 2005; Melucci 1996; Rucht 1996; Della Porta and Diani 2006; Buechler 2000). However, Ferree and Mueller (2007: 577) observe that "women's movements remain on the fringes of most theoretical efforts to understand 'social movements' generically, meaning that most theories still approach male-led movements as if they represented the normative case. Instead we argue that bringing in women's movements, feminist and otherwise, equally into the formulation of basic concepts poses interesting new theoretical challenges." The findings on women's movements from this chapter, therefore, can make an empirical contribution in support of this contention.

The RNGS data, focusing on the public positions women's movement actors take on policy debates, or microframes, across the last four decades in thirteen countries, enable us to compare women's movements across time and place systematically.[2] We develop a new women's movement actor dataset that we use for the analyses in this chapter. Additional women's movement variables in the RNGS dataset are also used to make generalizations about women's movements composition, development over time, attention to issues, and success. In this way, we will be posing some empirical challenges to a number of hypotheses derived from social movement theory.

First, this chapter analyzes the development of women's movements at the aggregate level over the past three decades in order to answer some recurring issues in social movement theory and research. Do women's movements follow the general pattern of the cycle of protest described for Western democracies in the social movement literature? Do they follow a cyclical pattern in their development over the last decades? Has there been a decline in movement activism in the 1990s, as is generally supposed? Are there significant state-specific patterns? To analyze these questions, we have constructed a timeline of all the RNGS debates and counted all ongoing debates during a year. We have also compiled a table of all women's movement actors who have presented a microframe over the entire period under study from the Text Appendices to the RNGS dataset to track changes over time (RNGS 2007b).

Along with the relevant variables on women's movements from the RNGS dataset, this timeline also serves to explore a second set of questions on patterns of women's movement actor development, such as the kinds of organizations and groups women produced, the mix of organizations (informal or formal), the issues these addressed over time, and whether feminist framings were expressed in the debates. From which location, inside or outside the policy arena, did women's movement actors operate? Does the overall composition of the movement change over time, from outsider to insider status, and from autonomous groups to an increasing number of organizations with ties to other political actors? What issue priorities did women's movement actors develop over time? Are there state-specific patterns in any of these processes? What can we learn about transnational women's organizations? Does the mix of groups expressing feminist framings or nonfeminist framings change over time?

Third, we will explore a question that has been highly salient for both social movement scholars and movement activists: whether movement actors, specifically women's movement actors, are more successful when they mobilize a high level of activism or when they take positions within conventional institutional arenas.

What Are Women's Movements?

This chapter follows the working definition of women's movements presented in Chapter 2, which consists of two elements. The definition refers to both the discourse of women's movements—the ideas, aspirations, and identities developed from gender consciousness that inspire collective behavior—and to the actors articulating these ideas in public. These actors can be individual women or informal and formal organizations that have been inspired by movement ideas and that act to advance what they see as women's interests. Women's movement actors are defined by their discourse; while they share with other social movements their engagement in collective behavior for social change, the major difference between women's movements (and men's movements, if they exist) is that they are consciously and explicitly gendered. They claim to represent the grievances of women as women, and set gender as the focal point of their mobilization. Women's movement actors develop a wide range of discourses and demands on what they define as women's interests in public debate and policy arenas.

The RNGS project found it necessary to distinguish between women's movement ideas and feminist ideas. There are women's groups that defend traditional female roles or vehemently oppose legalizing abortion or same-sex marriage. As discussed in Chapter 2, the distinction has been constructed on the basis of the discourses of the women's movement actors. Although all actors express explicit identity with women as a group, use gendered discourse, and claim to represent women, feminist ones also hold that there is something wrong with the status of women and challenge gender hierarchies and women's subordination. Feminist movements are, thus, a specific subset of the total population of women's movements—a basic tenet of the RNGS project, which also corresponds with the arguments made by Karen Beckwith (2000), Ferree and Aili Tripp (2006: vii), Ferree (2006: 6–7), and Ferree and Mueller (2007: 577).

The population of movements we will be investigating in this chapter are those that were active in the five series of policy debates that formed the substance of the RNGS issue books (Mazur 2001; McBride Stetson 2001a; Outshoorn 2004; Lovenduski et al. 2005; Haussman and Sauer 2007). To be more precise, we look at those actors presenting issue frames on the policy debates on the issues. Our data allow us to look in two ways at women's movement actors. First of all, a fair number of the variables in the dataset take into account the overall characteristics of the women's movement as a whole, such as stage, issue priority, and closeness to the Left ideologically and organizationally. Also included is cohesiveness—that is, to what extent women's movement groups and actors agree on the issue at hand. We were also able to distinguish women's movement actors from feminist actors by looking at what kind of frames they expressed in the debates studied.

Second, we have used the Text Appendices to develop the quantitative dataset, which contain abundant information about all women's movement actors active in the debates: the goals of the actors, their framing of the issue, their location, form, and activities A list of all women's movement actors (Women's Movement Actors dataset) from the Text Appendices was compiled, resulting in a large, but accessible, database of all actors in all the countries researched and over the entire period studied. Since our authors of the qualitative books who delivered the Text Appendices were asked to list the actors presenting issue frames in the selected policy debates, both the datasets underreport the number of formal groups and networks. Not included are those who were involved only in cultural activities and consciousness-raising and did not become involved in a debate. We are aware that this limits our generalizations to a certain extent.

Women's Movement Actors over Time

In order to analyze questions on the development of the women's movement and changes in its internal composition, we transposed the RNGS data and coded new variables from the Text Appendices to the Women's Movement Actors dataset.[3] This dataset contains women's movement actors by name, activities, location, form of organization, and agenda priorities during a debate. From the data on the beginning and end years of debates in the RNGS dataset and our new actor-based dataset, we compiled a timeline in which all the debates were arranged in chronological order. Our timeline, which also distinguished by issue, shows that more debates occurred in the 1990s than other periods, even if we ignore the fact that all the hot-issue debates were in the 1990s. The 1990s debates also seemed to have shorter durations at the aggregate level; a possible explanation may be that in earlier debates on the same issue, more alternatives were articulated and new discourses were produced. In the course of time, many of these get weeded out in the attempts to come to a decision on the issue, reducing the number of alternative solutions and therefore resulting in shorter debates.[4]

With the timeline, it then became possible, by eliminating the country dispersion, to count the number of ongoing debates during a year. It emerged that the number of ongoing debates has been continually increasing during the whole period, with only two dips, around 1980 and 1986–1989. These dips may, however, be an artifact of the way participants were asked to select the debates in the RNGS project, selecting three debates that were representative of the life cycle of each issue area over time. Our timeline also shows that the topics of the debates have shifted over time, indicating the shift of attention of women's movements over the whole time period. Abortion was the major issue in the early years; prostitution became an important issue in the 1990s. Job training debates were always low-profile and even diminished in the 1990s. We also see that debates on political representation increased at the beginning of the 1990s, and when the number of such debates stabilized in the mid-1990s, it was at a higher level than in the period before 1990.

This observation corresponds with the observations made by several authors in the study of women's movements and the reconfiguration of the state (Banaszak, Beckwith, and Rucht 2003), who point out that the state configuration in the late 1980s gave rise to electoral and constitutional demands of women's movements (Mueller and McCarthy 2003: 228; Jenson and Valiente 2003). David S. Meyer (2003: 276) observes that neoliberalism led to less state intervention and, therefore, less space on the political agenda. He, therefore, thinks it became easier to set process issues on the agenda than substantive issues. For women's movements, we indeed see the rise of demands concerning political representation—a process issue—in our data, but this can also be attributed to the rising levels of formalization of women's groups.

From the RNGS book on hot issues (Haussman and Sauer 2007), nine of the issues that the authors identified as being among the four most debated issues in the thirteen countries in the study can be said to belong to this category of procedural issues (these nine were about constitutional and electoral reform) (Haussman and Sauer 2007: 305–306). We have no similar data, however, on the two earlier decades to provide evidence for Meyer's observation.

Our data do not allow us to infer increased activity of women's movement activity over time. But by counting all women's movement actors active in all the debates, it becomes possible to arrive at some conclusions on the number of actors over the years. In order to do so, it was necessary to avoid double-counting: A women's movement actor may be simultaneously active in two or more debates, inflating the number of actors. To eliminate this, all movement actors were listed by name. This also made it possible to fill in their location and organizational form in our dataset.

We also calculated the number of active women's movement actors who participated in a debate in a given year—that is, presented their views on the issue. The assumption we had to make when compiling the data was that all actors were participating during the entire period of the debate. For instance, if six women's movement actors were active in the second Canadian abortion debate, under the condition that there is no overlap with other Canadian debates that year, it scores 6 points for each year the debates run.[5]

Cycles and Waves

Observers of social movements have long been aware of the phenomenon of clustering of protest in time; protest is contagious, and movements mobilize and expand in the same period before going into decline. Cycles of protest have been well-mapped at the aggregate level for Western Europe and America during the past 150 years (e.g., Tilly 1978; Tarrow 1989, 1994, 1998; Kriesi et al. 1995; Della Porta and Diani 2006). The last protest cycle started in the 1960s, and with an extra impetus in the early 1980s, is held to have run its course in the mid-1980s. Early studies assumed that social movements also follow stages in their life trajectories that were often described in organic terms of growth, maturity, and decay (i.e., having the form of a parabola), but this has been called into question in later work (e.g. Tarrow 1994, 1998; Koopmans 1995).

Ruud Koopmans already observed the variance between *protest waves*—a term he prefers to cycle—and noted that movements can radicalize or institutionalize, depending on the openness of the political system. Doug McAdam, Tarrow, and Charles Tilly (2001: 266–267) went further in questioning the "parabolic" model, noting that social movements do not go through invariant stages, and suggesting that the cyclical model may just be one of the possible empirical trajectories, a point also taken up by Donatella Della Porta and Diani (2006: 188–190). Koopmans later made the point that there is no "typical" way in which protest waves end; there are, in principle, "unlimited" ways (2007: 36). Declining protest can better be seen as a "process of re-stabilization" and the rerouting of patterns of interaction within one country. The term *decline*, in his view, leads to the wrong kind of question about the worsening opportunities, lesser resources, or inadequate framing (Koopmans 2007: 37).

The question, then, becomes to what extent women's movements fit into the "general" pattern of the protest wave that took off in the 1960s and is held to have run out of steam by the mid-1980s. Do women's movements in the period studied here follow a parabolic life trajectory? Moreover, to what extent is it true that women's movements and the second wave of feminism have been "in decline" since the early 1980s, as the common wisdom holds? Or are we dealing with a case of re-stabilization?

If we use the number of organizations active in debates as the indicator for overall women's movement mobilization, we can tackle these questions. Figure 7.1 shows the number of women's movement actors active for each year from 1966 until 2004. In this figure, we have distinguished between the hot-issue debates (black) and other debates (gray), in order to correct for bias, given the fact that the hot-issue debates were specifically selected from the 1990s and early 2000s.

At the aggregate level, there is little evidence that the women's movement has followed the "general" pattern of the protest wave of the 1960s and 1970s. Both the number of ongoing debates and the number of women's movements over the past decades remain high far beyond the mid-1980s, even if the hot-issue debates are not counted. There are two dips in our charting of debates and groups: around 1980 and 1989. Looking at the number of women's movement actors and taking this to be the women's movement, there is also no parabolic life trajectory of the movement; the decline since 2003 is an artifact of the selection process in which no new debates were selected for analysis beyond the start of the twenty-first century. The women's movement, therefore, in contrast to other social movements such as the student movement, several peace movements, the antinuclear movement, and the autonomous urban movements in Europe, is alive and kicking right into the twenty-first century. As Ferree and Mueller have observed, women's movements have been among the "most enduring" (and successful) social movements of the modern period (2007: 576).

A possible explanation for the differences observed can be found in Ferree's and Mueller's suggestion that the political opportunity structure itself is gendered, giving men and women "different advantages in mobilizing, at any given point" (2007: 590). We know that, in general, women's movement demands cover a much wider range of issues than many other social movements and are dealt with in many different policy arenas. It follows that women's groups can switch to more promising arenas and issues, and can thus take advantage of the different openings in these arenas. They can respond to perceived opportunities by raising different issues. This is reflected in the set of priorities documented in our data, where, as we show in greater detail below, shifts in movement attentions emerge. For instance, when abortion law reform was achieved in many

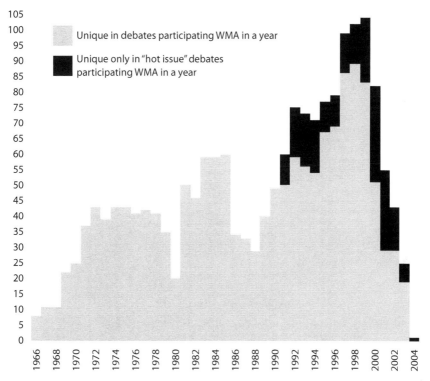

Figure 7.1 Active women's movement actors in a year.

countries, women's movement actors became involved in issues around prostitution and political representation, sustaining overall involvement. The latter was not a big issue in the 1970s, but demands on the topic were offered a window of opportunity when constitutional reform achieved a prominent place on the political agenda in a fair number of countries in the 1990s. Different opportunities can also account for the relatively constant numbers of actors at the aggregate level we have observed in our data into this century. It concurs with Mueller and John D. McCarthy's observations ascribing the longevity of the women's movement to its ability to adjust to the changing political circumstances, enabled by its decentralized nature and strong movement culture (2003: 238–240).

However, Mueller and McCarthy have also suggested that the resiliency of the women's movement is probably issue-dependent; if its issues are more suitable for bargaining, there would be more advantageous opportunity structures (Mueller and McCarthy 2003: 240). Contradicting this contention about bargaining are our findings about abortion. Abortion is generally regarded as a non-negotiable issue, yet it has been a continuing concern to women's movement groups, even when they met formidable opposition. Given the priority of the issue to women's movements, incentives to mobilize and lobby remained strong, even if the opportunities looked less promising.

What we see from our actor-based data is that women's movement actors have been consistently present at the national level in the most recent decade (read off from the numbers involved in national political debates), although this does not hold equally for all countries. This runs contrary to Meyer's contention that national mobilization of women's movements declined because activists looked elsewhere to redress their grievances when states reconfigured in the 1980s and early 1990s (2003: 287). Leaving out the women's movement actors coming forward on the hot issue, it is still striking to see the number of active groups on the other issues during the 1990s up to 2003 at the national level, where most of the debates we studied took place. No fewer than sixty-three separate women's movement organizations were active from 1991 to 2001, as compared with thirty-four in the period 1966–1980 and forty-five between 1981 and 1990.

National Trajectories

The question emerges to what extent state-specific patterns exist in movement trajectories, deviating from the general pattern. Here again, we take the number of women's movement actors as an indicator of the overall movement trajectory. A first analysis of all women's movement actors per country involved in policy debates showed high variation, most likely a result of the RNGS selection criteria for debates. This makes it risky to draw conclusions about single countries with only a few debates. More importantly, we do not have data for all issues for all the countries studied, so a cross-national comparison is not possible. We can, however, categorize the thirteen countries, not by comparing them to each other but by comparing the numbers of actors over time within one country. No fewer than five countries show the pattern of increasing activity during the 1980s and 1990s: Austria, Canada, Ireland, Italy, and Spain. Austria witnessed rapid institutionalization of the more moderate part of the early women's movement groups within several policy sectors when the Social Democrats were in power during this period. In Canada, groups rallied around the Charter of Rights and other constitutional reform matters in the early 1990s, as well as on abortion. In Ireland, women's movements recovered from the defeats of the divorce and abortion reform referendums in the 1980s and managed to consolidate themselves in the 1990s. In Italy, the interest in women's political participation sparked a wave of new activity in the late 1980s and the 1990s. The pattern for Spain can be explained by the fall of the Franco regime in the 1970s, making mobilization possible only after the democratic transition.

The number of women's movement actors involved in debates was more or less stable in seven of the countries studied, although in the majority of these there was a dip in the 1980s—particularly in Great Britain, France, and Germany. In France, the movement was in abeyance and continued to eschew the traditional political arena, not making much use of the window of opportunity offered by the Socialist victory in 1982 and the Mitterrand presidency. In Great Britain, there was closure of the political arena under the Thatcher government, and women's movements were forced into a defensive position. Women's groups in Germany remained highly fragmented and much divided over the issue of participating in traditional politics. Finland is the exception here; the number of active women's movement actors remained high in the period from 1979 until the early 1990s. Then the economic downturn put the movement on the defensive, leaving little energy for new initiatives (Holli and Kantola 2007: 99). While the United States and the Netherlands had the highest number of organizations in all three decades, in both countries the numbers declined significantly in the 1990s. This corresponds with the findings of McBride (2007) and Outshoorn and Jantine Oldersma (2007) about the women's movements in the two countries in a recent study of changes in state feminism since the mid-1990s (Outshoorn and Kantola 2007).

Our findings for France, Germany, and the Netherlands can be compared to the earlier findings of Hanspeter Kriesi and colleagues (1995), who analyzed the mobilization of several "new" social movements: the peace movement, the solidarity movement, the environmental movement, the gay movement, and the urban autonomous movement. In the study, they used protest event analysis and observed a high peak in protest activity for Germany and the Netherlands between 1980 and 1986, high (1980) and lower (1988–1989) peaks for Switzerland, and none in France.

From our data, we know that the number of women's movement organizations was much higher in the 1980s than in the 1970s. When we look at the three countries that are also in our dataset, France, Germany, and the Netherlands, we can observe that the pattern that Kriesi and colleagues observed indeed applies to the Netherlands. In our data, however, France and Germany show a pattern of women's movement organization different from the one observed for the other social movements.[6] France shows a complete disappearance of the women's movement in the 1980s, but some groups re-emerged along with the formation of new ones in the early 1990s when the parity campaign for women's political representation got underway. In Germany, women's movement groups, cherishing their autonomy, started to move into mainstream politics in the late 1980s, and the number of groups increased significantly into the 1990s. Since the mid-1990s, the movement has gone into decline.

Changes within the Composition of Women's Movements

Organizational Format and Location

We are also interested in the overall changes in the composition of the women's movement over time. The rise of second-wave feminism is associated with the emergence of new women's groups that were often informal in nature and not tied to any existing organization or political party. Loose structure and autonomy were highly prized. Moreover, many women activists eschewed the mainstream political channels for their activities. Generally speaking, in the social movement literature, informal and autonomous groups are held to be less likely to survive over time, since this requires organization and the mobilization of resources. Institutionalization and professionalization as responses to maintaining mobilization, as well as the less open political context of the 1980s, account for the decline in autonomous feminism, with its informal networks operating outside of the regular political channels. And as women's movement actors formalized, they also entered the established political arena in several ways, such as promoting certain candidates for electoral office, lobbying a department, or becoming part of a decision-making arena.

Are these trends visible in our data? We can plot them across all Western postindustrial democracies, but not at the national level because of the selection criteria for the debates in the study. Using our women's movement actor data, we can see how the mix between formal and informal groups has evolved over time, and we can chart the changes in location across the decades—whether groups worked outside of or inside the political arena.[7] First of all, how did the mix between formal and informal organizations change over time?

To enable us to interpret the structural change of types over time, the periods presented in Figure 7.2 reflect years of increased or decreased activity of women's movement actors compared to the overall positive trend line of movement actor activity presented in Figure 7.1. As Figure 7.2 shows, the percentage of informal groups of all women's movement groups active over the whole period we studied has indeed declined, independent of changes in general activity; but we also see that even in the 1970s, the supposed heyday of autonomous feminism, they were never in the majority. If we were to include the share of individual women in the total action, the decline would be even more striking, as their share never dropped under the 22 percent mark.

Second, we can plot shifts in the location of women's movement actors over time, denoting whether they are inside or outside of the policy arena. It can be seen that in the 1970s free-standing women's movement actors were clearly in the majority, but that the number declines sharply at the end of the decade. This corresponds to Dieter Rucht's (2003) findings on movement-state interaction in a comparison of four social movements (women's, environmental, labor, and peace) on the basis of protest events and the number of participants in social movements in France, the Netherlands, Switzerland, and Germany. He shows that the women's and the environmental movements have shifted from "more confrontational to more assimilative strategies" in this period (Rucht 2003: 273). Our data on the women's movement actors display a shift in location, with women's movements increasingly operating within policy arenas; this is indicative of the same trend observed by Rucht. Countries differ in how far they display this shift; both Rucht's and our data show that it is weaker in France and Germany. (It should be remembered that more debates for France than for Germany are present in our dataset.) Rucht also suggests that the women's movement (along with the labor movement) is more affected by the state

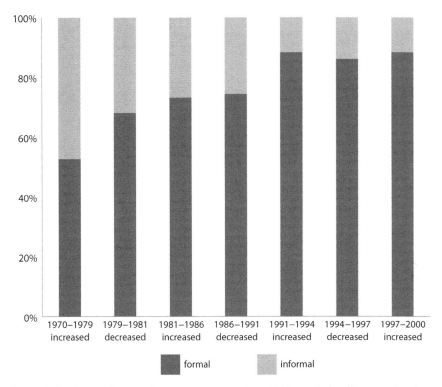

Figure 7.2 Types of women's movement actors (WMA) in periods of increased and decreased activity.

restructuring of the 1980s and the 1990s than other movements. However, our data show that the number of women's movement actors active over the period of state reconfiguration has actually increased, so that state reconfiguration may actually have been an incentive for movement activity.

When we looked at the location of women's movement actors across time, it emerged that the shift to insider politics started right at the beginning of the 1980s. Previously, 60 percent of all women's groups were free-standing groups; after 1981, they formed less than half of all actors until the mid-1990s, when their number shot up to beyond the 1970s figures, to 63 percent. This latter increase could point to a less hospitable climate for women's movement actors in decision-making arenas, forcing them to work from the outside. Another explanation for this rise could be the formation of new organizations on new issues. But our data show that, with some exceptions like the groups around the parity campaign in France, nearly all of them were already in existence before the 1990s decade. This makes more likely the thesis that the climate was less hospitable.

Our data show an undeniable decline of informal groups and increase of formal groups, indicative of a process whereby an overall movement becomes institutionalized over time. Many of the women's groups are no longer distinguishable from interest groups, taking part in the political arena and lobbying for certain issues. At the same time, free-standing groups remain strong, and, as we have seen, their number has actually increased in the last decade. But movement actors inside the political arena do resort to outsider tactics, if they perceive this to be necessary. Although we have no data on this point in our numerical dataset, the qualitative case analyses in the RNGS issue books provide abundant evidence of this flexibility. It is precisely this flexibility that calls into question the rigid division often drawn between interest groups and social movements. The question should not be about defining the essences of each but instead about examining empirically when actors resort to another strategy, either becoming bent on entering the decision-making arena or going outside to increase the pressure on decision makers.

Changes in Issue Priorities

Because it was theorized that women's movements would be more successful if a given issue were among the top priorities of the women's movement groups, our dataset allows us to make some observations about the issues in which women's movements as a whole have been involved over the past three decades. For this purpose, we used the list of top five movement priorities for each country, observed in three to four separate periods per country (forty-three total) from the mid-1960s to the early 2000s, provided by RNGS researchers for the original study.[8]

Among the most frequently listed priorities of women's movements since the mid-1960s, "equality at work" (42 listings) and "abortion and reproductive rights" (37 listings) stand out, being mentioned nearly twice as often as the third issue, "political representation." They can, therefore, justifiably be called the crucial issues of the last thirty years. "Combining work and family/child care" (22 listings), "violence against women" (21 listings), "political representation" (20 listings), and "sexual violence" (16 listings) also occur twice as often as the remaining issues listed. And if one argues that "violence against women" and "sexual violence" are, in fact, one issue, this category would actually be larger than the "abortion and reproductive rights" category.

Table 7.1 gives an overview of the changes of the six most frequently listed issues on the agenda of women's movements at the aggregate level. Since there is considerable variation in the number of years that an issue is on the agenda, we had to decide to compare only the relative importance of priorities in three decades: 1971–1980, 1981–1990, and 1991–2000. Moreover, our data do not allow us to assign weights to the priorities. We cannot say that the issue ranked first is five times more important than the issue ranked fifth.

Equality at work and abortion remain high on the agenda of women's movements during the whole period. Violence against women and sexual violence are relatively high on movement agendas in the 1980s, with a slight decline in the 1990s. The slight decline is hard to account for; possibly it is related to the

TABLE 7.1   FEMINIST INSIDERS AND OTHER INSIDERS BY ISSUE

Priority Issue	DECADE		
	1971–1980	1981–1990	1991–2000
Equality at work	16% (10)	21% (18)	18% (16)
Abortion/reproductive rights	16% (10)	16% (14)	19% (17)
Combining work and family/child care	11% (7)	11% (9)	10% (9)
Violence against women	8% (5)	12% (10)	9% (8)
Political representation	5% (3)	8% (7)	12% (11)
Sexual violence	5% (3)	11% (9)	7% (6)
Total	100% (63)	100% (85)	100% (89)

Note: Percentages are of all the issues mentioned as a priority in a given decade. Totals are the sum of all listed priorities in a decade. Absolute values are given in parentheses.

demise of radical feminism in the 1980s, the strand in feminism that originally politicized both issues. Not included in the table is the decline of priority given to the legal status of women after the mid-1980s, when it was listed frequently. This decline can most likely be ascribed to the many legal reforms, typical liberal feminist demands relatively easy to achieve.

The most spectacular change is to be seen in the rise of political representation as a priority issue. In the 1970s, most women's groups did not consider political representation to be important, distrustful as many women were of mainstream politics. There was, therefore, little inclination to campaign for "more women in politics." By the early 1980s, women's movements rediscovered the importance of mainstream politics and started to demand that more women be part of political bodies. This was fueled by the need for defensive action against the restructuring of the welfare state and the opportunities arising from various types of constitutional reform in the 1990s.

In addition to the overall pattern, in which most women's movements from different countries have the top issues in common, there are several interesting national "deviations," as emerged from the Women's Movement Actor dataset coded from the RNGS Text Appendices, presented in Box 7.1. Notable is the issue of divorce for the Irish women's movement actors, and the early status of immigrant women's rights on the French movement's priority list. The state of international feminism figures high on the agenda of the Austrian and the Belgian movements, but it is not a priority issue in the other countries' movements. Education is only a high priority in the Netherlands (in the 1970s) and Spain (in the 1990s), most probably because it was also a top government priority.

The Mix in Feminist–Nonfeminist Framings

Finally, we have analyzed the number of active women's movement actors expressing feminist frames over time.[9] These are framings that claim there is something wrong with the status of women and that challenge gender hierarchies

Box 7.1 Country-Specific Changes in Women's Movement Priorities

Austria	*International women's movements* were on the priority list in the 1970s and re-emerge in the early 2000s.
Belgium	Together with Austria, Belgium accounts for 80 percent of the occurrences of *international women's movements* on the agenda of women's movements. *Women's legal status* was an issue during the 1980s.
Canada	*Women's policy agency reform* was on the agenda for the 1970s and 1990s, but it disappeared in the 1980s. The women's movement in Canada also has country-specific issues on health care and government cutbacks on its agenda.
Finland	During the first decade of our timeline, the agenda of the women's movement in Finland consisted entirely of the top six issues of the cross-national priority list. In the next two decades, *women's legal status* (country-specific) and *prostitution* became important issues.
France	The agenda of the women's movement in France has changed three times. These agendas contain most of the six top priorities. *Immigrant women's rights* was a stable priority issue in the 1990s. *Sexism in the media* was a priority in the 1970s, and returned to the agenda after 1994. This issue had no priority in other countries.
Great Britain	All issues are within the general top six priorities.
Germany	All issues are within the general top six priorities.
Ireland	The agenda in Ireland shows issues other than the six top priorities (*divorce* and *social welfare*) only in the period 1979–1986.
Italy	The Italian women's movement had four different agendas during our timeline. The first agenda (1970–1979) shows *divorce* and *autonomous women's movement building*. The agenda from 1986 to 1995 held significant other issues than the other Italian agendas, with *social welfare* on it.
The Netherlands	An important issue of the women's movement in the 1970s in the Netherlands was education. From 1986 until 2002, the women's movement did not change their agenda. *Health care* was on that agenda
Spain	Apart from the six general top priorities, only two agendas have occurred in Spain: *divorce* in the early 1980s and *education* in the 1990s.
United States	During the 1980s, a *country-specific issue* was on the agenda. *Health care* and *women's legal status* were also on the agenda in the 1970s.

and women's subordination. Does the mix of groups expressing feminist micro-framings compared to nonfeminist microframings change over time?

Our data show that in all periods the majority of involved actors expressed feminist framings, a figure that has increased in the course of time. Of all groups, around 60 percent used feminist framing in the period between 1971 and 1981, and this percentage hovered around 75 percent between 1981 and 1997. It increased even more in the period after 1997, when more than 80 percent of all groups used feminist frames. This is somewhat surprising, as the common wisdom usually holds that feminism was waning after the period of the 1960s and 1970s. One might expect that free-standing groups are more likely to express feminist framing, but there is little correspondence between the number of free-standing groups and the number of those expressing feminist frames. A possible explanation of our findings may be that in the later periods women's movement actors increasingly turned to feminist framings to be able to make a difference to the debate, as other women's movement framings had become part of the mainstream discourse, while in previous periods, entering women's frames already provided a challenge to the dominant discourse.

Transnational Social Movement Organizations

The last decades have seen a vast increase in transnational social movement organizations or transnational social movement actors working on a range of issues internationally (Keck and Sikkink, 1998; Smith 2004, 2005). Generally, their purpose is to "change some elements of the social structure or renewed distribution, or both of a society" (Smith 2005: 231). Transnational social movements can be long-term federations with low involvement of participants or long-term campaigns with high involvement. In the short term, there can be a coalition around a certain event with high involvement or an instrumental coalition with low involvement (Tarrow 2005: 166–167).

The women's movement already had many international ties in the latter half of the nineteenth century, such as the organization around trafficking of women and the many branches of the women's peace movement, which lasted until World War II. In the 1960s, a plethora of new transnational organizations on many issues emerged, ranging from social justice and human rights to reproductive issues and sex work. Jackie Smith (2005: 233) counted sixteen "women's rights" organizations in 1973, or 9 percent of all transnational social movements she found; for 2000 she counted 94, accounting for 9 percent of all transnational social movements. As Tarrow (2005: 189, note 9) has observed, the actual numbers may be even higher, as many groups not listed as women's rights organizations have "strong interest" in women, such as those working on human rights, economic development, or religion.

In our data, we do observe an increasing number of debates over time in which instances of participation in transnational advocacy networks (TANs) by women's movement actors occur.[10] We have compared these instances with the periods of increased and decreased women's movement actor activity in debates. The overall trend is a dramatic increase of participation in TANs. In the 1970s, only 15 percent of women's movement actors participated in a TAN, but since 1997, 85 percent participated. This increase does not follow a linear pattern. When there is an overall increase of women's movement activism, we also see an increase in instances of participation in TANs as well; in a period of decreased activity, participation in TANs slows down or even decreases. This occurred in the mid-1990s. The transition into a new period of increased activity in 1997 resulted in a vast increase of instances of participation in TANs. Unfortunately, our data cannot explain whether the variations in instances of participation are a result of changing success or political opportunity structures of TANs as a whole, or of new possibilities of frame deliberation or resource pooling for national women's movement actors inside a TAN.

When we look into differences in participation in TANs by women's movement actors on the different issues, only the issues of political representation and prostitution show high levels. This does not imply that there is no TAN activity on job training and abortion, but the rate here is less than half the total number of women's movement actors participating in these TANs, even when we take into account the huge increase of TAN participation in the 1990s. The participation in these networks during debates on prostitution over time increases along with the increased attention for the issue in the 1990s. This raises the question of whether the issue of prostitution itself or the overall increasing TAN activity explains this increase. A look into the issue of political representation and participation in TANs can be enlightening here. The number of debates on political representation also increases in the decade of the 1990s, but there is no corresponding increase in TANs on the issue, the number of which remains relatively constant over the entire period of 1970 until 2000. This suggests that the specific character of the issue of prostitution accounts for the increase, with its link to trafficking of women, which in and of itself is an international phenomenon. Political representation debates focus mainly at the national level, therefore making transnational activity less likely.

Generally, the trend of internationalization has facilitated ties between national and international women's movement actors, with the growth of supranational institutions providing favorable opportunities for women's transnational social movement organizations (Tarrow 2005: 203). As a consequence, we think it can be argued that when an issue gains in popularity among local and national feminists today, it is highly likely to result in increased participation in transnational networks. Resources and outcome of the debates are also less likely to be restricted to the domestic realm. This is one of the reasons that Tarrow (2005: 213) argues that the traditional divide between local and international contention is diminishing.

Participation in transnational organizations or alliances can enable women's movements at the national level to articulate and frame successful demands by comparing with other women's movements in similar situations abroad, as well as by expanding issues and transplanting demands to other agendas. It is therefore very likely that the capacity for diffusion and externalization of transnational networks has contributed to the vast increase of the number of debates on prostitution in virtually all RNGS countries.

The Link between Success and High Activism

Much of the social movement literature suggests that heightened levels of mobilization lead to demands of social movements being met. Other scholars have tried to explain mobilization and success in terms of organizational resources. Recently, Elizabeth S. Clemens and Debra Minkoff have argued that scholars are moving beyond the long-dominant "organizations as resource" hypothesis toward a focus on "interaction": "Choices of organisational form are simultaneously vehicles of mobilisation, signals of identity to opponents and possible coalition partners, and 'etiquettes' for collective action" (2007: 158). They observe that local activists are faced with a severe dilemma: If one takes advantage of the access to resources and strategies that give them local legitimacy and leverage, one runs the risk of becoming "overincorporated," losing the spontaneity and energy that drives grass-roots activism (Clemens and Minkoff 2007: 163). But it may enhance their chances of having their demands met. Their choices, in turn, are the result of the dynamics between them and other organizations or institutions in the policy arena. Are women's movement actors more successful when they go for mobilizing a high level of activism or for obtaining positions within conventional institutional arenas? To find an answer to this crucial question, we use the RNGS State Response Typology presented in Chapter 1 and used throughout the book, with four types of movement impact and state response: Dual Response, Preemption, Co-optation, and No Response.

Movement actors have to decide on their strategy. They can mobilize their supporters and relevant publics to exert pressure on the decision makers, a strategy that can be characterized as an outsider strategy, leading to high activism. Movement actors can also rely on their institutional strength: that is, the degree to which movements have become part of institutions. They can then follow an insider strategy, entering the policy arena and becoming a partner in decision making, lobbying, and negotiating their demands in the process. For our evidence, we have used the information from the RNGS dataset on women's movement activism and women's movement mobilization across all thirteen countries in the study.[11] So what is the surest road to success?

Our data show some notable results indicating which strategy is more successful. Looking at Table 7.2 on the level of activism, it can be seen that the likelihood of achieving a Dual Response—that women's movement actors' demands were included in the final policy decision and the movement actors gained access to the decision-making arena—is greater when the level of activism is actually quite low. High levels of activism tend to result in a higher number of cases—over half of all Preemptions, in which case policy demands were more or less met, but women's movement actors did not participate in the policy arena. Thus, a more moderate level of activism does not lead to acceptance in the arena.

TABLE 7.2   ACTIVISM AND MOVEMENT SUCCESS

	LEVEL OF ACTIVISM			
Concept of Success	Low	Moderate	High	Total
No response	9	9	4	22
	40.9%	40.9%	18.2%	100%
Preemption	17	13	14	44
	38.6%	29.5%	31.8%	100%
Co-optation	4	0	3	7
	51.1%	0.0%	42.9%	100%
Dual Response	16	8	3	27
	59.3%	29.6%	11.1%	100%
Total number of cases	46	30	24	100
	46%	30%	24%	100%

Note: Total number of cases here does not include thirty cases of "mixed fit" between women's movement actors' frames and policy content. Cases of low-level activism scored 1–3; moderate, 4–7; and high, 8–10.

The level of institutionalization, presented in Table 7.3, displays other effects. With high levels of institutionalization, it is more likely that women's movement actors will have success. Being part of the "establishment" in the policy arena pays off; it leads to more success. An informally organized movement actor, poorly or moderately institutionalized, is likely to be excluded from the policy arena. The high percentages in the combination of low level of institutionalization and No Response (i.e., no policy response to women's movement actor demands and no actor participation) and Preemption categories confirm the proposition that poorly or moderately institutionalized actors have less success.

To be able to conclude whether *increasing* activism and institutionalization leads to *increased* success, we must apply a different method. Assuming that No Response is the least preferred outcome, Dual Response the most preferred, and both Preemption and Co-optation (actor participation with no policy response) equally preferred, an ordinal scale of success can be constructed. Calculating the correlation with the levels of activism and institutionalization produces the results shown in Table 7.4.

The correlations are compatible with our findings from Tables 7.2 and 7.3. We saw that low levels of activism are weakly connected to Dual Response and Co-optation; here there is no relation between the degree of activism and state response. We also found that high and low levels of institutionalization do correspond to high and low levels of movement success, respectively. In this table, that relationship is statistically significant: the higher the degree of institutionalization, the greater the likelihood of Dual Response. Nevertheless, the results point to the difficulty of solving the dilemma of an actor choosing a strategy. Both strategies may or may not lead to success, depending heavily on the context of an actor (Snow 2007: 401–403), yet probabilities tip toward going inside political institutions. Hardly any correlation exists between level of activism

TABLE 7.3 INSTITUTIONALIZATION AND MOVEMENT SUCCESS

| Concept of Success | LEVEL OF INSTITUTIONALIZATION | | | |
	Low	Moderate	High	Total
No response	8	13	1	22
	29.6%	21%	9.0%	22%
Preemption	13	27	4	44
	48.1%	43.6%	36.4%	44%
Co-optation	1	5	1	7
	3.7%	8%	9%	7%
Dual Response	5	17	5	27
	18.5%	27.4%	45.5%	27%
Total number of cases	27	62	11	100
	100%	100%	100%	100%

TABLE 7.4 CORRELATIONS BETWEEN ACTIVISM, INSTITUTIONALIZATION, AND SUCCESS

| | SPEARMAN'S RHO (N = 100) | |
	Activism	Institutionalization
Success	−.097	.184
Activism	1	.010

and institutionalization; thus, there is at least a clear choice between one strategy and the other. Although the coefficients are low, indicating no strong correlations, the direction of the correlations confirms our findings from Tables 7.2 and 7.3. The greater the level of activism, the less likely it is that a Dual Response will result. A higher level of institutionalization generates a greater chance of achieving Dual Response. The low correlation coefficients point to the difficulty of solving the dilemma of an actor choosing a strategy. Either strategy may or may not lead to success, depending heavily on the context of an actor (Snow 2007: 401–403).

In the highly controversial debates raging in most women's movements in the 1970s on the issue of formal versus informal organization, those who claimed that participation in the regular channels would make women's groups more effective were right. From our data, we can state that if one wants to be effective, the strategy for success is to go inside state institutions and gain access into conventional political arenas.

Conclusion

This chapter has analyzed three clusters of related questions. First, we were interested in several issues concerning the life cycle of the women's movement and the debate about its possible decline. Second, we analyzed several questions around the organizational characteristics of women's movement actors. Finally, we looked into the issue of the relation between mobilization and institutionalization of the women's movement and its chances of success, measured by policy outcomes and the presence of movement actors in the decision-making process.

The first conclusion we can draw is that women's movements have maintained a high level of activity since the 1960s, if we take as a measure of movement activity the public expression of microframes, or positions, by women's movement actors on particular policy issues. This involvement actually increased in the 1990s—when we do not count the hot-issue debates that were selected specifically from that decade. We also noted that the debates covered a shorter period of time in the course of the decades, probably because in earlier versions of the debates unfeasible solutions were teased out and later debates become more focused on viable proposals presented for decision making. The topics of the debates also shifted in the course of time, with abortion debates decreasing and those on political representation increasing, reflecting shifts in attention by women's movement groups.

By counting all women's movement actors who expressed positions on all the debates analyzed in the RNGS study, we were also able to draw some conclusions about the number of women's movement groups over time—even though our sample is somewhat biased toward groups that take positions on debates about government action, and we do not have the same number of issue observations for each of the thirteen countries in the dataset. From our data, we can conclude that there is little evidence that the women's movement paralleled the general pattern of the protest wave of the 1960s and 1970s, which is held to have dwindled in the mid-1980s. The number of active groups remained high right to the end of the century, even when we exclude the hot-issue debates. There is no overall pattern of decline; our data show that the contention of Ferree and Mueller (2007: 576)—that the women's movement is among the "most enduring" of the protest movements of the 1960s and 1970s—is well-founded. Our data also lend support to their idea of "gendered opportunity structures"—that opportunity structures differ in their barriers and opportunities depending on the social movement involved. Despite the reservations we had about drawing inferences about national patterns of movement activity, our data show some intriguing national differences, such as the increased activity of women's movement groups in Austria, Canada, Ireland, Italy, and Spain, and less activity in the United States and the Netherlands during the 1980s and 1990s.

A second cluster of questions concerns several organizational characteristics of women's movement actors. As many second-wave feminist scholars have observed, the proportion of informal groups among all women's groups has indeed declined, but our data also show that this proportion never constituted a majority, even in the 1970s. We also observed that free-standing groups—those groups outside the policy arena—were originally in the majority, but their proportion decreased sharply at the end of the 1970s. They formed fewer than half of all movement groups until the 1990s, when their numbers increased significantly—most likely resulting from closure of policy arenas within a more hostile political climate. The increase in the number of formal groups blurs any distinction between social movement actors and interest groups, calling into question the rigid division between the two represented in the literature.

Our data do support the idea that the life cycle of a social movement is not necessarily parabolic in form. We also show that in all periods a majority of women's movement actors involved in debates presented feminist framings, according to the operational definition developed by RNGS and used in this book. Their number actually increased over time, which also casts doubts on the thesis of feminism's so-called decline. Another important finding is the notable increase in transnational activity of the women's movement over the three decades studied, in line with the global increase in transnational social movement organization. This is most evident with regard to women's political representation and especially with regard to prostitution, in which case the vast increase in debates in the 1990s can be attributed to transnational diffusion and activity.

Abortion and equality at work have been the most important issues of the women's movements in the period studied, with the combination of work and family life, political representation, violence against women, and sexual violence listed as the next most important. The most important change in issue priority has been the rise of political representation in the 1980s. Women's movements then increasingly entered mainstream politics, fueled by the deterioration of the welfare state undermining women's rights and the need to be represented in the decision-making arena.

A third cluster of questions we explored focused on whether women's movement actors are more successful when they mobilize a high level of activism or when they take positions within conventional institutional arenas. Our data lend support to the conclusion that movement success, assessed in terms of outcomes and access in relevant political arenas, is indeed more likely when movement actors are incorporated in the decision-making process and the level of activism of the whole movement is actually quite low. High and moderate levels of activism tend to correspond to incidences of Preemption: Policy demands were satisfied, but women were not active in the process. Involvement in the policy arena yields more policy success; poorly institutionalized groups are less likely to be invited into the policy process and to achieve their goals. Finally, the higher degree of institutionalization over time does result in more Dual Responses, with fewer cases of Preemption. Thus, it is apparent that the best strategy to achieve one's aims is to take part in decision-making structures, such as political parties, legislatures, and interest lobbies.

8

Political Representation

JONI LOVENDUSKI
MARILA GUADAGNINI

Feminist empirical and theoretical work on representation has largely proceeded along separate paths.[1] The RNGS project offers a corrective, as it permits the simultaneous consideration of the effects of formal and informal channels of participation, patterns of women's presence in decision-making arenas, movement activities, and policy outcomes. Thus, it provides a rich source of data that can be analyzed to illuminate both substantive and descriptive representation, a distinction that is central to current feminist debates. We find evidence that feminists should not give up on presence, that women's substantive and descriptive representation are linked through the critical acts of women legislators and agency officials.

Our findings challenge various aspects of previous research on women's representation, four of which are contentious. First, they raise questions about the relationships between descriptive (procedural) and substantive representation. Second, they suggest a model of effective policy advocacy that does not quite correspond to the idea of the policy triangles of movement, agency, and legislature, or of autonomous and integrated women's movements and agency or legislature. Third, they suggest that the debate over critical mass–critical actor–critical acts should be revisited and respecified. Fourth, they raise important questions about accountability.

In this chapter, we first examine the varying dimensions of political representation found in recent feminist research and summarize these concerns into a series of nine researchable questions. Second, we show how we draw on RNGS concepts and data in an attempt to refine and provide initial answers to these questions. Third, we use the RNGS data to answer the questions. We conclude with a discussion of the relationships between different kinds of representation and different actors in contemporary policy debates.

Dimensions of Political Representation:
Theory and Research Questions

Much of feminist political representation scholarship that we address here draws heavily on Pitkin's four-part typology of representation (1967) and attempts to develop it theoretically for the analysis of instances of representation in particular, usually legislative, settings (Bratton and Ray 2002; Celis et al. 2008; Dovi 2002, 2007; Lovenduski 2005; Lovenduski et al. 2005; Mansbridge 1999, 2003; Phillips 1995; Schwindt-Bayer and Mishler 2005; Wängnerud 2000; Weldon 2002a). Such scholarship implies that the gender-blind standard operating procedures of research on representation mask the exclusion of women and women's interests from authoritative political deliberation and decision making.

This feminist scholarship is largely driven by a common concern to characterize representation in such a way as to allow a systematic assessment of contemporary experiences of women's representation. For example, recent studies include work that highlights the neglected interconnections among all of Pitkin's categories (Schwindt-Bayer and Mishler 2005), studies focusing on the relationships between substantive and descriptive representation (Bratton and Ray 2002; Lovenduski et al. 2005; Weldon 2002a), reformulations of Pitkin's categories in the light of feminist theories of representation and the requirements for research (especially on the United States; Dovi 2007), and proposals for new categories that consider the requirements of deliberative democracy particularly in an American political setting, but also in Great Britain (Campbell, Childs, and Lovenduski 2010; Mansbridge 2003).

A central problem is the measurement of the extent to which the interests of particular groups of voters (normally more or less differentiated groups of women) are represented in legislative decisions. Since Phillips (1995) argued so effectively for a "politics of presence," feminists have contended that a necessary condition for the representation of women's interests is the presence of women in decision-making bodies. Phillips contends that interests are realized in the course of deliberation and decision making as various options, implementation strategies, and competing concerns are discussed. Only those who take part in the deliberation can benefit from such realization and insert their interests. Leaving aside the vexing question of identifying "valid" group interests, the logic of Phillips' claim is inescapable. However, it has proved difficult to demonstrate empirically that the representation of women's interests necessarily follows from the presence of women representatives in legislatures, although a great deal of circumstantial evidence that this is the case has been assembled and presented (Chaney, Alvarez, and Nagler 1998; Childs 2004, 2005, 2007; Childs and Krook 2006; Lovenduski 2005; Mateo Diaz 2005). Repeated demonstrations of a strong association between increases in the presence of women legislators and enhanced agenda status of variously described women's issues or preferences does not convince some scholars, who insist (unfairly, we believe) that such studies merely read off substantive from descriptive representation.[2] Others reckon that the associations between presence and policy substance are limited and argue that it makes most sense to consider all four of Pitkin's dimensions of representation together (Schwindt-Bayer and Mishler 2005). Still others stress the necessity to move beyond legislatures as sites of representation to understand the totality of women's representation (Weldon 2002a). Finally, a repeating debate among feminist political scientists turns on the relationship between critical mass and critical acts. Briefly, the fundamental question is whether the presence of at least a certain number of women legislators will lead to a better representation of women's interests in politics. At the time of writing, the matter seems to be settled around agreement that it is the critical acts of representatives and not their numbers that matter (Childs and Krook 2006). Such agreement brings the debate back to its starting point in 1988, when Dahlerup argued that acts, not numbers, are critical (Dahlerup 1988). Agreement that acts matter has not yet been accompanied by much empirical testing of their relationship to numbers, however. RNGS data can be used to explore this relationship and move the debate forward.

Feminist scholars are concerned with differences between and among women, and have recently been especially concerned with intersectionality. Women are thought to be fully represented when deliberations about public policy explicitly consider the potential impact on different groups of women. In practice, the processes of making effective and properly differentiated claims to increase the representation of women in political processes are rudimentary. For the most part, institutionalized political processes were designed to aggregate politically salient differences among men. Hence, incoming women and women's interests are assumed to coincide with those of men and tend to be treated as unproblematic. We attribute this to the relatively early stage of the campaigns for the equal representation of women in most countries; such claims are not irrevocably essentialist but instead are starting points on the basis of which different identities will acquire political purchase as the processes of women's representation develop.

Feminist political scientists are attracted to the potential of descriptive representation to deliver at least a measure of substantive representation. However, there remains a division between those who allegedly claim that descriptive representation will lead to substantive representation and those who see no connection. To us, this argument represents a position that can be constructed in theory but for which no advocates can be found. Most students of political representation are all too aware of possible discrepancies between the characteristics of representatives and their actions. Pitkin herself is dismissive of descriptive representation, because she rejects its implicit assumption of such a conjunction. She believes that, in hands less competent than hers, concentration on descriptive representation leads to a focus on presence at the expense of action. If this were ever true, it no longer is. While she may be correct to identify such a danger, it is not an inevitable error, and if it was ever a common mistake, it no longer is. These days in empirical study, any curiosity about the relationship between action and personal characteristics is regarded as a topic for empirical research, not an assumption. Even so, the literature is awash with instances of feminists constructing fictional opponents from scholarship that allegedly reproduces mindlessly the error of simply assuming that women's presence in decision-making bodies is a good thing for women's interests. It is something of a trope, one that offers a convenient launching pad for an argument that might otherwise be more difficult to make.[3]

Representation takes place in the state and in civil society on executives, boards, and commissions, as well as in political parties, trade unions, and international organizations. Only a fraction of these positions are directly elected; many are appointed, and some are self-selected. Such representation is highly sensitive to context and is not necessarily democratic.

Several feminist scholars have attempted to research representation beyond legislatures. In a pathbreaking study, Weldon (2002a) claimed that representation in state bodies in conjunction with women's movement activism, in circumstances where the state body consults the women's movement, does outperform what she terms *descriptive representation*, but by which she clearly means legislative representation. Her formulation raises key issues about representation, as it equates accountability with consultation, a problem we discuss later in the chapter. Despite its theoretical value, this work only minimally considers political context, uses the terms *descriptive* and *legislative representation* interchangeably, and covers only the year 1994, when there was much less variation in women's legislative presence in her thirty-six countries than in the following decade; hence, a later study might have produced different conclusions.[4] In contrast, in their study of thirty-one countries over time, Leslie Schwindt-Bayer and William Mishler (2005) provide powerful evidence that increases in women's representation in legislatures tend to be associated with increased policy responsiveness to women's concerns.

Women's movement actors make alliances both within movements and between movements and civil society and the state. Such activity is recounted in feminist research, which reveals policy cooperation between women's policy agencies and movement advocates located in different arenas, such as autonomous women's movements, the media, political parties, trade unions, legislatures, government, and public administration. The literature includes discussions of strategic partnerships between women's movements and women's policy machinery (Holli and Kantola 2005). A common metaphor is that of the triangle, capturing the idea of an alliance linking movements, the state, and some other entity. Different terms have been used, including *strategic partnership, triangle of empowerment, velvet triangles,* and *feminist advocacy coalitions* (Halsaa 1999; Vargas and Wieringa 1998; Mazur 2002; Woodward 2003). Although there is no agreement on the definition of the triangle, its components, or its strategic location, most include state actors, legislators, and women's movement actors who are linked to each other through different organizations and political processes.

Thus, research demonstrates that representation is not confined to legislative structures and also identifies the variety of possible alliances between movement and state actors. It distinguishes between different sources of representation and draws attention to their combined impact on policy processes. In showing that a strong women's movement improves the representative function of policy agencies, it highlights the importance for movements of having allies in the state, combining and making more systematic the findings of previous studies of women's movements and the state. Although the metaphor is limited and may obscure complex processes of alliance making, it has considerable analytical utility if used sensibly (Holli 2008).

Arguably, both the theory and the practice of representation are in a complex phase of change that poses huge challenges for research. The divide between theoretical and empirical research has been recognized by scholars who call for detailed strategies of investigation that take into account the range of questions theorists have raised about women's representation. A good example is found in the work of Celis and colleagues (2008), and others who draw attention to the requirements of empirical research on political representation that they argue must answer at least four questions: Who represents or claims to represent women, what policies are put forward by representatives, where and why are they put forward? Our reading of feminist representation theory suggests five additional questions: Which women are represented (capturing difference and intersectionality); when does the representation take place; what are the processes through which claims are formulated, refined, and advanced (indicative of political context); to whom are the representatives accountable (a classic concern of representation theory); and to what effect are they made an indicator of effectiveness? The logical order of the questions becomes *how* is representation done, *who* does it, in relation to *which* women, *what* policies, *where*, *when*, *why*, and *to whom* accountable, and *how effective* is the representation?

Concepts, Data, and Definitions

We focus here on each question about representation in turn using RNGS data, which we contend offers new answers to many of the questions. RNGS supplies new data on representation in different kinds of institutions including movements, bureaucracies, agencies, and parties in conjunction with legislative representation, as well as in the context of temporal and specific policy settings. The RNGs project extends well beyond simply correlating the characteristics of representatives with their activities. The key innovation is the research design, in which the unit of analysis is the policy debate.[5] Debates were selected using criteria that included their importance at the time in terms of the issue. While it has its limitations (Celis 2008), the design generates a sample size sufficient for quantitative analysis, often impossible in studies of individual countries. It also offers a cleaner view of the existence and effectiveness of movement representation. Simply asking what movements achieve risks exaggerating their effects; in contrast, starting with debates allows empirical observation of movement actor intervention and effectiveness.

In this chapter, we use a common distinction between autonomous and integrated women's movements and organizations. Autonomous women's movements are a form "of women's mobilization that is devoted to promoting women's status and well-being independently of political parties and other associations that do not make the status of women their main concern. Autonomous organizations must be self-governing and recognize no superior authority nor be subject to governance of other political agencies" (Weldon 2002a: 1161). By contrast, "integrated women movement(s) [are] individuals and groups inside non women's movement organization (women in political parties, in trade unions, media, academia, etc.)" (Weldon 2002a: 1161). Women's movement actors, like social movements actors, may adopt a strategy of working within a variety of state institutions. Following Ferree and Mueller (2007), only when actors have *links* to organized collective women's movement entities may they be considered women's movement actors. Independent individuals (free of movement constraints) who happen to use feminist rhetoric are not movement actors. In the RNGS study, movements are diverse but may be thought to contain actors from either or both autonomous and integrated movements.[6] Both make claims for women. The RNGS definition of women's movement stipulates that all such actors must be women. Representation is fully successful when the state both includes movement actors in the policy process and makes decisions that reflect movement preferences (Dual Response), is partly successful when the state accepts either procedural or substantive representation by movement actors (Co-optation and Preemption), and is unsuccessful when the state makes no response (No Response).[7]

To explain political representation in relation to the theories discussed above, we developed several additional measures from the datasets. These are women's movement actor *presence* at the beginning and end of the debate, *legislator presence* in the debate, women's *policy agency representativeness*, women's movement actor *agreement, feminism of agency leadership, debate gendering*, and *legislator intervention*.[8]

- Women's movement actor *presence* is a scaled measure of procedural (or descriptive) representation defined as participation by movement actors at the beginning and end of the debate. It is a measure of the extent to which movement actors are accepted in the policy subsystem and is not exhaustive of those movement actors who put forward microframes in a debate.
- *Legislator presence* indicates whether one or more movement actors who were legislators took a stand in the debate.
- Women's *policy agency representativeness* scale is a simple measure of agency attempts to represent. Here we distinguish between strategic and delegate representation, where strategic representation is the independent advocacy of women's interests as understood by agencies

and delegate representation is the strict advocacy of women's movement preferences. Thus, the highest point on the agency representativeness scale is delegate representation, capturing the occasions when
agency officials advocate expressed movement preferences. The (perhaps arbitrary) placement of delegate above strategic representation
reflects feminist concern with accountability to movements, discussed
later in this chapter.
- *Women's movement agreement* simply distinguishes between debates
  in which both autonomous and integrated actors intervened and those
  in which only one or the other did.
- *Feminism of agency leadership* indicates any women's movement
  background of the agency head.[9]
- *Debate gendering* identifies the point at which a debate became
  gendered.
- *Legislator intervention* counts the number of legislators who intervened in each debate. It is the performance of a public act in the debate, including the public expression of an opinion.

These additional indicators enable us to distinguish the input and effectiveness
of different participants in policy debates. Movement actors, agency officials,
and legislators are corners of a hypothetical policy triangle. We determine the
circumstances under which each participates, the relative contributions of each
to the substantive and procedural representation of women, and the extent of
links between the three groups. In short, we can determine if such triangles
operated in the debates.

The remainder of this chapter follows the questions and distinctions developed above through the RNGS datasets. We next explore the activities and
effects of movement actors, women's policy agencies, and legislators. We use
both quantitative (bivariate correlations) and qualitative evidence to inform our
discussion of the representation questions and use the findings to draw conclusions about both the nature of women's political representation in various policy environments and the relationships between different policy actors.

Answering the Nine Questions about Representation

1. How Is Representation Done?

Representation is performed by elected and appointed actors, movements,
and individuals operating in different and changing circumstances at different stages of policy debates. In our data, representation is conceptualized in
terms of processes of framing. Women's representatives put forward gendered
ideas in attempts to frame or reframe a debate so that its discourse is gendered
or regendered in line with women's interests. These gendered frames may be
feminist but are not necessarily so. Debates on public policy issues have sev-

eral sources. They may emerge from public debate and be taken forward by in-dividuals working in different institutions and arenas. They may, for example, begin in discussions inside sections of political parties, interest organizations, social movements, or parts of the civil service, or within the political leader-ship, and later find their way into manifestos and achieve priority in political programs.

What does gendering do to a discourse? Most issues have gender dimen-sions, as they implicitly or explicitly reflect some notion of relations between women and men, and between masculinity and femininity. The strategy of gen-dering exposes the biases of debates by drawing attention to their gendered content or by offering a regendering of an already gendered debate. Women's representatives act in these processes. Although practices vary considerably, the case studies presented in Box 8.1 provide clear evidence of such involvement. Movement actors attempt to establish and maintain consultative relationships with policy agencies; policy agencies seek movement support and occasionally establish consultative groups that include movement actors. Recently, for exam-ple, Great Britain's Women and Equalities Unit established a Muslim women's forum to facilitate government consultation with this group of women (Loven-duski 2007a). Probably the most common relationship between agencies and movement turns on the research and expertise of movement actors. Contribu-tion to policy research by expert movement actors is one of several forms of lob-bying and a major site of framing. It feeds into deliberation in terms of content, and discourse, hence, is an attempt to gender subsequent debate.[10]

As predicted, movement actors, agencies, and women legislators attempted to gender debates. Agencies intervened in 80 debates, movement actors operat-ing autonomously or together with other organizations did so in 110 debates, and legislators intervened in 46 debates. The initial answer to the "how" ques-tion is that representation is done by all three sets of actors through standard repertoires of political intervention, both separately and together.[11]

2. Who Represents Women?

Movement actors prioritize women's movement concerns to the exclusion of other interests. Women legislators may present their party's view of women's interests, while, normally, the brief of a policy agency is to advocate for wom-en's interests as conceived by the appointing government when designing the agency's remit.

Table 8.1 classifies 217 representative acts found in the debates. It shows the number of interventions by women representatives in the most important deci-sional arenas of the 114 debates and indicates that actors from free-standing women's movement organizations (autonomous) made the most interventions.[12] However, these 87 interventions were still a minority of the total number of interventions.

Policy agencies were also active. At least one intervened in more than half (seventy-one) of the debates. In practice, the claims of agencies to speak for or to

Box 8.1 Two Case Studies on Diversity

The Debate on Ending Entitlements for Poor Families in the United States, 1992–1996

The U.S. welfare reform debates of the 1980s and 1990s were gendered with a focus on poor women. The Personal Responsibility and Work Opportunity Reconciliation Act of 1996 "instituted a paradigm shift in welfare policy, holding the poor individually responsible for poverty and for ending it" (McBride 2007: 293). This welfare-to-work policy was enacted after a protracted set of debates. The policy aimed at poor single mothers. The discourse mainly named single mothers as the proposed targets. Race was a subtext, and many of the participating welfare advocacy organizations were black women's groups. The long-term welfare recipients in the United States were mainly black. Hence the debate was saturated with class, race, and gender meanings. Women's movement actors made explicit the gender and class but not the race meanings. In the recorded testimony of actors, there are many accusations that middle-class feminists acquiesced to the plan to deny support to poor women, an accusation that McBride (2007: 292) regards as founded. Antifeminist gendering came from both right-wing movements and fathers' rights groups. In this debate, although the interests of poor black women were under threat, attention was focused mainly on class and gender interests. Despite long-standing and general recognition that campaigns against welfare benefits in the United States are racist, race does not appear to have been a preoccupation of the movement actors in the debate. The issue was not a priority for the movement, which was also divided about the goals of welfare policy. The near-silence on race may have reflected public discourse on race more generally. However, McBride argues that movement failure on the issue reflects a failure to focus on the interplay of race, gender, and class.

Canadian Jobs Strategy to Combat Unemployment, 1984–1985

Diversity was built into the debate on Canadian job training strategy. By the mid-1980s in Canada, state institutions were organized to take responsibility for diversity effects. Hence the initiating document on job training strategy stressed the "importance of addressing the specific needs of disadvantaged groups in particular women, people living with a disability, aboriginal people and immigrants" (Teghtsoonian and Grace 2001: 242). Provision was made for women's movement actors to participate in the debate, including representatives of immigrants and minority women. The final policy contained a fair number of elements that both matched their preferences and incorporated diversity. For example, the law included provision for participation targets for women and minority groups. In Canada at that time, the founding logic of agencies required them to consider diversity, and this was reflected in movement organization and debates (Teghtsoonian and Grace 2001: 242).

TABLE 8.1 WOMEN'S MOVEMENT ACTOR INTERVENTION BY
INSTITUTIONAL BASE AND ISSUE

Issue	INSTITUTIONAL BASE					
	Parliament/ Legislature	Political Party	Trade Union	Other Non–Women's Movement Organizations	Auton-omous	Total
Abortion	14	10	1	6	29	60
Job training	5	7	11	9	10	42
Prostitution	7	4	0	7	24	42
Political representation	14	11	2	8	15	50
Hot issue	6	3	1	4	9	23
Total	46	35	15	34	87	217

act for women are necessarily indirect. Agency relationships to women's movements are often left unspecified, given that RNGS concept definitions *assume* that movement actors speak for women.[13] Therefore, when other actors, like women's policy agencies, articulate ideas that coincide with those of movement actors, they represent women. For the agencies, such claims derive from mandates made by governments, usually on the basis of fairly specific briefs,[14] and may or may not involve regular consultation with movement representatives. Weldon (2002a) argues that agency interventions facilitate movement representation when reliable arrangements for consultation with autonomous movements are in place. Although we lack systematic evidence of the patterns of consultations with women's movements, we do have data on the presence of movement ideas in agency microframes and also on the presence of women's movement experience in the form of officials with movement experience. In sixty-three of the sixty-six cases for which we have evidence both on agency representativeness and on movement actor and agency microframe fit, agency microframes either match or are compatible with those of movement actors. In thirty-eight such cases, the microframes match; hence, agencies are representative of movement actors. The data also provide evidence that agency leaders may be influenced by women's movement and feminist ideas or may have backgrounds in women's movements.

Statistical correlations suggest the existence of a policy triangle linking some women legislators, movement actors, and agencies. Agency representativeness associates positively with movement actor presence at the end of the debate (.275*), which is also positively associated with the presence of women legislators in the debate (.429**), the number of women legislators who intervened (.412**), and with movement agreement (.347**), but not with the percentage of women in the lower house of the legislature—a finding that warrants further research.[15] Technically, women legislators are also movement actors and appear in the dataset as such. This raises the question of overlap in the data and means that we cannot be confident of the correlations. When the cases in which women legislators intervene are removed from the dataset, the correlations between agency representativeness and movement actor presence disappear—an effect that may suggest that those legislators who intervene are a key element to the relationships on which policy triangles are based. Although we are stretching the data beyond its reach, these findings suggest that intervention by women legislators enhances movement participation but the percentage of women in the legislature does not. Is this preliminary evidence of critical acts that enhance the representation of women? We return to these discussions in our conclusions.

3. Which Women Are Represented?

The question raises issues of difference among women. The data presented here describe instances of both feminist and nonfeminist representation, whereas the two case studies (see Box 8.1) include some consideration of diversity but not intersectionality, as such. To construct an answer to this question, we read off claims about who is represented in the different debates from their responsibilities to their organization or movement. In each debate, movement actors advocate for those women's movements interested in the issue, including sometimes feminist movements. Because the perceived interests of different groups of women vary by debate issues, so also does the pattern of intervention.

Table 8.1 indicates that interventions in abortion debates mobilized a range of movement actors concentrated in free-standing groups and, to a lesser extent, in parliaments. Job training debates predictably mobilized trade unions; eleven of the fifteen interventions by trade union movement actors were in job training debates. Prostitution debates most often engaged autonomous movements. Political representation debates engaged women legislators as well as party and autonomous movement actors, while hot-issue debates attracted the attention of autonomous and parliamentary women. Autonomous movement actors were the most consistently active, often speaking for issue-specific groups. Actors in legislatures, in trade unions, and with other institutional affiliations may have responsibilities to represent women within the context of their organization but will normally also be required to be responsible to wider membership, electors, and the goals of their organization. In other words, they operate within the normal lines of political contestation and are thereby constrained. In so doing, they may have responsibilities to act on behalf of particular groups of women and in opposition to the interests of other women.

As Table 8.2 shows, in thirty-six debates, agencies either did not represent women's movements or they advanced frames that threatened those of the women's movements. Agencies attempted representation in seventy-two debates, gendering thirty-eight of them. They were least likely to intervene in hot-issue debates. To interpret these findings in terms of the question of which women are represented, we need to turn to our qualitative evidence, which shows that the groups of women for whom claims to representation were made varied by

TABLE 8.2   POLICY AGENCY INTERVENTIONS BY DEBATE ISSUE
AND PERCENTAGES

Issue	No Intervention or Intervention Does Not Advance Movement Actors' Frames	Intervention Advances Movement Frames But Not Gender Debate	Intervention Advances Movement Frames and Gender Debate	Total Number of Debates
Abortion	11 (40.7%)	7 (25.9%)	9 (33.3%)	27
Job training	6 (27.2%)	12 (54.5%)	4 (18.2%)	22
Prostitution	6 (23%)	10 (38.5%)	10 (38.5%)	26
Political representation	6 (28.6)	3 (14.2%)	12 (57.1%)	21
Hot issue	7 (58.3%)	2 (16.7%)	3 (25%)	12
Total	36	34	38	108

debate and type of representative. This tells us a little about the different groups of women who are represented. Interventions in job training debates were designed to improve the position of employed women or women seeking employment (Mazur 2001). In the abortion debates, women's rights were framed in a variety of contexts. In Great Britain and the United States, some attention was given by advocates to the needs of those women who were dependent on public provision for abortions (poorer, therefore more likely to be young and to belong to an ethnic minority) (McBride Stetson 2001a,c). In Great Britain, minority women's movement actors explicitly asserted separate interests in abortion debates. In prostitution debates, some movement actors and some agencies advocated on behalf of prostitutes and of trafficked women and children and against their clients, but frames did not normally highlight differences among women. In a few cases, however (the Netherlands, Italy, Finland), it was noted that many prostitutes were foreign (Outshoorn 2004). In political representation debates, different roles, social characteristics, and interests of women were sometimes highlighted, as attention was drawn to the requirements of mothers, the relationships between women's claims and those of others (e.g., ethnic or linguistic minorities) (Lovenduski 2005). In the smaller sample of hot-issue debates, references to different groups of women varied by the issue under consideration (Haussman and Sauer 2007). Parliamentary women, often divided along party lines, were most likely to express movement microframes on political representation and abortion debates.

Because difference has been a consistently important concern in feminist movements, we expect that feminist interventions were sensitive to it. Feminist concerns were advanced by fifty-five agencies. To the extent that feminist and women's movement discourse was imbued with ideas about difference, and this was reflected in representation, then we can infer that ideas about different groups of women were taken into account. But this is an imperfect process, and we are not in a position to make a systematic quantitative assessment of which of the various categories of women were represented in discourse, in terms of their class, race, education, marital status, and so forth. While we can only infer so much from the classification of frames as feminist, we can explore the issue of diversity further, by looking at the two case studies described in Box 8.1.

Discourses of gender diversity seem to be confined mainly to considerations of class in the debates, with an occasional genuflection to race. The data do not suggest that diversity issues were central to representation. Though advocates did not deny, and indeed frequently affirmed, the diversity of women—with the exception of some of the political representation debates—and despite some mobilization of minority women's movements, intersectionality did not receive much attention. On these issues and at this level of decision making, women's movement actors are ineffective when they express concerns about diversity, and women continue to be treated as a unitary category. Outshoorn and Johanna Kantola note the slowness of governments to "recognise diversity among women and to take it into account in policy" and the tendency for "agencies to take women as an undifferentiated category . . . with the attendant danger of paying too little heed to minority voices" (2007: 279–280). Religious, class, and regional differences may be reflected in party systems that are more or less responsive to their women's advocates. However, in systems where the state and party institutions do not reflect a difference among women—often because there is no corresponding politically salient difference among men—neither does the agency. This is a pattern that began to change in the 2000s, especially after European legislation to protect various diversity strands came into force; but most of our debates took place before this change, and few of them portend it. The ideally gendered representation of diversity that is so central to feminist concerns translates only poorly through institutional political structures, which are designed to aggregate and not to differentiate interests.

4. What Policies Are Put Forward by Representatives; What Representations Are Made?

Feminist scholars argue that representatives should advance women's interests but falter when it comes to producing a reliable and accepted definition of those interests. Frequently, expressed preferences are treated as proxies for interests. Following this logic, the relevant research question here becomes: Do representatives put forward claims that are made by women's movements? In classic representation theory, representatives advance the interests of the represented either as delegates who act *as* those they represent, putting forward the policies advocated by their voters (or whoever appoints or elects them), or as trustees who act *for*, that is, attempt to learn and advance, or even to construct, the interests of those they claim to represent. Although we cannot determine if representatives see themselves as delegates or trustees without asking them, we can observe their interventions in relation to movement issues and infer from our observations that expressed movement interests are (or are not) represented.

The policies that are put forward by representatives are a significant part of the basis of their claims to represent. Our data indicate (1) the top five movement priorities at the time of the debate; (2) whether the interventions of movement actors were made on issues that were movement priorities; (3) which categories of movement actors intervened; and then (4) whether movement concerns were expressed by each category of representative.

Accordingly, we identify actor, agency, and legislator presence in each debate that took place while they were among the top five women's movement priorities. We then compare these with interventions on issues that were not top priorities. For each debate, we identify which types of actors participated. Finally, we inspect the content of the interventions to determine whether movement actor and agency official interventions were congruent and how congruence varied by type of actor.

All three expressed gendered microframes in both priority and nonpriority debates. These are presented in Tables 8.3 and 8.4.

Table 8.3 shows that in most of the seventy-nine debates that were on priority issues, agencies advanced gendered microframes; autonomous and integrated movement actors and legislators intervened in just under half of them, but separate interventions by autonomous and integrated actors were much less frequent.

In the thirty-five nonpriority debates shown in Table 8.4, the pattern is not the expected mirror image. The last row of the table gives interventions by each category of actor on nonpriority issues as a percentage of their total interventions. While this calculation is admittedly crude, it is quite instructive. If we could verify the patterns suggested by the tables, then the percentages would suggest that on the debate issues studied by RNGS, women legislators and coalitions of autonomous and integrated movement actors are more likely to act as delegates who put forward women's movement priorities than agencies and movement actors acting separately, who in turn are more likely to act as trustees taking a position on issues that were not movement priorities. This does not

TABLE 8.3   REPRESENTATION IN PRIORITY ISSUE DEBATES AND PERCENTAGE OF INTERVENTIONS

Issue	Agency Advances Gendered Microframe	Autonomous Movement Actors	Integrated Movement Actors	Autonomous and Integrated Movement Actors	Legislators	Number of Debates
Abortion	19 (31%)	11 (58%)	1 (8%)	18 (38%)	14 (37%)	30
Job training	12 (19%)	3 (16%)	6 (46%)	4 (9%)	3 (8%)	13
Prostitution	7 (11%)	1 (5%)	0 (0%)	6 (13%)	4 (11%)	7
Political representation	16 (25%)	1 (5%)	3 (23%)	14 (30%)	12 (32%)	8
Hot issue	8 (13%)	3 (16%)	3 (23%)	5 (13%)	5 (13%)	11
Total	62	19	13	38	38	79

TABLE 8.4   REPRESENTATION IN NONPRIORITY ISSUE DEBATES AND
PERCENTAGE OF NONPRIORITY ISSUE INTERVENTIONS
OF ALL INTERVENTIONS BY ACTOR

Issue	Agency Advances Gendered Microframe	Autonomous Movement Actors	Integrated Movement Actors	Autonomous and Integrated Movement Actors	Legislators	Number of Debates
Abortion	1 (3%)	0	1 (10%)	0	0	1
Job training	9 (31%)	2 (17%)	5 (50%)	1 (11%)	2 (25%)	9
Prostitution	15 (52%)	10 (83%)	2 (20%)	7 (78%)	3 (38%)	20
Political representation	4 (14%)	0	2 (20%)	0	2 (25%)	4
Hot issue	0	0	0	1 (11%)	1 (13%)	1
Total of nonpriority interventions	29	12	10	9	8	35
Percentage of all interventions	36% (N = 81)	39% (N = 31)	43% (N = 23)	19% (N = 47)	17% (N = 46)	N = 228

mean that the positions are not in movement interests, which may have been under construction. It means only that movements were not at the time giving priority to the issue being debated and may have preferred representatives to be spending their time on the issues that were priorities.

To deepen our understanding of the representativeness of the interventions, we also inspect the content of the microframes. Where both agencies and movement actors have microframes on debate issues, we can inspect their fit with each other. Policy agencies mainly attempted to gender debates that were about movement priority issues. In the majority of cases, agency officials attempted to represent the preferences expressed by women's movement actors by inserting matching microframes into policy debates, and, in a substantial minority of cases, the shared microframes were feminist. The pattern is clear. Agencies seemed more likely to advance movement frames on those movement priority issues on which both autonomous and integrated actors were active, and they did not intervene in cases where autonomous movements acted alone. Similarly, women legislators were most likely to express movement microframes where both autonomous and integrated movements and organizations were engaged. Otherwise, they expressed microframes in debates in which integrated movements acted alone but did not speak in support in those debates in which autonomous movements acted alone.[16]

Initial statistical testing of the associations indicates that more women legislators intervened when the issue was a movement priority (.207*). Movement actor presence at the end of the debate rose with movement actor agreement (.347**). However, although agency representativeness varied with movement actor presence (.275*), it did not vary consistently and significantly with movement issue priority or with movement actor agreement.

5. Where Are the Policies Put Forward?

Affecting representation are the political system or country in which the debate takes place, the institutional sites (especially their proximity to power) at which the debate is conducted, and the bases from which the debate's participants operate. We propose that the citizenship model, the policy environment, the institutionalization of the women's movement, the type of institution, and the proximity of agencies to power all affect actor behavior in debates.

Most of the debates took place in Western and Northern European democratic systems. Reasoning that citizenship models were important to the framing of representation debates, we classified these systems in ascending order according to their responsiveness to claims for group representation, with republican systems least likely, followed by liberal, hybrid, and consociational corporatist (Krook, Lovenduski, and Squires 2009).[17]

We found significant and strong positive associations between citizenship type and the percentage of women in the lower house (.457**). This is an expected effect of the tendency of hybrid and corporatist systems to have relatively high numbers of women in the parliament. The positive association of citizenship model with legislator presence in these debates is weaker but nonetheless significant (.233*), as it is with the intervention of women legislators (.234*). But we found no associations with movement presence in policy subsystems or agency representativeness, suggesting that women's representation is not well provided for via established systems of extraparliamentary group representation, and that women are outsiders in established interest group politics.

As several earlier chapters have indicated, theories of public policy highlight the policy sector as a crucial determinant of the nature and outcome of policy debates. Access to the policy subsystem is a crucial group resource. Where systems are closed, only those inside have access; hence, the relative openness of the policy subsystem in which a decision is made is an important element of the ability of movements to participate. As expected, women's movement presence in the policy subsystem was positively associated with the openness of the policy subsystem (.331**), a finding that was unaffected by the political complexion of the government in power at the time of the debate. The representativeness of the policy agency is not associated with the degree of openness of the policy subsystem. However, in cases in which the policy subsystem is closed, there is a strong association between movement actor presence and women legislator intervention (.664**). When compared to the correlation of .412** of these variables in all debates, this finding suggests that in closed systems, where access is at a premium, women legislators will be important points of access.

Debates were conducted and, in practice, were decided upon in a variety of locations, but for the most part, were eventually decided in the legislature (92 of 114), at least on a formal basis. In most legislatures, both women and men are likely to be represented by men who in all but a few countries operate in contexts that are constrained by party discipline and party manifestos, institutions that historically are dominated by men and male concerns. In such systems, women's movements and agency officials may actually have more scope to represent women than legislators bound by party discipline. For example, party discipline affects the behavior of parliamentary women, who may vote with their party and against movement preferences that they have otherwise supported, as did the women legislators of the Center Right in the Italian debate on constitutional reform between 1992 and 2001 (Guadagnini 2007).

The RNGS research strategy of debate tracing brings the legislature to the fore through its requirement that the debate must have an end point in an official authoritative decision. Constitutionally, this is often the legislature. However, in European party democracies, where legislatures do not necessarily hold the ultimate decision-making power, it is normal to give legitimacy to decisions made whether publicly or behind the scenes elsewhere in the system by the executive or the political parties, or both. Thus, the very high proportion of issues that were debated in parliament may be more an indicator of system type than of decision point, and we should, therefore, assume that other institutions were involved, especially political parties; this issue, for reasons of space, is not discussed in this chapter.[18] Although intervention by parliamentary women is important, it is only one aspect of the decision system.

In the ninety-two debates that were wholly or partly conducted in parliament, neither the presence of movement actors in the policy subsystem nor the interventions of women legislators were associated significantly with the percentage of women legislators. This finding suggests that numbers determine neither acts nor effectiveness, and, hence, has implications for the critical-mass debate. Have we demonstrated conclusively, then, that critical acts are independent of numbers? We return to this question in our conclusions.

Women's movement institutionalization is a measure of the relative degree of presence of movement activists representing ideas and agendas of the collective women's movement inside social, political, and authoritative state institutions. It refers to the extent to which movement actors are in legislatures, well-established lobby coalitions, bureaucratic and legislative commissions, political parties, unions, interest groups, academia, media, and formal campaigns. This conceptualization treats institutionalization in terms of levels or degrees. It is effectively a count of presence across an extensive range of key decision-making institutions and is, therefore, an indicator of descriptive representation.[19] The institutionalization of the women's movements was not significantly associated with movement actor participation or with agency representativeness. However, our expectation that high levels of women's movement institutionalization might overcome the barriers of a closed policy subsystem to movement actor presence in policy subsystems was confirmed with a significant positive association between them of .332** in closed policy systems.

In terms of their proximity to government power, most women's policy agencies were part of the top echelon of decision-making power in their institutional context. The closeness of the agency most involved in the debate to the center of power co-varies with the presence of women legislators (.204*) but is not associated with the number of women legislator interventions, movement actor presence, or agency representativeness.

To summarize, that citizenship models are associated with the presence of women in the legislature does not predict movement actor presence in the policy subsystem or agency representativeness. Open policy subsystems benefited movement actor presence. Debates in parliament provided a useful site to test arguments about critical mass. In such debates, the interventions of parliamentary women enhanced movement actor presence, but this effect was not associated with the percentage of women legislators. Women legislators were more likely to intervene in debates in which both autonomous and integrated movement actors engaged, one of several associations that support claims that cross-movement cooperation is more powerful than feminist separatism. Finally, neither movement institutionalization nor agency proximity to the center of power predicted movement participation or agency representativeness.

6. When Does Representation Take Place?

Political time is complex; hence, this question has several dimensions, including proximity to election years; the phases of the world and national economies; the public opinion cycle; the timetable of the decision process and sequence, or whether the debate followed a victory or defeat for the movement; favorable political climate and consensus around priorities, issues, and policy content. The most straightforward usage is the dates of debates. The RNGS sample of debates was selected to be representative of each decade since the emergence of the new women's movements in the 1960s. This period extends from the 1960s to the early 2000s, with some concentration of debates in the 1990s.[20] If policy agencies become more likely to act in concert with movement actors over time, we expect to see an increase in the degree to which they express the same microframes on movement priority issues. We found no statistically significant relationship between the fit of the movement actor and agency microframes and the decade in which the debate takes place.

The issue books offer insight into some aspects of sequence, the effects of which vary by issue type. For example, while the analysis of job training debates revealed a widespread context characterized by movement away from male breadwinner models of employment, this was not reflected in a change over time in the success of women's movements in gaining substantive and descriptive representation. Nor did the data on this issue suggest a link between economic cycles and variation in agency performance over time (Mazur 2001: 309–310). Sequence effects vary by issue. McBride Stetson found that sequence had some effect in abortion debates. Once debates were gendered, the frame tended to last through subsequent debates on the same issue, although this pattern was not universal (2001a: 274–275). On the issue of prostitution, however, the achievement of representation does not ensure access in subsequent debates (Outshoorn 2004: 270). No systematic sequential cross-national patterns were found in debates on political representation either (Lovenduski et al. 2005: 291).

We can infer changes in the political climate from the position of the government on the Left-Right political spectrum and the ideological and organizational closeness of the women's movement to the Left. We found that the ideological and organizational closeness of the movements to the Left increased over time (.270** and .267**, respectively) and expected that when the Left was in power and movements were close to the Left, they would have both procedural access and the benefit of having their microframes advanced by policy agencies. However, this prediction proved unfounded.

7. Why Are Representations Made?

Decisions to represent are, like any decisions to undertake political action, based on motivation, obligation, or opportunity—or a combination thereof. Motivation follows from interests and desire, obligation from legal and/or moral responsibility, and opportunity from a combination of capacity and position. For all actors, we expect motivation, obligation, and opportunity to vary by debate issue, citizenship model, the number of women in parliament, and the position on the Right-Left spectrum of the government in power.

The obligation of movement actors to represent movement interests is moral and in this research is a matter of definition. Agency obligations are legal and may also be moral; they do not necessarily include representation of women's movements but may vary with the feminism of the leadership. Legislators have opportunity in the sense that so many debates are decided in parliaments but, as we have seen, may be constrained by their party and perhaps by institutional convention and procedures. We explore the patterns for each category of actor.

There are at least four ways in which actor motivation to intervene may vary: according to cohesion, threat, feminism, and priority. If an issue is of high priority to the women's movement, we expect that its actors will make claims, and we hope that agencies and legislators will support them. Movement cohesion did not have predictive value. At least half of movement actors were in agreement on all but one issue, and on most issues there was complete agreement within the part of the movement that was interested in the issue. Despite their theoretical promise, motivation variables of cohesion, priority, and degree of threat did not add to the explanation of movement actor participation.

The concept of opportunity had more predictive value. We understand opportunity as a feature of the political configuration at the time of the debate and of the associated winnability of the debate. Relevant here are the relationships of the movement to the Left, the party in power, the proportion of women parliamentarians, the institutionalization of the movement, and the winnability of the debate. Movement actor presence rises with some indicators of the political opportunity structure but not others. In addition to legislator intervention and agency representativeness (already discussed), we found that actor presence in policy subsystems co-varies with the institutionalization of the women's movement (.235*) but not with the percentage of women in parliament or closeness of the movement to the Left or the presence of a left-wing party in government.

The winnability of the debate is a difficult condition to quantify in a convincing way. Arguably, some debates are more winnable than others, which may affect strategic decisions to intervene by representatives. Some issues are more susceptible to gender reframing. One aspect of debate winnability is that some policy subsystems are amenable to explicitly gendered debate frames. How well do the frames of movement actors match the frames of the policy subsystem in which the debate is resolved? It could be said that where movement and subsystem frames are matching or compatible, the debate is more winnable for the movement; yet tests for correlation do not confirm this notion. RNGS measures the compatibility of the microframe of movement actors with the issue frame that initially shapes the debate in the policy subsystem. In more than half the cases (58 percent), movement actors' frames were compatible with those of the policy subsystem actors. Table 8.5 shows that issue frames were most likely to be gendered at the end of debate when the initial subsystem frame matched that of the movement actors, while compatible frames predicted a less than even chance of debate frame gendering. Movement actor presence in the policy subsystem was not significantly associated with the frame fit between actors and policy subsystems, but it correlated strongly with the gendering of the issue frame by the end of the debate (.417**). These seemingly perverse findings may result from a greater reluctance on the part of decision makers to adjust policy when frames are compatible but not matching, a possibility that requires further investigation.

The data include observations of feminist issue frames at both the beginning and end of the debate. Twenty-five debate frames were feminist at the beginning of the debate and forty-five at the end. Movement actor presence in the policy subsystem was positively correlated to feminist frames at beginning (.395*) and at end of the debates (.369*).

We discussed priority at length in question 4 above. Here we extend that discussion to consider the question of why movement actors might support issues that are not among movement top priorities. This occurred most often in prostitution debates, where 56 percent of agency and 32 percent of movement nonpriority interventions were made. An issue that is difficult for women's advocates to ignore, prostitution touches on aspects of sexuality and, once under consideration, highlights the state habit of regulating sexual behavior, a habit of considerable importance to feminists. As Outshoorn (2004) and others have shown, prostitution debates feature many gradations of gender content that are stressed by women's movements seeking to gender debates on this issue. It is also an issue on which women's movements are not cohesive.

TABLE 8.5   ISSUE FRAME AT THE END OF DEBATE BY ISSUE FRAME FIT

| Issue Frame Fit | ISSUE FRAME GENDERED AT END OF DEBATE | | Total |
	Yes (%)	No (%)	
Threatening	10 (71)	4 (29)	14
Mixed	27 (77)	8 (23)	35
Compatible	23 (48)	25 (52)	48
Matching	15 (88)	2 (12)	17
N	75 (66)	39 (34)	114

Prostitution debate frames are polarized and controversial. The rights of prostitutes are interpreted either as sex work or in terms of sexual oppression. Outshoorn points out that the few women's movements that did give high priority to the prostitution issue did so in debates that took place after 1990. Prostitution debates tend not to be high priorities for movements, which find it difficult to agree to a common problem definition and to maintain agreement once achieved. The relationship between agreement and priority is well illustrated by the Italian debate on prostitution that took place in 1998 presented in Box 8.2.

When we consider the contested and complex frames of the prostitution issue and its conjunction with the importance to movements of what is at stake, it becomes more understandable why movement actor presence, agency representativeness, and movement priority may not coincide. As already discussed, opportunity for agencies is related to their capacity and their location. Policy agency representativeness may also be affected by motivation, obligation, and opportunity. Officials may be *motivated* by the beliefs of their leadership at the time of the debate. They may be *obliged* to intervene by their terms of reference; they may, as professionals charged with advancing women's interests, seek to advance women's movement concerns especially where issues are of high priority to the movements. They may respond to a particular *opportunity* when a public debate of some kind illuminates a women's concern—including those not currently on the movement agenda. Policy agency officials may be inhibited or encouraged by their capacity.

Policy agencies rarely act when the debate is outside of their remit; only ten put forward microframes during debates outside of their remit. Agency representativeness could not be explained by agency capacity, movement issue priority, or feminist leadership.[21] Nor could it be explained by any of the political opportunity variables, except the organizational closeness of the movement to the Left, with which it was negatively associated (–.200*).

For women legislators, opportunity is a function of whether a debate is decided in parliament and of the views of their party on the issue. Legislator intervention was associated with the organizational closeness of the movement to

---

Box 8.2   Case Study: Criminalization of Clients of Underage Prostitutes in Italy, 1998

Changes in ideas during the years before the debate seem to explain women's movement ambivalence about the policy. By the early 1990s, blaming clients for the existence of prostitution was common among both Catholics and feminists, an awkward political combination at best. From 1994 onward, many city mayors ordered municipal traffic police to fine clients in order to reduce street prostitution. At first, feminists welcomed the shift in blame from women to men. However, as the effects of such policies became apparent, feminists withdrew their support, arguing that the resulting measures worsened the working conditions of women on the streets. So, by the time the 1998 bill was debated, punishment of clients was not on the movement agenda, and neither women's movement actors nor women's policy agencies participated in the debates (Danna 2004).

---

the Left (.221*) and could possibly be explained by the impact of party affiliation on motivation and opportunity.

To summarize, except when microframes are feminist at the beginning or end of the debate, movement presence is not predicted by indicators of motivation or opportunity. Agency representativeness is not explained by changes in the opportunity variables, but legislator intervention may depend on opportunity.

8. To Whom Are the Representatives Accountable?

Although not an explicit focus of the RNGS project, the data include useful information about the accountability of representatives to movements. RNGS defines women's and feminist movements in terms of ideas and identifies women's movement actors accordingly. Accountability to ideas may potentially be a powerful constraint but raises questions about who determines what criteria need to be met and if the requirements are satisfied. Representatives have two main modes of acting, which we conceptualize as the poles of a parameter of representativeness. At one pole, we find representatives who are specifically mandated by those represented on an issue to be debated—the delegates. At the other pole, representatives are mandated to act on behalf of those represented by discovering their interests if these are not already agreed upon—the trustees. In practice, delegate representation would be secured only by regular and effective consultation between movements and representatives, including between movement actors and other members (see Weldon 2002a).

At the system level, accountability is a function of the institution in which representatives act. So, where movement actors are in the legislature they are accountable to their electorate, their parties, and their constituencies. Where movement actors are in trade unions, they are accountable to their members and co-workers, whereas in parties they are answerable to their fellow members but also more indirectly to the electorate and to the interests that are the basis of party support. The accountability of a representative to women's movements is not normally constitutionally specified and may or may not figure large in decision making.

While policy agencies may be accountable to women's movements at the level of ideas, movements do not have legal purchase over agency officials; hence, there is very little formal or legal basis for agency accountability to women's movements. Most policy agency leaders owed their jobs not directly to women's movements, but to elected governments; almost all were political appointments. In general, the recruitment of staff and lower level appointments in the agencies followed the appointments conventions of the relevant system (e.g., civil service procedures or corporatist nominees). Thus, whereas women's movements may have been influential in getting agencies established and are often involved in the formal or informal nomination of leaders, they do not have the last word about who are the decision makers and are not in a position to recall unsatisfactory officials. There are exceptions; some agencies are committees of movement representatives or include designated places for movement representatives (Guadagnini and Dona 2007). In addition, many agency officials try to represent women's movements, if only as a means of legitimating their activities by securing movement support.

To return once again to the distinction between trustees and delegates, if agency officials are movement delegates, then we expect them to advance issues that are movement priorities using microframes that match those of movement actors, and in so doing advocate for the movement except when the discourse is adopted solely for symbolic reasons. We have shown that agency officials sometimes do this. At such times, they directly support movement goals. On other occasions, however, agencies make claims on issues that are not movement priorities or advance frames that are not congruent with those of movement actors. On such occasions, they may be acting as trustees—that is, discovering or constructing interests that movements have not yet expressed. Alternatively, they may decide to advocate interests expressed by some movement actors on nonpriority issues. Either way, agencies act as trustees. They might also, of course, act against women's interests and express frames that are opposed to those of women's movement actors.

When agencies intervene on issues that are movement priorities and advance microframes that are congruent with those of movement actors, they are advocates for the women's movement. May we infer accountability because ideas match? This seems a step too far, as crucial elements of accountability are missing. As stated above, generally movements are not invited to select officials and are not in a position to recall them from their roles in state decision-making positions, so traditional accountability is not present. Indeed, autonomous movements are especially constrained, as they have by definition no formal part in the powerful established decision-making institutions and can control only their own delegates where they have such delegates.

Integrated movements may well be in a different position. Party and trade union women's organizations, for example, often determine who are the movement actors within that institution, whereas organized-party women sometimes have considerable influence over who the legislative representatives are and sometimes over who is appointed to a policy agency. Integrated movement actors, by virtue of their presence in channels of representation, have some purchase over traditional levers of accountability. We can stretch this a little farther and state that when women's movements are institutionalized into the traditional institutions that are formally accountable to the electorate via the legislature, they may be able to influence levers of accountability through the activity of movement actors in these contexts. Thus, we can illuminate some dimensions of accountability by exploring the institutionalization of women's movements into decision-making structures.

"Institutionalization is the process by which claims-making by social movements becomes repetitive, revitalized and self-sustaining in response to the internal dynamics of social movements and the imperatives of the external environment" (Mueller and McCarthy 2003: 233). This is not a unitary concept, and different movements achieve different levels of institutionalization that may vary by policy subsystem, by issue type, and by country. We measure this on two related scales: Our distinction between autonomous and integrated movement actors captures some of the variation in women's movements' institutionalization into civil society, while the RNGS institutionalization variable can be used to probe presence in civil society and state institutions together. The data show that only a few movements enjoyed relatively high levels of institutionalization (7 of 114); most movements (79) were at a medium level of institutionalization, and 28 were at a low level of institutionalization.[22] Movement institutionalization rose consistently with the openness of the policy subsystem (.194*), with the ideological (.419**) and organizational (.192*) closeness of the movement to the Left, and with movement presence in the policy subsystem at the end of the debate (.235*), but not with agency representativeness, the receptivity of the citizenship model to group representation, or the presence of the Left in government. The variation with the openness of the policy subsystem suggests that movement actors, who are often outsiders, may benefit from the greater political hospitality of open policy sectors. Of course, relatively greater institutionalization may also portend relatively greater access in closed policy systems.

To summarize, although attention to women's movement ideas about women's interests may affect the representativeness of policy agencies and definitionally inform the microframes of movement actors, ideas are porous channels of accountability. Strictly speaking, agencies are accountable to movements only insofar as the working of the particular democratic system in which they are embedded provides for them to be so accountable. In most democratic systems, that provision is via the legislature and is normally indirect.

9. How Effective Is the Representation?

So far, we have explored the connections predicted by feminist representation theory, testing associations where the data permit by running bivariate correlations. This exploratory research suggests that women's movement actor presence in policy subsystems is explained by movement actor agreement, intervention by women legislators, policy agency representativeness, issue priority, the openness of the policy subsystem, and relative movement institutionalization. The percentage of women in the lower house of the legislature at the time of the debate seems to have no explanatory power for either movement presence or agency representativeness. However, because of its theoretical importance to the critical-mass debate, we will test it in our final models.

To conclude our analysis, we entered each variable into an Ordinal Regression or PLUM, an extension of the linear model to ordinal categorical data.[23] The full model was not substantiated by further statistical testing, which found only the number of women legislator interventions and agency representativeness to be significant, confirming that the acts of women legislators and policy agencies increase the presence of women's movement actors. This result is reported in Table 8.6. As explained in Chapter 4, the last column of the table shows the exponential ratio, $EXP(\beta)$, for each level of the predictor variables. An $EXP(\beta)$ of less than 1 indicates a negative effect, whereas an $EXP(\beta)$ of greater than 1 is a positive effect. Table 8.6, thus, shows that the absence of agency representativeness has an independent negative effect and that legislator intervention has an independent positive effect on movement presence. The likelihood of women's movement actor presence in the policy subsystem at the end of the debate is more than twice as great when women legislators intervene in the debate than when they do not. When the policy agency neither supports nor contradicts movement microframes, the likelihood of movement actor presence is about 80 percent less than when agency and movement actors' frames match and about 89 percent less likely than when the agency does nothing. Thus, we confirm that movement actor presence is enhanced by the acts of legislators and policy-making officials.

Finally, we turn to the interplay between substantive and descriptive representation to consider whether policy agencies and legislators also facilitate substantive representation. The variable State Response counts the occasions when movements achieve either a procedural or a substantive response, neither, or both.[24] Exploratory bivariate analysis indicates that one or more interventions by women legislators is associated (.213*) with the achievement of substantive and descriptive representation—full success for the movement—and this effect is also positively associated (.200*) with the percentage of women in the lower house of parliament. However, there is no association between women's policy agency representativeness and the successful achievement of both substantive and descriptive representation together.

TABLE 8.6   ORDINAL REGRESSION OF WOMEN'S MOVEMENT ACTOR
PRESENCE MODEL

Independent Variable Measures	Parameter Estimate	EXP(β)
Legislator intervention	.846**	2.253
No legislator intervention	Reference category	N/A
Policy agency representativeness: agency microframe incompatible with women's movement actors	− .484	Not significant
Policy agency representativeness: agency does nothing	−2.145***	.1171
Policy agency representativeness: agency advances microframe neither matching nor conflicting	−1.568*	.2008
Policy agency representativeness: agency matches movement actor's microframe	Reference category	N/A

Pseudo R²: Cox and Snell, .299; Nagelkerke, .359; McFadden, .199.

To unpack this further, we created indicators of outcomes of substantive representation (defined as the state meeting movement actor demands without permitting their participation, i.e., Preemption) and descriptive representation (defined as the state permitting movement actor participation without meeting their policy demands, i.e., Co-optation). There were twenty-two cases of substantive representation only and twelve cases of descriptive representation only. These outcomes were not associated with agency representativeness, parliamentary intervention, characteristics of the policy system, or movement institutionalization. Half of the substantive representation debates were on prostitution, underlining the points made above about this issue, but otherwise there was no particular issue-based pattern.

Hence, the final step in our analysis is to test the impact of agencies, legislators, and movements on the achievement of both substantive and descriptive representation, again using the PLUM Ordinal Regression technique and State Response as the dependent variable. We entered movement actor agreement, the presence of women legislators, intervention by women legislators, policy agency representativeness, issue priority, the openness of the policy system, movement institutionalization, and percentage of women in the lower house of the legislature into the regression, finding that only agency representativeness was independently positively associated with successful movement actor representation on both descriptive and substantive representation. However, legislator intervention was almost as significant, and, when entered into a streamlined model, it proved to be a predictor of movement success independently of agency representativeness.

Table 8.7 shows a significant positive association between women legislator presence and the achievement of both procedural and substantive movement success in systems in which a women's policy agency exists. Where one or more women legislators take a stand in the debate, movements are more than twice as likely to achieve both substantive and descriptive representation than

TABLE 8.7 ORDINAL REGRESSION OF THE ACHIEVEMENT OF BOTH
SUBSTANTIVE AND DESCRIPTIVE REPRESENTATION

Independent Variable Measures	Parameter Estimate	EXP(β)
Women legislators present	.835*	2.305
Women legislators not present	Reference category	N/A
Policy agency representativeness: agency microframe incompatible with women's movement actors	Not significant	N/A
Policy agency representativeness: agency does nothing	−1.158*	.3141
Policy agency representativeness: agency advances microframe neither matching nor conflicting	Not significant	N/A
Policy agency representativeness: agency matches movement actor's microframe	Reference category	N/A

Pseudo R^2: Cox and Snell, .09; Nagelkerke, .104; McFadden, .047. Link function: Logit.

when no legislators do so. Where an agency does nothing, movements are about one third less likely to achieve both kinds of representation than when agency frames match movement frames.

Conclusion

One version of the policy triangle model is partly supported by our research, which identifies three important components: movement actors, policy agencies, and women legislators. But the linkages within this triangle exist only under certain conditions. Intervention by women legislators is not associated with agency representativeness. The pattern is not triangular but consists of converging lines in which agencies act independently, while movement actor success is boosted by the acts of women legislators. The association between interventions by parliamentary women and the agreement of autonomous and integrated movement actors suggests yet a different type of linkage and indicates that effective action is most likely to come from a division of labor between autonomous and integrated feminists and other feminist policy actors, including politicians and state officials.

Thus, we add to the evidence that substantive and descriptive representation are linked through the critical acts of women legislators and of policy agencies that assist their achievement by women's movement actors, independently of the nature of the policy system and the percentage of women in the legislature. We suggest that the standard critical-mass account of representation does not pay enough attention to the nature of the institutions in which representation takes place. The political affiliations and preferences of women legislators may be crucial to their position and capacities as critical actors. Our research reinforces the contention that it is critical acts and not critical mass that determine movement success, but it also points to the need for further work that is sensitive to the interplay between actors in different institutional contexts. Moreover, the full RNGS dataset provides some evidence that the percentage of women legislators in conjunction with their political party affiliations may be especially important to policy success, although this discussion is beyond the scope of this chapter.[25] The analysis in Chapter 4 confirms that important alliances are formed between left-wing legislators and women's movement actors.

Accountability is the hidden dragon of feminist representation theory, some of which can be read as a catalogue of justifications for demands for the accountability of state actors to women's movements. But that is not how democratic political systems are constructed. Accountability exists through imperfect, formally democratic processes, in which movement voices are absorbed into aggregating electoral politics that were not designed to take account of the interests of women. Women's movements aim to correct the resulting imbalances, but their effectiveness is limited by the nature of the systems in which they operate. There is very little feminist political representation theory that acknowledges this problem in real political systems. Jane Mansbridge's discussion of accountability is an honorable and useful exception (2003). However, although her theories are advanced as though they are of general applicability to democratic deliberation, it is difficult to fit them to the cases of party government that are characteristic of the eleven European democracies in our research, in which voters have little choice of candidate and legislators are subject to party discipline. Policy agencies cannot make up the shortfall. The accountability of movement to agency is rarely direct and is generally a matter of the arrangements in whatever part of the state women's policy agencies are located.

The claims of movement actors also raise accountability issues. The representativeness of movement actors observed in the research is an issue frequently raised by RNGS critics, who argue that the project does not take account of all parts of the women's movement but only of those active on a particular issue (Squires 2007). This, it is argued, privileges certain kinds of actors and certain parts of the movement. In fact, the concern with movement actors who have a microframe on the issue results from the debate focus of the research design. We study movements in relation to debates because it gives a clearer picture of the existence and effectiveness of movement representation. This specificity has the advantage of accuracy. By starting with debates and naming movement actors within them, we keep the question of movement actor intervention a research question, a matter for empirical observation.

Does our analysis support the contention that the descriptive representation of women is necessary for their substantive representation? It seems so. We find that legislator and agency interventions enhance the achievement of movement representation. Such interventions depend on the presence of women legislators. Moreover, combinations of autonomous and integrated women's movement actors are more effective than either acting independently. It is difficult to resist the conclusion that for successful political representation, the women's movements need both presence and action in representative institutions to achieve their goals.

Although this chapter has provided some of the answers to all of the questions it raises, it has inevitably highlighted new avenues of research. Each research question suggests an extensive research project of its own and generates a set of data requirements, some of which require new survey instruments and fieldwork. Yet each also offers a starting point for extending research on political representation. Viewed through the lenses of representation theories, the RNGS research contributes to knowledge of processes and effects of the intervention in policy debates by movement actors, agency officials, and women legislators, and offers some support for movement engagement with the state.

9

Framing and Gendering

Birgit Sauer

The concept of framing is an essential component of the state feminism framework examined in the first part of this book, but it is not the central focus of the analysis. The aim of this chapter is to use information collected about the 130 policy debates from the RNGS study to explore propositions about framing as an important strategy for political actors and, in doing so, contribute to the accumulation of knowledge about movements, framing, and policy in political science. There are several strands of interest. In the last decade, the struggle over definitions and meanings of public policy moved to the center of the study of democracies (Gamson and Meyer 1996). Political ideas are not given; to the contrary, they are contested. Therefore, society-based groups and state actors align themselves with definitions of policy issues that might reflect their positions and aims. Political scientists have found that discourses, ideas, and frames are important sources of power. The struggle over their meaning (i.e., discursive politics) has increasingly become the focus of political analysis. This chapter considers different approaches to frame analysis and discursive policy analysis found in the fields of social and women's movement research (Zald 1996; Whittier 2002; Kenney 2003; Beckwith 2005; Schoen and Rein 1994; Snow and Benford 1992; Kingdon 1995), discursive institutionalism (Schmidt 2008), discursive policy analysis (Fischer 2003; Hajer and Wagenaar 2003), and feminist policy research (Bacchi 1999, 2005; Ferree et al. 2002; Squires 2005; Verloo and Lombardo 2007; Lombardo, Meier, and Verloo 2009a).

Frames are "organized ideas" that provide at least some "coherence to a designated set of elements" (Ferree et al. 2002: 105). Framing organizes perceptions of social and political problems and gives meaning to specific situations and issues. In the studies of social movements, frames are seen as modes of defining problems and as structures of organized meanings (Snow and Benford 1992; Gamson 1988). Framing refers to the way in which actors define policy issues in terms of problems (diagnosis) and policy goals (prognosis) (Benford and Snow 2000; Zald 1996).

Analysts agree that there is an important connection between the definition or framing of a policy problem and, eventually, policy outcomes (Schattschneider 1960; Kingdon 1995; Cobb and Elder 1983; Schneider and Ingram 1993; Muller 1990). Frames shape agenda-setting processes as well as decision making, and might also influence policy implementation. The opportunity to shape the overall idea of a policy gives power to collective actors from outside state institutions. They can, thus, insert their ideas into the policy process and realize their interests by changing the policy discourse and the underlying ideas in a specific policy environment in which the policy decisions are prepared. Such a change in framing constitutes one form of process change because it brings ideas and interests of new groups into the policy discourse and changes substantive representation. Moreover, outside actors are at the same time "constructed" as participants by the specific framing of an issue. In other words, a specific framing of an issue might mobilize collective action and allow these actors, and not others, to participate in a policy debate. Thus, since framing might open the door to power for women's movements, it becomes a political strategy to gain substantive and descriptive representation. Frames produce political action (Benford and Snow 2000: 631) and compose part of the cultural or discursive opportunity structure (Burstein 1999; Ferree et al. 2002). The cross-issue, cross-time, and cross-country analyses of this chapter seek to contribute to the fast-growing political science literature on framing by giving detailed empirical evidence on how women's movements and policies, as well as civil society and state, are connected through framing.

As described more fully in Chapter 2, the research plan of the RNGS project discerns *general frames, issue frames,* and *microframes.* A *general frame* refers to wide-range definitions, that is, to a "universe of political discourse" (Jenson 1989), or what Bob Jessop (1994) calls the "state project," for instance, the "welfare state." Gender equality might be such a wide general frame of the women's movement (Lombardo, Meier, and Verloo 2009a). The *issue frame* is the meaning of a specific policy area, used by actors in this specific policy subsystem in a specific policy debate, such as employment, health, or environment policy. Typical issue frames in abortion debates, for example, are health frames; in prostitution debates, we find crime frames. Such frames can be welcoming to the women's movement activists' ideas, or they can be hostile.

A *microframe* is the position that specific actors, both inside and outside of the state (e.g., bureaucratic agencies, political parties, interest groups, and women's movements) seek to insert into the issue frame to change the definition of the issue and policy content. Microframes express discourses and ideas of individuals or organizations. Individuals and organizations in women's movements are such actors who, with their microframes, attempt to weigh into the debates at the level of the policy subsystem.

The concept of state feminism used in this book places certain aspects of framing as indicators as well as drivers of women's movement success and agency effectiveness. For example, movement success is defined as the compatibility of policy content with movement microframes expressed in the debate.

The compatibility of ideas of women's movement actors who take a position in a debate with the frames that characterize the given policy environment is explored as a central explanatory factor in the success of women's movements. Moreover, it is shown, in Part II of the book, that the role of women's policy agencies in mediating between women's movements and the policy environments may also be crucial—namely, the gendering or de-gendering of an issue by the agencies in a way that the perceptions of the issue by policy actors coincide with the movement frames in the debate (also see Ferree and Gamson 2003). Women's policy agencies that effectively insert women's movement frames into policy debates are influential in enhancing Movement State Feminism in two respects: They facilitate the entry of women's movement actors in the policy arena, and they shape the policy outcome according to the women's movements ideas and goals. Alliances between women's movements and women's policy agencies are likely to occur through an agreement on frames—that is, on the definition of the policy issue at stake and on the vision of the policy solution.

The state feminism framework also assumes that gendered issue frames help to put the aims of women's movement actors on the political agenda and that the gendering of an issue is important for the substantive and descriptive success of the women's movement. The major assumption is that frames are the "glue" to policy change, for the participation of women's movement actors, and for state feminism. The framing of a policy issue is a way to enhance the likelihood that women's movement actors will be able to change the content of a policy and to bring forward the quantitative representation of women in a policy arena.

This chapter seeks to fill in the blanks relating to the content of women's movement framing in the RNGS policy debates, classifying the content of microframes expressed by women's movement actors.[1] Then it uses information from the RNGS dataset to examine changes in issue frames and their relation to women's policy agency frames. While the role of framing is widely acknowledged in the political science literature, not much systematic empirical research has been conducted on the influence of frames in a policy process in which women's movements were involved. The first section investigates in detail how these frames attempt to gender policies in the issues of abortion, job training, prostitution, political representation, and hot issues of state restructuring over the last three decades. Did the frames change over time? Are there country-specific patterns of frames? Do clusters of countries exist that show commonalities in framing a specific policy issue and across the five issues? Are there specific groups of frames that shape specific issues? Case studies will show how women's movement actors brought issues onto the agenda by strategic framing of policy problems.

Second, the chapter looks at patterns of the issue frames of policy actors. Given that changes in issue frames are an indication of cultural change inside the state, it explores patterns in the frames over time and whether cultural change toward gender equality has occurred. Is there cross-country variation in framing issues? To what extent were women's movements able to change frames in policy debates over time? What leads to a gendered or de-gendered issue frame?

The third section examines the important nexus between women's movement microframes and policy actors' issue frames. The data on the congruence of these types of frames suggest factors that might explain the likelihood that women's movements microframes will be compatible with the frames used by policy actors and, thus, be more welcome in a specific policy environment. Finally, the chapter submits the major assumptions of the state feminism framework to empirical analysis. Are these assumptions warranted by the data from the debates?

Women's Movement Discourse since the 1970s: Data and Findings

Women's movements, like other movements, use frames to mobilize constituencies and to address policy makers with the aim of influencing policy decisions. Frames, thus, indicate and express the movement discourse on a specific issue and the meanings of a policy problem at a given time and in a given country. Women's movement frames also refer to a wider set of meanings and strategies that might change over time and vary across countries. At the same time, Emanuela Lombardo, Petra Meier, and Mieke Verloo (2009b) point out that women's movement frames might shrink, stretch, or bend gender equality framing in a conscious or unconscious way. In this section, the Women's Movement Frames dataset is the basis for looking at patterns and trajectories of frames according to issue and country, and over time. The goal is to determine whether there is a convergence of frames and whether cross-country "families" of frames exist.

The Women's Movement Frames Dataset

The RNGS dataset has only a few measures of women's movement actors' microframes, and none of these pertain to their content, but rather, cohesion (the degree to which movement actors agreed on a single idea) and location of movement actors using feminist frames. The data show one notable finding: A fairly high proportion of movement actors involved in policy debates agreed on at least one single microframe (in 74 of 114 debates, that is, 64.9 percent of all debates). To study the movement frames systematically, however, it is necessary to analyze the content of the microframes of all movement actors; these are found in the Text Appendices to the RNGS dataset, found on the RNGS Web site, in a way that permits valid and reliable comparisons across issues, countries, and over time.

As discussed earlier, women's movement actors' microframes are composed of the issue definition—views of the nature of problems raised in policy discussions—and the solution (i.e., the policy goals that will fix the problem); these categories correspond to the diagnostic and prognostic types of frames (Benford and Snow 2000). The Women's Movement Frames dataset includes 1,002 separate observations: 512 issue definitions and 490 policy goals presented.[2] For the analysis in this chapter, we focus only on the issue definition component of actors' microframes grouped into three categories, described below in more detail: equality, difference, and transformative frames.[3] As previous research shows, issue definition has the greatest potential to change policy culture and thus policy outcomes in the long term (Bacchi 1999).

The three types of issue definitions correspond to gender-specific strategies identified in feminist theory: (1) framing oriented to equality and rights, (2) difference framing, (3) a gender relation–power frame or transformative frame (Squires 2005). The *equality and rights frame* claims that what is at stake in a policy debate on a particular issue is a matter of equality or inequality between men and women. Whether the issue is abortion, job training, or prostitution, the problem to be solved is how to treat women in such a way that they will attain equal rights with men and become more autonomous of men. The *difference frame*, by contrast, may begin with a goal of equality of men and women but focus on ways that women are different from men. What women can contribute as women is at the center of the problem definition as well as the solution. Because women have special qualities and capacities in comparison to men, special policy solutions for women are necessary to achieve an egalitarian result. The *gender relation–gender power* or *transformative frame* takes the power positions of men and women into account. This frame also explicitly focuses on the role of men in producing gender inequality and on gendered power relations. Such issue definitions often include a critique of institutionalized unequal hierarchical relations between men and women. Thus, the policy solutions aim at transforming and overcoming such bipolar gender roles. Moreover, this category includes a notion of diversity and intersectionality on different axes of inequality.

By definition, in the RNGS study, women's movement frames are gendered. Women's movement actors explicitly refer to the situation of women and to gender relations in the description of a policy problem and in the suggested policy solutions. In only two debates were movement issue definitions presented in a de-gendered way: in an abortion debate in the Netherlands from 1981 to 1984 (brought into the debate by the women's group "We Women Demand"), stressing the doctors' responsibility, and in the debate in Belgium on naturalization and citizenship in 2000 where the women's movement activists (the Dutch Council of Women and the French Council of Women) referred to migrants in an explicitly de-gendered way. Detailed case studies below examine each of these instances of gender-free framing. Although the issue definition component of the microframe was gendered in all of our cases, the policy goal part tended not to be gendered, such as the plea for change of legislation or new policy programs in general.

Trends in Framing by Issue Area

In the 114 debates, we found 512 microframes of women's movement activists, defining the specific issues. These microframes shape the women's movement discourse since the 1970s. What is the result?

As Table 9.1 shows, a majority of the frames in the debates conformed to the equality and women's rights frame: 66 percent referred to equality and women's rights (338 microframes). Only 15 percent of women's movement actors frames were difference frames (77 of all microframes), while transformative frames made up 19 percent (97 microframes) across the debates. The most common frame in *abortion* debates is the women's rights and especially the autonomy frame, with 77.9 percent (102 of 131 microframes in abortion debates). The main message here is that movement actors claim that women should have the right to decide on their own about their bodies. The difference frame is not very common in abortion debates (16 percent, or 21 microframes), and transformative frames have an even lower frequency in abortion debates (6.1 percent, or 8 microframes). One example of transformative problem definition was expressed by the women's section of the Austrian Social Democratic Party (SPÖ) in the debate on the People's Initiative to overturn legal abortion (1975–1978). They claimed that when a woman seeks an abortion, men are responsible. Another example comes from the German debate from 1993 to 1995 on the recriminalization of abortion. Then, Alice Schwarzer, one of the most famous German feminists, blamed "patriarchal judges" in abortion decisions. This might be explained by the important role of the abortion debate in both countries since the nineteenth century and the importance of the issue for the mobilization of the second-wave women's movement, which claimed to be autonomous from male institutions and organizations.

In *hot-issue debates on state restructuring*, women's movement actors also often used equality and rights frames (61.5 percent, or 48 microframes out of 78). In the U.S. debate on welfare reform from 1992 to 1996, for example, seven of the twelve women's movement actors framed the problem as a matter of female inequality and poverty. As another example, in the German debate on bioethics from 1995 to 2002, ten of twenty-six women's movement actors framed the issue as a question of women's reproductive rights. Eighteen women's movement frames found in the hot-issue debates introduced the problem emphasizing women's difference (23.1 percent). For instance, in the Austrian debate on child care allowances that took place from 1999 to 2001, one microframe (from the Conservative Party's women's section) described the problem with allowances as that they forced women into waged labor so that they could not stay with their children. Twelve women's movement microframes in hot-issue debates aimed at deconstructing gender relations (15.4 percent). In the same Austrian debate, for instance, three actors criticized the sexual division of labor. In the Canadian health care debate from 2000 to 2003, the notion of diversity was stressed by one women's movement actor (National Coordinating Group on Health Care Reform and Women) as important for the health

TABLE 9.1   FRAMES IN ISSUE DEFINITION BY FIVE POLICY ISSUE AREAS

Issue	Rights	Difference	Transformative	Total Number of Frames
Abortion	102	21	8	131
	77.9%	16%	6.1%	100%
Job training	54	6	8	68
	79.4%	8.8%	11.8%	100%
Political representation	91	24	12	127
	71.7%	18.9%	9.4%	100%
Prostitution	43	8	57	108
	39.8%	7.4%	52.8%	100%
Hot issue	48	18	12	78
	61.5%	23.1%	15.4%	100%
Total	338	77	97	512
	66%	15%	19%	100%

issue. The higher number of deconstructive or transformative frames, compared to abortion and political representation, might be due to the time factor: The RNGS project analyzed debates on state restructuring only since the 1990s, and in this decade the sensibility for transformative gender equality frames was rising.

Among 127 frames found in *political representation debates*, we identified 91 equality frames (71.7 percent). The major frame in all political representation debates was a plea for equal political representation of women. Twenty-four women's movement frames can be labeled as difference frames (18.9 percent), arguing that women should represent women. This emphasis on difference is characteristic of Germany, Austria, Great Britain, and the Netherlands. All in all, we found 12 transformative frames (9.4 percent). For example, in the Austrian debate on overcoming underrepresentation of women in the civil service from 1981 to 1993, the SPÖ women challenged the "male character" of politics; in the Finnish debate on party gender quotas from 1986 to 1987, women's movement actors claimed that patriarchal structures are responsible for women's political under-representation.

In the twenty-three *job training debates*, women's movement actors introduced fifty-four equality frames of a total of sixty-eight frames (79.4 percent). For example, the problem of unequal labor market participation is used as an argument in Finland, France, and Spain. Six women's movement microframes presented the issue in terms of gender difference (8.8 percent). In two Finnish debates (1975 and 1987), women's movement actors from the Conservative Party section, as well as from the women's studies movement, wanted to value women's care work. Eight microframes presented job training in a deconstructive way (11.8 percent), relating the issue to structural problems and to men. In the Canadian Jobs Strategy debate from 1984 to 1985, the National Action

Committee on the Status of Women and the Fédération des Femmes du Québec blamed structural discrimination of women on the labor market.

Among the 108 women's movement microframes found in *prostitution debates*, only 43 women's rights or equal rights frames appeared (39.8 percent), mainly in defining prostitution as sex work. Even fewer (8) definitions of the problem labeled prostitution as an issue of female difference (7.4 percent). A majority of the frames (57 or 52.8 percent) presented prostitution in the context of a patriarchal, male-dominated society that oppresses women. This perspective is central to the abolitionist approach to prostitution.

This analysis shows some interesting framing patterns according to the different issues. Except for prostitution, a majority of frames are equality and rights frames. For these, the strategy of demanding equal rights for women and men and giving women citizenship rights prevails. Prostitution is the only issue for which transformative frames were most frequent. The abolitionist frame, which has a long tradition in prostitution debates since the nineteenth century, defines prostitution as oppression of women by men (Outshoorn 2004). This is still the most common perception of prostitution in postindustrial societies. However, also somewhat common is the rights frame, which is a new definition in the debate claiming a woman's right to sex work.

In political representation and in debates on state restructuring, women's movements actors are more likely than in other policy issues to emphasize the idea of female difference (18.9 percent and 23.1 percent). In political representation debates, the idea often prevails that women might bring something different to the political realm and that women should formally represent women. This finding arises from the realization that women have long had the same legal political rights as men but have not been able, thus far, to actively realize their rights. This triggers a reference to women's difference and to a strategy focusing on the specific role of women in politics. However, one could also expect a more transformative problem definition. Still, there are few references to male structures and patriarchy as a reason for permanent female political under-representation—only in twelve microframes (9.4 percent).

Trends in Framing by Country

In a country-based comparative perspective, the analysis of frames sheds light on "ideational themes," which were "especially resonant" in different national contexts (McAdam, McCarthy, and Zald 1996: 19).[4] The women's movement microframes show interesting country patterns.[5] While in all countries the equality and rights frame predominates in comparison to difference and transformative frames, some countries show specific characteristics. In Belgium and France, women's movement actors refer to women's rights and equality in a greater proportion than in other countries. In the Belgian debates, 100 percent, and in French debates 89.4 percent of the women's movement frames referred to the equality of men and women and to women's rights. This might be explained by the French republican tradition, which is also strong in the French part of the Belgian women's movement. The difference frame is significant in Germany, Italy, and the Netherlands. In these countries, difference often refers to biological differences of women as women and mothers, or to specific qualities of women. Although in German abortion debates the rights frame is predominant, we find quite a few frames asking for women's responsibility and women's choice only to have an abortion. Similarly, the difference frame in the Dutch debates stresses the choice of the woman in case of abortion. Another example is the German bioethics debate, where some women's movement actors stress the interaction of the mother's body with the embryo as most important to decide on the issue. Also, in debates about political representation, the idea that women should represent women was common in the German and Dutch women's movements. In the Italian debate on political representation, we also find a strong reference to the special contribution that women can make to politics. These findings resonate with the history of the women's movements in Germany and Italy, which have strong traditions of "feminism of difference" (for Germany, Holland-Cunz 2003; for Italy, Dalla Costa 1988).

In Belgium, France, and Spain, the difference frame is absent or underrepresented. Here, the equality frame is dominant. The deconstructive or transformative frame is significant in Sweden, Finland, and Italy, and it is present, but not dominant, in Great Britain and the United States. These results on national differences of strategic framing suggest that women's movement actors employ framing strategies that are located in national women's movement traditions (McAdam, McCarthy, and Zald 1996: 19).

Trends in Framing by Decade

The data also reveal changes in strategic framing by women's movements over time, presented in Table 9.2. Fifty-four frames (67.5 percent) out of the 80 frames expressed at the time of debates in the 1970s defined the policy problems as equality and rights issues. In this decade, there are 20 difference (25 percent) and 6 transformative frames (7.5 percent). In the 32 debates that took place in the 1980s, 89 of 129 frames (69 percent) were oriented to rights, 20 to difference, and another 20 to transformative frames (15.5 percent each). The 46 debates in the 1990s contain 240 women's movement microframes. One-hundred fifty-nine frames were equality and rights oriented (66.3 percent), 24 can be labeled as difference frames (10 percent), and 57 as deconstructive frames (23.7 percent). Only 18 debates started after the year 2000, with 39 microframes: 19 were oriented to rights (48.7 percent), 10 to difference, and 10 to transformative frames (25.7 percent).

In the 1990s, the deconstructive or transformative perspective on gender policy issues became more prominent in the women's movement discourse than in the decades before. Since the 1990s, women's movement actors have increasingly presented the problem of female discrimination as something other than a matter of equal rights. They have often been just as likely to locate discrimination and marginalization in basic structures of gender inequity, which

TABLE 9.2 FRAMES IN ISSUE DEFINITION BY DECADE

Issue	Rights	Difference	Transformative	Total Number of Frames
1970s	54	20	6	80
	67.5%	25%	7.5%	100%
1980s	89	20	20	129
	69%	15.5%	15.5%	100%
1990s	159	24	57	240
	66.3%	10%	23.7%	100%
2000s	19	10	10	39
	48.7%	25.7%	25.7%	100%
Total	321	74	93	488
	65.8%	15.2%	19%	100%

Note: The difference between the number of frames here and the total number of frames in the dataset is due to the exclusion of frames expressed in the 1960s.

might not be addressed by equal rights measures alone. The frames attack male-dominated systems more openly and make men responsible for the discrimination that women experience. This trend reflects the success of women's studies' approaches to inequality, which since the late 1980s focused not only on women but also on gender relations.

Case Studies of Strategic Framing in Austria, France, the Netherlands, and Belgium

The case studies provided here illustrate the importance of strategic framing by the women's movements (Lombardo, Meier, and Verloo 2009a), where women's movements define policy issues as women's and gendered issues, and have them placed on the government's agenda.

The two case studies in Box 9.1 show important impacts of the women's movement framing. In the two Dutch abortion debates, the equality and women's rights frames were presented against the image of women as being mere victims of illegal practices and poor social conditions, and as morally underdeveloped beings who do not have the ability to make moral decisions. The framing of the Dutch movement placed the question as a women's issue on the agenda. The same transformation of a nongendered issue took place in the second and third Austrian prostitution debates. The gendering of prostitution as a women's rights issue helped the organization of prostitutes to become a publicly visible actor, and the frame also involved women's movement activists as well as women's policy agencies.

The two case studies in Box 9.2 show the causal mechanisms for the expression of nongendered microframes by women's movement actors—two of the few cases of such strategic de-gendering or "shrinking" women's movement frames (Lombardo, Meier, and Verloo 2009b) found in the RNGS study.

Box 9.1 Two Case Studies of Agenda Setting by Women's Movement Actor Framing

Debate in the Netherlands on Bill to Liberalize Abortion, 1971–1973

The debate started during a national election campaign in April 1971 (Outshoorn 2001). Until that time, the abortion practice was illegally providing women with abortion on demand. On the one hand, a cabinet reform was inevitable because of social changes, but doctors on the other hand showed ever more sympathy for women's demands for abortion. Liberals and Christian Democrats became active on the issue, as part of the cabinet coalition pact, and Social Democrats tried to push through a radical reform with some of the Liberals, hoping for a positive election turnout. While the Liberals and Social Democrats framed abortion as a social issue and a medical problem, making doctors experts, the confessional parties saw abortion as a moral problem that had to be carefully policed and thus controlled. All parties aimed at bringing the illegal abortion practice under control. It was the emerging women's movement that introduced a new feminist meaning into the policy debate, seeing women not only as victims of social conditions and illegal practices but as moral agents with the right to abortion. As a result of the framing of the women's movement, party actors could no longer ignore women's involvement in abortion and their "interest" in the matter. Whereas the compromise of this first debate was a law that tried to contain abortion within the frame of public morals, in the following years abortion became linked to women's status and rights (Outshoorn 2001: 211). The Dutch feminists framed the next debate on the legalization of abortion from 1977 to 1981 with the argument that women seeking an abortion are mature and moral persons who make their own responsible decisions (Outshoorn 2001: 215). The 1981 act allowed abortion until viability of the fetus. Thus, the doctors had a major say in the decision, but the women seeking an abortion had the final say. However, in both debates the *rights frame* was successfully changing the meaning of the policy, and the frame was at the same time compatible with the social-democratic frame.

Prostitution Debates in Austria, 1980s to 1997

Debates over prostitution were de-gendered. The issue came on the agenda during the social democratic modernization "from above" in the course of a major reform of the Austrian penal code in the 1970s (Sauer 2004: 43). This decriminalization led to hot debates about pimping and to the amendment of the penal code at the beginning of the 1980s. None of the Austrian women's movement actors included prostitution on the political agenda. Thus, women did not come into the picture (nor did men); the issue was seen as a crime and as a threat to public security, public health, and public morals. The picture changed during the 1980s, however. Austrian provinces reacted to the

(continued on next page)

Box 9.1 *Continued*

liberalization of prostitution with restrictive laws, and debates on AIDS pushed prostitution into the media. Moreover, after the fall of the Iron Curtain, street prostitution was on the rise. Also, taxation of sex work led to an organization of prostitutes in the second half of the 1980s. This organization—along with Viennese women's movement activists and the then minister for women's affairs—gendered the issue in the public and media debate: They presented prostitution as legal work, which must be regulated by the state. The lack of women's rights in the sex business—again the rights frame—was one of the major frames in the two Austrian debates in the 1990s, and it was successfully introduced to put the issue again on the agenda and to change the legal situation of sex workers.

Box 9.2 Case Studies on Strategic De-gendering: Debates in the Netherlands and Belgium

Regulations and Services for Abortion in the Netherlands, 1981–1984

In the first two Dutch abortion debates, women's movement actors were actively gendering the debate in order to make policy makers, doctors, and the public aware that the issue was a women's issue and, moreover, that women are morally responsible citizens who need the right to make their own decisions over their lives. With this strategy of gendering the issue, Dutch women's movement actors were successful in changing the legal situation. However, in the third debate, women's movement activists from the group We Women Demand took another approach. In a coalition with actors opposing the new act, they worked to remove gendered reference and defined women seeking abortion as "normal patients" (Outshoorn 2001: 220). How can we explain this strategic de-gendering or frame-shrinking? The 1981 act defined abortion as a women's issue and provided abortion on demand, the debates emerging after the law covered implementation measures. The Christian Democrats tried to restrict the scope of the law by obstructing the implementation and restricting the licenses for hospitals. Therefore, they reframed abortion as a special medical procedure to be handled by medical experts only. It was, thus, wise not to frame the implementation of the abortion law as a women's issue but as a "normal" medical issue in which the patients have rights to decide. The framing strategy resulted in November 1984 in an abortion law that made abortion on demand available for all women.

Immigration Reform Bill in Belgium, 1999–2000

During the 1990s, immigration posed new question about how migrants and majority populations should live together and what it meant to be a Belgian

Box 9.2 *Continued*

(Woodward 2007: 60). The Flemish Far Right "Vlaams Block" mobilized against immigrants and challenged social peace. The implementation of EU citizenship in the Belgian legislation made it possible to acquire both Belgian citizenship and the duty (not only the right) to vote through a rather simplified procedure of naturalization (Woodward 2007: 67). This was a success for the women's movement. To keep the debate purely in legalistic terms and to avoid populist right-wing debates, Belgian women's movement activists (the VOK, Dutch and French Council of Women), who for years had been demanding improvement in the political status of the non-EU female population did not exploit the gender argument but de-gendered the issue as an issue of human rights (Woodward 2007: 69), knowing that immigration had taken on an increasingly feminized face.

To sum up, the case studies show that it is an important strategy of women's movement actors to frame policy issues in a gendered way to put an issue on the political agenda—that is, to "stretch" the framing toward gender equality (Lombardo, Meier, and Verloo 2009b). However, we find also some cases in which their strategic de-gendering of an issue helped to push through the aims of the women's movement activists involved in a debate. The analysis of the content of women's movements actors' microframes shows that framing relied on a variety of strategies—on equality, on difference, and on transformation—throughout the last thirty years. We do find some country-specific trends in how national women's movements perceive policy problems, such as the dominance of the difference frame in Germany and Italy. The data also provide evidence of changes over time. Gender studies did have an impact on movement actor framing through emphasizing gender relations as power relations and criticizing actively male dominance since the 1990s. Also, portions of each of the five issue areas are likely to be presented by actors in conventional ways. However, framing did not meet expectations in political representation, where the difference frame tends to predominate more than in other issues. The reason for this is that formal equality has been achieved but has not been successful in the equal representation of women. Therefore, women's special contribution to politics is actively brought into the debate. This is also an example of strategic framing by women's movement actors; different issues require different framing strategies.

Issue Frames and Cultural Change

The focus now turns to issue frames—the explicit way the majority of actors in a policy subsystem defines the meaning of issues. Issue frames influence the process and outcome of policy debates, and they give voice to specific actors during the policy process. The analysis of issue frames over time—when and how gender equality becomes part of the mainstream perception of a policy problem—shows the development of gender knowledge, gender consciousness, and gender awareness in policy environments. More generally, it may indicate mechanisms of cultural change in political systems toward gender equality, especially more openness to women's movement ideas and aims, and more gendering of dominant issue frames. This section examines the patterns of change in how abortion, prostitution, job training, political representation, and hot issues are framed by major actors in policy subsystems. Measures of frames at the beginning and end of each debate found in the RNGS dataset are analyzed over time, across issues, and across countries.[6] To what extent do debate frames become gendered, stay gendered, or become de-gendered from the beginning to the end of a policy cycle?

In 41 percent of all debates, the issue frame was gendered at the beginning. This means that in more than half of the debates the problem at stake was not seen as a problem of men and women. By the end of the debates, 68 percent of the policy issue frames were about gender; this means that women's movements and women's policy agencies were able to raise gender awareness in the policy arena. Looking at the pattern of change during the debates, nearly half of the issue frames changed to become gendered or more gendered, as shown in Table 9.3. In 29 percent of all 130 cases, the issue frame evolved from nongendered to gendered, and in 18 percent it moved from gendered to more gendered. Fifteen percent remained gendered similarly throughout the course of the debate. In only 8 percent of the cases were there reversals in gendering, with 5 percent going from gendered to less gendered and 3 percent from gendered to nongendered. In 30 percent of all debates, the issue frame remained unchanged and nongendered throughout the debate. So we can conclude that once the debate has become gendered at the beginning, it remains gendered until the end, and that the framing of an issue in terms of gender relations is becoming "mainstreamed."

Returning to the question of gendering issue frames at the beginning and at the end of a policy debate, there are variations by issue area. The abortion and political representation debates are more likely to be gendered at the beginning and at the end than the other issues. Job training has especially low rates of gendered issue frames, both at the beginning (13 percent of debates) and at the end (39 percent of debates). Debates about state restructuring (hot-issue debates) in the 1990s are also relatively low at the beginning (25 percent) but show a higher success rate at the end than job training (58 percent). While abortion and political representation were seen as women's issues with a good chance of becoming more politicized by women's movement actors, the issues of job training and state restructuring presented difficulties in this regard. Nevertheless, the change in gendering from beginning to end in job training debates was dramatic. If change in issue frames is an indication of cultural change in policy processes in political systems, then both job training and prostitution debates saw the most dramatic shifts (threefold increases). The smallest change is found in the political representation debates, which entered the political agenda as gendered issues.

TABLE 9.3   TYPES OF CHANGES IN ISSUE DEFINITION BY POLICY ISSUE

Issue	Non-gendered to Gendered	Gendered to More Gendered	Gendered to Less Gendered or Non-gendered	Similarly Gendered Throughout	Non-gendered Throughout	Total Number of Debates
Abortion	11	7	6	5	3	32
	34%	22%	19%	16%	9%	
Job training	6	2	0	1	14	23
	26%	9%	0%	4%	61%	
Political representation	5	10	2	10	5	32
	15%	30%	6%	30%	15%	
Prostitution	12	1	2	3	12	30
	40%	3%	6%	10%	40%	
Hot issue	3	4	0	0	5	12
	25%	33%	0%	0%	42%	
Total	38	24	10	19	39	130
	29%	18%	8%	15%	30%	

The types of changes also show similar *trends by issue*. Issue frames in abortion and debates over state restructuring have the highest rates of overall changes toward gendering, with 88 percent of the abortion debates and 58 percent of the hot-issue debates becoming gendered for the first time or more gendered. Abortion also showed the highest rates of de-gendering at 19 percent (Table 9.3). Prostitution frames present both the greatest change overall with 40 percent of frames changing from nongendered to gendered, but also a high rate of frames remaining nongendered throughout at 40 percent—second only to job training, in which the issue frames remained nongendered in 61 percent of the debates.

There are some *country patterns*, but most are likely to be affected in the particular mix of issues covered in each country in the RNGS study—given the differences, for example, between job training and political representation. Thus, here we present patterns only for the four countries where all debate issues were covered—France, Italy, Spain, and the United States—investigating differences in the extent to which policy subsystem cultures have changed as a result of gendering of issue frames. Two indicators of such changes in the data are: (1) the difference in the number and percentage of debates that have gendered issue frames at the end in relation to those with gendered frames at the beginning, and (2) the increase in the overall number of debates that have progressed from nongendered to gendered in relation to those for which the frames have been de-gendered during the debate.

The patterns in Italy and the United States show the greatest increase in gendered issue frames from the beginning to end of policy debates. In Italy, the issue frame was gendered in 50 percent of the debates when the problem arrived on the political agenda, and 83 percent of the issue frames were gendered at the end of the policy debate. In the United States, the pattern goes from 38 percent to 62 percent. France and Spain, on the other hand, show very little difference in the number and proportion of cases gendered at the beginning and those gendered at the end of a policy debate. Looking at the patterns of frame change, France, Italy, and the United States each has three or four debates showing a complete change from nongendered at the beginning to gendered at the end. In France, however, the overall indicator of a cultural shift in terms of gendering the issue frame of debates is limited, because two other debates were de-gendered; we examine in more detail the dynamics of these two de-gendered debates below. Although Italy had one reversal in a debate, it also had three additional debates that became more gendered to offset this loss. Thus, we can conclude that Italy and the United States show the greatest cultural shifts in policy subsystems toward more gendered content as a result of the politics of state feminism. In France and Spain, whether or not gender became part of issue frames is more likely a function of whether the frame is gendered in the agenda-setting process at the beginning.

In three French debates—two in abortion and one in political representation—the issue frame went from gendered to nongendered from the beginning to the end of the debate; in other words, all three issues were de-gendered. Does this mean that cultural change was limited in France? The two case studies in Box 9.3 provide some answers to this question.

Gendering Issue Frames over Time

Are issues more likely to be considered in gendered terms if they have been discussed for a longer time? If the women's movement actors and women's policy agencies are having any effect over the decades, such a pattern is likely to appear. However, the rates of change across five-year increments reveal no discernible pattern of increased gendering over time. Women's movement actors and women's policy agencies have continued to realize that, on average, between 50 percent and 64 percent of the proposals come to the public agenda with no references to women or gender. In fewer than half of the debates analyzed in the RNGS study—issues that were politicized by the women's movement—was the issue frame gender-sensitive at the beginning of the debate. Gendering of an issue frame is thus an activity undertaken by movement actors and by women's policy agencies. However, we can see that in abortion debates as well as in debates on political representation, gender knowledge and awareness were greater from the beginning than they were in prostitution, job training, and state restructuring (hot issues).

Our findings show that there was a rising sensibility during the life cycle of the debates for the gendered structure of the policy issues. Changing political culture by gendering policy issues has been an ongoing process since the 1970s, without much variation by decade. However, there is an ongoing need for active gendering by women's movement actors and women's policy agencies.

Box 9.3   Case Studies of De-gendering Issue Frames in France

Abortion Debates

The debate on the public reimbursement of abortion expenses from 1981 to 1983 was placed on the public agenda after the Socialist Party had won the presidential election. The Deputy Minister of Woman's Rights, Yvette Roudy, changed women's policy dramatically. She was determined to bring even controversial issues to the political agenda—like the question of reimbursement of abortion costs. Roudy and abortion activists framed abortion at the beginning of the debate as a problem of women's rights and class struggle, against pro-natalist and pro-life arguments. In order to push through a compromise for reimbursement, the Socialist government decided to avoid framing abortion as a women's issue, instead defining it in the same manner as any other medical procedure in order to legitimate reimbursement. This led to a success of the women's movement activists; the costs of abortion were covered by the state (Robinson 2001: 95f).

The debate over sanctions for antiabortion activism from 1991 to 1993 dealt with the issue of antiabortion commandos. The government issued a communication that blockades of hospitals would not be tolerated. The Deputy Ministry of Women's Rights and Daily Life, Véronique Neiertz, at the beginning of the debate used the rhetoric of women's right to abortion. However, when she realized that the feminist gender frame was not effective in eliciting support from the Minister of Justice, she reframed the issue and de-gendered it, saying that the problem at stake was an issue of the state's legal authority to safeguard public hospital service (Robinson 2001: 102f).

Political Representation Debates

The process of de-gendering in the case of the debate around the constitutional court challenge to municipal election quotas from 1981 to 1982 was different. Promising to improve the democratic process, the Socialist government in 1981 proposed the introduction of a proportional electoral system. The pledge for a quota for women in municipal elections in the Socialist platform was a way to demonstrate the party's support of feminist principles and actors. However, the government bill "forgot" the gendered dimension in the change of the electoral system, and the topic became de-gendered. The public debate was nevertheless explicitly gendered, and a quota of 25 percent on municipal candidate lists was introduced into the law by Gisèle Halimi, a feminist MP, not the activist, Roudy (Baudino 2005: 87ff). The final law, however, was overturned by the Constitutional Court and ended in a failure (No Response) for the women's movement actors.

Opening the Door:
Issue Frame Fit

Women's movement actors seek to convince policy makers to adopt their framing of a specific issue in order to change the content of policy to better reflect their demands and claims. The compatibility of women's movements actors' microframes with the frames used by policy makers (issue frame), therefore, is an indicator for the substantive success of the women's movement in terms of policy outcomes. The notion of issue frame fit, a concept used in the RNGS study, is based on the notion "goodness of fit" developed by Thomas Risse, Maria Green Cowles, and James Caporaso (2001). It is defined as the compatibility of the microframe of the women's movement actors with the issue frame that initially shaped the debate in the policy subsystem. Issue frames can be welcoming to the women's movement problem definitions, or hostile and threatening—in RNGS terms, matching, compatible, threatening, or mixed (a combination of threatening and/or compatible) (RNGS 2007a). Moreover, the state feminism framework developed and assessed in this book assumes that movement activists will find it extremely difficult to influence debates when the issue frame is opposed to the women's movement views. Occasionally, especially when a new policy problem emerges, state actors and movement actors will not agree on a common set of norms and perspectives. In those cases, the policy debate itself may be not only about a policy proposal but also about the proper frame in which to deal with it.

The RNGS data indicate a positive and significant correlation between issue frame fit with women's movement actors' goals and the degree of women's movement actors' presence at the beginning of the debate. If the issue frame at the beginning of a debate fits with the movement's perceptions, then a greater percentage of subsystem actors will be from the women's movement. We find also a positive correlation between the issue frame fit with the women's movement goals and the percentage of women's movement actors present at the end of a debate. If the issue frame at the beginning of the debate fitted the women's movement actors' microframe, a higher percentage of movement actors were part of the subsystem at the end of the debate. We expand on these findings in greater detail in the next section.

The analyses of state feminism in the chapters in Part II of the book treat issue frame fit as a possible explanatory condition for the occurrence of state feminism. In this chapter, the goal is to explore which factors might be conducive to a fit favorable to women's movement actors. There are several possibilities. Fit of policy definitions may be more likely when women's movement actors make strategic decisions to frame their demands in a way that will be compatible with the prevailing points of view of policy actors. While we do not have data on women's movement actors' motivations for framing, we can look at the different conditions for fit between movement and issue frames, and in this investigation, one pattern did turn up: the importance of the governing majority—Right, Center, or Left.[7]

TABLE 9.4   ISSUE FRAME FIT BY GOVERNING MAJORITY

Governing Majority	Threatening	Mixed	Compatible	Matching	Total
Right	7	16	14	4	41
	44%	40%	26%	20%	32%
Center	4	8	11	6	29
	25%	20%	21%	30%	22%
Left	5	16	28	10	59
	31%	40%	52%	50%	46%
Total	16	40	53	20	129
	100%	100%	100%	100%	100%

Table 9.4 shows the distribution of issue frame fit by the governing majority at the time of the debate. Here, fit tends to be more compatible or matching when the Left is in power, whereas fit tends to be more mixed or threatening to movement actor goals when the Right is in power. There is little variation under Center governments. To better understand the mechanisms of issue frame fit, we present two case studies in Sweden and Germany that illustrate path-dependent processes (Box 9.4). In the prostitution debates in Sweden and the abortion debates in Germany, the same issue frame fit carried over from one debate to the next to produce similar levels of women's movement success across the time period covered by the debates, although in Sweden that path dependency led to movement success and in Germany the process produced limited success for the movement actors.

Assumptions of the State Feminism Theory: Empirical Assessment

As Chapter 1 points out, assumptions about the role of debate framing are an important foundation for the state feminism framework laid out in this book. The framework assumes that movement success is dependent on the frame of the policy debate being gendered. Framing an issue in gendered terms is seen as a way to enhance the likelihood that women's movement actors will gain substantive and procedural response from the state. In this section, we submit these assumptions to empirical analysis. The results confirm the assumption that gendering has an effect on the participation and procedural access of women's movement actors in policy subsystems. Table 9.5 presents the association between the gendering of the issue frame at the beginning of a policy debate and the participation of women's movement actors in the policy subsystem, also at the beginning of a debate. These results support the assumption that the issue frame affects opportunity for movement actors to have influence.

Table 9.6 shows a similar association with respect to the end of the debate. If the issue frame is gendered at the end of the debate, we find a greater likelihood that women's movement actors will receive descriptive representation.

Box 9.4 Case Studies of Path Dependency and Issue Frame Fit in Sweden and Germany

Prostitution Debates in Sweden, 1981–1999

The first Swedish debate on prostitution, which began in 1981, came to an end when a law prohibiting public pornographic shows came into force (1982). The dominant perception placed prostitution in a framework of gender equality, but politicians involved also included men in the "human question" of prostitution and located the problem in patriarchal structures as well as in the commercialization of sexuality (Svanström 2004: 230). Thus, movement actors' frames and issue frames matched. Also, the coalition of autonomous and party women gendered the debate in a similar direction, framing prostitution as patriarchal and both men and women as commercialized by the sex business (Svanström 2004: 230f). The third prostitution debate beginning in 1997 stood at the end of a series of bills since 1983, which had tried to criminalize clients of prostitutes. Finally, the 1999 law was adopted, which criminalized "buying of sexual service" (Svanström 2004: 236); in other words, the law criminalized the "johns." As with the earlier debate, the frame of the major policy actors as well as the women's movement actors' microframe defined prostitution as a problem of patriarchal exploitation, which had to be banned. Neither frame called for punishment of women as prostitutes but instead the men who were clients. Thus, there was evidence of path dependency in both the women's movement microframe and the issue frame. The "problem" of men buying sex had been on the agenda since the early 1980s and henceforth was a part of the problem as defined by major policy actors. Women's movement activists also pushed the issue in the same direction in the 1980s and early 1990s. In the end, framing prostitution as a "men's issue" helped the women's movement not only to bring the issue to the agenda but also to match the overall approach of the mainstream actors in the policy subsystem.

Abortion Debates in Germany, 1969–1995

Path dependency was also at work across the three abortion debates in Germany, where the microframes of the women's movement were threatening to the policy makers and the success of the movement was low. In the late 1960s and early 1970s, the issue of abortion came to the West German political agenda through the emerging women's movement. Although the movement saw abortion as an issue of a woman's self-determination, the dominant issue frame was about preventing illegal abortion and about protecting life as required of the state by the German Constitution. In a long struggle for compromise, the "indication model," which allowed abortion for specific indications including the social situation of the woman, was adopted into law in 1974. Yet abortion remained in the criminal code. The issue did not come to the agenda again until German reunification challenged this West German

---

Box 9.4 *Continued*

---

compromise, because abortion was legal in East Germany. The new 1992 law tightened abortion regulations. Again, the dominant frame was about protecting the unborn life, whereas women's movement actors debated abortion again in terms of female autonomy and self-determination (Kamenitsa 2001: 118n). We can also see path dependency at work in the third abortion debate on recriminalizing abortion from 1993 to 1995, where the protection of unborn life was again the focus; here the women's movement was essentially absent from the debate, with the exception of East German members of Parliament, who continued to emphasize women's self-determination (Kamenitsa 2001: 127).

TABLE 9.5 GENDERING ISSUE FRAMES AND WOMEN'S MOVEMENT ACTORS' (WMA) PARTICIPATION AT BEGINNING OF DEBATES

Issue Frame	WMA Participation at Beginning	No WMA Participation at Beginning	Total Number of Debates
Gendered at beginning	23 53%	20 47%	43 100%
Not gendered at beginning	19 27%	52 73%	71 100%
Total	42 37%	72 63%	114 100%

Pearson chi square = 8.222; $p < .004$.

TABLE 9.6 GENDERING ISSUE FRAMES AND WOMEN'S MOVEMENT ACTORS' (WMA) PARTICIPATION AT END OF DEBATES

Issue Frame	WMA Participation at End	No WMA Participation at End	Total Number of Debates
Gendered at end	56 75%	19 25%	75 100%
Not gendered at end	9 23%	30 77%	39 100%
Total	65 57%	49 43%	114 100%

Pearson chi square = 29.481; $p < .0001$.

The analyses support another part of these core assumptions: If the issue frame is gendered at the end of the debate, there is a greater likelihood that women's movement actors will receive substantive representation. Table 9.7 shows a strong association between the gendering of an issue frame at the end of the debate and the policy content that results from the debate. On the other

TABLE 9.7   GENDERING ISSUE FRAMES AND WOMEN'S MOVEMENT ACTOR
(WMA)–POLICY CONTENT FIT

Issue Frame Gendered at End of Debate?	WMA–Policy Content Fit Threatening/ Incompatible	WMA–Policy Content Fit Matching/ Compatible	Total Number of Debates
No	17	14	31
	61%	23%	35%
Yes	11	47	58
	39%	77%	65%
Total	28	61	89
	100%	100%	100%

hand, if the issue frame is not gendered, there is a strong possibility that the policy results will be threatening or incompatible with women's movement actors' goals.

Thus, so far, the results show that, with respect to women's representation, changes in the framing of debates to recognize gender roles not only bring interests of women into the policy-making arena but also set the stage for substantive representation in the policy outcome. At the same time, the gendered framing gives groups of women justification for participation in a policy debate and facilitates their procedural access. Policy debates that ignore gender relations deny women the basis for increased descriptive and substantive representation.

Next, we examine whether a particular gendering (i.e., one that is matching or compatible with women's movement actors' microframes) increases the degree of movement actors' participation, measured here as the percentage of actors in the policy subsystem at the beginning of the debate and at the end of the debate. Analyses of issue frame fit—ranging from threatening, to compatible, to matching (mixed-fit cases are not included) in relation to the percentage of subsystem actors who were women's movement actors at the beginning of the debate and at the end of the debate—produced positive and significant correlations. This result gives empirical support to the assumption that the type of gendering can increase the presence of women's movement actors. Thus, if the issue frame at the beginning of the debate fits the women's movement actors' microframe, then they will have a greater presence among subsystem actors at the beginning and at the end of the debate.[8]

The final assumption that we examine addresses the relation between initial issue frame fit and final policy content fit with women's movement actors' microframes. This analysis shows the importance of issue frame fit to the measures of state substantive response to women's movement goals. There is a significant correlation between the issue frame fit with women's movement actors' microframes (from threatening to matching) at the beginning of the debate and substantive response at the end as measured by the fit of the policy content (from threatening to matching) with women's movement microframes.[9] If the issue frame fits the women's movement actors' microframe at the beginning of the debate, therefore, it is more likely that the policy content will fit the women's movement actors' microframe at the end of the debate.

The Politics of Framing: Conclusion

This chapter has presented data to support the assumptions of the state feminism project. Gendering a policy issue, presenting policy problems in gender-sensitive frames, is a way to bring in women's movement ideas into the policy arena. Moreover, framing an issue in terms of gender equality identifies women as potential target groups in a given policy and, thus, is a strategy to insert women's movement actors into the policy-making process. Therefore, to be successful, women's movement actors would be wise to frame issues in gendered terms.

Taken together, this study shows that frames are important factors in policy processes and that framing is important for policy outcomes. Frames shape the policy agenda by putting problems on the agenda or, alternatively, can define certain social problems to be unimportant. The data show that the assumptions of discursive policy analysis hold true (Hajer and Wagenaar 2003; Bacchi 1999; Verloo and Lombardo 2007; Lombardo, Meier, and Verloo 2009a); the claim, "frames matter" has stood the test of systematic empirical analysis. Significant evidence was marshaled to demonstrate that the framing of a policy helped women's movement activists gain substantive responses from the state and that movement actors can change the major frames and the content of a policy. The study also demonstrates that women's movements have been able to put new frames on the political agenda since the 1970s, namely, frames that address women's social inequality, women's political under-representation, women's rights, and gender hierarchies. Moreover, the active framing "constructed" women's movement activists as political actors in a specific policy area and helped them to gain representation in the policy debate. The analyses also found a significant association (chi square with $p < .005$) between gendered agenda setting (i.e., gendering the dominant frame) and the presence of women's movement actors.

In the last thirty-five years, women's movement actors have adopted a wide range of frames in different policy areas. Whereas the rights and equality frame was the predominant definition across all issues and countries in the study and over time, movement actors strategically used other frames in various debates to influence policy content. The best example is political representation, where formal equality between men and women had been achieved in all countries during the first half of the twentieth century. Here, the movement used the difference frame as a tool to raise awareness of female inequality, which goes beyond formal equal rights. The findings also resonate with work that identifies "national patterns" in women's movements, at least in some of the countries in the study. Germany and Italy, for instance, have a long tradition of "difference feminism," and these findings support national path dependency in framing.

Also, these findings indicate a shift in framing, which mirrors a transformation in the focus of gender studies and women's movements more generally speaking, regarding the shift from a sole focus on women to the intersection of different types of inequality.

The chapter shows that women's movement actors have been successful in affecting cultural change in Western democracies by making the discussion of policy issues more gendered. While for some issues, policy environments and issue frames were gendered from the beginning (e.g., abortion), other issues, like prostitution, job training, and state restructuring (hot issues), show the necessity of "active gendered framers" in the policy process. Gender mainstreaming, thus, requires women's movement actors as well as women's policy agencies that actively gender the perception of an issue throughout a policy debate. The study also identified the conditions for women's movement actors to be successful framers. One of these conditions is the fit of women's movement actors' microframes with the issue frames. Here we found positive correlations between issue frame fit and the content of the policy. Future research, however, will have to determine what women's movements actually do to make their frames compatible with the frames of major political actors.

10

Gendering New Institutionalism

AMY G. MAZUR
DOROTHY E. MCBRIDE

P olitical institutions are central to state feminism theory. In turn, findings from this study of state feminism make important contributions
to theories associated with "new institutionalism," an approach that
typically ignores the complex interplay linking gender, change, and political institutions. The goal of this chapter is to add to ongoing efforts by
feminist scholars to gender new institutional approaches. It begins with an
overview of this feminist research and lays out the components of new institutional theory. Next, using the RNGS-based dataset of women's policy
agencies (see Chapter 3), we assess propositions from new institutionalism
about change over time and across sector, country, and region. The analysis
first focuses on propositions based in historical institutional theories. Then,
we turn to agency-movement alliances as they inform theories of discursive
institutionalism in terms of Movement State Feminism and Transformative
State Feminism. The chapter concludes with a review of the implications
of the findings for a better integration of feminist and nonfeminist institutional work.

Approaches to Gendering
New Institutionalism

Since the late 1980s, social scientists have turned their attention to institutions as major factors in explaining political and social outcomes, and
have sought to understand how, why, and to what end institutions change.[1]
Within political science, new institutionalism has been associated with
"bringing the state back-in" (Skocpol 1985) through a focus on formal political institutions both inside and outside of government, ranging from parliamentary commissions and bureaucratic agencies to political parties and
interest groups. In this literature, institutions are defined as systems of rules
and norms that structure political behavior: "codified rules of political

contestation" (Pierson 2004: 21). Although there is often overlap, three general approaches have emerged: (1) *rational-choice institutionalism* conceptualizes institutional change and dynamics in terms of the logic of individuals maximizing opportunities; (2) *historical institutionalism* seeks to explain the changes of formal political institutions and patterns of institutional interaction across time; and (3) *discursive institutionalism*, a more recent variant, approaches institutional change in terms of set patterns of discourses and ideational logics or frames that structure political action within the state (Schmidt 2008).

All of these theories virtually ignore issues of gender (Chappell 2006; Mackay and Waylen 2009). One of the more notable examples of this omission is the *Oxford Handbook of Political Institutions* (Rhodes, Binder, and Rockman 2006). This inventory of the field of institutional analysis has no separate entry on gender or feminist institutionalism, and only one of thirty-eight chapters mentions feminist analyses of the state (Jessop 2006).[2] While the new institutionalism has become a well-developed area of study despite ignoring gender, feminist theorists and analysts have produced an equally impressive body of work, beginning in the early 1990s, to advance theories of gender, state, and institutional change.[3] From the beginning, their central question has been whether the contemporary state and its various institutions could help women and promote the cause of gender equality and if so how, why, and to what end.

Feminist scholars agree that state institutions are inherently gendered (Acker 1992) and *gender-biased*—either patriarchal or driven by organizational masculinism (Lovenduski 1998). Early feminist theorists argued that the state is a monolithic patriarchy that women's advocates and feminists should avoid. In the late 1980s, Australian feminist scholars deconstructed the state and asserted that there are different state arenas, some of which could be effective sites for feminists and women's rights activists to gain entry and promote women-friendly policy (e.g., Connell 1987; Pringle and Watson 1992). This conceptualization of the state as a more porous and disaggregated entity allowed analysts to consider it as a potential vehicle for feminist change. Still, feminist analysts saw the need to focus on the specific gendered culture of many individual state structures, like commissions or bureaucratic agencies, and identified the so-called culture of neutrality in many agencies as highly gender-biased (Cockburn 1991; Ferguson 1984; Chappell 2002b; Stivers 1993). Whatever the label, it is in the nature of institutions, according to this perspective, to ignore gender equality and women's issues, setting up barriers to women's participation.

Feminist engagement with the state is an attempt to change the inherently gender-biased dynamics of state institutional processes. A new generation of scholars, using the Australian poststructural analyses as a point of departure, saw that feminist activists have the potential to enter certain state arenas to *change the gendered nature of institutions* and achieve a range of *women-friendly outcomes*, including policies, programs, effective women's policy agencies, gender equality in society, and women-friendly administrative cultures, to name a few. Learning when, where, and why feminist and women's movement actors mobilize to gender the state is part of the research agenda. Through qualitative comparisons especially, scholars have explored whether such feminist engagement has in fact changed gender-biased norms and patterns of state institutions to favor women's interests, feminist goals, and gender equality.

The term *feminist engagement* with the state is a loose one, used by feminist institutionalists (e.g, Chappell 2002b, 2006; Kantola 2006; Gelb 1995) to capture a variety of interactions between women and women's movement activists (both as individuals and representatives of groups) on the one hand, and state institutions and structures on the other. Such engagements can include, for instance, women bureaucrats, femocrats, activists from women's movement organizations, gender experts, women members of Parliament, or women's policy agencies that pursue a generally feminist agenda.[4] The new feminist institutionalist literature examines a wide range of state-government action to assess feminist engagement—lobbying, voting on legislation, formulating laws in the cabinet, implementing policy, policy deliberation, consultation, court decisions, and policy discourse and framing. Feminist institutionalists are also interested in bringing a feminist perspective into the design of government: "the scope for ensuring that institutions acknowledge gendered difference and deliver more equitable outcomes" (Gatens and Mackinnon 1998: cover). As Louise Chappell (2006: 225) points out, a priority is to learn how established patterns of norms and standard operating procedures of political structures, called "logics of appropriateness" (March and Olsen 1989), affect the treatment of gender issues and women as political actors within the state.

Despite an apparent gap between the two, feminist approaches have many areas of overlap with new institutionalism. Feminist engagement with the state necessarily involves political institutions either as actors—through women's policy machineries or through women's participation in political institutions like legislatures, bureaucracy, or courts—or through policy frames and discourse of institutional actors.[5] Any assessment of whether feminist engagement actually brings about institutional change necessarily focuses on the building blocks of institutions—rules, structure, and discourse. Like new institutionalism, much of the feminist institutional literature takes a comparative perspective over the long term to assess how different forms of government design and patterns of state-society relations can provide different opportunities and access points for women's-feminist movement actors to enter the state and achieve women-friendly outcomes (Chappell 2006; Mazur 2002; Weldon 2002b).

Beyond the importance of institutions and their characteristics to explaining the process and outcome of feminist engagements with the state, the study of such engagements in turn provides a means of assessing theories of institutional change and development. Beginning in the 1970s, feminists have increasingly addressed states and their institutions even through periods of neoliberal state retrenchment. This engagement has had the potential to bring about institutional change through establishment of women's policy agencies, shifts in "organizational logics of appropriateness" that remove gender-biased institutional rules and norms, and the increased presence of women and/or feminist advocates in bureaucracy and in elected office. Investigations of any and all these changes speak to the various theories of institutional change that focus on "big" explanations for "macro social processes" (Pierson 2003).

Gendering New Institutionalism through Studying Women's Policy Agencies and State Feminism

As Lovenduski (1998) indicated early on, gendering institutional analysis is complex and multifaceted. It ranges from bringing in gender-specific institutions as objects of analysis, to posing gendered institutions as drivers and outcomes, to examining how institutions affect feminists' engagements with the state, to testing theories of institutional change with gendered political processes over time. The analysis in this chapter contributes to this complex endeavor by focusing on women's policy machineries as an object of institutional analysis and using their characteristics and activities to amend theories associated with historical institutionalism, policy change, and discursive institutionalism.

Opening the Black Box:
Agencies as the Object of Study

The study of women's policy offices responds to the call from new institutional scholars to focus on formal or "parchment" institutions (Carey 2000) and "codified rules of political contestation" (Pierson 2004: 25) as causal mechanisms and as objects of analysis in historical and comparative contexts (e.g., March and Olsen 1984; Thelen 2003). Given the potential of these agencies to represent non-state actors from women's movements and democratize the state and policy formation processes, their study opens the black box of government to reveal its inner workings. Such work has the potential to increase understanding of state action, broadly speaking, or, in other words, to "shed light on democracy's critical processes" (Kettl 1993: 409) and to fill the empirical gap on "the role of bureaucracies in making policy" (Peters 1992: 285).

The state feminism framework, the literature on women's policy agencies, the comprehensive map of agencies in Chapter 3, and the research and analysis of policy debates presented thus far in this book have already contributed to knowledge about gendering the state and made a strong case for treating women's policy agencies as an important population of political institutions. In this section, we bolster the case by focusing on the patterns of institutional change in fifty-seven national-level agencies, ten quasi agencies, and six subnational offices, using six structural dimensions across four decades, thirteen countries, and five policy sectors.

Assessing Theories of Institutional Change

Women's policy machineries appeared on the scene in significant numbers across all postindustrial democracies in the early 1970s, not forgetting earlier incarnations in the United States, France, and Canada, as well as in the United Nations. They have remained in place and, for the most part, have become more numerous and more powerful. Thus, they serve as a terrain on which to examine change over what historical institutionalists call the *longue durée*, or long haul. As such, studying these state-based agencies provides an opportunity to assess theories of change that are associated with historical institutionalism, policy change, and discursive institutionalism.[6] This overview of these theories lays the groundwork for the empirical assessment found in the later sections of the chapter.

Historical Institutionalism

Scholars using this approach seek to understand institutional *change* and *choice* over time, as exhibited by state-based structures and rules rather than societal norms. The goal is to explain when, how, and why institutional dynamics pertaining to the state and its policies change or, in many cases, stay the same. Such institutional dynamics include formal political institutions both inside and outside of the state, as well as the established patterns of interactions between state and society. There are several different explanations for changes of great magnitude, "big, slow-moving and . . . invisible" (Pierson 2003), such as changes in welfare states (Palier 2000), in Europeanization (Pierson 1996), or in entire areas of policy like family policy (Morgan 2006).[7]

Theories of path dependency assert that state action is limited by the way in which "increasing returns" (Pierson 2004) develop around a specific policy. These returns create patterns of interactions linking state and societal actors and institutions that are mutually reinforcing over time. According to the path-dependent perspective, new institutions and institutional dynamics appear at specific moments during the process of development—sometimes called "critical junctures"—which set the pattern of institutional interactions until the next juncture. The outcome is that even many years after these critical junctures, it is difficult to alter political dynamics; in other words, there is a certain "stickiness" to institutions and the policy dynamics around them (Pierson 2004). To illustrate, Kimberly Morgan (2006) shows how path dependencies in family policies developed in the Netherlands, the United States, Sweden, and France, according to the way state-religion relations crystallized in each country at a certain moment in time. The set pattern of institutional relations in each country explained the differences in the extent to which family policies promoted gender equality. It is interesting to note that the particular way in which family policy emerged has meant that women's policy agencies have not intervened in this area of policy in any of the countries in her study.

Another theory, called constant cause, assesses the factors that led to the original establishment of state structures and processes, not key moments along the path of development, as the most important in explaining institutional dynamics over time.[8] In a constant-cause argument, institutions can change or stay the same, and these dynamics can be traced to the moment of establishment. Take the previous example of family policy: One can understand change in family policies from a constant-cause perspective by knowing the circumstances of their adoption at the end of the nineteenth and the beginning of the twentieth centuries. It is important to note, as historical institutionalists often do, that neither of these theories tells us precisely when change occurs, nor do they reveal much about the content of the institutional change or its direction. Using information about women's policy offices and state feminism to examine constant-cause and path-dependent propositions is a step toward clarifying the application of these theories.

Theorizing Policy Change

Scholars who focus on institutions as a way of understanding public policy formation are also interested in explaining institutional change and resistance to change over the long haul. To that end, Jack Hayward (1992) offers the notion of "sectoralization" in functional policy areas in agriculture or industry. Similarly, Pierre Muller (1990) has noted the creation of a sectoral "*référentielle*," what discursive institutionalists would call a dominant frame.[9] Sectoralization forces actors in certain domains to follow a particular set of policy approaches and actions instead of their own goals and also suggests the themes of resistance (Muller 1990). If a policy area is sectoralized, there is a specific lineup of state- and society-based actors that mobilize around a general area of policy formation and with its way of approaching policy issues.[10]

In an initial study of agenda setting in the United States that was later extended to other Western democracies, Frank R. Baumgartner and Bryan D. Jones (2002) applied the idea of "punctuated equilibrium" as a slightly different way of understanding policy change. Their argument is that change occurs at particular moments when government agendas reconfigure patterns of actors and politics at subsystem levels (Baumgartner, Green-Pedersen, and Jones 2006). This notion of change is similar to path dependency but is more case-specific and individualized, depending on the political dynamics of each policy decision.[11]

Other theories of public policy analysis show more flexibility in their predictions about the potential for change. At the same time, they are based on the notion of permanence at given moments and involve political institutions to a certain degree. The theory of "advocacy coalition frameworks," first elaborated by Paul Sabatier and Hank Jenkins-Smith (1993), shows how advocacy coalitions emerge through policy learning to affect the direction of institutional dynamics and policy outcomes around discrete issues, like water policy. Similarly, applications of John Kingdon's agenda-setting model (1995), in a comparative perspective, show that policy windows can open as a result of shifts in political context and the presence of "policy entrepreneurs" to incur "macro reforms" and hence change the direction of policy across governments as a whole (Keeler 1993; Mazur 1995). Hall and others have also shown that a combination of ideas, interests, and institutions can lead to important changes in long-established patterns of state action (1997).

Discursive Institutionalism

The discursive approach to institutional change aims not only to bring the state in as a focus of political science research but to bring ideas back in when trying to understand state institutions. As Vivien Schmidt (2008) argues, most new institutional theories (historical, rational choice) seek to explain dynamics of institutions from the outside—the context in which institutions operate. To complement this exogenous research, discursive studies look at agency change from the inside, that is, the way individuals and groups in the institutions develop and communicate ideas, and the patterns and effects of their discourse. The focus is to examine how and why the actors themselves frame the problems, seek solutions, and follow through. Such information explains not only the pattern of change, but also the timing, substance, and process of that change.

The theory of state feminism elaborated in this book has a strong component of discursive institutionalism. Assumptions about framing have a central place in understanding the interactions between state and non-state actors, the influence of state agencies, and successes and failures in gendering the state. In Chapter 9, Sauer describes the range and diversity of frames representing women's movement discourse and their fit with the dominant discourse of policy actors across debates on a variety of issues.[12]

In this chapter, we focus on the impact of agencies on changing the dominant discourse of policy actors. According to the state feminism theoretical framework, women's policy machineries, as new political institutions, have the potential to introduce gendered perspectives into state processes, change the discursive frameworks of policy arenas, and enable routine consideration of issues of gender equality. In addition, the extent to which agency frames coincide with those of women's movement groups, whether feminist or not, links ideational change to actors inside and outside the state, expanding the discursive institutional dynamics. Those agencies that gender policy discourses with women's movement frames are Insiders; thus, the frequency of Insiders across policy debates is an indicator of discursive institutional change. The analysis of agency activities therefore contributes to understanding the role of discursive institutions in state change, yet another indicator of feminist engagement and institutionalization within the state.

To sum up, this review of theories of institutional change brings us to the study of the presence and structural change of women's policy agencies and their activities over time as well as across issue sectors and across countries. The goal is to assess the applicability of these theories in understanding patterns in the data. What happens after institutions are created? Do agencies become more formalized, hierarchical, professionalized with clearly outlined rules, and more successful? Or do they remain static or decline? How useful are notions of path dependency, punctuated equilibriums, and constant cause to understanding the fate of these state-based offices? Are there established patterns of sectoralization and framing within the state that prevent the new agencies from being powerful players? To what extent can institutional actors change prevailing policy discourse? Can we identify a single configuration of institutional change and impact in each country or across a similar regional grouping of countries? To address these questions, we begin with an assessment of agency characteristics over time and then turn to considering the trajectory of Insider agencies and their success rates as indicators of discursive change.

Exploring New Institutionalism through Patterns of Agency Characteristics

Two general aspects of institutional change are examined here. The first aspect uses the presence of women's policy offices as an indicator of institutional change within the state. Creating a new agency reflects the state's ability to take on gendered approaches to public policy. When agencies persist over time, they disprove the notion that all state institutions are forever frozen into a gender-biased logic of appropriateness. A significant upward trajectory in the number of agencies over time suggests that the state has empowered a new type of institutional actor not only to be present in the state but also to become numerous enough to mark a critical juncture of change. Similarly, the resilience and institutionalization of structures specifically charged with women's rights issues indicate "institutional layering," where new institutions and administrative systems are established on top of or outside of existing ones. This layering process is different from "institutional conversion," where existing politico-administrative structures become used in a new way (Thelen 2003: 226–230).

The second aspect of institutional change evaluated in this section is the timing and pattern of change of the structural features of agencies from the early 1970s to the early 2000s in each country and across regions. Here, the question of whether agencies follow a constant-cause or path-dependent model of change is relevant: Do agency characteristics present at its creation continue over time, or are there moments during the process when they change significantly? The structural features of agencies as a whole identify overall trends of institutionalization by time period, country, and region. For example, are certain countries or regional groupings of countries more amenable than others to structurally complex and well-resourced agencies?

We use the dataset of seventy-three agencies developed from the RNGS study and used in Chapter 3 to compare structural characteristics of agencies in thirteen countries from the 1970s to the early 2000s.[13] This quantitative information shows whether, when, and to what degree agencies have become established institutional actors within the state. At the same time, it is important to note that this information does not allow for a direct analysis of the determinants of that change or the specific timing and content of the patterns after the agencies appeared—what institutionalists identify as "the sequences of events and processes that shaped their development" (Pierson and Skocpol 2003: 721).

Agency *presence* is tracked through information on the number and proportion of agencies in each decade in relation to all agencies, and by country and regional grouping. The *level of formalization* follows the idea of "organizational institutionalization" (Meyer and Rowman 1991), based on a Weberian notion of bureaucracy: the existence of formal rules and regulations, hierarchy, and professionalization. Here, formalization is measured by the degree to which a given agency has any or all of the following six resources: separate budget, separate full-time staff, administrative divisions and/or field offices, separate research staff, and subsidies for women's groups. Scores for administrative capacity indicate the number of these resources for each agency.

Proximity to decision-making power, along with resources of administrative staff and budget measures the *relative power* of agencies. Agencies closer to decision-making centers in government with high levels of budget and staff are considered to be more powerful than agencies with low levels. There are two measures to indicate the *links with constituencies*: the proportion of overall budgets dedicated to subsidies for women's groups and the experience of agency heads in women's movement or feminist movement activities. Higher levels of subsidies for women's groups and agency heads with links to women's movements and/or feminist movements can sustain constituencies that support agency presence.[14]

Presence, Power, Formalization, and Links to Movements

The 1970s represents the takeoff period for women's policy agencies.[15] The presence of the agencies studied in the RNGS project increased over time: Nearly half (twenty-six or 46 percent) of all agencies are found in the 1990s to early 2000, from fourteen or 25 percent of all agencies in the 1970s, and seventeen or 30 percent of all agencies are in the 1980s. Such an abrupt increase suggests state responses to a critical juncture, shifting the gender-biased institutional culture to allow entry to new administrative players. The pattern of change is also clearly that of institutional layering and not institutional conversion; all but seven of the seventy-three agencies in the study, fewer than 10 percent, were created uniquely to target women's–gender equality issues. Most of these converted structures are found in the 1990s, when established ministries were given the additional portfolio to attend to women, gender equality, or emancipation.[16] Only one converted agency was created before 1990; thus, their limited trend begins in the 1990s and extends to the early 2000s.

The rate of structural formalization over time reveals a nuanced pattern of institutionalization alongside institutional retrenchment. Both the number and proportion of agencies with high numbers of administrative resources, four to six, increased over the three decades from three of thirteen, or 23 percent, in the 1970s, to eight of thirteen, or 62 percent, in the 1980s, to nineteen of twenty-seven, or 70 percent, in the 1990s to early 2000s. This trend was complemented by a steady decline in the proportion of agencies with lower resources—ten of thirteen, or 77 percent, in the 1970s, to five of thirteen, or 38 percent, in the 1980s, to eight of twenty-seven, or 30 percent,in the 1990s to 2000s. Nevertheless, while there was a steady expansion of capacity, the small proportion of less formalized agencies persisted well into the 1990s.

There was a trend toward more power over time; agencies moved closer to centers of power and built staffs as the years passed. Offices close to decision-making centers went from 50 percent (seven of fourteen) of all offices in the 1970s, to 53 percent (nine of seventeen) in the 1980s, to 62 percent (sixteen of twenty-six) in the 1990s to 2000s. Agencies with large staffs (100–229 employees) composed only 17 percent in the 1970s but increased to 38 percent by the 1990s to early 2000s. At the same time, most agencies did not have large full-time staffs; in fact, 40 percent in the 1990s to 2000s had fewer than 20 employees. In addition, a small number persisted in locations distant from or moderately close to centers of power into the early 2000s. Finally, while there were some modest variations in budgets, none of the agencies had more than a tiny fraction of the overall government budget—yet another sign of the institutional fragility of women's policy agencies more generally speaking.

Trends in agency links to women's movements through their subsidies to women's groups show limited institutional change over time as well. Over half of the agencies had no budget allocated to subsidizing women's groups, and one quarter funded women's groups at less than 15 percent of the total agency budgets. Across the three decades, the proportion of machineries that had no funds earmarked for women's groups declined but remained at 35 percent in the 1990s to 2000s. Although data on the subsidies indicate some trend toward greater connection with women's movement groups, experience of agency leadership moved away from that base. The great majority of agencies in the 1970s and 1980s had leaders with movement experience (and half had feminist contacts). By the 1990s, barely half of the leaders of agencies had movement connections, and only 25 percent had feminist movement connections. Thus, the potential that subsidies represent for bringing a women's movement perspective into the state is offset by a decrease in the proportion of office heads with women's movement experience.

There were similar mixed trends of institutionalization in the quasi state offices and agencies below the national level. Overall scores of administrative capacity of quasi agencies reflect their positions at the margins of the state: All had a low number of administrative resources—zero to two. At the same time, most of these agencies were close to centers of decision-making power— only two of the ten were distant—indicating that they were not entirely without potential influence. For subnational agencies, levels of formalization and capacity vary significantly: Two subnational agencies were at high levels of administrative resources, two at a moderate level, and two at low levels. Four of six subnational agencies were close to decision-making centers, one was distant, and the other functioned at a moderate distance. Two agencies had no staff, three had the lowest level of staff, and one was in the highest category. Similarly, links to the women's movement varied—three agency heads with no women's movement links, three with feminist movement links. Four of the six agencies had no subsidies, and two had limited funds allocated for women's groups.

These aggregate findings on presence, bureaucratization, power, and relations to women's groups therefore show a mixed pattern of institutionalization. On one hand, the postindustrial state has changed: Events in the 1970s provided a critical juncture permitting the formation of new agencies inside gender-biased state arenas, setting the stage for a break with the path dependency of the gender-neutral state and launching a new institutional dynamic. On the other hand, the institutional change of the agencies themselves conforms more to a constant-cause perspective: There were some shifts in agency characteristics, but these were within the parameters of their creation—increases in some institutional resources but limited budgets and power alongside some institutional backsliding. The similar situation with quasi agencies reinforces the constant-cause argument. One could argue that persistence of gendered hierarchies and bias in the state—path dependency, if you will—also explains the continued marginal position of agencies. Thus, both theories seem to apply—path dependency to explain both the arrival of agencies on the scene at a critical juncture and the resistance of the state to institutionalization of the agencies, and constant cause to understand their evolution across the decades and the Western postindustrial countries as a whole.

Timing of Agency Change by Country: Path-Dependent or Constant Cause?

Here we apply historical institutional propositions to agency change within countries. To what extent do country patterns reflect the dynamics of change overall? Do the structural and political dynamics flow from the circumstances of establishment—a constant-cause argument? Or are there certain moments since the establishment when political dynamics changed permanently as a result of a critical juncture or punctuated equilibriums toward a new pattern—a path dependency argument?

The appearance of women's policy agencies in the 1970s indicates an important moment or critical juncture of institutional change in postindustrial states, but the timing of shift varies across the countries in this study. Before the 1970s, the United States, France, and Canada had national-level agencies. Governments in six countries—Finland, Great Britain, the Netherlands, Belgium, Sweden, and Ireland—established agencies for the first time in the 1970s; in Spain, Italy, Austria, and Germany, however, national offices did not appear on the scene until the 1980s.[17] The continued presence of offices in all countries through the 1990s and early 2000s must be seen in terms of path-dependent and not constant-cause explanations. Political circumstances, the increased mobilization of the women's movements, and the attention of the United Nations and European Union to gender equity policies broke the gender-biased logic of the individual states to include new structures.

At the same time, the pattern of agencies within each country varies with respect to the usefulness of constant-cause explanations in understanding the institutional change. Agencies in the Netherlands, Spain, Finland, and Germany retain similar forms and characteristics from their establishment forward. In the 1970s, governments in the Netherlands and Spain created administrative offices inside ministries—Spain's Women's Institute and the Netherlands' Department for Coordination of Equality Policy. These administrative offices have no powers to propose policy, only to review and recommend, and are only moderately close to centers of decision making. Yet they are endowed with high numbers of administrative resources—three to five. In Germany, the form of choice is the "converted" ministry, charged with more than women's issues, yet having proposal powers, close proximity to power, and high levels of resources. The Finnish Council for Equality dates from the 1970s, and although there is another agency in the period,[18] the Council is the most important. As an executive commission, it is moderately close to power and has low levels of resources, but it retains policy proposal powers throughout. For all four countries, the attributes, once established, tend to persist—supporting constant-cause arguments.

Agencies in France also follow a national pattern beginning in the 1970s, but the constant-cause argument does not help us to understand the institutionalization of French agencies. Although seven of the ten agencies were ministries, they did not retain the same levels of resources throughout the three decades. Instead there was a steady increase in capacity. The three agencies in the 1970s had low levels of administrative capacity—two to four resources. In the 1980s, the two ministries were at high levels at five resources; in the 1990s, four of the five offices were at high levels of administrative capacity and one at a very low level, with one resource.

There are no national patterns in the trajectories of offices in the remaining eight countries—Austria, Belgium, Canada, Great Britain, Ireland, Italy, Sweden, and the United States. In many of these, the idea of a women's policy agency persists in policy design; however, few agencies last beyond a change in governing majority (e.g., Austria), or they are adapted to specific policy issues (United States). In some countries, there is a trend from small temporary or remote offices toward more centrally located ministries (Belgium, Great Britain, Ireland, Italy, Sweden). In any case, constant-cause explanations do not apply, and without more data about the circumstances of agency creation we cannot say whether critical junctures are responsible for the appearance of more resourced ministries or not.

To conclude the country analysis, constant-cause explanations are useful in understanding agencies in the Netherlands, Spain, Germany, and Finland. In France, it is possible that path dependency may be more useful, but that proposition requires further study. Neither theory provides adequate insight into the disjointed shifts over time in agency characteristics in most countries. What is certain is that more information about the content and context of the changes within each country might allow us to specify which model works better or indeed whether a completely different model should be used.

Few National or Regional Patterns

Few country patterns of institutionalization persist over time, and there are no regional groupings of countries over time.[19] Only in Spain and the Netherlands does the same agency exist from the 1970s through the 1990s.[20] Eight of the thirteen countries have a variety of types of agencies—ministry, administrative office, commission, judicial body, advisory council, or legislative council— and although in France there are mostly ministries, three of ten French agencies have other forms. Moreover, in no country do all the agencies have the same characteristics. Offices in Ireland and Sweden have no similar attributes on any dimensions, with each having a type of agency not found in other countries—a legislative committee in Ireland and a judicial office in Sweden.

Even in countries where similar types of offices are found across all periods (e.g., France and Germany), or where the same agency exists across all time periods (e.g., Spain and the Netherlands), agencies share no more than half of the range of structural attributes. At the same time, common characteristics of the Department of Coordination for Equality Policy in the Netherlands and the Women's Institute in Spain constitute the three principal indicators of institutionalization: Both have moderate to high levels of decision-making power, administrative capacity and staffing, and funding for women's groups in all time periods of the agencies' evolution. However, given the absence of patterns in the other countries, this is the exception and not the norm.

Comparativists taking both gendered and nongendered perspectives (e.g., Orloff 1993; O'Connor 1999; Esping-Andersen 1993; Castles 1993) typically designate regions of postindustrial democracies as Anglo-American, Nordic, Southern European, and Continental European. Here we find no regional patterns in agency institutional characteristics. In the first place, the only two country cases where offices show national structural similarities—Spain and the Netherlands—are in different regional groupings. In the second place, almost none of the agencies from similar regions share even a single characteristic. There were only two instances of regional trends on discrete structural dimensions: (1) Agencies in both Finland and Sweden tend to be moderately close or close to the centers of power; and (2) all party quasi agencies are active in parliamentary systems in Western Europe. Thus, theories of institutional change pointing to country or regional variations find little support in light of these findings, which suggests that explanations will *not* be found by looking at regional variations. The drivers that break gender-biased path dependencies in postindustrial democracies come neither from the national context nor from shared institutional legacies, sociohistorical patterns, or cultural norms in a given regional configuration.

Putting New Institutionalism
to the Test with State Feminism

Analytical Parameters

Complementing the structural analysis, we now examine the activity of women's policy agencies from the perspective of institutional change over the long haul across countries, and, for the first time in this chapter, by policy sector. This analysis uses the presence of Insider agencies—those that adopt women's movements' positions and introduce them into issue frames of policy debates— as an indicator of discursive institutionalization. On one hand, gendering policy debates and presenting women's movement demands in official policy discussions brings institutional change to an individual policy debate. On the other, accumulation of Insider activity over time within countries, across all countries, and within specific policy sectors brings a higher level of institutionalization of gender in the state.

We examine both the incidence of Insiders compared to less successful agencies and the trajectory of Insider activities across time, sector, and country. To gauge the impact of that success, we show the degree to which Insider agencies coincide with Dual Response (women's movement actors were part of the policy subsystem and policy outcomes fitted their demands), a combination that means Movement State Feminism. The analysis also includes information on Feminist Insiders and outcomes where agency activities and state responses incorporate feminist positions, or Transformative State Feminism. Scholars of gender and institutions assert that feminist stances lead to a more effective treatment of gender inequality, because only feminism identifies the sources of inequality in the gender-biased, patriarchal norms in society and has the explicit goal of improving women's rights by overcoming these norms. Thus, one could argue that examining the incidence of Transformative State Feminism is the ultimate institutionalization of feminist engagement with the state through women's policy agencies.

Using the 123 cases of agency-movement interplay in policy debates across job training, abortion, political representation, prostitution, and hot issues means that we can address issues of institutional change by sector as well as over time and across countries.[21] More specifically, the questions include the following: Are there patterns of discursive institutional change—incidence of Insider success—by issue sector? What are the patterns in time periods and in countries? We also revisit questions of constant cause versus path dependency by looking at the timing of sectoral patterns by country and across all postindustrial democracies.

Incidence of Insiders

More agencies are Insiders (47 of 123 or 38 percent) than any other type. Thirty-six (29 percent) are Marginals, which support women's movement positions but do not gender the debate, and 33 (27 percent) are Symbolics—those that take no position in the debate.[22] Only 6 percent (7 of 123) of agencies act against women's movement actors by adopting positions threatening to or incompatible with women's movement positions—the Anti-Movement agencies. Just as there are no patterns in the structural attributes of agencies by country or region, there is no country that has a single type of agency performance. All four types of offices are found in Great Britain, Finland, France, and the United States. Austria, Canada, Italy, the Netherlands, and Spain have agencies distributed across three categories, whereas those in Belgium, Ireland, and Sweden fall into only two categories. All countries except Ireland have more than one Insider agency, ranging from two to five.[23] There are twice as many Insiders in political representation debates as in other issues; thus, the rate of Insiders will tend to be lower in Canada and Ireland, where there were no debates on that issue.

Agencies have much higher rates of success in political representation debates than any other area, nearly twice as high as the next two successful areas in abortion and prostitution debates; 65 percent (20 of 31) of all agencies in political representation debates were successful, as compared to 36 percent (10 of 28) in abortion debates, 31 percent (9 of 29) in prostitution debates, 26 percent (6 of 23) in job training debates, and 17 percent (2 of 12) in the hot-issue debates. The high rate of success for agencies in political representation debates is due in part to the higher incidence of debates taking place in party arenas and the success of agencies inside of the parties. Job training issues and discussions of policies at high levels of national significance are the most resistant. Significant numbers of agencies fail to gender debates and to introduce women's movement demands in all areas, but the highest rate of Symbolic agencies is in hot-issue debates—42 percent (5 of 12). The lowest failure rate is in political representation—19 percent (6 of 31), with around one third of all agencies in abortion, job training, and prostitution debates showing Symbolic performance.[24] Thus, once again the trend toward institutionalization in each policy sector must be tempered by a trend away from institutionalization, although not at similar levels of magnitude.

Examining agency activity over time, there is a clear trend toward discursive institutionalization after the 1970s, with the proportion of Insiders stabilizing around 40 percent of the cases in the 1980s, 1990s, and early 2000s. The proportion of Symbolics is not linear; it shifts between 23 percent to 34 percent over the decades. Here we see a pattern of increased institutionalization that tends to confirm the path dependency of the Western postindustrial state over time. With the arrival of women's policy machineries in the 1970s, there is an increase in both their presence and their success, at least in terms of gendering debate frames and supporting women's movement demands in those debates, alongside a persistence of failed agencies at somewhat lower levels.

Trajectory of Insiders

The sectoral trends are also evident when looking at the forty-seven Insider agencies across issues, time, and country. Nearly half of Insiders are in political representation debates (43 percent), while 21 percent are in abortion debates and 19 percent in prostitution debates. At the low end are agencies in job training debates, which constitute only 13 percent of all Insiders, and hot-issue debates, with 4 percent, showing once again the resistance of these two sectors to discursive institutionalization. Agencies have a greater chance of making an impact in political representation debates, perhaps because of the way discursive histories treat these issues. In comparison with job training, for example, proposals for changes in political representation policy were often gendered when they arrived on the national agenda, and agencies are more likely to be justified in promoting issue definitions and goals compatible or matching with dominant issue frames of policy actors. The party arenas, as we have already seen, are also especially welcoming to party agencies, and half of the debates took place in these at the margins of the state. Thus, although the agencies have more discursive success in political representation debates, the barriers they face are less formidable than dominant discourses in areas like job training and several hot issues more central to the economy and employment.

There is also a pattern of discursive institutionalization across time: from 13 percent of successful Insiders found in the 1970s, to 29 percent in the 1980s, to over 50 percent of all Insiders from the 1990s to early 2000s. It is important to note that this increase over time is, to a certain degree, an artifact of the debate coverage in the RNGS study; more than half of the debates take place in the 1990s and 2000s. Furthermore, increased institutionalization over time does not occur in all countries. In Austria, the number of Insiders actually decreases from three in the 1970s to zero in the 1980s, and back to two in the 1990s, while the Netherlands had one Insider in the 1970s, three in the 1980s, but one in the 1990s. In the United States and Spain, the numbers of Insiders initially increase from the 1970s to the 1980s but then remain at similar levels in the 1990s to early 2000s—two Insiders in Spain and one in the United States. The pattern of Insiders—an initial increase and then a leveling off in both countries—suggests a constant-cause model of change.

These country pairings indicate, once again, the absence of regional trends. Similarly, the success rates of Insiders in the most recent period reveal differences by country but little regionalization. Great Britain had the highest rate of success in the 1990s to early 2000s, with 75 percent (three of four) of its Insiders, and the Netherlands had the lowest success rate, with 25 percent (one of four) of its Insiders in this period. Sixty percent (three of five) of Insiders in France had success in this latest period, 50 percent each for Germany, Ireland, Spain, and the United States, 40 percent for Austria and Finland, and 33 percent for Sweden.

The frequency of Insider agencies is fairly even in each sector across the different decades with the exception of political representation debates. A majority of the Insiders in the political representation debates are in the 1990s. This is probably due to the peculiarities of debate selection on this issue. As Outshoorn shows in Chapter 7, political representation issues did not have a high priority for women's movements until the 1990s. Thus, once again we see that political representation policy debates stand out. They lend themselves to higher degrees of success and hence overall institutionalization. Sectoralization seems to be a more powerful explanation for patterns of institutional change than country or region. A constant-cause model may apply here as well, with dynamics being set from the beginning in a particular sectoral area and patterns of agency success being restrained to that dynamic over time; agencies allied with the women's movement actors to the greatest extent in political representation and the least in job training and the hot-issue debates. We now turn to evaluating this trend toward sectoralization and constant causes in looking at the rates of successful Insiders.

The Success of Insiders: The Effect of Discursive Change

Movement State Feminism

The ultimate test for discursive institutionalization is the degree of state feminism—the extent to which Insider agencies enable state action, giving procedural access and policy satisfaction to women's movement actors—in other words, Dual Response. We find a high rate of Movement State Feminism: Thirty-one of the forty-seven Insider agencies (66 percent) achieved Dual Response from the state. Only one Insider failed to bring about some positive state response for the women's movement: a 1990s Canadian debate on job training, which we examine in more detail below. In the remaining fifteen cases (31 percent), Insiders coincide either with women's movement procedural access (Co-optation) or policy satisfaction (Preemption). Complete Movement State Feminism occurred in all countries. In Belgium, Ireland, Sweden, Great Britain, and the United States, there are no Insiders without Dual Responses. There is less variation across sectors in rates of Movement State Feminism than the incidence of Insiders overall. Insider agencies achieved Dual Responses at similar levels in abortion, job training, prostitution, and political representation debates. All of the Insiders achieved a Dual Response in hot-issue debates.

Reflecting the trend toward institutionalization of Insiders more generally over time, the frequency of cases of Movement State Feminism steadily increased from two in the 1970s to ten in the 1980s to nineteen in the period 1990s to 2000s. Thus, these patterns of effective agencies and successful women's movements suggest that institutionalized agencies, as Insiders, have a strong potential for success regardless of issue area, and that the institutionalization of agencies has become more pronounced over time. This pattern of discursive institutionalization through state feminism is stronger than structural institutionalization based on agency characteristics; moreover, and even more importantly, the sectoral trends are no longer present.

It is useful to examine the one exceptional case where a well-resourced Insider agency produced No Response from the state to the demands of women's movement actors. The women's policy agency, Status of Women Canada, had the highest level of administrative resources, a large staff, and strong links to the women's movement; 66 percent of its budget was devoted to subsidies for women's groups. Furthermore, the debate occurred in the 1990s, when women's policy offices generally were more powerful, bureaucratized, and successful.

Case Study: Insider Outlier in Canada: Reform of Job Training and Unemployment Insurance, 1994–1996

In 1994, the new Liberal government, with an agenda of neoliberal downsizing, announced its plans to conduct a significant reform of the social security system (Teghtsoonian and Grace, 2001). A part of the proposed reform would finance job training programs. A range of women's groups working directly with Status of Women Canada and the Canadian Advisory Committee on the Status of Women[25] saw this as a chance to promote women's training opportunities by challenging the gendered structural impediments to women's advancement in the work force. The microframes of most of the women's groups participating in the debate were feminist, as were those of Status of Women Canada.

The head of Status of Women Canada, Hedy Fry, introduced a gendered frame, based on the women's groups' positions, into the discussions around the law even during the closed-door Cabinet sessions. The general tactic of the Liberal government of the time also encouraged open public hearings. At the hearing on job training held by the Standing Committee on Human Resources Development, a wide range of nongovernment groups made submissions—more than 200. Among the submissions were briefs from feminist and nonfeminist groups. Although the Committee produced a "green paper," meaningful policy formulation took place behind closed doors in the Cabinet with no participation from non-state actors or groups.

The final outcome, a bizarre twist of events, was that although the Status of Women Canada and women's movement groups and actors were in agreement and the agency gendered the private policy discussions with a feminist frame, women's movement groups did not participate at the heart of the policy subsystem. As a result, the final law included none of the demands for better opportunities for training funding for women. Instead, the new law treated women like any other applicants for training, and a set of stipulations made it difficult to acquire even that funding. For many, the policy outcome posed a threat to the demands articulated by Status of Women Canada and the women's movement groups.

In this case, we see that despite the presence of a well-established and quite powerful Insider agency with links to the women's movement, movement actors were still unable to get access to the policy decision-making arena, which was closed to outside participants—a hallmark of the job training arena in all of the countries in the study. This occurred even when the women's movement was at a high point of institutionalization. Instead, the neoliberal, right-wing government ignored proposals made in the open forum, avoided any actors with alternative voices, and kept the real policy discussions behind closed doors. In the final analysis, a well-resourced Insider agency could not push the government to open the policy arena to women's movement actors.

Feminist Insiders and Transformative State Feminism

To what extent is feminist ideology a part of discursive institutional success of agencies producing Dual Responses? In the vast majority of debates (80 percent), women's movement actors expressed explicit feminist policy frames and goals.[26] Ninety national agencies and quasi agencies supported women's movement demands; among those ninety agencies, more than half were feminist (57 percent). Agencies were most active in promoting feminist frames in debates on job training and least active in those involving hot issues. The 1980s was the high point of agency feminism, with 74 percent of the agencies seeking to advance feminist claims.

Of the fifty-two agencies with feminist frames in debates, twenty-four or 46 percent became Feminist Insiders; that is, they gendered the policy debate with feminist frames matching those of the feminist movement actors. There was a wide sectoral difference in the likelihood of agencies allying with feminist actors and succeeding in changing the policy discourse. The most successful were in the abortion debates, where the rate of agency feminist success was 72 percent. The least successful were in job training at 23 percent, and in prostitution at 33 percent. There were only three agencies with feminist goals in the hot-issue debates, but two of them became Feminist Insiders, for a proportion of 67 percent. In the political representation debates, unlike the high incidence of Insiders, the proportion of agencies with feminist frames that became Feminist Insiders was average—46 percent.

The rates of institutionalization of feminist ideas in the agency activities do not, however, extend to the incidence of Transformative State Feminism, where Feminist Insiders achieve Feminist Dual Responses. As elaborated in Chapter 6, the measure of Transformative State Feminism (from 0 to 6) tallies the extent to which agencies gender debates with feminist frames that match women's movement actors frames and the state responses incorporate feminist actors and goals. Complete Transformative State Feminism requires a score of 6, and partial Transformative State Feminism requires a score of 5. This means that the agencies are Feminist Insiders and they achieve either feminist policy or feminist participation or both. Going beyond the analysis in Chapter 6, we include here the nine party debates with quasi agencies along with the national state debates in the analysis. Only 20 percent (23 of 117) of debates showed complete or partial Transformative State Feminism; 76 percent (89 of 117) of the cases received the lowest scores. The highest proportions of Transformative cases are in abortion and political representation debates, together making up 57 percent (13 of 23) of all the cases. Job training (3) and prostitution (5) compose around 34 percent of the cases of Transformative State Feminism, with the hot issue having the lowest share, reflecting in part the smaller proportion of hot-issue debates. Beyond these issue differences, it is difficult to assess trends in Transformative State Feminism given the low number of cases—23 of 117. Still, the analysis shows that although agencies have successfully brought feminist ideas into the state—a change reflected as well in the feminist movement experience of agency heads—it has not often been transposed into successful feminist outcomes.[27] This indicates that gender-biased norms within the state persist, making feminist success difficult to achieve.

Conclusion

This empirical analysis of the institutionalization of agencies in terms of structural characteristics and state feminism provides several insights for new institutional theories as well as for work that seeks to gender new institutionalism. First, the general pattern of institutionalization is mixed. Overall, since the early 1970s, women's policy agencies have become increasingly formalized and powerful with respect to structural dimensions, Insider success, state feminism, and the presence of feminist ideas within the state. There have, however, been key reversals and setbacks along the way. Upward trends in more powerful, bureaucratized, and successful agencies in Western postindustrial democracies have been offset by the continued presence of less powerful, less bureaucratized, and less successful agencies. Outcomes that combine Insider agencies with Dual Response to movements—in other words, complete Movement State Feminism—have increased over time. While Insiders as effective women's movement allies have increasingly achieved Dual Responses, their financial support for women's groups through subsidies remains low. Furthermore, whereas Movement State Feminism has grown, Transformative State Feminism remains quite rare.

What can we conclude from this review about theories of new institutionalism and the model of feminist engagement with the state described at the beginning of the chapter? First, the 1970s represents an important tipping point for the institutionalization and layering of agencies and advancing state feminism that changed established gendered patterns within states. At the same time, while the arrival of women's policy offices on the political scene produced a new pattern of feminist engagement and challenged gender bias, it has not overturned the gender-biased logic of appropriateness that persists in institutions.

Second, both path dependency and constant-cause explanations add to our understanding of the patterns of change and development of agencies. New women's movements fueled the critical juncture of the 1970s, followed by path dependency, explaining the abrupt arrival and persistence of agencies. Constant-cause models of change may provide the key to understanding patterns of institutionalization in some countries (i.e., Germany, the Netherlands, Finland, and Spain). At the same time, with mixed institutionalization in others, further study is required to determine the forces at work in the development of women's policy offices in each country over the long haul.

Third, this analysis has brought into question assumptions about national or regional patterns of political change. National styles of agency structure and success occur only in a few cases, and there is no indication of regional patterns. Reflecting the findings of other comparative scholarship from both gendered and nongendered perspectives, national legacies over time are not important determinants for understanding institutional change.

Fourth, sectoralization does appear to have some significance in explaining discursive institutional dynamics of agencies, at least with regard to Insiders and Feminist Insiders, but less so with Transformative State Feminism. Agencies have the highest rates of success both as Insiders and in achieving movement outcomes in debates in abortion and political representation, and the lowest in job training and hot issues. About one quarter of the political representation debates occurred in party arenas at the margin of the state involving quasi agencies. In contrast, the subsystem dynamics on hot issues were at the center of the state in policy areas, many of which had set rules for participation and decision-making that complicated entry for outsiders. The case study of the Insider outlier in job training policy in Canada in the 1990s illustrates the importance of such closed policy subsystems, especially in the hands of a ruling party with a neoliberal approach. Even a powerful agency ally could not overcome a subsystem so hostile to women's movement actors and goals. Therefore, while on the one hand the second-wave women's movement mobilization was a driving force in the opening of the state in the 1970s–1980s producing the women's policy agency moment, on the other hand, subsystem structure and dynamics at the sectoral level may be important explanatory factors in understanding why agencies continue to have difficulty in achieving success for movement actors.

A fifth contribution of this chapter is the clarification and operationalization of concepts and propositions that, up to now, have been imprecise and undeveloped. There is now a clear definition of institutionalization based on four aspects of the structures of women's policy agencies—presence of agencies, level of formalization, level of power, and links with constituencies—that could be applied to other types of governmental agencies. This strategy suggests that researchers should pay closer attention to the context of structures in developing indicators for institutional change. Indicators have also been identified to differentiate between constant-cause and path-dependent explanations, models that clarify the differences in the way these theories elucidate processes over time. This chapter has applied state feminism concepts to clarify aspects of discursive institutionalism and operationalized the concept of sectoralization in terms of institutional patterns and processes.

The state feminism framework and the RNGS data provide the means to make strides toward gendering new institutionalism. By showing how information about women's policy agencies contributes to theory building, the results of this analysis place the study of agencies and state feminism on the agenda of new institutionalist research. With a foundation in the feminist literature on gender and institutions as well as the nonfeminist new institutionalist scholarship, these findings can foster steps toward better integration of the two approaches and hence produce more systematic theorizing about gender, politics, and the state.

IV

Conclusion

This last part of the book comprises a single chapter that brings together the findings from all previous chapters to arrive at a theory of state feminism, assess the mixed-methods approach, and set an agenda for further research. Writing the final chapter has been challenging because of the range of research questions and propositions in the various chapters and the richness of the source materials from the debates collected by the RNGS project. Thus, we have set forth clear goals and developed a balanced organizational plan to reach those goals. With these considerations in mind, Chapter 11 is designed to follow from Part I, especially Chapter 1, "The State Feminism Project," and the two parts can be read together. We hope readers will also return often to the intervening chapters: the investigation and testing of state feminism propositions in Part II and the expert analyses of social movement, representation, framing, and institutional propositions in Part III.

11

The New Politics of State Feminism

This book's mixed-methods exploration of the state feminism framework and the unpacking of its component parts have cleared the way toward a new theory defining and explaining the politics of state feminism in Western postindustrial democracies. In this concluding chapter we offer this theory, reflect upon the study's contributions to the foundational bodies of theory for the project, suggest a future agenda for state feminism research, and summarize the lessons for practitioners and citizens. As we show at the end of the chapter, the state feminism project ultimately contributes to making social science research more scientific and reveals how democracies become more democratic.

The results of this study of policy debates reject broad generalizations about the impact of women's policy agencies and of other key social and political forces on women's movement success. The record is clear: In Western postindustrial democracies, women's movements have had remarkable success in achieving procedural access and policy response since the 1960s. However, contrary to social movement theories as well as the state feminism framework propositions, there is no one recipe for success—not resource mobilization, not political opportunity structure, not support of the Left, and not alliances with women's policy agencies inside the state. Movement actors make their claims on government in a variety of contexts, some more favorable than others. While agencies may help from time to time, they are often not necessary but instead have tended to have a backup role, stepping in to make the difference in the absence of such favorable conditions as open policy arenas, supportive governing majorities, or welcoming policy cultures.

Nevertheless, a majority of women's policy agencies support women's movement goals that oppose the status quo, and many of those help gender the terms of policy debates. Thus, they represent the women's movement despite their place inside the state and their closeness to traditional structures of power. Agencies rarely work to bury women's movement aims; they are, however, Symbolic in a number of debates and, thus, disappoint those seeking women-friendly outcomes. There are no easy explanations for different levels of agency activity, and there are no regional groupings where agencies conform to specific patterns. There is also no blueprint for designing a movement ally inside the state. Administrative resources and policy capacity do not portend agency effectiveness, nor do identifiable levels of Women's Movement Resources, Favorable Policy Environments, or Left Support. The new politics of state feminism is complex, context specific, and conditional.

In this final chapter, we first summarize the findings of the mixed-methods assessment of state feminism propositions and set the stage for a more nuanced theory. Next, we comb the four chapters in Part III that unpack the component parts of state feminism—social movement, representation, framing, and new institutionalism—for insights that *deepen* and *broaden* the state feminism framework. Putting it all together, we offer a theory of the politics of state feminism along with a discussion of its implications for the bodies of foundational theory identified in Chapter 1. The final section assesses the contribution of the mixed-methods approach to theory development, advances a research agenda, and shows the significance of this study of the politics of state feminism to the academic community in the pursuit of better social science and to practitioners in pursuit of a more gender-just democratic polity.

Results of the Mixed-Methods Investigation of State Feminism

Chapter 1 presented the propositions for investigating state feminism in terms of six topics: the importance of state feminism to women's movement success; the conditions for state feminism; effects on patterns of democratization; characteristics of Insider agencies; the special features of Transformative State Feminism; and the importance of policy sectors, countries, and regions to state feminism. Here, we address each topic and integrate the findings from the mixed-methods investigations in Part II to confirm, modify, or revise the initial research propositions.

How Important Is State Feminism?

There is no doubt that women's movement actors have been successful in gaining favorable state responses and that these successes have increased over time. Women's policy agencies have taken up women's movement causes in a majority of cases across all issues. The degree of agency involvement in policy debates on behalf of movement actors is linked to the degree to which the state responds to movement claims for access and policy content, based on the results of Ordinal Regression. This finding confirms a central proposition of state feminism theory: Activity of agencies is a significant cause of more favorable state responses to movement demands.

Agencies tend to be advocates, but they are not always Insiders in the policy process. Insiders—those that gender the issue frame of the debates in ways that match or are compatible with the frames of women's movement actors—are present in about half of the cases of complete movement success, Dual Response, where movement actors are present at the end of the debate and their demands are included in the policy decision. Based on csQCA, Insiders are neither necessary nor sufficient causes of Dual Responses overall; women's movement actors achieve success with the state based on a variety of combinations of favorable conditions that vary across policy areas, countries, and even by case. However, when such favorable conditions are not present, Insider agencies seem to function as a backup to bring positive state responses. Thus, in some debates, Insiders are found to be necessary but not sufficient to women's movement success with the state.

This finding suggests the following modification of the central state feminism proposition: Although agencies form alliances with movement actors to achieve procedural access and policy change in favor of movement goals, movement actors need not depend on Insider agencies to reach success with the state. If typically favorable conditions are not present, however, success is likely to be furthered through alliances with Insider agencies.

There is little reason to fear that women's policy agencies will work against women's movement actors. The few Anti-Movement agencies who do work against movement goals are often the closest to the centers of decision-making power—usually ministries responsible to political executives. In other debates, these more powerful agencies tend to be the most dependable allies of movements. The rare cases of opposition are due to the relationship between the agency and the ruling government's views about the issue under discussion; if the government in power—and it can be either right- or left-wing—opposes the women's movement demands, the agency too turns against the movement. There is more reason to fear that agencies will be Symbolic—that is, remain silent while women's movement actors make their claims in policy debates. When compared to the agencies that support women's movement positions, including both Insiders and Marginals, there is no pattern, identified through csQCA, to explain why some agencies do not respond. Failure can be understood only in terms of the way conditions combine in specific cases, through tracing causal mechanisms in case studies.

What Conditions Are Favorable for State Feminism and Movement Success?

The original framework looks at three explanatory clusters of social forces outside of agency activities and characteristics: Women's Movement Resources, Favorable Policy Environment, and Left Support. The original propositions predict (1) that these clusters will explain movement success on their own and in combination with agency activities, and (2) that they will explain the overall effectiveness of women's policy agencies as allies of movement actors. Statistical analysis shows that some variables, but not all, from each of these clusters contribute to our understanding of what leads to both movement success and the likelihood that agencies will become Insiders on behalf of the movement. However, when using csQCA, we find that these clusters do not provide consistent paths to movement success on their own. To find formulas for

Dual Responses, any explanatory model applied to the five issues must include the presence or absence of Insider agencies along with other conditions and variables. Even with the addition of Insiders, the models provide explanations only in two out of the five debate areas covered in the state feminism project—job training and the hot issues. These findings lend some support to the initial propositions made to explain outcomes, but they do not justify sweeping generalizations about the driving factors behind them.

Putting all the different analyses together—across time, sector, and country, as well as through csQCA, Ordinal Regression, and case studies, there are certain characteristics from these clusters that show promise in explaining movement successes and state feminism. With respect to Women's Movement Resources, the *priority of the issue* to the movement as a whole appears as an independent influence on state responses to the movement in statistical analysis and, in the case studies, as an important causal mechanism that provokes leaders to bring their agencies to effective Insider status. The importance of priority for the activities of women's movement actors and women's movement representation in policy debates is supported by analysis in Chapters 7 and 8. Cohesiveness of actors and movement activism and institutionalization play a part only in specific cases or countries; there are no common trends.

Two conditions of the Favorable Policy Environment cluster explain both movement success and agency effectiveness. The *degree of openness to outside actors in policy subsystems* where debates occur has a significant and independent influence (based on Ordinal Regression results) on the degree of state response. A crisp-set measure of subsystem openness also appears as one of the central conditions for movement success in job training debates and is a necessary and sufficient condition for success in debates in Great Britain. Another important feature of the environment turns out to be *issue frame fit*—the fit at the beginning of a debate between the microframes of the women's movement actors and those of the policy actors. In the Ordinal Regression, issue frame fit has a significant effect on the likelihood that women's policy agencies will be more active and effective in debates. It also turns out to be an important causal mechanism, found in the case studies, that has a path-dependent effect on whether agency leaders insert themselves into debates and become Insiders. Gendered issue frames at the beginning of a debate cycle may be carried over from previous debates on the issue. Often in such cases, agencies do not have to intervene, because movement frames are already in the dominant policy frame. We do not find that the strength or weakness of a countermovement has any explanatory effect in the debates.

Finally, the analysis suggests a more nuanced look at the Left Support cluster of factors, which combines left-wing parties and unions that are very close both organizationally and ideologically to the women's movement, with the presence of a left-wing governing majority as the ticket to success. In the csQCA of hot-issue debates as well as case studies of causal mechanisms, there is evidence that the important connection to the Left is not between the movement, the left-wing parties, and the government, but between the movement, the left-wing parties, and their members of Parliament. Detailed examination of these cases reveals the importance of compromises and alliances among women parliamentarians. The important role of individual MPs also appears in the case studies of Transformative State Feminism in Chapter 6 and in the correlational analysis on representation in Chapter 8.

To sum up, we have found that none of the proposed clusters—Women's Movement Resources, Favorable Policy Environments, or Left Support—on their own increase the chances of women's movement success with the state. Instead, individual characteristics from these clusters, often in combination with activities of women's policy agencies, show promise as explanations for movement success. Thus, propositions that avoid proposing broad clusters of variables to explain movement success and state feminism but instead recognize the nuances and interrelations among conditions are appropriate. The most promising explanations for movement success will be found by examining a variety of combinations of characteristics of participants and contexts of policy debates with the activities of women's policy agencies on behalf of women's movement goals.

Does State Feminism Make Democracies More Democratic?

Women's movement success signifies the expansion of democracy by achieving both substantive and descriptive representation. As successes accumulate within a given country, representation expands, making democracies more inclusive and thus more democratic. The state feminism framework proposed that women's policy agencies are key players in the achievement by women's movements of substantive and descriptive representation. That is, a Dual Response to women's movements would occur when there is an Insider Agency. In this light, if agencies are effective allies in achieving such movement success over time within a given country, then state feminism makes democracies more democratic.

The csQCA and case study analysis in Chapter 4 shows that movement success and, thus, increasing inclusiveness and representation varies by country. Among those with high (Sweden, the United States, Canada, Austria, and Italy) and moderate success rates (Belgium, Ireland, Finland, and Great Britain), movements tend to benefit consistently from various specific combinations of favorable conditions (most of which pertain to just one or two countries) of Women's Movement Resources, Favorable Policy Environments, or Left Support regardless of the presence or absence of Insider agencies. However, often when such conditions are not present, Insiders act as a backup. For those countries with low levels of movement success over time (Germany, France, the Netherlands, and Spain), case studies of the few successes show the necessary, not merely secondary, role for Insiders. Thus, the modification of the original proposition is that women's policy agencies on their own are not a cause of expanded representation of women in democracies. Instead, agencies tend to be effective allies in a given country where women's movement actors confront conditions that are unfavorable to their success in particular debates at a given point in time; they are not a continuing influence over time.

What Is the Recipe for an Insider Women's Policy Agency?

Women's policy agencies are important allies for women's movements, and in some debates, Insiders make the difference between success and failure in gaining positive state responses. Many scholars suggest that the structure, powers, administrative resources, and leadership have a significant impact on what agencies are able to accomplish within a political system. The state feminism framework proposed that such agency characteristics would explain agency effectiveness alone or in combination with the Women's Movement Resources, Favorable Policy Environment, and Left Support clusters. However, statistical analysis shows that individual agency characteristics do not independently account for agency activities. Configurational analysis with csQCA found that, in combination with other conditions, such characteristics explain agency effectiveness only in political representation debates. These characteristics include type of agency, proximity to power, and feminist leadership, and depend on their relationship to issue frame fit, the shape of the decision system, and priority of the debate issue to the women's movement. This pattern was also found in the case studies conducted in Finland, Italy, and the United States, where the carryover of some conditions from previous debates was also important There is no explicit recipe for either successful Insider agencies or the inactive Symbolic agencies.

These findings suggest a more open-ended proposition: The influence of agency structure, powers, leadership, and administrative capacity depends on the relation of those features to the arenas where debates occur. Agency effectiveness may also be affected by path-dependent dynamics: the characteristics of previous debates on the issue and of previous coalitions with women's movement actors.

Is Transformative State Feminism the Same as Movement State Feminism?

The state feminism framework proposed that the processes of Transformative State Feminism are the same as those of Movement State Feminism—that feminist movement actors are successful in gaining procedural and policy content state responses, and that they form alliances with feminist-oriented women's policy agencies to achieve that success. Previous research on state feminism had not differentiated between general women's Movement State Feminism and specifically feminist outcomes. As such, this analysis is exploratory and is limited to suggesting new propositions, rather than confirming or rejecting aspects of the framework. The findings demonstrate a much lower incidence of feminist success with the state than women's movement success generally. However, Feminist Insider agencies have a strong record of success in debates; that is, they always achieve some feminist state response. At the same time, feminist movement actors can achieve feminist response without Insiders, but Feminist Dual Response coincides with Feminist Insiders at a much higher rate than in the movement debates. Thus, women's policy agencies have the potential to be effective in countering patriarchal ideas and processes, but empirical observations of Transformative State Feminism are isolated over time and across countries. There is no trend or pattern.

Given the low number of cases of Transformative State Feminism (18 percent of debates), the analysis is limited to qualitative methods. The results provide components for a theory of state feminism that includes transformational outcomes. Feminist movement actors are likely to gain partial feminist responses from the state without the help of Feminist Insiders, but alliances with Feminist Insiders increase the chances of Feminist Dual Responses. As the csQCA shows, this is especially so when the policy subsystem is closed and when the issue frame fit is mixed or threatening to feminist actors, echoing the backup role of agencies found more generally. According to the case studies, ministries with feminist leadership are the most promising agencies to play the role of Feminist Insider, and feminist movement actors with close ties to left-wing parties and unions can rely on supporters inside the Parliament as well as both quasi and full-fledged agencies.

These initial findings lead us to wonder: Why is there such a small incidence of Transformative State Feminism? There is no lack of feminist demands. On the contrary, as Joyce Outshoorn shows in Chapter 7, a majority of women's movement actors offer feminist frames in debates and the number has increased over time, becoming more prominent in the 1990s. Indeed, feminist frames have become less "radical" and more mainstream in the women's movement. Nearly half of the agencies take up a feminist frame in the debate. Thirty-three promote frames that match feminist actor goals, yet only nineteen of these become Insiders. Thus, the barrier to increasing Transformative State Feminism is the difficulty that agency feminist allies face in bringing those perspectives into the dominant policy culture.

Although there is a general upward trend in the adoption of feminist frames among women's movement actors, there is not a similar magnitude shift of agencies adopting feminist frames and gendering debates with them. Possible barriers to agencies becoming Feminist Insiders may include reluctance of policy actors to adopt frames that challenge long-standing gender arrangements; governing majorities' preference that agencies take more moderate and less threatening positions; a decline in the proportion of agency leaders with feminist experience or ties to feminist movement actors.

Does State Feminism Vary by Policy Sector, Country, or Region?

A proposition of the state feminism framework that affects all other propositions is that political dynamics vary by policy sector but not according to country or region. A variety of findings support the conclusion that movement success depends on the issue considered in policy debates: the degree of women's movement success with the state; the likelihood that movement actors will form effective alliances with women's policy agencies; the role of Insiders as a backup where favorable conditions such as priority and cohesiveness of movement actors, subsystem openness, or issue frame fit are not present. Favorable environments for women's movement success also vary according to the issue under consideration. There is a sectoral finding that abortion, prostitution, and hot-issue debates involve higher numbers of Feminist Insiders than do political representation debates. For job training debates, subsystem openness and issue frame fit are important for women's movement success; Left Support tends to lead to positive outcomes in political representation and hot-issue debates. In addition, whether a particular characteristic, such as proximity to centers of power, policy proposal powers, or administrative capacity will give agencies an advantage in promoting movement goals depends on the policy arena, which in turn depends on the policy sector. For abortion and prostitution debates, no consistent paths to success could be found, another sectoral finding. The roles of Insider agencies in those issues are so diverse that only tracing causal mechanisms shows promise.

These findings suggest that there are features of each policy sector across postindustrial democracies that influence women's movement activism and state feminism in different ways; many of these are brought out in more detail in the five issue-based books from the RNGS project. For example, there are few permanent powerful players in debates on abortion and prostitution policy; thus, the subsystems tend to be more open to autonomous women's groups (McBride Stetson 2001a; Outshoorn 2004). The policy arenas in job training are much more structured, usually tripartite relations between the state, labor, and management; such networks are closed to women's groups, and feminist experts, hence, are more predictable and resistant than abortion and prostitution subsystems (Mazur 2001). Many of the hot-issue debates involve economic development and state restructuring, arenas that reflect the same predictability and structure as job training (Haussman and Sauer 2007).

One of the reasons for selecting the policy debate and not the nation-state as the unit of analysis for this study was to determine whether or not movement success and state feminism followed country or regional patterns across the issues. At the same time, we were not able to cover all issues in all countries: Some have only six or seven debates on two or three issues, whereas others have as many as fourteen debates on all five. That said, the results presented in Chapter 4 show that there are country differences in patterns of state feminism, but these are useful primarily in understanding the extremes, rather than any single pattern or national style of state feminism politics. For example, Sweden had a perfect record of women's movement success in six debates, while Austria, Italy, and the United States had success rates greater than 60 percent. At the low end, the Netherlands had only one Dual Response in nine state debates, and France and Spain had success rates of only 20 percent each. In between, however, the remaining countries—Belgium, Ireland, Finland, Great Britain, and Germany—cluster between 40 and 60 percent success rates. In countries with a low success rate, Insiders tend to be more important to women's movement actors. Countries with higher success rates depended less on Insiders. There are few differences by country in the characteristics of women's policy agencies or rates of Transformative State Feminism.

Alongside the strength of sectoral dynamics and the weakness of national patterns in understanding state feminism is the near absence of tendencies according to groupings of countries. Both feminist and nonfeminist comparative politics scholars have developed taxonomies of countries to identify regional trends across the Western industrialized world. Some of the more prominent include patterns in welfare state development, both gendered and nongendered (Esping-Andersen 1993; Stephens and Huber 2001; Orloff 2002); in institutional design (Stephens and Huber 2001; Epstein and O'Halloran 1999; Laver and Shepsle 1996; Lijphart 1999); in historical cultural foundation (e.g., Castles 2003); and in the "varieties of capitalism" (Hall and Soskice 2001). Few such schemes are useful in understanding state feminism. Finland and Sweden, usually grouped together as highly developed welfare states with a focus on gender equality, have quite different levels of women's movement success and state feminism more generally. Similarly, the Anglo-American liberal welfare states—the United States, Great Britain, Ireland, and Canada—have different levels of state feminist performance. So, too, do the southern European countries of Spain, France, and Italy, and the Christian Democratic "conservative" countries—the Netherlands and Germany. Given that the underlying assumption of the comparative classification systems is based on national path dependencies where political dynamics follow similar patterns over time within countries with similar traditions, the results of the state feminism project put into question this country-centered path-dependent logic.

An assumption in much comparative politics literature on Western postindustrial democracies is that the best means of explaining country patterns is to compare the institutional designs. This assumption offers little assistance in understanding the dynamics and determinants of state feminism and women's movement impact. The classic comparison of presidential versus parliamentary systems predicts, for example, that politics follows the type of executive-legislative relations: Presidential systems have "multiple veto points" (Stephens and Huber 2001); parliamentary systems are closed (Lijphart 1999). Such propositions gain little traction in explaining cross-national variation in state feminism. Grouping countries according to these indicators reveals no common patterns. Territorial distribution of power also does not seem to be the decisive factor: The federal systems of Spain, the United States, Germany, and Canada spread across the range of women's movement success and state feminism.[1] Thus, clearly it is not so much regional or national variation, but the subsystem and sectoral levels within countries that are theoretically salient for state feminism. Variables of institutional design, welfare state dynamics, and religious-cultural dimensions may be important, but their importance varies by sector. It is interesting to note that this coincides with other findings and theories of comparative gender and policies that show sectoral dynamics to be more meaningful than national or regional trends (Htun and Weldon 2010; Mazur and Pollock 2009; Mazur 2002).

Expanding the State Feminism Framework

By conducting separate empirical studies of women's movements, representation, gendering, and institutions, the authors of the chapters in Part III of the book offer important insights that *deepen* our understanding of component parts of the state feminism framework. In addition, their research raises ideas that *broaden* its reach as a basis for further exploration. The insights gleaned from these contributing chapters add to the modifications of propositions reviewed above and move the study closer to a new theory of the politics of state feminism.

Deepening the Framework

Examining Assumptions

The core assumption in the state feminism framework is that if policy actors use a definition of the issue gendered in ways that coincide with women's movement goals, it will facilitate the entry of women's movement actors into the policy arena so that their ideas can become part of policy outcomes. This assumption provided the starting point for the development of the state feminist propositions but was not itself assessed through empirical testing or qualitative analysis in the chapters on the state feminism framework. In Chapter 9, Sauer unpacks this core assumption into five component parts and conducts correlational analysis using the RNGS data. She finds that all are supported.

Similarly, the RNGS research design designates four policy sectors assumed to represent the range of interests of women's movement actors over the span of four decades: abortion, job training, prostitution, and political representation. These choices were not based on a detailed examination of women's movement demands in the various countries of the study. Instead, it fell to Outshoorn, in Chapter 7, to examine this assumption in her analysis of the priorities of women's movements over time. Her study shows that abortion and equality at work have been top priorities across the decades, followed by political representation and sexual violence, which match the four policy areas covered in the debates; hence, this study does examine some of the top priority issues of the women's movements in Western democracies over the past forty years.

Women's Movement Characteristics over Time

The state feminism framework, although applied to policy debates over time, made no explicit assumptions about the variations in women's movement characteristics over time. Outshoorn takes the question of temporal change as the focus of her explorations into the women's movement actors in debates and the entire movement during periods of the debates. Her findings deepen our understanding of changes in movement characteristics, a central component of the state feminism framework. Women's movement actors come in all forms and locations throughout the period of the study. Nevertheless, formal organizations have increased in proportion to informal organizations. By the 1990s, many women's groups could be classified as interest groups participating regularly in political arenas and lobbying. There has also been a trend in the locations for their expression of ideas about debates. In the 1970s, actors tended to speak from free-standing organizations, both formal and informal. Since then, there has been an increase in the proportion of actors presenting ideas from non–women's movement organizations (such as political parties) and from inside parliament.

There is a mixed pattern of change with respect to the issues that were priorities for the women's movement as a whole. Goals of equality at work and abortion rights have been high on movement agendas from the 1970s through the 2000s. Violence against women and sexual violence were especially important in the 1980s, with some decline after that. Outshoorn labels the rise of the importance of political representation after the 1970s as "spectacular." She concludes that the initial lack of interest may be due to the distrust many early movement activists had of mainstream politics. After 1980, however, government became the focus of interest, and many saw low women's representation in public office as a barrier to achieving goals. The movements have not lost interest in feminist frames for priority issues. Contrary to many expectations, a majority of actors involved in the debates from the 1970s on have expressed feminist microframes challenging gender hierarchies, and the proportion has steadily increased.

Finally, contrary to the findings of conventional studies of social movement change that emphasize the "cycles of protest," the patterns of women's movement change with respect to activism and institutionalization are not cyclical. As Figure 11.1 shows, while some countries may have high and low points, overall there is very little difference between the means of activism-mobilization scores and the means of institutionalization scores over forty-three country/periods.[2] Activism spikes in the late 1970s, and the means are parallel in the 1980s; in the 1990s, institutionalization trends higher, but the change is not linear.

Thus, until the turn of the twenty-first century, the women's movement in postindustrial democracies had shown no signs of dying or withering away. This resilience of women's movement activism over the long haul—and most likely into the future, if predictions based on the past hold—makes women's

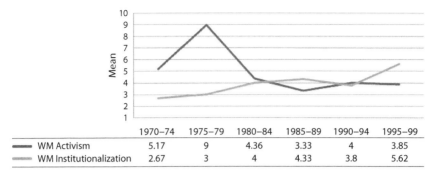

Figure 11.1 Mean scores of women's movement (WM) activism and institutionalization over time.

policy agencies and state feminism relevant for a long time to come. As long as women's movements seek to influence state action, agencies will have a key role in the challenging process of turning demands into policy and in reaching the larger goal of state democratization.

Women's Policy Agency Characteristics over Time

The 1970s served as a critical juncture, where democracies added women's policy agencies to the formerly gender-biased state arena, breaking the path dependency and logic of appropriateness of the gender-neutral state. After that, characteristics of agencies followed a similar track from the time of establishment, with increases in institutional strength but with limited power and permanence alongside some institutional backsliding. As Mazur and McBride point out in Chapter 10, path dependency explains both the arrival of women's policy agencies and the resistance of the state to the institutionalization of these offices.

Constant-cause theories contribute to our understanding of the aggregate evolution of agencies in all countries across the decades. Overall, the agencies have become more institutionalized and powerful, but not extremely so; the power and capacity of agencies remains circumscribed and mixed. Still, they have come closer to decision-making centers and are more likely to have staff members and separate budgets. They have gained powers as well, as more are able to make policy proposals as well as recommendations within policy subsystems. This increasing institutional strength coincides with the increase in the frequency of the ministry form, as opposed to weaker executive commissions, into the 1990s. At the same time, there is a decline in the likelihood that leaders in these agencies have had either women's movement experience or specific feminist experience before taking office. A minority of agencies remain small, weak, and distant from power. Others are subject to the whims of changes in governing majorities. In both Austria and Spain, for example, fairly well-resourced agencies were swept away by right-wing governments, only to be reestablished when the Left took power again.

Country versus Sectoral Patterns

In their efforts to unpack state feminist ideas, the authors of Chapters 7 through 10 also explore the question of sectoral versus country-regional patterns, with similar results to those obtained in assessing the state feminist propositions—in other words, that sector matters more than national or regional patterns. In Chapter 7, covering women's movements, sectoral differences show up in the frequency of debates over time. There were more abortion debates in the 1970s than later, whereas prostitution came to the agendas in the 1990s. The incidence of debates on political representation rose in the 1980s. Job training retained a low profile during the entire span of the study. Outshoorn also finds that, while there has been an increase in the contacts between women's movement actors and transnational advocacy networks over time, most links are found in political representation and prostitution debates and the fewest in abortion, job training, and the hot-issue debates.

In Chapter 9, Sauer shows that women's movement actor framing in political representation debates changed from an attachment to equality and rights ideas to emphasizing differences between women and men—specifically, the potential of women's special contribution to politics as justification for their greater presence in formal office. One can find the same actors promoting equality and rights frames in debates other than those on representation. This finding suggests that strategic framing pertains to characteristics of issues on the agenda and not to the mix of women's movement actors as a whole that take public positions in a country.

Among the various dynamics of representation processes studied in Chapter 8, Lovenduski and Guadagnini demonstrate that the sequence of actions across debates varies by issue. For example, in job training, the movement representatives shifted away from male breadwinner models of employment to shared partnership ones, although this had little effect on their fortunes vis-à-vis the state. The authors reported evidence of path dependency in abortion debates, where gendered issue frames tended to enhance opportunity for success in subsequent debates.

In Chapter 10, Mazur and McBride show higher rates of discursive institutionalization with greater frequency of Insider agencies in political representation, compared with less frequency in job training and the hot issue. There is also a wide sectoral difference across 117 debates in the proportion of agencies taking feminist positions, their success in becoming Feminist Insiders, and the achievement of transformative outcomes.

The findings of all of these authors, with respect to country patterns, are consistent with the state feminism findings in the second part of the book. That is, there are differences across the countries on some characteristics of movement actors and agencies, framing, and representation, but it is difficult to find commonalities, and there are no regional groupings. Outshoorn classified countries according to the patterns of activity of women's movement actors in policy debates over time. She found "intriguing national differences" that did not correspond to conventional comparative classification systems. It is difficult to explain why Austria, Canada, Ireland, Italy, and Spain should show increasing activity over the decades, while the United States and the Netherlands show less activity. Similarly, Lovenduski and Guadagnini did not find any correlation between different models of citizenship—republican systems versus liberal, hybrid, and corporatist—and agency representativeness of women' movement participation.

Some authors looked for "national styles" of dynamics. Sauer wondered if women's movement actors in each country followed discernible framing strategies across debates and issues. She found only four examples: In Italy and Germany, the difference frame dominated women's movement discourse, and in Belgium and France she found mostly rights frames. Mazur and McBride also found some national styles in the area of agency structure and success, but only in five of the thirteen countries: Germany, the Netherlands, Spain, Finland, and France. They identified few national trends in the development of discursive institutions, either in terms of the presence of Insider agencies or in the patterns of Transformative State Feminism. All countries had anywhere from two to four types of agencies—Insider, Symbolic, Marginal, or Anti-Movement agencies. Similarly, while discursive institutionalization increased over time, this longitudinal institutionalization did not occur in all countries, and patterns of discursive institutions did not follow any regional groupings.

The number of Insiders decreased in Austria and the Netherlands over time; Insiders increased and then leveled off in Spain and the United States. Great Britain had the highest rate of Insiders from the 1990s to 2000s at 75 percent of all agency activities in debates; Sweden (33 percent) and the Netherlands (25 percent) had the lowest levels. Moderate success rates were seen by agencies in this last period in the remaining countries: France at 60 percent; Germany, Ireland, Spain, and the United States at 50 percent; and Austria and Finland at 40 percent. Thus, to sum up, elements of state feminism—including women's movements, women's policy agencies, and policy subsystems—are too complex to conform to consistent patterns in countries or regions. They are better understood by the type of policy sector in which they operate common to all countries in the study.

Broadening the Framework

Agency Activity in Representation

The exploration of the state feminism framework in Chapter 4 focuses on the significance of women's policy agency activity in policy debates in helping women's movement actors achieve success with the state. We use measures of agency activity that combine both the degree to which their microframes coincide with those of women's movement actors as well as agency success in inserting those microframes into the dominant issue frame in the policy subsystem (i.e., Insider agencies). The treatment of women's movement success focuses on two measures: a nominal category of Dual Response (both procedural and policy content success) and an ordinal measure: Dual Response, Preemption or Co-optation, or No Response. The statistical and qualitative studies in Chapter 4 do not, however, separate the outcomes of Co-optation (procedural response) or Preemption (policy response) for special attention.

Lovenduski and Guadagnini (Chapter 8) do unpack the central proposition of the state feminism framework to focus directly on those aspects of agency activities and state responses that show or facilitate descriptive representation or the presence of women. They develop a measure of agency representativeness that includes only the degree to which agency microframes match those of women's movement actors in the debates. For the dependent variable, the concept of movement actor participation measures their presence in policy subsystems from none to continued presence from beginning to end of the debate. Their statistical analysis confirms the influence of agency representativeness on women's movement actors' success in infiltrating arenas where important decisions are made. In other words, the more agencies take up the demands of women's movement actors, the greater the likelihood that the state will expand to include representatives of women's interests. Their analysis also identifies the importance of critical actors over any critical mass of women elected to parliament.

Lovenduski and Guadagnini also explore the idea that women's policy agencies can be understood as part of a "triangle of women's empowerment" along with movement actors and women legislators. Did the triangle idea find traction among the debates in this study? To answer this question, they used their measure of agency representativeness and developed two new measures: women's movement agreement between autonomous and integrated types of actors, and legislator intervention based on whether or not women legislators were among the women's movement actors presenting microframes. They examined the connections between and among the three and their effect on overall movement success. They found not a triangle with links among all three groups, but instead two separate streams where agencies act independently while legislators work together with autonomous and integrated movement actors.

Cultural Change

The state feminism framework conceptualizes state responses to women's movement success in terms of policy content and procedural access to policy subsystems for women's movement actors. This ignores a third kind of state response suggested by Rochon (1998)—cultural change. In Chapter 9, Sauer looks at changes in the content of issue frames—the definitions of issues used by participants in policy subsystems—as evidence of cultural change inside the political system. She takes the extent to which issue frames become gendered or more gendered, especially in sync with the microframes of women's movement actors, as evidence of movement impact on culture. By this indicator, Sauer finds significant cultural change as a result of movement activists and agency allies. The issue frames tended to be gendered at a higher rate at the end than at the beginning and, in general, became more gendered, although there is some variation by issue area. The most dramatic shifts toward more gendering were in prostitution debates, followed by abortion. She concludes that movement actors and agencies have been successful in sensitizing policy makers to the gendered aspects of the problems they confront. Such cultural change has been ongoing since the 1970s, with little variation by decade. Lovenduski and Guadagnini also identify the correlation between movement actor participation and gendering at the end of the debate.

There is a question, however, of the extent to which such change is permanent. In many cases, the gendered issue frame is not path-dependent; it does not carry over to the next time the issue reaches the agenda. Since the cultural change has occurred due to the frequent cooperation of women's movement actors and women's policy agencies, it is unlikely that gendering issue frames will persist without the presence of Insider agencies and Dual Responses occurring together—in other words, state feminism.

Based on these findings, it would be interesting to explore the sources of women's movement actors' microframes and how they change in relation to other changes in women's movement discourse. Sauer examines the shift in women's movement actors' frames that mirrors a similar shift in academic gender studies—that is, from a focus on women's equality and status to an awareness of gender and intersecting axes of inequality and race, sexuality, ethnicity, and religion. In addition, her work directs our attention to the place of what she calls "active gender framers" in the policy process. These are not just women's policy agencies but experts who are vigilant throughout policy processes.

International Influences on State Feminism

The state feminism framework did not include ideas about international influences on the women's movement–women's policy agency alliances and their efforts to gain state responses. A list of such influences would certainly include "transnational advocacy networks" (Keck and Sikkink 1998). Other avenues could be the relations between national-level women's policy agencies and international agencies, such as those in the United Nations and European Union. Although RNGS gathered some data about these influences beyond the nation-state through the participation of women's movement actors in TANs and national compliance with CEDAW (Convention for the Elimination of Discrimination against Women) in the United Nations and with European Union policy requirements, none of these proved to be important in cross-tabulations or regression analysis.

The lack of salience of these factors must also be placed within the context of the actual development of international and supranational influences during the decades covered by the cases that comprise the RNGS data, beginning in the late 1960s and early 1970s. Although there have long been international contacts and networks across issues, the phenomena of global movements did not emerge until the late 1990s (Keck and Sikkink 1998; Smith 2005; Ferree and Tripp 2006). Outshoorn takes a systematic look at the international arena in Chapter 7 and shows that there was an increase over time in the contacts between women's movement actors at the national level and transnational networks active in the political representation and prostitution debates, but not in the other three issue areas in the study. Similarly, influence from the United Nations was present but did not become an important factor at the national level until after the Fourth World Conference on Women in Beijing in 1995 (Rai 2003a). Member states of the European Union became more responsive to policy directives and gender mainstreaming in the mid-1990s after the adoption of the Treaty of Amsterdam (Hantrais 2000; Haffner-Burton and Pollock 2009). Thus, future studies of state feminism must include consideration of the importance of extranational influences beginning in late 1990s and early 2000s.

Diversity and Intersectionality

This study has little to say on the issue of whether women's movements and women's policy agencies deal with the full diversity of women's interests as they cross-cut or "intersect" with racial, ethnic, religious, linguistic, age, and other group differences. As an emerging literature on gender and diversity began to show in the 1990s, these differences among groups of women undermine notions of a single monolithic set of women's interests.[3] The study's conceptualization of women's movements and feminism, detailed in Chapter 2, does take into account differences among women by defining movement actors in terms of a variety of ideas and frames. However, the RNGS design does not consider diversity as a distinct policy area or direct researchers to look for explicit frames that incorporate identities other than those based on sex and gender.

As a result, only about 5 percent of all women's movement actors' microframes in the study include claims of ethnic groups of women, and only a few of the hot-issue debates address race discrimination: the immigration debate in Belgium and the welfare reform debate in the United States. A handful of agencies cover axes of discrimination other than gender inequities. It is important to note that these silences on diversity in the state feminism theoretical framework stem primarily from the timing of the RNGS study. The network selected the five issues for study in 1995, several years before the systematic attention to diversity issues on the European scene (Squires 2007); similarly, governments were slow to take them into account in policy (Outshoorn and Kantola 2007: 279).

The four chapters that unpack state feminism treat intersectionality in a similar peripheral fashion. Lovenduski and Guadagnini show that while women's movement advocates did not deny and indeed frequently affirmed the diversity of women, they did not pay the question much attention in these debates. Sauer asserts that shifts in framing over time toward more difference framing across all countries mirrors a similar shift in women's studies and gender studies, as well as a general rising awareness about how different forms of discrimination intersect.

Clearly, there is much work to be done to bring in issues of ethnic, racial, and cultural diversity into state feminism theory. Squires (2005, 2007) and others insist that it is essential to incorporate diversity into gender and the state research more broadly. Not only has intersectionality become increasingly relevant politically and in scholarly circles in recent years, but more women's policy agencies have been transposed into "diversity" agencies that treat in one unit all forms of discrimination. In some cases, this is a strategy to address inequalities in their full complexity, as in Great Britain (Lovenduski 2007a; Squires and Wickham-Jones 2002); in others it tends to marginalize the treatment of gender equality, as in the case of recent developments in women's policy machinery in France.

From a Framework to a Theory of State Feminism

With the modifications from the exploration of state feminism propositions and results of unpacking state feminism components at hand, we propose a more theoretically powerful and empirically robust set of propositions, which move the state feminism framework to the level of a theory. The result is a more nuanced and complex statement of the relationships among women's movement actors, women's policy agencies, and state policy-making processes that can be put to the test in future explorations into the process of gendering the postindustrial democratic state. After presenting the theory, we discuss its implications for the foundational theories of state feminism.

The Theory

Women's policy agencies can and do form alliances with women's movement actors to achieve procedural access and policy change in favor of movement goals. If policy actors use a definition of an issue gendered in ways that coincide with women's movement goals, it will facilitate the entry of movement actors into the policy arena and of their ideas into policy outcomes. Thus, agencies can facilitate movement success by adopting microframes that are compatible with or match women's movement actors' frames: Gendering issue definitions used by policy actors with those frames brings about access, policy success, and political cultural change in specific policy subsystems and in the state, more broadly speaking. The degree of activism of agencies is a significant cause of more favorable state responses to movement demands. The most effective agencies—Insiders—play a necessary backup role in gaining complete movement success, Dual Responses, if other conditions are not favorable. Agencies also may form partial alliances or fail completely while women's movements are still successful in achieving their goals. The result is women's movement success but not state feminism.

The patterns of successful agency-movement alliances are the patterns of state feminism. Alliances that achieve specifically feminist goals are cases of Transformative State Feminism; those that achieve movement goals more broadly are Movement State Feminism. There is limited ability of feminist movement actors to gain complete success in debates, but the likelihood is greater when agencies gender policy debates in feminist terms that match movement actor claims. With the accumulation of women's movement successes over time in a given country, democratic governments become more democratic through increased substantive and descriptive representation of advocates for women, a previously excluded constituency. Women's policy agencies on their own are not a cause of expanded inclusiveness of women in democracies in this broad sense. Instead, agencies tend to be effective allies when women's movement actors confront conditions that are unfavorable to their success in particular debates, but are not a continuing influence over time—once again a backup role.

Agencies that take up women's movement microframes increase the likelihood that movement actors will gain access to policy subsystems; thus, agencies, apart from their effect on gendering issue frames, have an influence on women's descriptive representation. Rather than existing as part of a policy triangle, agency activism occurs at the same time but is not necessarily linked with the activism of three types of women's movement actors: autonomous, integrated, and individuals in legislatures. In relation to this, women's movements gain representation when women legislators intervene regardless of their number in that legislature: "Critical acts" are more important than "critical mass" in the representation of women and their interests.

Particular configurations of movement actors seeking responses from the state in policy debates may vary over time, but from 1990 on, they are more likely to be formally organized, in free-standing and non-movement organizations, and inside parliament; their microframes are more likely to be feminist than not. The levels of activism and institutionalization of women's movements are not cyclical but vary little from the 1970s to the present; thus, state feminism is likely to remain a permanent feature of postindustrial democracies. At the same time, successful engagement on the part of the women's movement with the state is not related to existing levels of activism. State responses are more likely to be favorable for movements that have higher levels of institutionalization. Women's movement success is affected by but not entirely dependent on the level of women's movement strength.

The most promising explanations for movement success are likely to be combinations of agency activities and characteristics with features of Women's Movement Resources, Favorable Policy Environments, and Left Support within the contexts of specific policy sectors or even individual debates. These features include the type of agency and its leadership, the priority of the debate issue to the women's movement as a whole, the support of women members of Parliament, the degree of openness of the policy subsystem, and the degree to which the issue frame at the beginning of the debate fits with women's movement microframes. Agency effectiveness may also be affected in a path-dependent manner by characteristics of previous debates on the issue and of previous coalitions with women's movement actors. Patterns of state feminism vary by types of policy sectors; any path-dependent effects occur by sector and not by country or by regional groupings of countries. Country patterns in state feminism may exist but will not be as important as patterns within different policy sectors that transcend national or regional contexts.

Implications for Foundational Theories

Institutionalism and the State

This study has clearly shown the permeability of the state to social change; women's movements have gained access to decision-making arenas in the state and received positive responses, and women's policy agencies, often speaking for those movements, have become permanent fixtures within the state since their appearance in the 1970s. Mainstream institutionalists, still outside a gendered purview, must now consider women's policy agencies as political actors in their own right and important objects of analysis to test their theories. Two of these—path dependency and constant cause—explain the development of agencies across all postindustrial democracies; at the same time, these theories do not hold up when institutional change is studied by country or regional grouping. Clearly, institutionalists need to expose their theories to the world of gendered institutions.

For feminist institutionalists, women's policy agencies play important, but not necessary roles in weakening the gender-biased logic of appropriateness in state institutions; they frequently have an impact by enhancing women's representation and changing the discourse of the state itself. This role applies in the context of specific policy sectors and debates and not by countries or certain state-society traditions. At the same time, state feminism theory raises doubts about the link between high levels of capacity and power and the success of agencies as movement allies. Furthermore, when determining the degree to which engagement with the state challenges gender hierarchies and promotes women's rights and equality, agencies are often willing but not typically effective allies; barriers to achieving feminist cultural change remain.

Social Movements and Women's Movements

Analysis that is comparative, cross-national, and longitudinal can be enhanced and thus be more useful for advancing knowledge if researchers conceptualize the idea of *social movement* in a way similar to the way women's movement is defined in this study. Two features of this approach are key to its usefulness: (1) the separation of the elements of movement discourse from that of movement actors who present the discourse in public life (gathering data on the latter) and (2) removal of the element of protest from the essential dimensions of a social movement, allowing observation of the range of confrontations with the state. These two innovations, used to our knowledge for the first time in this research, remove many of the obstacles to theory-enriching empirical research on social movement impact on states.

Scholars who focus on women's movements and social movements more broadly can no longer speak in sweeping generalizations about the impact of political opportunity structures, movement resources, or left-wing influences on women's movements outcomes. Indeed, this study shows that conventional theories of resource mobilization and political opportunity structures have little traction to explain the relations between agencies and movements. Studies that

have insisted on the importance of left-wing governments or women's movement relations with the Left seem to be flawed. Instead, a mid-range approach
that unpacks and operationalizes the constituent elements of these broad categories of drivers is more likely to yield theoretical knowledge of movement
impacts. To make progress in understanding movement success or failure, it
is important to look for the nuanced and contextual effects of combinations
of resources, political environments, policy arenas, and policy sectors instead
of general theories. Such a mid-range approach has already been captured in
Edwin Amenta's political mediation model: "To be influential, challengers need
not always employ some specific strategy of action or hope for [the] right political conditions, but they must match mobilization and strategy to specific political contexts" (2006: 14).

Finally, the state must be taken seriously in research on social movement
success. Not only does this study operationalize that success in terms long-term
process change in the state; the findings show that women's policy agencies are
potential key ingredients, in tandem with other drivers and depending on the
constraints of the subsystem, to women's movement success.

Democracy and Representation

Contemporary democratic states have indeed become more democratic over the
past forty years through the enhancement of women's representation in terms
of presence and policy content. Once and for all, the feminist criticism that
the state is resistant to gendering and the inclusion of women must be laid to
rest. At the same time, the degree of women's representation is not uniform in
all countries in all policy areas or across all time periods. Studies of women's
representation therefore must take the same mid-range approach as studies of
movements by going beyond the nearly exclusive focus on women's presence in
national legislatures; government agencies and movements also serve representative functions. Agencies are not, however, the only means of expanding representation of women and women's interests as defined by movement actors;
democracies can become more inclusive without active agencies when conditions are favorable. Nevertheless, agencies have an important backup role.

More inclusiveness through women's substantive and descriptive representation in policy debates does not necessarily undermine gender bias and underlying structures of gender power. This question, of course, becomes relevant only
if researchers differentiate between feminist and nonfeminist actions and outcomes. Similarly, our findings confirm new theories showing that critical acts
by individual women in public office are more important than a magic number
of women elected to office; the confirmation of that proposition here affirms the
complexity of links between descriptive and substantive representation.

Policy Conflict and Framing

E. E. Schattschneider's (1960) famous assertion, "the definition of alternatives
is the supreme instrument of power," can now be modified to include the ca-
veat that outside actors must be able to gain access to the discourse in arenas

where decisions are made to be able to take control of issue definition. The assumption that gendering discourse and policy frames is important has proven to be true: Placing a gendered microframe into the issue frame of a policy subsystem usually gets women's representatives a place at the table. The content and outcome of framing, however, vary across policy sectors, less by country or by regional groupings, and women's movements choose strategic or motivational frames depending on the issue. Getting access to the discourse usually requires allies, and once again women's policy agencies must be included in the theoretical mix. Half of the observations of women's movement success occurred when agencies gendered the policy debate frame, thus confirming social movement framing theories that show a link between the frame of the debate and the lineup of actors that are able to come forward in formal policy arenas. Here, when policy debates were gendered by agencies, movement actors participated.

Methodological Pragmatism: Conceptualization and a Mixed Methods Approach

Clearly the pragmatic approach to selecting methodologies has fulfilled its promise. From the beginning, we chose methods that were most appropriate for particular research propositions and adopted an integrated approach to understanding the findings of each method. Following the standards for conceptualization set by qualitative researchers, we took care to place central ideas of state feminism in the context of research in Western postindustrial democracies as a necessary step toward conceptualization. The reexamination and operationalization of key concepts has been the means to better observe, record, analyze, and compare components of the new politics of state feminism. A first step was to deconstruct the idea of the state from a monolithic entity into different arenas across policy sectors and to assume, following feminist theorizing from Australia, that there are women-friendly arenas with the potential to change the gender-biased logic of appropriateness. RNGS researchers developed and refined the central concepts of the state feminism framework—women's policy agencies, women's movements, feminism, feminist movements, women's movement change, and framing—for use in cross-national, cross-sectoral, and longitudinal analyses.

The project also combined the logic of large N quantitative analysis with qualitative approaches. Quantitative logic led RNGS to increase the number of observations by selecting the policy debate as the unit of analysis, to identify five issues for study, to sample issues and policy debates for study in each country and to produce a dataset of 130 debates. Qualitative logic underlies the study of each policy debate through process tracing, interviews, and archival research. Thus, methods of inquiry and the results reported in this book build on the early decision of RNGS to "choose not to choose" (Mazur and Parry

1998) between qualitative and quantitative research strategies and to combine the "two cultures of research" (Mahoney and Goertz 2006).

The application of a concurrent integrated mixed-methods strategy in Part II allows us to take the framework of state feminism and bring it to the level of a theory. These chapters present results of statistical inference, csQCA, and causal-mechanism case studies not just to validate each other but to present a more full and accurate picture of the role and causes of women's policy agencies activities in promoting women's movement access to the state. For example, while the Ordinal Regression in Chapter 4 indicates that the degree of activism of agencies is linked to women's movement success and that certain variables are more important than others within the three clusters in explaining that link, it is the csQCA that brings forward the central finding that Insiders play a backup role. Adding agency Insiders to the mix of multiple configurations clearly shows distinct pathways to movement success and clarifies the ways that agencies work in the politics of state feminism. The QCA method requires that researchers return again and again to the rich detail of the individual cases, thus leading to a deeper understanding of the relation between women's movement actors, left-wing parties, unions, and left-wing government. Contradictory results direct us to cases where the vital role of left-wing women members of Parliament becomes clear. Similarly, we find cases that reveal the salience of new conditions not included in the original framework, like path dependency of issue frames and the importance of the policy arena, in understanding why some agencies are more effective allies than others. By looking at results across the methods, we see which variables in the framework are important.

Where there are not enough observations to run statistical models, a combination of csQCA and case studies reveals important patterns in the data. Thus, we find the different place of state feminist alliances in accounting for patterns of democratization in each country and develop new propositions to explain agency failure as well as limits of Transformative State Feminism. Sometimes gaps in csQCA lead to additional case studies that expand the newer areas of theory. For example, a contradictory configuration of conditions— the same combination produces both the presence of Insider agencies and the absence of Insider agencies—covers the Minister for Equal Opportunities in three prostitution debates in Italy. A closer examination suggests new conditions for explaining agency effectiveness that are incorporated into state feminism theory—that is, leadership experience in the context of policy arenas, path dependency of issue frame fit, and path dependency of relations with women's movement actors. A fully integrative strategy is not the only approach to multimethods research by any means (Creswell 2003; Lieberman 2005), yet it has potential for a more complete understanding of research results. Thus, the state feminism project can be a model, or at the least can provide insight and a set of guidelines, for pursuing research that combines both quantitative and qualitative approaches.

Chapters that unpack and study the components of the state feminism framework in Part III follow a sequential mixed-methods approach using different large N datasets to explore discrete questions. These include descriptive analyses and cross-tabulations over time, across countries, and across issues (Chapters 3 and 10), correlations (Chapters 7 to 9), and statistical analysis (Chapter 8). They also use case studies of causal mechanisms, selected to confirm the findings of the quantitative analysis and/or identify important causal conditions omitted by the large N analysis. The taxonomy of women's policy agency profiles in Chapter 3 is the basis for theoretical analysis of critical junctures and path-dependent assertions of institutional change in Chapter 10. In all the chapters, trends in policy debates over time, across countries, and across regions provide solid stepping stones in the theory-building process.

Moving toward Better Science

The state feminism project makes several innovative theoretical and methodological contributions. It proposes a new theory of state feminism that differentiates between feminist and women's movement action. The theory offers enhanced knowledge and interpretation of the new phenomenon of women's policy agencies in Western postindustrial democracies and documents their backup role in aiding women's movements. The theory also emphasizes the importance of placing explanations for social movement impacts and state feminism in the context of specific policy sectors rather than nation-states or regional groupings. The integration of qualitative and quantitative methods helps to delineate the complex and variegated agency-movement link: more precise conceptualization, valid and reliable measures amenable to both quantitative and qualitative operations, and refined and robust analyses. Similarly, the findings contribute not only to theory building in state feminism but also to foundational theories of institutionalism, democracy, movements, and framing—a direct product of this integrated and pragmatic methodological strategy.

The integrative strategy applies to the way in which feminist approaches can have a dialogue with nonfeminist scholarship to deepen and expand the general knowledge of politics in postindustrial democracies. Inspired by other work that takes a "feminist empirical" approach, first identified by Sandra Harding in 1987 in *Feminism and Methodology* (Orloff 1993; Goertz and Mazur 2008), the state feminism project amends and strengthens nongendered social science. Research and writing continue to document the stubborn resistance of the fields of comparative politics and institutionalism to feminist ideas, approaches, and research (Beckwith 2010; Mackay and Waylen 2009). This study of the politics of state feminism not only improves the understanding of gender, politics, and the state; it proposes a way to improve social science through a better integration of both feminist and nonfeminist analysis and qualitative and quantitative approaches in those fields that have not benefited from knowledge gained through gender research.

We offer the following steps as ways to continue innovation and promote better science by contributing to the cumulative process of empirical theory building and raising new questions. In other words, we propose the next stage in a research agenda that builds on and refines the theory of state feminism as it applies to Western postindustrial democracies:

- Explore the sources of women's movement actors' microframes in the larger women's movement and how they change in relation to other changes in the more general movement discourse.
- Complete theory-driven cases studies that systematically use configurational logic to locate and map the combinations of conditions that explain agency activities and women's movement success in policy debates. Expand these to policy issues not covered in this study.
- Trace the patterns of institutional change of agencies within countries over time and apply theories of institutional change to explain the patterns.
- Investigate women's policy agencies in the twenty-first century and how they have adapted to social and political changes. Locate the process, critical junctures, and causal drivers of the critical junctures for women's policy agencies in specific cases at the country and sectoral levels.
- Bring in concepts of diversity, intersectionality, and international influences in all research on questions relating to state feminism.
- Expand the study of Transformative State Feminism to find barriers to agencies' effectiveness and women's movement success; include attention to the role of women legislators in promoting feminist movement goals.

There is a growing body of work on women's movements and women's policy machineries around the world. At the same time, the concept of state feminism is rarely used in these studies because of its origins and association with the Western countries (Mazur and McBride 2008; Valiente 2007). Until now, however, there has not been a systematic treatment of the theory and concepts, so it remains to be seen whether the innovations in this study will be of use to scholars interested in policy machineries and movements outside the West. Following good practices in conceptualization, we have grounded the theory and its terms in the context of countries we studied. Experts in other regions who wish to use some of the ideas here will have to consider how well these concepts will travel and adapt them to other political contexts.

To conclude, one of the most important outcomes of the state feminism project is its value for the problem-driven feminist perspective of social science research. In other words, what are the lessons for practitioners who seek to pursue gender equality and social change through the state? State feminism—the notion that women's policy agencies are important for women's movement success and democratic change—will remain an important idea for activists in the future. First of all, the study shows that women's movement institutionalization and activism, specifically feminist movement activities and the demand for social change and gender equality, are not dying away; they remain robust and growing. Second, the resilience of women's policy agencies has been proven: a gradual increase in administrative capacities over time, despite remaining weak in comparison with other institutions. Third, while agencies are not a necessary condition for women's movement success, they play essential roles—making the difference between movement success and failure—when usually favorable conditions are not present. Fourth, given that the state remains disaggregated and that policy sectors will continue to pose challenges to women's movement actors for participation and influence, agencies will remain important allies for those actors. Fifth, individual women experts and elected officials through critical acts can work with women's policy agencies to further women's claims. Thus, in the final analysis, women's policy agencies and women's movements can continue their alliances to make democracies more inclusive and better perform their democratic functions for years to come.

Notes

CHAPTER 1: THE STATE FEMINISM PROJECT

1. For a preview of the study's results, skip to Chapter 11.

2. The concept *postindustrial democracy* is used instead of *advanced industrialized democracy* to avoid normative implications of comparing the first world to the third world. For more on the concept see, for example, Esping-Andersen 1993 and 1999.

3. For a detailed chronology of the evolution of the use of state feminism as a concept in research, see Mazur and McBride 2008.

4. We use the term *women's policy agency* to incorporate the widest possible range of these structures. For more on our operational definition of the concept, see Chapter 2.

5. First identified in the 1990s in Australia (Eisenstein 1996; Sawer 1990; Watson 1990) and in the Netherlands (Outshoorn 1994), the term *femocrat* is used to describe feminist bureaucrats in general as well as agents of women's policy machineries.

6. The complexity in this differentiation is due to the long tradition of assuming that women's movements and feminist movements were the same. However, our conceptualization of feminist movements as a subset of women's movements with a particular gendered discourse compels this distinction. Instead of changing the name of the core concept state feminism, we opted for this solution.

7. The separation between women's movement feminist ideas—where feminist movements are a subset of more general women's movements—runs throughout the book and is operationalized in many of the analytical variables, including policy outcomes, women's movement actors, agency and policy frames, and the leadership of agencies. For more on our operationalization of feminism in relation to women's movements, see Chapter 2.

8. Gendering refers to the process whereby phenomena—such as identities, observations, entities, frames, and processes—acquire symbols based on ideas about men and women. Gendered frameworks are those described explicitly in terms of how the problem and proposed solutions will affect women in comparison with men. For more on how gendering is used in exploring state feminism, see Chapter 2, and in unpacking state feminism, see Chapter 9.

9. The shift away from the state (that permitted a return) was characteristic of behavioral approaches that swept political science in the United States and to some extent in Great Britain. The state did not disappear from European political science to the same extent.

10. For a review of the state-focused literature, see Jessop 2006.

11. More empirical studies of state-movement nexus and movement outcomes have appeared in the 2000s. See, for example, Meyer, Jenness, and Ingram 2005 and Amenta 2006.

12. Weldon (2002a) and others argue that policy processes are often neglected in representation and democracy studies in favor of analyses of elections and legislatures.

13. Much recent scholarly attention has been given to the link between the presence of women and policy outcomes—descriptive and substantive representation. Lovenduski provides an extensive overview of this literature in Chapter 8. For a review of the concept of representation in a gendered perspective, see Celis 2008; for a discussion of the "critical mass" debate, see the "Critical Perspectives" section of the journal *Politics and Gender* (2006: 2/4); and for current comparative research on substantive representation, see the special issue of *Representation* (2008: 44/2).

14. For more on this assertion see the discussion of this study's conceptualization of women's movements in Chapter 2.

15. Collaboration is the hallmark of the RNGS "process." Although McBride and Mazur were the administrative conveners of the network—managing communications, drafting documents, and organizing meetings—every component of the research plan was the result of collective deliberation and agreement among those researchers who did the work. For more on the work of the network, see http://libarts.wsu.edu/polisci/rngs/.

16. For more on transnational advocacy networks (TANs), see Outshoorn's discussion in Chapter 7.

17. The components of both typologies are amenable to ordinal measures, useful for statistical analysis.

18. Gamson (1975) used the term *policy change*; however, we have found that over time, movement success may be fending off proposals that change existing policy against movement demands; thus, in certain cases "Non-decisions" (Bachrach and Baratz 1970) are considered a success as well as policy decisions.

19. Originally, the typology called an agency that influences the frame in a way that does not coincide with women's movement goals *antifeminist*, and then *nonfeminist*, and *nonfeminist* was used in all the issue books. But with further refinements in the definition of *feminist*, we have adopted *Anti-Movement* agency to name this category of debate.

20. Research was conducted by country-based teams of experts in Australia, Austria, Belgium, Canada, Finland, France, Germany, Great Britain, Ireland, Israel, Italy, Japan, the Netherlands, Spain, Sweden, and the United States. In the dataset used for this book, debates for all of the countries except Australia, Israel, and Japan, where only one debate was studied per country, were included. Not all issue areas were covered in each country in the study because of the availability of experts at the time of the study. See Box 2.1 for the precise coverage of issues.

21. RNGS decided to take the issue findings from these books and transpose them into a unified numerically based dataset. Both forms of data are used in this book. For the codebook and complete RNGS dataset, go to the network Web site: http://libarts.wsu.edu/polisci/rngs/. Toward the end of the project RNGS members decided to revisit the book that had launched the larger study, *Comparative State Feminism*, with a second look at women's policy agencies in each country ten years later. While many members of RNGS contributed to the second book (Outshoorn and Kantola 2007), it did not follow the RNGS framework and was not formally a RNGS project.

22. These debate case studies and eleven studies of individual women's policy agencies are identified, with specific locations, in the index under each country.

CHAPTER 2: CONCEPTS AND MIXED METHODS

1. While agencies did exist before the 1970s—for example, the Women's Bureau in the United States, created in 1920, and in Canada, created in 1954, or the Study Group on Women's Work in France, created in 1965, or the Committee of the Status of Women in the United Nations, founded in the 1940s—governments across a large number of postindustrial democracies did not establish agencies until the early 1970s. For a list of dates of establishment in fourteen Western democracies, see the Appendix in McBride Stetson and Mazur 1995a. Thus, before this takeoff period, women's policy machineries were the exception and not the rule.

2. Chappell 2006 points out that institutions have a certain gender-biased "logic of appropriateness"—a concept first introduced by March and Olsen (1984) in their definition of political institutions—that constrains actors operating within those organization from pursuing gender equality and women's rights.

3. For a full discussion of conceptualization of women's movement and feminism see McBride and Mazur 2008. Other papers on the RNGS Web site, http://libarts.wsu.edu/polisci/rngs/, record the search for research definitions of these key concepts in the literature.

4. Gendered references include the following: images of women and what they are like; how women are different from men; how women are different from each other; the ways in which gender differences shape identities (Katzenstein 1995).

5. The difference between formal and informal organizations is the presence or absence of written rules and policies.

6. Not all scholars make this distinction. Banaszak, for example, argues that agencies can be viewed as part of the movement (2005, 2009).

7. For a complete discussion of the concept of state feminism, see Mazur and McBride 2008.

8. All measures for periodization, activism, and institutionalization can be found listed under Chapter 2 in the book's Web Appendices.

9. For additional descriptions of these debates see, for example, Brady and Collier (2004); Caporaso (1995); King, Keohane, and Verba (1994); Ragin (1987); McBride and Mazur (2006); Mazur and Parry (1998). For more on issues in mixed methods research see the newsletter of the Qualitative and Multi Methods Research Section of the American Political Science Association.

10. The field is in the early stages of development and has not been institutionalized among social science scholars (Lohmann 2007). To set some ground rules, a number of texts to guide graduate students and others have appeared recently (e.g., Creswell 2003).

11. Henry Brady and David Collier (2004: 310) define triangulation to mean the same as mixed methods: "employs empirical evidence derived from more than one method or more than one type of data." Triangulation, a metaphor based on the methods used by surveyors to map terrain, has taken on a variety of meanings. Therefore, we prefer to use *integration*.

12. All cases in the issue books are included except for those that took place in Australia, Israel, Japan, and at the European Union level. The worksheets involved information on each policy debate. In addition, there were worksheets on the women's movements during three to four periods of debates in thirteen countries that describe the movements as a whole, not just the actors involved in the debates. Examples of these worksheets are available on the RNGS Web site.

13. The original RNGS Codebook (RNGS 2007a), dataset, and Text Appendices (RNGS 2007b) are available on the RNGS Web site. There, readers will find full nominal and operational definitions of all concepts and related variables in the study.

14. For a more detailed discussion of how csQCA is used in the study, see our discussion of the "Logic of csQCA" in Chapter 4.

15. We opted for crisp sets because so many measures of the concepts in the descriptive and quantitative sources are dichotomous. Fuzzy sets measure the numerical degree of membership in a set from 0 to 1; multi-value QCA uses ordinal points such as low, medium, and high (Rihoux and Ragin 2008).

16. Most notable among these other debates are intersectional issues that combine gender and other identities such as race, ethnicity, or class. If RNGS were selecting the debate topics today, we would definitely explore issues of intersectionality.

17. These reasons include the small number of gender and politics researchers in political science departments in the 1990s and the heavy research responsibilities of those experts who were active.

18. See Table 1.2 for the list of all debates in the original RNGS study.

19. Typically the concepts of standard error and sampling error are used to assess the confidence with which one can assume that a particular sample represents the true values of

the larger population. Here, we make no claims that our list of debates is a sample in that sense. At the same time, we recognize that error plays a part. While our sources of information are comprehensive, they are not exhaustive, and measurements based on such qualitative information are estimates subject to error. There is also the inevitable human error that arises from mistakes in coding or entering codes or recording measures from one dataset to another. In the course of preparing this book, we have already found and corrected such errors, and, to the best of our knowledge, few remain.

CHAPTER 3: MAPPING WOMEN'S POLICY AGENCIES

1. Whether a particular configuration of such characteristics helps or hinders their effectiveness in helping women's movement actors is the subject of Chapter 5.

2. We trace the attributes of agencies across three decades: the 1970s, 1980s, and 1990s to early 2000s.While agencies did exist before the 1970s, governments across a large number of postindustrial democracies did not establish agencies until the early 1970s (McBride Stetson and Mazur 1995a: Appendix). Some of the earlier agencies include the Women's Bureau in the United States (created in 1920) and the Women's Bureau in the Ministry of Labour in Canada (created in 1954), or the Study Group on Women's Work in France created in 1965, or the Committee of the Status of Women in the United Nations, founded in the 1940s. Thus, before this takeoff period, women's policy machineries were the exception and not the rule.

3. We used cross-tabulation tables to determine the composites; available in the Web Appendices for Chapter 3.

4. We count only one agency here in Austria for the 1970s, but the same agency was active in two abortion debates and one political representation debate.

5. For an analysis of women's policy machineries in postindustrial democracies that has an explicitly multi-level approach, see Outshoorn and Kantola 2007. For work on Spain, see, for example, Ortbals 2008. For work on the United States, see Parry 2000 and Stewart 1980.

6. See tables in Web Appendices for Chapter 3 on characteristics by time.

7. See tables in Web Appendices for Chapter 3 on characteristics by country.

8. See Summary Table of Agency Characteristics by Country and Table of Distinctive Structural Attributes of Agencies over time in Chapter 3 in the Web Appendices.

CHAPTER 4: WOMEN'S POLICY AGENCIES
AND WOMEN'S MOVEMENT SUCCESS

1. For more on this mixed-method approach see Chapter 2.

2. The logic of csQCA is explained later in the chapter when it used.

3. Not included are ten debates that took place within parties, five debates at the subnational level, and one debate with no women's movement actors.

4. 0 = The agency does nothing or has a microframe that is threatening or incompatible with movement actors; 1 = the agency has a microframe that is compatible or mixed with movement microframe(s); 2 = the agency has a microframe that matches movement microframes; 3 = the agency has a compatible or mixed microframe and genders the debate; 4 = the agency has a matching microframe and genders policy debate.

5. For the numbers from Figures 4.1 to 4.4, see the tables in the Web Appendices for Chapter 4.

6. See "Agency Activity Table by Decade" in the Chapter 4 Web Appendices.

7. We thank Rosie Campbell (Birkbeck College) for her invaluable assistance in interpreting the results of the statistical analysis in this section as well as in Chapter 5.

8. For conceptualization and measurement of these variables see RNGS (2007a) and the Web Appendices for Chapter 4.

9. 0 = No Response; 1 = either Preemption or Co-optation Response; 2 = Dual Response.

10. Some of the categories of variable measures were collapsed to accommodate requirements of the technique. See Chapter 4 Web Appendices for full results of all SPSS Ordinal Regression runs.

11. In one of the categories of Agency Activity, the results indicated that the small size of the sample may undermine the significance.

12. For a description of movement priorities over time, see Chapter 7.

13. For a more general discussion of QCA in the mixed-methods logic of the state feminism project, see Chapter 2.

14. QCA techniques use crisp sets (dichotomous categories of presence [1] and absence [0]), multi-value form of crisp sets with more than two values, or fuzzy sets (placement of cases according to degrees of presence or absence along a scale from 0 to 1). All the QCA here uses crisp sets. For a justification for our decision to use crisp sets and not fuzzy sets, see Chapter 2. For more on QCA see Ragin 1987, 2000, 2008; Berg-Schlosser and Cronqvist (2005); Amenta, Carruthers, and Zylan 1992; Rihoux and Ragin 2008.

15. While the QCA literature uses the term *sufficient*, we opt for the label *consistent path* to avoid any confusion with *sufficient conditions*, another key concept of QCA presented later.

16. Truth tables are descriptions of configurations found in the observed cases. The truth tables for all csQCA results reported in this book are in the Web Appendices.

17. This process is called "Boolean minimization"; see Rihoux and Ragin 2008: 56–64.

18. A condition is *necessary but not sufficient* if it is contained in all combinations linked to an outcome but does not produce the outcome alone. A condition is *sufficient but not necessary* if it is capable of producing the outcome on its own and at the same time there are other combinations linked to the outcome. A condition is *necessary and sufficient* when it is the only causal condition for all cases of the outcome. These definitions also apply to combinations of conditions (Grofman and Schneider 2009).

19. See the Chapter 4 Web Appendices for measures of all conditions.

20. We use the TOSMANA (Tool for Small-N Analysis) program (Cronqvist 2005) to run the csQCA. This program reports the solutions or paths using Boolean notation: + means OR; * means AND; → means LEADS TO. The presence of a condition is shown with uppercase letters and the absence in lowercase. An example of solutions showing the causal configurations using the Women's Movement Strength and Insider Typology is written: priority * COHESIVE * INSIDER * active_wm → DUAL_RESPONSE. This particular solution means that the combination of conditions that leads to DUAL_RESPONSE is: presence of an Insider agency and cohesive movement actors when the issue is not among the top priorities of the movement as a whole nor is the movement highly active and mobilized.

21. The program compares these remainders to the configurations producing the outcome in the observed cases and includes those that logically would be expected to lead to the same outcome.

22. For more information on logical remainders and why they are important to include, see Ragin 2008; Rihoux and Ragin 2008. We accept solutions only after a careful examination of the hypothetical combinations (called simplifying assumptions) to ensure that the particular combinations in these cases could logically be found through observation.

23. In QCA notation, this model is: COHESIVE * SUBSYSTEM_OPENNESS * FIT * INSIDER → DUAL_RESPONSE.

24. For all QCA solutions, it is important to report *coverage* (the proportion of cases to which a particular solution applies) and *consistency* (the proportion of all cases with the outcome that also have a particular condition).

25. The evidence for the importance of an absence of Insider agencies to the absence of Dual Response is stronger, however. The combination of a closed subsystem with the absence of an Insider explains the lack of success (outcome of Not Dual Response) in thirteen of fifteen cases for coverage of .87 in job training debates.

26. The model also includes Insider and Left in power: ORGL * IDEOL * LEFT * INSIDER → DUAL_RESPONSE.

27. This solution does not include the logical remainders and pertains only to the cases in this study. The solutions with the logical remainders were inconclusive.

28. Given the split governance in the United States in 1996, with a Left president and a Right legislature, it is a judgment call as to whether the Left was in power or not. Because leadership on the welfare reform debate shifted to the Republican-controlled Congress in 1994, it was measured as 0 or absence of Left in power. However, if that measure is changed to 1 or Left-governing majority present, the United States would join the Italy case and the solution would be IDEOL * LEFT * INSIDER, meaning that for those two cases, the presence of organizational closeness did not matter.

29. This is reinforced by the solution for two of the three cases of Not Dual Response: orgl * LEFT * insider → dual_response. This combination explains women's movement actor failure in hot issue debates in France and the Netherlands.

30. See Chapter 5 for more on the Anti-Movement agencies.

31. See "Table of Country Summaries of State Responses and Insiders" in the Web Appendices for Chapter 4.

32. Not all issues are covered in all countries. See Box 2.1.

33. Because all the outcomes are Dual Responses, we cannot do csQCA. That technique requires cases both with and without the outcome of interest.

34. The more complex solution without remainders is: PRIORITY * COHESIVE * ACTIVE_WM → DUAL_RESPONSE, emphasizing the importance of women's movement strength in the observed cases in Italy.

35. Without logical remainders, the path combines fit with movement priority: PRIORITY * FIT → DUAL_RESPONSE.

36. A corporatist structure provides for institutionalized representation by interest groups into formal decision making processes. In this case, the women's movement actors had formal presence on important consultative bodies.

37. The solution without remainders shows that Issue Frame Fit is a necessary condition for Dual Response in the observed cases: SUBSYS * FIT + COHESIVE * FIT * INSIDER → DUAL_RESPONSE. When hypothetical cases are included, however, this condition becomes irrelevant.

38. Without remainders, there is a solution that makes Insider a sufficient condition in a path that covers three cases: COHESIVE * OPEN_SUBSYSTEM * INSIDER → DUAL_RESPONSE, for a coverage of .60.

CHAPTER 5: WOMEN'S POLICY AGENCY SUCCESS AND FAILURE

1. Thus, the state debates with quasi women's policy agencies are not included in this dataset. There were four state-level debates with quasi agencies: the second abortion debate in Austria; the third abortion debate in Great Britain; the third political representation debate in the United States; and the hot-issue debate in the United States. See Chapter 3 for more on the quasi agencies in state debates as well as in party debates and state agencies. Chapter 6 includes case studies of two quasi agencies that achieved transformational feminist outcomes. These cases are included in the csQCA datasets analyzed in this chapter.

2. Ideological closeness to the Left is measured in terms of whether left-wing trade unions and political parties make women's movement goals important priorities. Organizational closeness asks whether unions and parties of the Left have formal women's sections or women's movement actors in leadership positions.

3. For the indicators of this variable, see note 4 in Chapter 4.

4. See the Web Appendices for Chapter 5 for specific indicators used in the Ordinal Regression as well as our results.

5. All categories of the issue frame fit variable were significant at $p < .10$.

6. See the tables comparing the characteristics of Marginal to Insider agencies in the Web Appendices for Chapter 5.

7. In early csQCA runs, we examined a model that combined women's movement strength with agency characteristics: inst * capacity * priority * cohesiveness * feminist leadership → insider. The solution was not useful, but it did uncover these interesting cases.

8. See tables in Web Appendices for Chapter 5.

9. The csQCA notation for this model is: bureau * capacity * proximity * proposal-power * feml → SYMBOLIC_AGENCY. The model produced one contradictory configuration covering three prostitution cases in Italy. They provide the basis for process-tracing comparisons later in this chapter.

10. The csQCA analysis of Symbolic agencies in the hot-issue debates including remainders produced four groups of solutions. We selected the one with the fewest number of simplifying assumptions (eight). All others were based on twelve.

11. This is the second job training debate in Finland. Researchers could locate only two individual women who spoke about job training in any way, and their positions did not pertain directly to the job training question in the debate. Data on individual women's movement actors were included in the dataset; however, for a case study we consider the movement activity to be too weak.

12. Feminist analysts before the 1980s were generally suspicious of the state and, by extension, women's policy machinery—for example, Elshtain 1983; MacKinnon 1989; Ferguson 1984.

13. Lovenduski and Guadagnini focus on women legislators in promoting representation in Chapter 8.

CHAPTER 6: WHAT'S FEMINIST ABOUT STATE FEMINISM?

1. For more on this conceptualization of feminism see Chapter 2.

2. For recent collections of scholarship on the comparative politics of gender, see Beckwith (2010), and on feminist institutionalism, see Mackay and Waylen (2009).

3. This became especially clear in the RNGS project when activists promoting what they claimed were women's interests opposed proposals such as liberalized abortion laws or sexual harassment policies. Part of the women's movement? Yes, by definition. Feminist? No, but we needed a definition of feminism to know for sure.

4. Claiming that one's definition of a concept captures the true meaning and trumps others' approaches is one of the three measurement validity traps noted by Robert Adcock and David Collier (2001). It is wise to remember that definitions always pertain to specific research contexts, and other choices are likely to be just as defensible.

5. The information on feminist frames of women's movement actors and women's policy agencies for each debate is found in the Text Appendices to the RNGS dataset (RNGS 2007b).

6. Both Outshoorn (Chapter 7) and Sauer (Chapter 9) present detailed analyses of the feminist frames in the RNGS dataset.

7. For a breakdown of the 108 cases by the Transformative State Feminism measure, see the Web Appendices for Chapter 6.

8. See the tables used to identify sectoral and temporal trends in Transformative State Feminism in the Web Appendices for Chapter 6.

9. Tables of these comparisons can be found in the Web Appendices for Chapter 6.

10. We used various combinations of likely conditions, and the following model produced findings: proximity * FEML * LEFT * FIT * → COMPLETE_FEMINIST_SUCCESS. All of the csQCA solutions reported here are solved with remainders both for the outcome of complete success (1) and the outcomes of partial success (0). There is one contradictory configuration covering three cases.

11. Tables of cross-tabulations can be found in the Web Appendices for Chapter 6.

12. Unlike earlier investigations, these characteristics do not compose a single pathway in the csQCA; they produce too many contradictory configurations.

13. See the Web Appendices for Chapter 2 for more on the institutionalization scale.

CHAPTER 7: SOCIAL MOVEMENTS AND WOMEN'S MOVEMENTS

1. This writer acknowledges the work of Remco van der Laan for the statistical analysis and preparation of the tables and figures of this chapter, and Sanne Rijkhoff, research assistant at the Department of Political Science, University of Leiden, for helping to revise the tables and figures and prepare the final manuscript.

2. For issue coverage by country, see Box 2.1.

3. The RNGS dataset shows characteristics of 130 debates in thirteen countries over a period of more than thirty-five years. From this dataset, it was not possible to answer questions about the women's movement itself, because the data were based on the debates.

4. See Web Appendices for Chapter 7 for the figure illustrating the trends.

5. See the Web Appendices for Chapter 7.

6. See the Web Appendices for Chapter 7.

7. Information gathered for Concept 18, Women's Movement Actor Location, in the RNGS dataset was used (RNGS 2007a).

8. For more on how the list of women's movement priorities was established, see the Web Appendices for Chapter 7.

9. This measure was developed from the data collected for Concept 1, Policy Response in the RNGS dataset (RNGS 2007a).

10. See information gathered for Concept 26.1, Women's Movement Actors Participation in Transnational Advocacy Networks, in the RNGS dataset (RNGS 2007a).

11. Concepts C21b for activism and C22 for institutionalization (RNGS 2007a). For more on the operationalization of these two measurements see Chapter 2.

CHAPTER 8: POLITICAL REPRESENTATION

1. We are grateful to Rosie Campbell, Karen Celis, Fiona Mackay, and, as always, Dorothy McBride and Amy Mazur, who gave valuable feedback on earlier versions of this chapter.

2. For a discussion of these arguments, see Squires 2007.

3. A recent example is Dovi 2007, who draws attention to this apparent problem, but names none of its putative practitioners.

4. Weldon's argument depends on an intervening variable that indicates an interaction between movement and policy agency. While this intervening variable explains everything that her model does not explain and is, thus, an important part of her argument, unfortunately its description does not allow one to test it for validity and reliability. Even so, the work has analytical potential and implicitly alerts us to the potential importance of policy triangles.

5. The principles of debate selection are explained in Chapter 2.

6. See Chapter 2 for more on the operational definition of women's movements from RNGS used here and throughout the book.

7. For more on these four types of movement representation, see discussion of the State Response Typology in Chapter 1.

8. A new dataset was developed of the specific location of the women's movement actors active in policy debates: parliament, political party, trade union, autonomous women's movement groups, and other non–women's movement groups. The Women's Movement Actor Location dataset classifies 217 women's movement actors and their activities into these different locations. See the Web Appendices for Chapter 8 for full details of the scales and measurements discussed in these paragraphs.

9. Unlike the analysis in Part II, this operationalization does not differentiate between women's movement leadership and feminist leadership; agency leaders with either feminist experience or women's movement experience are counted here.

10. Sauer, in Chapter 9, draws attention to the importance of gender experts, as well as many of the country-based analyses in the five RNGS issue books (McBride Stetson 2001b; Mazur 2001; Outshoorn 2004; Lovenduski et al. 2005; Haussman and Sauer 2007).

11. This is an operational definition; hence, these findings do not take into account undiscovered women's interests, which are beyond the scope of the RNGS project.

12. Interventions are instances where women's policy agencies or women's movement actors expressed a position or a microframe in policy debates.

13. The RNGS definition of women's movement actor is based on discourse. If an actor is a woman, articulates movement discourse in public by expressing explicit identity with women as a group, uses explicitly gendered language, and claims to be representative of women, then she is acting for women.

14. For more on the formal mandates and briefs of the agencies in this study, see Chapter 3 and our analysis below. For a more general discussion of women's policy machineries, see, for example, Outshoorn and Kantola 2007.

15. All bivariate significance tests discussed in this chapter are nonparametric bivariate correlations. The test of significance is Spearman's rho: * significant at .05; ** significant at .01; *** significant at .001. See the Web Appendices for Chapter 8 for full correlation tables.

16. See the Web Appendices for Chapter 8 for details of frequency and cross-tabulation of microframe fits.

17. Liberal models are Canada, Ireland, Great Britain, and the United States; hybrid ones are Sweden and Finland; a republican one is France; and consociational corporatist models are Belgium, Italy, the Netherlands, and Spain.

18. Party debates from the RNGS study are examined in Chapter 10; party women's policy agencies, (usually what RNGS calls quasi agencies), are discussed in Chapter 3.

19. For more on how institutionalization is operationalized in this book, see Chapter 2 or the RNGS *Codebook*, Concept 22 (RNGS 2007a).

20. This concentration is partly an effect of the hot-issue debates, which were intended to capture issues of importance in the 1990s and were mostly resolved in the 2000s; hence, the full dataset does not adequately reflect debates in the 2000s, which were, therefore, subsumed into the 1990s category.

21. Feminist leadership varied negatively with agency capacity (-.224*), suggesting that the less powerful agencies were more likely to have leaders with feminist experience.

22. The institutionalization measure is of movements in relation to each other. The three different levels of low, moderate, and high were calculated from the 10-point scale developed by RNGS, where low instances of institutionalization scored 1–3; moderate, 4–7; and high, 8–10 points. For the correlations, the full 10-point scale was used.

23. Polytomous Universal Model in SPSS. See Chapter 4 for a more in-depth discussion of its use in this book and Norušis (2007) for a useful guide to Ordinal Regression in SPSS. To run the regression, we collapsed movement institutionalization and percentage of women in the legislature into bands of low, moderate, and high.

24. State Response: 0 = state does nothing (No Response); 1 = movement actors achieve policy change or procedural access (Preemption or Co-optation); 2 = movement actors achieve policy change and procedural access (Dual Response).

25. The full RNGS dataset includes an additional sixteen debates that were excluded from this analysis either because there was no policy agency at the time of the debate or because the debate was decided in a political party or at the subnational level. If we run the same statistical tests using the 130-case dataset, the percentage of women legislators is a significant predictor of State Response. See the Chapter 8 Web Appendices for these results.

CHAPTER 9: FRAMING AND GENDERING

1. Using information in the Text Appendices to the RNGS dataset, this writer and Eva Miklautz mapped the microframes of all women's movement actors in 114 debates (those at the national level where women's policy agencies existed). Altogether, we found 1002 frames and used the 490 frames that described issue definitions. We used the RNGS datasets of 114 and 130 debates for the rest of the analysis.

2. The RNGS operationalization of movement microframes, following the literature, broke down frames into these two component parts: issue definition and policy goals (RNGS 2007a: Concept 1). Information on both dimensions for each of the 130 debates, reported by the researchers, is in the Text Appendices at the RNGS Web site for most of the women's movement actors that expressed a position on the debate issue; in some cases, there were no policy goals reported. For an overall breakdown of the two different types of 1002 frames in general and the issue definition component by country and by decade, see the Web Appendices for Chapter 9.

3. In the RNGS project, rights and equality frames as well as transformative frames were included in the general feminist category; in each Text Appendix entry, the feminist frames presented by actors in the debate were identified. See Chapter 2 for the RNGS operational definition of feminist. For the analysis in this chapter, we decided to categorize women's movement activist frames through a more differentiated threefold categorization to better capture the nuances of the gender-based framing process.

4. These are general summaries based on the particular mix of debates for each country. For a more detailed country breakdown, see the table in the Web Appendices for Chapter 9. It is important to keep in mind that generalizations are limited, because some issues (e.g., prostitution, which has a high frequency of transformational themes) are not included in all countries.

5. See Web Appendices for Chapter 9 for data tables.

6. For more on the definition and operationalization of Concept 2, Procedural Response, see the RNGS *Codebook* (RNGS 2007a).

7. See the Web Appendices for Chapter 9 for cross-tabulations between issue frame fit and other factors.

8. At the beginning of the debate, the Pearson correlation of .244 with a significance level of .030, and at the end of the debate, .253 with a significance of .024.

9. Spearman's rho of .291 with significance of .014.

CHAPTER 10: GENDERING NEW INSTITUTIONALISM

1. See Rhodes, Binder, and Rockman 2006 for one of the most comprehensive analyses of the full range of new institutional approaches.

2. This mention is in a short section that cites two pieces from the 1980s.

3. For a discussion of the evolution of feminist theories of the state, see McBride Stetson and Mazur 1995b; also see Weldon 2002b; Chappell 2002b and 2006 for discussions of gendering institutional analyses. The Feminism and Institutionalism International Network at http://www.femfiin.com provides information on current research projects as well.

4. Not all of the engagement by women and women-friendly actors is necessarily feminist. Nonetheless, the concept *feminism* is used to indicate that the ultimate goal of these interactions with the state is to improve women's rights and status; whether those ideas are strictly feminist is a question for research.

5. See Chapter 9 and Kantola's 2006 study of Finland and Great Britain for another example of discourse as institutions.

6. The theories examined here provide particular insight into change in state structures and policy processes from a complex actor-oriented and structural perspective. Not included are other more comprehensive theories of change, such as rational choice or Marxist theo-

ries, because of space limitations and, perhaps more importantly, because such theories do not provide the flexible explanations that are necessary to study policy and institutional change.

7. See Pierson and Skocpol 2003, for a review of the historical institutional approach in political science, and Mahoney and Dietrich-Rueschemeyer 2003, for issues of methodology related to this approach.

8. For more on the differences between path-dependent and constant-cause arguments for institutional change, see Thelen 2003.

9. The concept of issue frame used in the RNGS project was developed from this work on dominant frames and *référentielles*.

10. Sectoralization is an important finding of the exploration of the state feminism framework in Chapters 4 to 6. Other studies of feminist policy development have identified the importance of sectoral trends within countries as well (e.g., Mazur 2002; Htun and Weldon 2010).

11. It is interesting to note that punctuated-equilibrium models are also used in understanding path dependency (Thelen 2003).

12. Sauer also empirically assesses the assumptions about framing in the state feminism theory, finding them supported by the data.

13. Though by no means an exhaustive inventory, this sample of fifty-seven national-level agencies is quite representative of the full range of women's policy offices within each country and across the three decades in Western postindustrial democracies, more broadly speaking. In cross-checking with an inventory of agencies up to the mid-1990s that covered ten of thirteen countries, only eight agencies were covered in that inventory but were missing from this dataset—three in Canada, three in France, and two in Sweden (McBride Stetson and Mazur 1995a: Appendix). In addition, including ten quasi women's policy agencies in eight countries and six subnational agencies in four countries expands the coverage of agencies in postindustrial democracies across a full range of locations. For the complete list of agencies listed by country, see Box 3.1.

14. See the Web Appendices for Chapter 10 for the cross-tabulations used.

15. Prior to the 1970s, only Canada, France, and the United States had national-level offices.

16. These include: in Belgium, the State Secretary for the Environment and Social Emancipation (1987) and the Ministry for Labour and Equality of Opportunity (2000); in Germany, the Ministry for Women and Youth (1991), the Ministry for Family, Women, and Youth (1995), and the Ministry for Family Affairs, Senior Citizens, Women and Youth (2001); in France, the Deputy Minister of Women's Rights and Job Training (1978); and in Ireland, the Department of Equality and Law Reform (2002).

17. In Germany, equality offices were established in many Länder and in some larger cities in the 1970s prior to the national-level agencies (Ferree 1995; Lang 2007).

18. See the Finnish case study on the quota debate in Chapter 5.

19. See tables for analysis of agencies over time in the Web Appendices for Chapter 3.

20. In both countries there were other agencies (in Spain the Consejo Rector and in the Netherlands the Emancipation Council); neither was counted in this dataset, which includes the agencies most active in the policy debates under study in that country in the RNGS study. For more on the Emancipation Council, see the Dutch case study in Chapter 4.

21. Unlike the analysis of only national-level state debates in the exploration of state feminism theory conducted in the second part of the book, here *all* but one of the debates with women's policy agencies in the RNGS study are analyzed, whether they involve subnational, national, or quasi agencies. The exception is the first prostitution debate in Austria, where there were no women's movement actors. Thus, conceptually, the entire potential range of discursive institutional change is taken into account at all levels of the state.

22. The figures for the analysis of discursive institutionalization can be found in the tables in the Web Appendices for Chapter 10.

23. More than the actual performance of agencies in Ireland, this is probably due to the low number of issue areas covered in the Irish case (only two), as well as the difficult and divisive abortion issue.

24. If job training debates had been studied in the six countries that had no job training debates in the RNGS research, this trend toward Symbolic agencies would be even higher, with patterns of Symbolics involved in hot-issue and job training debates being less divergent.

25. The CACSW and Status of Women Canada were fused into one entity in 1995.

26. For analysis of Transformative State Feminism we use the dataset developed for Chapter 6 adding the scores for nine party debates: $N = 117$.

27. Analysis of the Spanish cases shows that while the state and agencies have resisted feminist outcomes at the national level, not only was the Socialist Party women's agency a Feminist Insider in three debates, but it coincided with complete feminist policy-participation response in two debates. These are the only cases of Insider–Dual Response among twelve Spanish policy debates in this study.

CHAPTER 11: THE NEW POLITICS OF STATE FEMINISM

1. The only instance of significant variations in terms of design of national institutions is in the case of quasi women's policy agencies. All except one of the quasi agencies in the study are found in parliamentary systems, where parties play a more central role in political dynamics generally speaking; they are important primarily in political representation debates.

2. As indicated in Chapter 2, the measure of women's movement activism and institutionalization is based on 3 to 4 periods in each country, during which the policy debates in the study occurred.

3. For an overview of this concept and the contributing scholarship, see Weldon 2008.

Glossary

Activism of women's movement: One of two measures of women's movement change that focuses on the growth in participation of women in informal networks, protests, cultural centers, new organizations, and policy campaigns.

Administrative resources: The summation of staff, administrative divisions, field offices, separate budget, subsidies for women's groups, and funding for research assigned to women's policy agencies.

Agency Activity: An ordinal variable that measures the extent to which women's policy agencies formed effective alliances with women's movement actors in policy debates.

Agency allies: a term used to refer to both Insider and Marginal agencies.

Alliance typology: A classification of women's policy agencies according to two measures: whether or not they adopt women's movement actors' microframes in the policy debate and whether or not they gender the issue frame of the policy debate with those microframes: Insider, Marginal, Symbolic, Anti-Movement agencies.

Anti-Movement agencies: Women's policy agencies that influence debates with microframes that do not agree with the views of movement activists.

Appointment of agency head: One of the characteristics of women's policy agencies that classifies agencies according to whether the agency director is appointed politically, bureaucratically, or by a lay panel.

Autonomous women's movements: A form of mobilization that is independent of parties and other associations.

Capacity: A measure of administrative strength of agencies by counting staff, administrative divisions, budgets, subsidies, research, and leadership.

Case: A unit of analysis or observation where researchers provide information according to a theoretical model.

Case study: An in-depth investigation that explores every possible aspect of a subject and stands alone without reference to other cases.

Collective action frames: Hierarchy of meanings that hold a social movement together with three elements: diagnostic (grievances), prognostic (solutions), and motivational (mobilizing).

Concurrent integration strategy: The mixed-methods approach used in Part II of this book that focuses on synthesizing results from both quantitative and qualitative methods; this approach is also called triangulation.

Consistency of a sufficient condition: A measure used in QCA that shows the proportion of cases in which a relation between condition X and outcome Y holds relative to the number or cases with condition X.

Contradictory configurations: In Qualitative Comparative Analysis (QCA), the combinations of conditions that lead to both the presence and the absence of the outcome.

Co-optation: A policy response that brings movement actors into the policy subsystem but does not produce policy that coincides with movement demands.

Corporatism: A form of interest group/state relations where interest groups have permanent representation on consulting and advisory commissions to policymakers.

Coverage of a sufficient condition: A measure used in QCA that shows the proportion of cases that display condition X in relation to the number of cases to be explained, that is, all cases with the given outcome Y present.

Crisp sets: Measures used in QCA that show the presence (1) or absence (0) of a particular condition or outcome. Other types of measures are multivalue and fuzzy sets.

Descriptive representation: A form of representation where the representative stands for a group by virtue of sharing similar characteristics such as race, gender, ethnicity, or residence.

Dual Response: A policy response that fits women's movement demands and brings movement actors into the policy subsystem.

Equifinality: An underlying assumption of QCA that there is more than one pattern of conditions that result in a particular outcome.

Favorable Policy Environment: One of three clusters of explanatory variables that includes openness of the subsystem structure, issue frame fit, and countermovement strength.

Feminist Insiders: Women's policy agencies that effectively gender policy debates with demands and frames that match feminist movement actors' microframes.

Feminist institutionalism: An area of study that seeks to introduce gender as a category of analysis into institutional approaches to analysis and theory building.

Feminist movement: A type of women's movement with an explicit feminist discourse—that is, to advance the status of women and to challenge gender hierarchies and forms of women's subordination.

Femocrats: A term used by Australian and Dutch researchers to refer to administrative-bureaucratic actors involved in gender-specific state actions.

Frames: Structures of organized ideas; definitions of policy problems that include a diagnosis and a solution.

Gendering the issue frame: Process of incorporating explicit references to women alone or women in relation to men as part of policy alternatives and meanings used by policy actors.

Gender mainstreaming: Any action, usually government-based, that aims to introduce the treatment of gender equality in a systematic fashion across all areas of action (public policy).

Hot issue: One of the five areas of policy action analyzed in the state feminism project, which includes the top-priority national-level issues in the 1990s and early 2000s in each country covered in the study.

Insiders: Women's policy agencies that effectively gender policy debates with women's movement demands and frames.

Institutionalism: A broad-based approach in the social sciences that places institutions and the rules of the political game at the center of analysis.

Institutionalization of women's movement: One of two measures of women's movement change that measures the extent to which movement actors participate in legislatures, bureaucracies, political parties, unions, interest groups, and academia.

Institutionalization of women's policy agencies: The process by which agencies become more permanent and powerful fixtures within a state.

Integrated women's movements: Women's movement actors located inside non–women's movement organizations such as political parties, trade unions, government entities.

Interventions in debates: Instances where women's policy agencies or women's movement actors expressed a position or a microframe in policy debates.

Issue frame: The definition of alternatives used by actors a policy subsystem in a particular issue area.

Leadership: One of the characteristics of women's policy agencies that classifies them according to the experience of the agency head in women's movement or feminist movement organizations.

Left Support: One of three clusters of explanatory variables that includes organizational closeness of women's movement to left-wing parties and trade unions, ideological closeness of women's movement to left-wing parties and trade unions, and a left-wing governing majority.

Logical remainders: In QCA, the cases with combinations of conditions that are not found in the observed cases, also called "hypotheticals."

Logic of appropriateness: The set of rules of a given political institution, first identified by March and Olsen (1989), that Chappell (2006) argues has the potential to constrain actors operating within that institution from pursuing gender equality and women's rights.

Marginals: Women's policy agencies that express frames that coincide with women's movement frames but do not gender the policy debate with those frames.

Microframes: Frames presented by individuals and organizations composed of an issue definition and policy goals.

Mixed methods: The use of both qualitative and quantitative approaches in a single study or program of inquiry.

Models: Proposed configuration of conditions expected to lead to a particular outcome; used in QCA.

Movement State Feminism: The situation in which a women's policy agency supports ideas and demands based on gender consciousness, women's solidarity, and the cause of women and women's movement actors participate in a meaningful way in a policy debate that leads to policy outcomes that reflect women's movement goals.

Multiple conjunctural causation: The assumption that an outcome of interest depends on a variety of conditions working together and not on a single independent cause.

Necessary conditions or causes: Conditions that are always present with a particular outcome but that cannot produce the outcome on their own.

No Response: A policy action that fails to bring movement actors into the policy subsystem and to produce policy content that coincides with movement demands.

Ordinal Regression: A method of statistical inference that uses variables with ranked measures.

Policy debate: Unit of analysis in RNGS project design and datasets; starts from the time proposals came to a national agenda and lasts until they are settled by government action.

Policy-making powers: One of the characteristics of women's policy agencies that classifies them according to their formal responsibilities.

Policy orientation: One of the characteristics of women's policy agencies that classifies agencies according to their mandates or remits as single-issue, multi-issue, or cross-sectional.

Political opportunity structure theory: Explanations of social movement effectiveness in terms of external environment (e.g., state organization, party configurations, political culture).

Postindustrial democracies: The approximately twenty-three countries with relatively similarly high levels of national wealth, similarly large service (or "post-Fordist" economies), stable nation-states, and well-established traditions of representative democratic institutions, and/or the emergence of stable democratic institutions since World War II.

Pragmatism: The tendency to choose methodologies that will best answer research questions and not by ideological adherence to a particular method.

Preemption: A policy action that produces policy content that coincides with movement demands but does not bring movement actors into the policy subsystem.

Procedural response: The recognition and acceptance by state actors of movement activists as legitimate representatives of social interests in policy processes.

Proximity: One of the characteristics of women's policy agencies that classifies them according to the closeness or distance from decision-making power in their institutional settings.

Qualitative Comparative Analysis (QCA): One of the configurational comparative methods that looks for explanations in the combination of conditions that lead to an outcome of interest. Most QCA analysis uses Boolean algebra techniques.

Quasi women's policy agencies: Institutions that act in the policy process like full-fledged women's policy agencies but that lack the formal governmental directive of establishment. There are two types: party bodies and legislative caucuses.

Resource mobilization theory: Explanations of social movement activism and effectiveness in terms of internal qualities such as leadership, organization, and members.

RNGS: The Research Network on Gender Politics and the State, established in 1995. RNGS designed and executed the research project that provides the data for this book.

RNGS data: The observations of women's movements and women's policy agencies acting in 130 policy debates made by RNGS and used as the substantive core of this book.

Sequential mixed methods: A mixed-methods approach that uses different datasets to explore and explain discrete questions.

State feminism: The extent to which women's policy agencies have been effective partners for women's movements and their actors in gaining access to policy-making arenas and influencing policy outcomes.

State feminism project: The study that uses the RNGS data and project design to conduct a mixed-methods analysis of state feminism theory and the four adjacent areas of institutionalism, representation, movements, and frames.

State Response Typology: A classification of outcomes of policy debates according to two variables: whether or not the microframes of women's movement actors are matching or compatible with policy content, and whether or not women's movement actors are part of the policy subsystem at the end of the debate: Dual Response, Co-optation, Preemption, or No Response.

Strategic frames: Frames used by movement actors to accomplish specific goals especially with policy makers.

Subnational agencies: Women's policy agencies located at regional or municipal levels of government.

Substantive representation: A form of representation where the representative advances a group's policy preferences and interests.

Substantive response: The incorporation of movement claims into the content of public policy.

Sufficient conditions or causes: A condition or configuration of causes that are capable of producing an outcome on their own, while other conditions or causes may also produce the same outcome.

Symbolic agencies: Women's policy agencies that are in a position to participate in a policy debate but take no position and have no influence.

Transformative State Feminism: The outcome where women's policy agencies ally with feminist movement actors to gender policy debates with feminist ideas and demands—that is, recognize patriarchy and gender-based hierarchies and promote gender equality; the alliance results in procedural access for feminist movement actors and policy outcomes that reflect feminist movement goals.

Type: One of the characteristics of women's policy agencies that classifies them according to form; the most common types are ministry, administrative office, commission, and advisory council.

Women's movement: Discourse that uses gendered language to express identity with women and represents women in public life and the actors who present that discourse.

Women's Movement Actor dataset: Compiled by Joyce Outshoorn for her analysis in Chapter 7 and containing information on activities of all women's movement actors in the RNGS policy debates.

Women's Movement Actors' Frames dataset: Developed by Birgit Sauer, the dataset classifies the substantive content of microframes expressed by women's movement actors in policy debates in the RNGS dataset Text Appendices.

Women's Movement Location dataset: Developed by Joni Lovenduski and Marila Guadagnini, the dataset that identifies the specific institutional location of 217 women's movement actors in policy debates in the RNGS dataset Text Appendices.

Women's Movement Resources: One of three clusters of explanatory conditions and variables that includes women's movement activism and institutionalization, priority of the issue to the movement as a whole, and the cohesiveness of women's movement actors in the debate.

Women's policy agencies: A structure that meets both of the following criteria: (1) any agency or governmental body formally established by government statute or decree, and (2) any agency or governmental body formally charged with furthering women's status and rights or promoting sex-based equality.

References

Aalto, Terhi, and Anne Maria Holli. 2007. "Debating Day Care in Finland in the Midst of an Economic Recession and Welfare State Downsizing." In *Gendering the State in the Age of Globalization*, edited by Melissa Haussman and Birgit Sauer, 101–120. Lanham, MD: Rowman and Littlefield.

Acker, Joan. 1992. "Gendered Institutions: From Sex Roles to Gendered Institutions." *Contemporary Sociology* 1: 565–569.

Adcock, Robert, and David Collier. 2001. "Measurement Validity: A Shared Standard for Qualitative and Quantitative Research." *American Political Science Review* 92(3): 529–546.

Amenta, Edwin. 2006. *When Movements Matter: The Townsend Plan and the Rise of Social Security*. Princeton, NJ: Princeton University Press.

Amenta, Edwin, and Neal Caren. 2004. "The Legislative, Organizational, and Beneficiary Consequences of State-Oriented Challengers." In *The Blackwell Companion to Social Movements*, edited by David A. Snow, Sarah A. Soule, and Hanspeter Kriesi, 461–488. Oxford: Blackwell Publishing.

Amenta, Edwin, Bruce G. Carruthers, and Yvonne Zylan. 1992. "A Hero for the Aged? The Townsend Movement, the Political Mediation Model, and U.S. Old-Age Policy, 1934–1950." *The American Journal of Sociology* 98(September): 308–339.

Bacchi, Carol Lee. 1999. *Women, Policy and Politics: The Construction of Policy Problems*. Thousand Oaks, CA: Sage.

———. 2005. "The MAGEEQ Project: Identifying Contested Meanings of 'Gender Equality.'" *The Greek Review of Social Research* 117: 221–234.

Bachrach, Peter, and Morton S. Baratz. 1970. *Power and Poverty: Theory and Practice*. New York: Oxford University Press.

Banaszak, Lee Ann. 1996. *Why Women's Movements Succeed or Fail: Opportunity, Culture and the Struggle for Woman Suffrage*. Princeton, NJ: Princeton University Press.

———. 2005. "Inside and Outside the State: Movement Insider Status, Tactics, and Public Policy Achievements." In *Routing the Opposition: Social Movements, Public Policy, and Democracy*, edited by David S. Meyer, Valerie Jenness, and Helen Ingram, 149–176. Minneapolis: University of Minnesota Press.

———. 2009. *The Women's Movement Inside and Outside the State*. Cambridge: Cambridge University Press.

Banaszak, Lee Ann, Karen Beckwith, and Dieter Rucht, eds. 2003. *Women's Movements Facing the Reconfigured State*. Cambridge: Cambridge University Press.

Bashevkin, Sylvia. 1998. *Women on the Defensive: Living through Conservative Times*. Chicago: University of Chicago Press.

Baudino, Claudie. 2005. "Gendering the Republican System: Debates on Women's Political Representation in France." In *State Feminism and Political Representation*, edited by Joni Lovenduski et al., 85–105. Cambridge: Cambridge University Press.

Baumgartner, Frank R. 1996. "The Many Styles of Policymaking in France." In *Chirac's Challenge: Liberalization, Europeanization, and Malaise in France*, edited by John Keeler and Martin Schain, 85–104. New York: St. Martin's Press.

Baumgartner, Frank R., Christoffer Green-Pedersen, and Bryan D. Jones. 2006. "Comparative Studies of Policy Agendas." *Journal of European Public Policy* 13(7): 959–974.

Baumgartner, Frank R., and Bryan D. Jones. 2002. *Policy Dynamics*. Chicago: University of Chicago Press.

Beckwith, Karen. 1985. "Feminism and Leftist Politics in Italy: The Case of UDI-PCI Relations." *Western European Politics* 8(4): 19–37.

———. 2000. "Beyond Compare? Women's Movements in Comparative Perspective." *European Journal of Political Research* 37: 431–468.

———. 2005. "The Comparative Politics of Women's Movements." *Perspectives on Politics* 3: 583–596.

———, ed. 2010. *"Symposium: A Comparative Politics of Gender."* *Perspectives on Politics* 8(1): 159–240.

Benford, Robert D., and David A. Snow. 2000. "Framing Processes and Social Movements: An Overview and Assessment." *Annual Review of Sociology* 26: 611–630.

Bennett, Andrew, ed. 2007. "Symposium: Multi-Method Work, Dispatches from the Front Lines." *Organized Section on Qualitative Methods: Newsletter of the American Political Science Association* 5(1): 34–47.

Bergqvist, Christina, Anette Borchorst, Ann-Dorte Christensen, Viveca Ramstedt-Silén, Nina C. Raum, and Auour Styrkársdoótir, eds. 1999. *Equal Democracies*. Oslo: Scandinavia University Press.

Berg-Schlosser, Dirk, and Lasse Cronqvist. 2005. "Multi-Value Qualitative Comparative Analysis (MV-QCA)—A New Tool for Cross-National Research." Paper presented at the annual meeting of the American Political Science Association, Washington, September 1–4.

Brady, Henry, and David Collier, eds. 2004. *Rethinking Social Inquiry: Diverse Tools, Shared Standards*. Lanham, MD: Rowman and Littlefield.

Bratton, Kathleen, and Leonard Ray. 2002. "Descriptive Representation, Policy Outcomes and Municipal Day-Care Coverage in Norway." *American Journal of Political Science* 47(2): 428–437.

Buechler, Steven M. 2000. *Social Movements in Advanced Capitalism: The Political Economy and Cultural Construction of Social Activism*. New York: Oxford University Press.

Burke, Johnson R., and Anthony J. Onwegbuszie. 2004. "Mixed Methods Research. A Research Paradigm Whose Time Has Come." *Educational Researcher Journal* 33(7): 14–26.

Burstein, Paul. 1979. "Public Opinion, Demonstrations, and the Passage of Anti-Discrimination Legislation." *Public Opinion Quarterly* 43: 157–172.

———. 1999. "Social Movements and Public Policy." In *How Social Movements Matter*, edited by Marco Giugni, Doug McAdam, and Charles Tilly, 3–21. Minneapolis: University of Minnesota Press.

Campbell, Rosie, Sarah Childs, and Joni Lovenduski. 2010. "Do Women Need Women Representatives?" *British Journal of Political Science* 40(1): 171–194.

Caporaso, James A. 1995. "Research Design, Falsification, and the Qualitative-Quantitative Divide." *American Political Science Review* 89(2): 457–460.

Carey, John M. 2000. "Parchment, Equilibria, and Institutions." *Comparative Political Studies* 33(6–7): 735–761.

Castles, Francis G. 1993. *Families of Nations: Patterns of Public Policy in Western Democracies*. Aldershot, England: Dartmouth.

Celis, Karen. 2008. "Representation." In *Politics, Gender, and Concepts: Theory and Methodology*, edited by Gary Goertz and Amy G. Mazur, 71–93. Cambridge: Cambridge University Press.

Celis, Karen, Sarah Childs, Johanna Kantola, and Mona Lena Krook. 2008. "Rethinking Women's Substantive Representation." *Representation* 44(2): 101–110.

Chaney, Carole, Michael R. Alvarez, and Jonathan Nagler. 1998. "Explaining the Gender Gap in U.S. Presidential Elections." *Political Research Quarterly* 51(2): 311–339.

Chappell, Louise. 2002a. "The 'Femocrat' Strategy: Expanding the Repertoire of Feminist Activists." In *Women, Politics, and Change*, edited by Karen Ross, 85–98. Oxford: Oxford University Press.

———. 2002b. *Gendering Government: Feminist Engagement with the State in Australia and Canada*. Vancouver: University of British Columbia Press.

———. 2006. "Comparing Political Institutions: Revealing the Gendered 'Logic of Appropriateness.'" *Politics and Gender* 2(2): 223–225.

Childs, Sarah. 2004. *New Labour's Women MPs: Women Representing Women*. London: Routledge.

———. 2005. "Feminising British Politics: Sex and Gender in the 2005 General Election." In *Britain Decides: The UK General Election 2005*, edited by Andrew Geddes and Jonathan Tonge, 150–167. Basingstoke, England: Palgrave.

———. 2007. "Representation". In *The Impact of Feminism on Political Concepts and Debates*, edited by Valerie Bryson and Georgina Blakeley, 94–118. Manchester: Manchester University Press.

Childs, Sarah, and Mona Lena Krook. 2006. "Should Feminists Give Up on Critical Mass? A Contingent 'Yes.'" *Politics and Gender* 2(4): 522–530.

Clemens, Elizabeth S., and Debra Minkoff. 2007. "Beyond Iron Law: Rethinking the Place of Organizations in Social Movement Research. In *The Blackwell Companion to Social Movements*, edited by David A. Snow, Sarah A. Soule, and Hanspeter Kriesi, 155–170. Oxford: Blackwell.

Cobb, Roger, and Charles D. Elder. 1983. *Participation in American Politics: The Dynamics of Agenda-Setting*. Baltimore: Johns Hopkins University Press.

Cockburn, Cynthia. 1991. *In the Way of Women: Men's Resistance to Sex Equality in Organizations*. New York: ILR Press.

Collier, David, and James E. Mahon. 1993. "Conceptual 'Stretching' Revisited: Adapting Categories in Comparative Analysis." *American Political Science Review* 87: 845–855.

Connell, Robert. 1987. *Gender and Power*. Cambridge: Polity Press.

Costain, Ann. 1992. *Inviting Women's Rebellion: A Political Process Interpretation of the Women's Movement*. Baltimore: The Johns Hopkins University Press.

Creswell, John W. 2003. *Research Design: Qualitative, Quantitative, and Mixed Methods Approaches*, 2nd ed. Thousand Oaks, CA: Sage.

Cronqvist, Lasse. 2005. "Tosmana User Manual." Paper prepared for the 2nd European Consortium for Political Research General Conference, Marburg, Germany. Available at http://www.tosmana.net/.

Dahlerup, Drude, ed. 1986. "Introduction." In *The New Women's Movement*, 1–26. Bristol, England: Sage.

———. 1988. "From a Small to a Large Minority: Women in Scandinavian Politics." *Scandinavian Political Studies* 11: 275–298.

Dalla Costa, Marie Rosa. 1988. "Domestic Labour and the Feminist Movement in Italy since the 1970s." *International Sociology* 3(1): 23–34.

Danna, Daniela. 2004. "Italy: The Never-Ending Debate." In *The Politics of Prostitution: Women's Movements, Democratic States and the Globalisation of Sex Commerce*, edited by Joyce Outshoorn, 165–184. Cambridge: Cambridge University Press.

Davis, Gerald F., Doug McAdam, W. Richard Scott, and Mayer N. Zald, eds. 2005. *Social Movements and Organization Theory*. New York: Cambridge University Press.

Della Porta, Donatella, and Mario Diani. 2006. *Social Movements: An Introduction*, 2nd ed. Oxford: Blackwell.

Diani, Mario. 1997. "Social Movements and Social Capital: A Network Perspective on Movement Outcomes." *Mobilization: An International Quarterly* 2(2): 129–147.

Dovi, Suzanne. 2002. "Preferable Descriptive Representatives: Will Just Any Woman, Black or Latino Do?" *American Political Science Review* 96(4): 729–743.

———. 2007. "Theorizing Women's Representation in the United States." *Politics and Gender* 3(3): 297–319.

Edelman, Murray. 1985. *The Symbolic Uses of Politics*. Urbana: University of Illinois Press.

Eisenstein, Hester. 1996. *Inside Agitators: Australian Femocrats and the State*. Philadelphia: Temple University Press.

Elman, R. Amy. 1996. *Sexual Subordination and State Intervention: Comparing Sweden and the United States*. Providence, RI: Berghahn.

Elshtain, Jean Bethke. 1983. "Antigone's Daughters: Reflections on Female Identity and the State." In *Families, Politics and Public Policy: A Feminist Dialogue on Women and the State*, edited by Irene Diamond, 300–311. New York: Longman.

Epstein, David, and Sharyn O'Halloran. 1999. *Delegating Powers: A Transaction Cost Politics Approach to Policy Making under Separate Powers*. Cambridge: Cambridge University Press.

Esping-Andersen, Gøsta, ed. 1993. *Changing Classes: Stratification in Postindustrial Societies*. London: Sage.

———. 1999. *Social Foundations of Postindustrial Economies*. London: Oxford Press.

Everett, Jan. 1998. "Indian Feminists Debate the Efficacy of Policy Reforms: The Maharashtra Ban on Sex-Determination Tests." *Social Politics* Fall: 314–337.

Fainsod Katzenstein, Mary. 1995. "Discursive Politics and Feminist Activism in the Catholic Church." In *Feminist Organizations*, edited by Myra Marx Ferree and Patricia Yancey Martin, 35–52. Philadelphia: Temple University Press.

Fainsod Katzenstein, Mary, and Carol McClurg Mueller, eds. 1987. *The Women's Movements of the United States and Western Europe*. Philadelphia: Temple University Press.

Feick, John. 1992. "Comparing Comparative Policy Studies—A Path toward Integration?" *Journal of Public Policy* 12(3): 257–285.

Ferguson, Karen E. 1984. *The Feminist Case against Bureaucracy*. Philadelphia: Temple University Press.

Ferree, Myra Marx. 1995. "Making Equality: The Women's Affairs Offices in the Federal Republic of Germany." In *Comparative State Feminism*, edited by Dorothy McBride Stetson and Amy G. Mazur, 95–113. Thousand Oaks, CA: Sage.

———. 2006."Globalization and Feminism: Opportunities and Obstacles for Activism in the Global Arena." In *Global Feminism. Transnational Women's Activism, Organizing and Human Rights*, edited by Myra Marx Ferree and Aili M. Tripp, 3–23. New York: New York University Press.

Ferree, Myra Marx, and William A. Gamson. 2003. "The Gendering of Governance and the Governance of Gender: Abortion Politics in Germany and the USA." In *Recognition Struggles and Social Movements. Contested Identities, Agency and Power*, edited by Barbara Hobson, 35–63. Cambridge: Cambridge University Press.

Ferree, Myra Marx, William A. Gamson, Jürgen Gerhards, and Dieter Rucht. 2002. *Shaping Abortion Discourse: Democracy and the Public Sphere in Germany and the United States*. Cambridge: Cambridge University Press.

Ferree, Myra Marx, and Beth B. Hess. 2000. *Controversy and Coalition: The New Feminist Movement*, 3rd ed. New York: Routledge.

Ferree, Myra Marx, and Carol Mueller. 2007. "Feminism and the Women's Movement: A Global Perspective." In *The Blackwell Companion to Social Movements*, edited by David A. Snow, Sarah A. Soule, and Hanspeter Kriesi, 576–607. Oxford: Blackwell Publishing.

Ferree, Myra Marx, and Aili M. Tripp, eds. 2006. *Global Feminism: Transnational Women's Activism, Organizing and Human Rights*, New York: New York University Press.

Fischer, Frank. 2003. *Reframing Public Policy: Discursive Politics and Deliberative Practices.* Oxford: Oxford University Press.

Franzway, Suzanne, Diane Court, and Robert W. Connell. 1989. *Staking a Claim: Feminism, Bureaucracy and the State.* Sydney: Allen and Unwin.

Gamson, William A. 1975. *The Strategy of Social Protest.* Homewood, IL: The Dorsey Press.

———. 1988. "Political Discourse and Collective Action." *International Social Movement Research* 1: 219–246.

Gamson, William, and David S. Meyer. 1996. "Framing Political Opportunity." In *Comparative Perspective on Social Movements: Political Opportunities, Mobilizing Structures, and Cultural Framings,* edited by Doug McAdam, John D. McCarthy, and Mayer N. Zald, 275–290. Cambridge: Cambridge University Press.

Gatens, Moira, and Alison Mackinnon, eds. 1998. *Gender and Institutions: Welfare, Work and Citizenship.* Cambridge: Cambridge University Press.

Gelb, Joyce. 1989. *Feminism and Politics: A Comparative Perspective.* Berkeley: University of California Press.

———. 1995. "Feminist Organization Success and the Politics of Engagement." In *Feminist Organizations: Harvest of the New Women's Movement,* edited by Myra Marx Ferree and Patricia Yancey Martin, 128–136. Philadelphia: Temple University Press.

———. 2003. *Gender Policies in Japan and the United States: Comparing Women's Movements, Rights and Politics.* New York: Palgrave Macmillan.

George, Alexander, and Andrew Bennett. 2005. *Case Studies and Theory Development in the Social Sciences.* Cambridge: Cambridge University Press.

Giugni, Marco G. 1995. "Outcomes of New Social Movements." In *New Social Movements in Western Europe: A Comparative Analysis,* edited by Hanspeter Kriesi, Ruud Koopmans, Jan Willem Duyvendak, and Marco Giugni, 207–237. Minneapolis: University of Minnesota Press.

———. 1998. "Was It Worth the Effort? The Outcomes and Consequences of Social Movements." *Annual Review of Sociology* 98: 371–393.

———. 1999. "How Social Movements Matter: Past Research, Present Problems, Future Developments." In *How Social Movements Matter,* edited by Marco Guigni, Doug McAdam, and Charles Tilly, xv–xxxiii. Minneapolis: University of Minnesota Press.

Giugni, Marco, and Sakura Yamasaki. 2007. "The Policy Impact of Social Movements: A Replication of Findings through Qualitative Comparative Analysis." Paper presented at the annual meeting of the American Sociological Association, New York.

Goertz, Gary. 2006. *Social Science Concepts: A User's Guide.* Princeton, NJ: Princeton University Press.

Goertz, Gary, and Amy G. Mazur, eds. 2008. *Politics, Gender and Concepts: Theory and Methodology.* Cambridge: Cambridge University Press.

Goldstone, Jack A., ed. 2003. *States, Parties and Social Movements.* Cambridge: Cambridge University Press.

Good, Anne. 2001. "Femocrats Work with Femocrats and the EU against Gender Bias in Ireland." In *State Feminism, Women's Movements, and Job Training: Making Democracies Work in the Global Economy,* edited by Amy G. Mazur, 213–234. New York: Routledge.

Gordon, Linda, ed. 1990. *Women, the State and Welfare.* Madison: University of Wisconsin Press.

Grofman, Bernard, and Carsten E. Schneider. 2009. "An Introduction to Crisp Set QCA, with a Comparison to Binary Logistic Regression." *Political Research Quarterly* 62(4): 662–672.

Guadagnini, Marila. 2007. "The Reform of the State in Italy". In *Gendering the State in the Age of Globalization,* edited by Melissa Haussman and Birgit Sauer, 169–188. Lanham, MD: Rowman and Littlefield.

Guadagnini, Marila, and Alessia Dona. 2007. "Women's Policy Machinery in Italy between European Pressure and Domestic Constraints." In *Changing State Feminism*, edited by Joyce Outshoorn and Johanna Kantola, 164–181. New York: Palgrave Macmillan.

Haffner-Burton, Emilie, and Mark A. Pollock. 2009. "Mainstreaming Gender in the European Union: Getting the Incentives Right." *Comparative European Politics* 7(1): 114–138.

Hajer, Maarten, and Hendrik Wagenaar. 2003. *Deliberative Policy Analysis: Understanding Governance in the Network Society*. Cambridge: Cambridge University Press.

Hall, Peter A. 1997. "The Role of Interests, Institutions and Ideas in the Comparative Political Economy of the Industrialized Nations." In *Comparative Politics*, edited by Allan S. Zuckerman and Mark Irving Lichbach, 174–207. Cambridge: Cambridge University Press.

———. 2004. "Beyond the Comparative Method." *APSA-CP* 15(2): 1–4.

Hall, Peter A., and David Soskice, eds. 2001. *Varieties of Capitalism: The Institutional Foundations of Comparative Advantage*. Oxford: Oxford University Press.

Halsaa, Beatrice. 1999. "A Strategic Partnership for Women's Policies in Norway." In *Women's Movements and Public Policy in Europe, Latin America, and the Caribbean*, edited by Geertje Lyclama à Nijeholt, Virginia Vargas, and Saskia Wieringa, 157–169. New York: Garland.

Hantrais, Linda, ed. 2000. *Gendered Policies in Europe*. London: MacMillan.

Harding, Sandra. 1987. *Feminism and Methodology*. Bloomington and Indianapolis: Indiana University Press.

Haussman, Melissa, and Birgit Sauer, eds. 2007. *Gendering the State in the Age of Globalization. Women's Movements and State Feminism in Postindustrial Democracies*. Lanham, MD: Rowman and Littlefield.

Hayward, Jack. 1992. "The Policy Community Approach to Industrial Policy." In *Comparative Political Dynamics: Global Research Perspectives*, edited by Dankwart A. Rustow and Kenneth P. Erickson, 381–407. New York: HarperCollins.

Heclo, Hugh. 1978. "Issue Networks and the Executive Establishment." In *The New American Political System*, edited by Anthony King, 87–124. Washington: American Enterprise Institute.

Hernes, Helga Maria. 1987. *Welfare State and Woman Power: Essays in State Feminism*. Oslo: Norwegian University Press.

Holland-Cunz, Barbara. 2003. *Die alte neue Frauenfrage*. Frankfurt: Suhrkamp.

Holli, Anne Maria. 2004. "Towards a New Prohibitionism? State Feminism, Women's Movements and Prostitution Policies in Finland." In *The Politics of Prostitution: Women's Movements, Democratic States and the Globalization of Sex Commerce*, edited by Joyce Outshoorn, 103–122. Cambridge: Cambridge University Press.

———. 2008. "Feminist Triangles: A Conceptual Analysis." *Representation* 44(2): 169–186.

Holli, Anne Maria, and Johanna Kantola. 2005. "A Politics for Presence: Finland." In *State Feminism and Political Representation*, edited by Joni Lovenduski et al., 62–84. Cambridge: Cambridge University Press.

———. 2007. "State Feminism Finnish Style: Strong Policies Clash with Implementation." In *Changing State Feminism*, edited by Joyce Outshoorn and Johanna Kantola, 82–101. New York: Palgrave Macmillan.

Htun, Mala, and Laurel Weldon. 2010. "When and Why Do Governments Promote Women's Rights? A Framework for a Comparative Politics of Sexual Equality." *Perspectives on Politics* 8(3): 207–216.

Imig, Doug, and Sidney Tarrow, eds. 2001. *Contentious Europeans: Protest and Politics in an Emerging Polity*. Lanham, MD: Rowman and Littlefield.

Inglehart, Ronald. 1990. *Culture Shift in Advanced Industrial Society*. Princeton, NJ: Princeton University Press.

Jenson, Jane. 1989. "Paradigms and Political Discourse: Protective Legislation in France and the United States before 1919." *Canadian Journal of Political Science* 2: 235–258.

Jenson, Jane, and Celia Valiente. 2003. "Comparing Two Movements for Gender Parity: France and Spain" In *Women's Movements Facing the Reconfigured State*, edited by Lee Ann Banaszak, Karen Beckwith and Dieter Rucht, 69–94. Cambridge: Cambridge University Press.

Jessop, Bob. 1994. "Veränderte Staatlichkeit. Veränderungen von Staatlichkeit und Staatsprojekten." In *Staatsaufgaben*, edited by Dieter Grimm, 42–73. Baden-Baden, Germany: Nomos.

———. 2006. "The State and State-building." In *The Oxford Handbook of Political Institutions*, edited by R.A.W. Rhodes, Sarah A. Binder, and Bert A. Rockman, 90–110. Oxford: Oxford University Press.

Kamenitsa, Lynn. 2001. "Abortion Debates in Germany." In *Abortion Politics, Women's Movements, and the Democratic State*, edited by Dorothy McBride Stetson, 111–134. Oxford: Oxford University Press.

Kamenitsa, Lynn, and Brigitte Geissel. 2005. "WPAs and Political Representation in Germany." In *State Feminism and the Political Representation of Women*, edited by Joni Lovenduski et al., 106–129. Cambridge: Cambridge University Press.

Kane, Melinda D. 2003. "Social Movement Policy Success: Decriminalizing State Sodomy Laws, 1969–1998. *Mobilization: An International Journal* 8(3): 313–334.

Kantola, Johanna. 2006. *Feminists Theorize the State*. New York: Palgrave Macmillan.

Kantola, Johanna, and Joyce Outshoorn. 2007. "Changing State Feminism." In *Changing State Feminism*, edited by Joyce Outshoorn and Johanna Kantola, 1–19. New York: Palgrave Macmillan.

Kaplan, Gisela. 1992. *Contemporary Western European Feminism*. London: UCL Press/ Allen and Unwin.

Keck, Margaret, and Kathryn Sikkink. 1998. *Activists beyond Borders: Transnational Advocacy Networks in International Politics*. Ithaca, NY: Cornell University Press.

Keeler, John T. S. 1987. *The Politics of Neo-corporatism in France: Farmers, the State and Agricultural Policy-making in the Fifth Republic*. New York: Oxford University Press.

———. 1993. Opening the Window for Reform: Mandates, Crises and Extraordinary Policy-Making." *Comparative Political Studies* 24: 433–486.

Kenney, Sally J. 2003. "Where Is Gender in Agenda Setting?" *Women and Politics* 25(1–2): 179–206.

Kettl, Donald F. 1993. "Public Administration: The State of the Field." In *Political Science: The State of the Discipline*, edited by Ada Finifter, 409–428. Washington: American Political Science Association.

King, Gary, Robert O. Keohane, and Sidney Verba. 1994. *Designing Social Inquiry: Scientific Inference in Qualitative Research*. Princeton, NJ: Princeton University Press.

Kingdon, John. 1995. *Agendas, Alternatives and Public Policies*. New York: HarperCollins.

Kitschelt, Herbert P. 1986. "Political Opportunity Structures and Political Protest: Anti-Nuclear Movements in Four Democracies." *British Journal of Political Science* 16: 57–85.

Kittelson, Miki Caul. 2008. "Representing Women: The Adoption of Family Leave in Comparative Perspective." *The Journal of Politics* 70(2): 323–334.

Koopmans, Ruud. 1995. "The Dynamics of Protest Waves." In *New Social Movements in Western Europe: A Comparative Analysis*, edited by Hanspeter Kriesi, Ruud Koopmans, Jan Willem Duyvendak, and Mario Giugni, 111–144. London: UCL Press.

———. 2007. "Protest in Time and Space: The Evolution of Waves of Contention." In *The Blackwell Companion to Social Movements*, edited by David A. Snow, Sarah A. Soule, and Hanspeter Kriesi, 19–46. Oxford: Blackwell Publishing.

Köpl, Regina. 2001. "State Feminism and Policy Debates on Abortion in Austria." In *Abortion Politics, Women's Movements and the Democratic State: A Comparative Study of State Feminism*, edited by Dorothy McBride Stetson, 17–38. Oxford: Oxford University Press.

——. 2005. "Gendering Political Representation: Debates and Controversies in Austria." In *State Feminism and Political Representation*, edited by Joni Lovenduski et al., 20–40. Cambridge: Cambridge University Press.

Kriesi, Hanspeter. 1996. "The Organizational Structure of New Social Movements in a Political Context." In *Comparative Perspectives on Social Movements. Political Opportunities, Mobilizing Structures, and Cultural Framings*, edited by Doug McAdam, John D. McCarthy, and Mayer N. Zald, 152–184. Cambridge: Cambridge University Press.

Kriesi, Hanspeter, Ruud Koopmans, Jan Willem Duyvendak, and Mario Giugni, eds. 1995. *New Social Movements in Western Europe. A Comparative Analysis.* London: UCL Press.

Krook, Mona Lena, Joni Lovenduski, and Judith Squires. 2009. "Gender Quotas and Models of Political Citizenship." *British Journal of Political Science* 39(4): 781–803.

Lang, Sabine. 2007. "Gender Governance in Post Unification Germany: Between Institutionalization, Deregulation and Privatization." In *Changing State Feminism*, edited by Joyce Outshoorn and Johanna Kantola, 134–134. New York: Palgrave Macmillan.

Laver, Michael, and Kenneth A. Shepsle. 1996. *Making and Breaking Governments: Cabinets and Legislatures in Parliamentary Democracies.* Cambridge: Cambridge University Press.

Lieberman, Evan. 2005. "Nested Analysis as a Mixed-Method Strategy for Comparative Research." *American Political Science Review* 99(3): 435–452.

Lijphart, Arend. 1999. *Patterns of Democracy: Government Forms and Performance in Thirty-Six Countries.* New Haven, CT: Yale University Press.

Lohmann, Susanne. 2007. "The Trouble with Multi-Methodism." *Qualitative Methods* 5(1): 13–17.

Lombardo, Emanuela, Petra Meier, and Mieke Verloo, eds. 2009a. *The Discursive Politics of Gender Equality. Stretching, Bending and Policymaking.* New York: Routledge.

——, eds. 2009b. "Stretching and Bending Gender Equality: A Discursive Politics Approach." In *The Discursive Politics of Gender Equality. Stretching, Bending and Policymaking.* New York: Routledge.

Lovenduski, Joni. 1998. "Gendering Research in Political Science." *Annual Review of Political Science* 1: 333–356.

——. 2005. *Feminizing Politics.* Cambridge: Polity Press.

——. 2007a. "Unfinished Business: Equality Policy and the Changing Context of State Feminism in Great Britain." In *Changing State Feminism*, edited by Joyce Outshoorn and Johanna Kantola, 144–163. New York: Palgrave Macmillan.

——. 2007b. "The UK: Reforming the House of Lords." In *Gendering the State in the Age of Globalization. Women's Movements and State Feminism in Postindustrial Democracies*, edited by Melissa Haussman and Birgit Sauer, 263–280. Lanham, MD: Rowman and Littlefield.

Lovenduski, Joni, Claudie Baudino, Marila Guadagnini, and Petra Meier, eds. 2005. *State Feminism and Political Representation.* Cambridge: Cambridge University Press.

Lovenduski, Joni, and Pippa Norris, eds. 1993. *Gender and Party Politics.* London: Sage.

Lovenduski, Joni, and Vicky Randall. 1993. *Contemporary Feminist Politics: Women and Power in Britain.* Oxford: Oxford University Press.

Lycklama, Geertje, Saskia Wieringa, and Virginia Vargas, eds. 1998. *Women's Movements and Public Policy in Europe, Latin America, and the Caribbean.* New York: Garland.

Mackay, Fiona, and Georgina Waylen, eds. 2009. "Critical Perspectives on Feminist Institutionalism." *Politics and Gender* 5(2).

MacKinnon, Catharine. 1989. *Toward a Feminist Theory of the State.* Cambridge, MA: Harvard University Press.

Mahon, Evelyn. 2001. "Abortion Debates in Ireland: An Ongoing Issue." In *Abortion Politics, Women's Movements and the Democratic State*, edited by Dorothy McBride Stetson, 157–180. Oxford: Oxford University Press.

Mahoney, James. 2003. "Strategies of Causal Assessment." In *Comparative Historical Analysis in the Social Sciences*, edited by James Mahoney and Dietrich Rueschemeyer, 337–372. Cambridge: Cambridge University Press.

Mahoney, James, and Gary Goertz. 2006. "A Tale of Two Cultures: Contrasting Quantitative and Qualitative Research." *Political Analysis* 14(3): 227–249.

Mahoney, James, and Dietrich Rueschemeyer, eds. 2003. *Comparative Historical Analysis in the Social Sciences*. Cambridge: Cambridge University Press.

Malloy, Johnathon. 1999. "What Makes a State Advocacy Structure Effective? Conflict between Bureaucratic and Social Movement Criteria." *Governance* 12(3): 267–288.

———. 2003. *Between Colliding Worlds: The Ambiguous Existence of Government Agencies for Aboriginal and Women's Policy*. Toronto: University of Toronto Press.

Mansbridge, Jane. 1999. "Should Blacks Represent Blacks and Women Represent Women: A Contingent 'Yes.'" *Journal of Politics* 61(3): 628–657.

———. 2003. "Rethinking Representation." *American Political Science Review* 97(4): 515–528.

March, James G., and Johan P. Olsen. 1984. "The New Institutionalism: Organizational Factors in Political Life." *American Political Science Review* 78: 734–749.

———. 1989. *Rediscovering Institutions: The Organizational Basis of Politics*. New York: Free Press.

Mateo Diaz, Mercedes. 2005. *Representing Women? Female Legislators in West European Parliaments*. Colchester, England: ECPR Press.

Mazur, Amy G. 1995. *Gender Bias and the State: Symbolic Reform at Work in Fifth Republic France*. Pittsburgh: University of Pittsburgh Press

———, ed. 2001. *State Feminism, Women's Movements, and Job Training: Making Democracies Work in the Global Economy*. New York: Routledge.

———. 2002. *Theorizing Feminist Policy*. Oxford: Oxford University Press.

Mazur, Amy, and Dorothy McBride. 2008. "State Feminism." In *Politics, Gender and Concepts: Theory and Methodology*, edited by Gary Goertz and Amy G. Mazur, 244–269. Cambridge: Cambridge University Press.

Mazur, Amy G., and Janine Parry. 1998. "Choosing Not to Choose in Comparative Policy Research Design." *Policy Studies Journal* 26(3): 384–387.

Mazur, Amy G., and Mark A. Pollock. 2009. "Gender and Public Policy in Europe: An Introduction." *Comparative European Politics* 7(1): 1–11.

McAdam, Doug. 1996. "The Framing Function of Movement Tactics: Strategic Dramaturgy in the American Civil Rights Movement." In *Comparative Perspectives on Social Movements*, edited by Doug McAdam, John D. McCarthy, and Mayer N. Zald, 338–355. Cambridge: Cambridge University Press.

McAdam, Doug, John D. McCarthy, and Mayer N. Zald, eds. 1996. *Comparative Perspectives on Social Movements: Political Opportunities, Mobilizing Structures, and Cultural Framings*. Cambridge: Cambridge University Press.

McAdam, Doug, Sidney Tarrow, and Charles Tilly. 2001. *Dynamics of Contention*. New York: Cambridge University Press.

McBride, Dorothy E. 2007. "Welfare Reform: America's Hot Issue." In *Gendering the State in an Age of Globalization: Women's Movements and State Feminism in Postindustrial Democracies*, edited by Melissa Haussman and Birgit Sauer, 281–300. Lanham, MD: Rowman and Littlefield.

McBride Stetson, Dorothy. 1987. *Women's Rights in France*. Westport, CT: Greenwood Press.

———, ed. 2001a. *Abortion Politics, Women's Movements and the Democratic State: A Comparative Study of State Feminism*. Oxford: Oxford University Press.

———. 2001b. "Federal and State Women's Policy Agencies Help to Represent Women in the United States." In *State Feminism, Women's Movements, and Job Training: Making Democracies Work in a Global Economy*, edited by Amy G. Mazur, 271–292. New York: Routledge.

———. 2001c. "Women's Movements Defence of Legal Abortion in Great Britain." In *Abortion Politics, Women's Movements and the Democratic State: A Comparative Study of State Feminism*, edited by Dorothy McBride Stetson, 41–61. Oxford: Oxford University Press.

———. 2004. "The Invisible Issue: Prostitution and the Trafficking of Women and Girls in the United States." In *The Politics of Prostitution: Women's Movements, Democratic States and the Globalization of Sex Commerce*, edited by Joyce Outshoorn, 245–264. Cambridge: Cambridge University Press.

McBride Stetson, Dorothy, and Amy G. Mazur, eds. 1995a. *Comparative State Feminism*. Thousand Oaks, CA: Sage.

———, eds. 1995b. "Introduction." In *Comparative State Feminism*, 1–21. Thousand Oaks, CA: Sage.

———. 2006. "Building a (Data) Bank While Crossing the Bridge: RNGS Strategies to Integrate Qualitative and Quantitative Methods." *British Journal of Political Science Anniversary Conference, London*. June.

———. 2008. "Women's Movements, Feminism and Feminist Movements." In *Politics, Gender and Concepts: Theory and Methodology*, edited by Gary Goertz and Amy G. Mazur, 219–243. Cambridge: Cambridge University Press.

McCammon, Holly J., Karen E. Campbell, Ellen M. Granberg, and Christine Mowery. 2001. "How Movements Win: Gendered Opportunity Structures and the U.S. Women Suffrage Movements 1866–1919." *American Sociological Review* 66(1): 49–70.

McCarthy, John, and Mayer Zald. 1977. "Resource Mobilization and Social Movements: A Partial Theory." *American Journal of Sociology* 82(6): 1212–1241.

McClurg Mueller, Carol, and John D. McCarthy. 2003. "Cultural Continuity and Structural Change: The Logic of Adaptation by Radical Liberal and Socialist Feminists to State Reconfiguration." In *Women's Movements Facing the Reconfigured State*, edited by Lee Ann Banaszak, Karen Beckwith, and Dieter Rucht, 219–242. Cambridge: Cambridge University Press.

Meier, Petra. 2005. "The Belgian Paradox: Inclusion and Exclusion of Gender Issues." In *State Feminism and Political Representation*, edited by Joni Lovenduski et al., 216–238. Cambridge: Cambridge University Press.

Melucci, Alberto. 1996. *Challenging Codes: Collective Action in the Information Age*. Cambridge: Cambridge University Press.

Mény, Yves. 1992. *La Corruption de la République*. Paris: Editions Fayard.

Meyer, David S. 2003. "Restating the Woman Question: Women's Movements and State Restructuring." In *Women's Movements Facing the Reconfigured State*, edited by Lee Ann Banaszak, Karen Beckwith, and Dieter Rucht, 275–294. Cambridge: Cambridge University Press.

Meyer, David S., Valerie Jenness, and Helen Ingram, eds. 2005. *Routing the Opposition: Social Movements, Public Policy, and Democracy*. Minneapolis: University of Minnesota Press.

Meyer, David S., and Sidney Tarrow. 1998. *The Social Movement Society: Contentious Politics for a New Century*. Cambridge: Cambridge University Press.

Meyer, David S., Nancy Whittier, and Belinda Robnett, eds. 2002. *Social Movements: Identity, Culture, and the State*. Oxford: Oxford University Press.

Meyer, John W., and Brian Rowman. 1991. "Institutionalized Organizations: Formal Structure as Myth and Ceremony." In *The New Institutionalism in Organizational Analysis*, edited by Walter W. Powell and Paul J. DiMaggio, 41–62. Chicago: University of Chicago Press.

Molyneux, Maxine. 1998. "Analysing Women's Movements." In *Feminist Visions of Development*, edited by Cecile Jackson and Ruth Pearson, 65–88. London: Routledge.

Morgan, Kimberly J. 2006. *Working Mothers and the Welfare State: Religion and the Politics of Work-Family Policies in Western Europe and the United States*. Palto Alto, CA: Stanford University Press.

Muller, Pierre. 1990. *Les Politiques Publiques*. Paris: PUF.

Naples, Nancy. 1998. "Toward a Multiracial, Feminist, Social Democratic Praxis: Lessons from Grassroots Warriors in the US War on Poverty." *Social Politics* Fall: 286–313.

Nelson, Barbara, and Najma Chowdhury. 1994. *Women and Politics Worldwide*. New Haven, CT: Yale University Press.

Nettl, J. P. 1968. "The State as a Conceptual Variable." *World Politics* 20: 559–591.

Norris, Pippa. 1987. *Politics and Sexual Equality: The Comparative Position of Women in Western Democracies*. Boulder, CO: Lynne Reiner.

Norušis, Marija J. 2007. *SPSS 15.0 Advanced Statistical Procedures Companion*. New York: Prentice-Hall.

O'Connor, Julie S. 1999. "Employment Equality Strategies in Liberal Welfare Regimes." In *Gender and Welfare State Regimes*, edited by Diane Sainsbury, 47–74. Oxford: Oxford University Press.

Orloff, Ann Shola. 1993. "Gender and the Social Rights of Citizenship: The Comparative Analysis of Gender Relations and Welfare States." *American Sociological Review* 58: 303–328.

———. 2002. "Women's Employment and Welfare Regimes: Globalization, Export Orientation and Social Policy in Europe and North America." Social Policy and Development Paper. United Nations Research Institute for Social Development, 12.

Ortbals, Candice. 2008. "Subnational Politics in Spain: New Avenues for Feminist Policy-making and Activism." *Politics and Gender* 4(1): 93–120.

Outshoorn, Joyce. 1994. "Between Movement and Government: 'Femocrats' in the Netherlands." In *The Yearbook of Swiss Political Science*, edited by Hanspeter Kriesi, 141–165. Bern: Paul Haupt Verlag.

———. 2001. "Policy-making on Abortion: Arenas, Actors, and Arguments in the Netherlands." In *Abortion Politics, Women's Movements and the Democratic State*, edited by Dorothy McBride Stetson, 205–228. Oxford: Oxford University Press.

———, ed. 2004. *The Politics of Prostitution: Women's Movements, Democratic States, and the Globalization of Sex Commerce*. Cambridge: Cambridge University Press.

Outshoorn, Joyce, and Johanna Kantola, eds. 2007. *Changing State Feminism: Women's Policy Agencies Confront Shifting Institutional Terrain*. New York: Palgrave Macmillan.

Outshoorn, Joyce, and Jantine Oldersma. 2007. "Dutch Decay: The Dismantling of the Women's Policy Network in the Netherlands." In *Changing State Feminism*, edited by Joyce Outshoorn and Johanna Kantola, 182–200. New York: Palgrave Macmillan.

Palier, Bruno. 2000. "Defrosting the French Welfare State." *West European Politics* 23(2): 113–136.

Parenti, Michael. 1974. *Democracy for the Few*. New York: St. Martin's Press.

Parry, Janine A. 2000. "Putting Feminism to a Vote: The Washington State Women's Council (1963–1978)." *Pacific Northwest Quarterly* 91:171–182.

———. 2005. "Women's Policy Agencies, the Women's Movement, and Representation in the U.S." In *State Feminism and Political Representation*, edited by Joni Lovenduski et al., 239–259. Cambridge: Cambridge University Press.

Pateman, Carole. 1988. *The Sexual Contract*. Stanford, CA: Stanford University Press.

Peters, B. Guy. 1992. "Public Policy and Public Bureaucracy." In *History and Context in Comparative Public Policy*, edited by Douglas Ashford, 283–316. Pittsburgh: University of Pittsburgh Press.

Phillips, Anne. 1991. *Engendering Democracy*. University Park, PA: University of Pennsylvania Press.

———. 1995. *The Politics of Presence*. Cambridge: Oxford University Press.

Pierson, Paul. 1993. "When Effect Becomes Cause: Policy Feedback and Political Change." *World Politics* 45(4): 595–628.

———. 1996. "The Path to European Integration: A Historical Institutionalist Analysis." *Comparative Political Studies* 29(2): 123–163.

————. 2003. "Big, Slow-Moving, and Invisible: Macro-Social Processes and Contemporary Political Science." In *Comparative Historical Analysis in the Social Sciences*, edited by James Mahoney and Dietrich Reuschemeyer, 177–207. Cambridge: Cambridge University Press.

————. 2004. *Politics in Time: History, Institutions, and Social Analysis*. Princeton, NJ: Princeton University Press.

Pierson, Paul, and Theda Skocpol. 2003. "Historical Institutionalism in Contemporary Political Science." In *The State of the Discipline*, edited by Ira Katznelson and Helen Milner, 693–721. New York: Norton.

Pitkin, Hanna Fenichel. 1967. *The Concept of Representation*. Berkeley: University of California Press.

Pringle, Rosemary, and Sophie Watson. 1992. "Women's Interests and the Post Structuralist State." In *Destabilizing Theory: Contemporary Feminist Debates*, edited by Michèle Barrett and Anne Phillips, 53–73. Cambridge: Polity Press.

Ragin, Charles C. 1987. *The Comparative Method: Moving beyond Qualitative and Quantitative Strategies*. Berkeley: University of California Press.

————. 2000. *Fuzzy-Set Social Science*. Chicago: University of Chicago Press.

————. 2008. *Redesigning Social Inquiry: Fuzzy Sets and Beyond*. Chicago: University of Chicago Press.

Ragin, Charles C., and Benoît Rihoux. 2004. "Qualitative Comparative Analysis (QCA): State of the Art and Prospects. *Qualitative Methods. Newsletter of the American Political Science Association Organized Section on Qualitative Methods* 2(2): 3–12.

Rai, Shirin, ed. 2003a. *Mainstreaming Gender, Democratizing the State? Institutional Mechanisms for the Advancement of Women*. Manchester: Manchester University Press.

————, ed. 2003b. "Institutional Mechanisms for the Advancement of Women: Mainstreaming Gender, Democratizing the State?" In *Mainstreaming Gender, Democratizing the State? Institutional Mechanisms for the Advancement of Women*, 15–39. Manchester: Manchester University Press.

Rhodes, R.A.W., Sarah A. Binder, and Bert A. Rockman. 2006. *The Oxford Handbook of Political Institutions*. Oxford: Oxford University Press.

Rihoux, Benoît, and Charles Ragin. 2008. *Configurational Comparative Methods: Qualitative Comparative Analysis (QCA) and Related Techniques*. Los Angeles: Sage.

Risse, Thomas, Maria Green Cowles, and James Caporaso. 2001. "Europeanization and Domestic Change: Introduction." In *Europeanization and Domestic Change: Transforming Europe*, edited by Thomas Risse, James Caporaso, and Maria Green Cowles, 1–20. Ithaca, NY: Cornell University Press.

RNGS. 2005. *RNGS Project Description*. Available at http://libarts.wsu.edu/polisci/rngs.

————. 2007a. *Codebook*. Available at http://libarts.wsu.edu/polisci/rngs.

————. 2007b. *Text Appendices*. Available at http://libarts.wsu.edu/polisci/rngs.

Robinson, Jean C. 2001. "Gendering the Abortion Debate: The French Case." In *Abortion Politics, Women's Movements and the Democratic State*, edited by Dorothy McBride Stetson, 87–110. Oxford: Oxford University Press.

Rochon, Thomas R. 1998. *Culture Moves: Ideas, Activism, and Changing Values*. Princeton, NJ: Princeton University Press.

Rochon, Thomas R., and Daniel A. Mazmanian. 1993. "Social Movements and the Policy Process." *Annals of the American Academy of Political and Social Science* 528: 75–87.

Rosenfeld, Rachel A., and Kathryn B. Ward. 1996. "Evolution of the Contemporary U.S. Women's Movement." *Research in Social Movements, Conflict and Change* 19: 51–73.

Rucht, Dieter. 1996. "The Impact of National Contexts on Social Movement Structures: A Crossmovement and Cross-national Comparison." In *Comparative Perspectives on Social Movements: Political Opportunities, Mobilizing Structures, and Cultural Framings*, edited by Doug McAdam, John D. McCarthy, and Mayer N. Zald, 185–204. Cambridge: Cambridge University Press.

———. 2003. "Interactions between Social Movements and States in Comparative Perspective." In *Women's Movements Facing the Reconfigured State*, edited by Lee Ann Banaszak, Karen Beckwith, and Dieter Rucht, 242–274. Cambridge: Cambridge University Press.

Sabatier, Paul A., and Hank C. Jenkins Smith, eds. 1993. *Policy Change and Learning: An Advocacy Coalition Approach*, Boulder, CO: Westview.

Sainsbury, Diane. 2005. "Party Feminism, State Feminism and Women's Representation in Sweden." In *State Feminism and Political Representation*, edited by Joni Lovenduski et al., 195–215. Cambridge: Cambridge University Press.

———. 2008. "Gendering the Welfare State." In *Politics, Gender and Concepts: Theory and Methodology*, edited by Gary Goertz and Amy G. Mazur, 94–112. Cambridge: Cambridge University Press.

Sartori, Giovanni. 1970. "Concept Misformation in Comparative Politics." *American Political Science Review* 74: 1033–1053.

Sassoon, Anne Showstack, ed. 1987. *Women and the State: The Shifting Boundaries of Public and Private.* London: Unwin Hyman.

Sauer, Birgit. 2004. "Taxes, Rights and Regimentation: Discourse on Prostitution in Austria." In *The Politics of Prostitution: Women's Movements, Democratic States and the Globalization of Sex Commerce*, edited by Joyce Outshoorn, 19–38. Cambridge: Cambridge University Press.

———. 2007. "What Happened to the Model Student? Austrian State Feminism since the 1990s." In *Changing State Feminism*, edited by Joyce Outshoorn and Johanna Kantola, 41–61. New York: Palgrave Macmillan.

Sawer, Marian. 1990. *Sisters in Suits, Women and Public Policy in Australia.* Sydney: Allen and Unwin.

Schattschneider, E. E. 1960. *The Semisovereign People: A Realist's View of Democracy in America.* New York: Holt, Rinehart and Winston.

Schmidt, Vivien A. 2008. "Discursive Institutionalism: The Explanatory Power of Ideas and Discourse." *Annual Review of Political Science* 11: 303–326.

Schneider, Anne Larason, and Helen Ingram. 1993. "Social Constructions of Target Populations." *American Political Science Review* 87(2): 334–347.

Schoen, Donald, and Martin Rein. 1994. *Frame Reflection.* New York: Basic Books.

Schwindt-Bayer, Leslie A., and William Mishler. 2005. "An Integrated Model of Women's Representation." *The Journal of Politics* 67(2): 407–428.

Siim, Birte. 1991. "Welfare State, Gender Politics and Equality Policies: Women's Citizenship in the Scandinavian Welfare States." In *Equality Politics and Gender*, edited by Elizabeth Meehan and Selma Sevenhuijsen, 175–192. London: Sage.

Skocpol, Theda. 1985. "Bringing the State Back In: Strategies of Analysis in Current Research." In *Bringing the State Back In*, edited by Peter B. Evans, Dietrich Rueschemeyer, and Theda Skocpol, 3–37. Cambridge: Cambridge University Press.

Smith, Jackie. 2004. "Transnational Processes and Movements." In *The Blackwell Companion to Social Movements*, edited by David A. Snow, Sarah A. Soule, and Hanspeter Kriesi, 311–336. Oxford: Blackwell Publishing.

———. 2005. "Globalization and Transnational Social Movement Organizations." In *Social Movements and Organization Theory*, edited by Gerald F. Davis, Doug McAdam, W. Richard Scott, and Mayer N. Zald, 226–249. New York: Cambridge University Press.

Snow, David A. 2007. "Framing Processes, Ideology and Discursive Fields." In *The Blackwell Companion to Social Movements*, edited by David A. Snow, Sarah Soule, and Hanspeter Kriesi, 380–412. Oxford: Blackwell Publishing.

Snow, David A., and Robert D. Benford. 1988. "Ideology, Frame Resonance, and Participant Mobilization." *Journal of International Social Movement Research* 1: 197–218.

———. 1992. "Master Framers and Cycles of Protest" In *Frontiers in Social Movement Theory*, edited by Aldon D. Morris and Carol McClurg Mueller. New Haven, CT: Yale University Press.

————. 2000. "Framing Processes and Social Movements. An Overview and Assessment." *Annual Sociological Review* 26: 611–639.

Snow, David A., Sarah Soule, and Hanspeter Kriesi. 2007. *The Blackwell Companion to Social Movements.* Oxford: Blackwell Publishing.

Soule, Sarah A., and Brayden G. King. 2006. "The Stages of the Policy Process and the Equal Rights Amendment, 1972–82." *American Journal of Sociology* 111(6): 1871–1909.

Squires, Judith. 2005. "Is Mainstreaming Transformative? Theorizing Mainstreaming in the Context of Diversity and Deliberation." *Social Politics* Fall: 366–388.

————. 2007. *The New Politics of Gender Equality.* Basingstoke, England: Palgrave.

Squires, Judith, and Mark Wickham-Jones. 2002. "Mainstreaming in Westminster and White-hall: From Labour's Ministry for Women to the Women and Equality Unit." In *Women, Politics, and Change,* edited by Karen Ross, 57–70. Oxford: Oxford University Press.

Staggenborg, Suzanne. 1991. *The Pro-Choice Movement: Organization and Activism in the Abortion Conflict.* New York: Oxford University Press.

Staudt, Kathleen, ed. 1997. *Women, International Development and Politics: The Bureaucratic Mire.* Philadelphia: Temple University Press.

Stephens, Evelyne, and John D. Huber. 2001. *Development and Crisis of the Welfare State: Parties and Policies in Global Markets.* Chicago: University of Chicago Press.

Stewart, Debra. 1980. *The Women's Movement in Community Politics in the U.S.: The Role of Local Commissions on the Status of Women.* New York: Pergamon.

Stivers, Camilla. 1993. *Gender Images in Public Administration: Legitimacy and the Administrative State.* Newbury Park, CA: Sage.

Stone, Deborah. 2002. *Policy Paradox: The Art of Political Decision Making,* revised edition. New York: Norton.

Svanström, Yvonne. 2004. "Criminalising the John—A Swedish Gender Model?" In *The Politics of Prostitution: Women's Movements, Democratic States, and the Globalisation of Sex Commerce,* edited by Joyce Outshoorn, 225–244. Cambridge: Cambridge University Press.

Tarrow, Sidney. 1983. *Struggling to Reform: Social Movements and Policy Change through Cycles of Protest.* Western Societies Program. Ithaca, NY: Cornell University.

————. 1989. *Struggle, Politics, and Reform: Collective Action, Social Movements, and Cycles of Protest.* Western Societies Program. Occasional Paper No. 21. Ithaca, NY: Cornell University Press.

————. 1994. *Power in Movement: Social Movements, Collective Action and Politics.* Cambridge: Cambridge University Press.

————. 1998. *Power in Movement. Social Movements, Political Opportunities, Mobilizing Structures, and Cultural Framings.* Cambridge: Cambridge University Press.

————. 2005. *The New Transnational Activism.* New York: Cambridge University Press.

Tashakkori, Abbas, and John W. Creswell. 2007. "Editorial: The New Era of Mixed Methods." *Journal of Mixed Methods Research* 1(3): 3–7.

Teghtsoonian, Kathy, and Joan Grace. 2001. "'Something More Is Necessary': The Mixed Achievements of Women's Policy Agencies in Canada." In *State Feminism, Women's Movements, and Job Training: Making Democracies Work in a Global Economy,* edited by Amy G. Mazur, 235–270. New York: Routledge.

Thelen, Kathleen. 2003. "How Institutions Evolve: Insights from Comparative Historical Analysis." In *Comparative Historical Analysis in the Social Sciences,* edited by James Mahoney and Dietrich Rueschemeyer, 208–240. Cambridge: Cambridge University Press.

Threlfall, Monica, ed. 1996. *Feminist Politics and Social Transformation in the North.* New York: Verso.

Tilly, Charles 1978. *From Mobilization to Revolution.* Reading, MA: Addison-Wesley.

Tolleson Rinehart, Sue. 1992. *Gender Consciousness and Politics.* New York: Routledge.

Tripp, Aili Mari. 2006. "The Evolution of Transnational Feminisms: Consensus, Conflict, and New Dynamics." In *Global Feminism: Transnational Women's Activism, Organiz-*

ing, and Human Rights, edited by Myra Marx Ferree and Aili M. Tripp, 51–75. New York: New York University Press.

Valiente, Celia. 1995 "The Power of Persuasion: The Instituto de la Mujer in Spain." In *Comparative State Feminism*, edited by Dorothy McBride Stetson and Amy G. Mazur, 221–236. Thousand Oaks, CA: Sage.

———. 2005. "The Women's Movement, Gender Equality Agencies and Central-State Debates on Political Representation in Spain." In *State Feminism and Political Representation*, edited by Joni Lovenduski et al., 216–238. Cambridge: Cambridge University Press.

———. 2007. "Developing Countries and New Democracies Matter: An Overview of Research on State Feminism Worldwide." *Politics and Gender* 3(4): 530–542.

Van Waarden, F. 1992. "Dimensions and Types of Policy Networks." *European Journal of Political Research* 21(1–2): 29–52,

Vargas, Virginia, and Saskia Wieringa. 1998. "The Triangle of Empowerment: Processes and Actors in the Making of Public Policy for Women." In *Women's Movements and Public Policy in Europe, Latin America, and the Caribbean*, edited by Geertje Lyclama à Nijeholt, Virginia Vargas, Saskia Wieringa, 3–23. New York: Garland.

Verloo, Mieke, and Emanuela Lombardo. 2007. "Contested Gender Equality and Policy Variety in Europe: Introducing a Critical Frame Analysis Approach" In *Multiple Meanings of Gender Equality. A Critical Frame Analysis of Gender Policies in Europe*, edited by Mieke Verloo, 21–49. New York: Central European University Press.

Wängnerud, Lena. 2000. "Testing the Politics of Presence: Women's Representation in the Swedish Riksdag." *Scandinavian Political Studies* 23(1): 67–91.

Watson, Sophie, ed. 1990. *Playing the State: Australian Feminist Interventions*. London: Verso.

Weldon, Laurel. 2002a. "Beyond Bodies: Institutional Sources of Representation for Women in Democratic Policymaking." *Journal of Politics* 64(4): 1153–1174.

———. 2002b. *Protest, Policy and the Problem of Violence against Women: a Cross National Comparison*. Pittsburgh: University of Pittsburgh Press.

———. 2008. "Intersectionality." In *Politics, Gender and Concepts: Theory and Methodology*, edited by Gary Goertz and Amy G. Mazur, 193–218. Cambridge: Cambridge University Press.

Whittier, Nancy. 1995. *Feminist Generations: The Persistence of the Radical Women's Movement*. Philadelphia: Temple University Press.

———. 2002. "Meaning and Structure in Social Movements." In *Social Movements: Identity, Culture, and the State*, edited by David S. Meyer, Nancy Whittier, and Belinda Robnett, 289–307. New York: Oxford University Press.

Wilson, Elizabeth. 1977. *Women and the Welfare State*. London: Tavistock Publications.

Woodward, Alison E. 2003. "Building Velvet Triangles: Gender and Informal Governance." In *Informal Governance in the European Union*, edited by Thomas Christiansen and Simona Piattoni, 76–93. Cheltenham, England: Edward Elgar.

———. 2007. "Speedy Belgians: The New Law of 2000 and the Impact of the Women's Movement." In *Gendering the State in the Age of Globalization: Women's Movements and State Feminism in Postindustrial Democracies*, edited by Melissa Haussman and Birgit Sauer, 59–77. Lanham, MD: Rowman and Littlefield.

Zald, Mayer N. 1996. "Culture, Ideology and Strategic Framing." In *Comparative Perspective on Social Movements: Political Opportunities, Mobilizing Structures, and Cultural Framings*, edited by Doug McAdam, John D. McCarthy, and Mayer N. Zald, 261–274. Cambridge: Cambridge University Press.

Index

Dorothy E. McBride (formerly Stetson) is Professor Emerita of Political Science at Florida Atlantic University and co-convener of the Research Network on Gender Politics and the State (RNGS). She is author of *Women's Rights in France* (1987), *Women's Rights in the U.S.A.* (2004), and *Abortion in the United States* (2008) and coeditor of *Comparative State Feminism* (1995).

Amy G. Mazur is C. O. Johnson Distinguished Professor in the Department of Political Science at Washington State University and co-convener of the Research Network on Gender Politics and the State and of the French Politics Group of the American Political Science Association. She is author of *Theorizing Feminist Policy* (2002) and coeditor of *Political Research Quarterly; Politics, Gender, and Concepts* (2008); and *The French Fifth Republic at Fifty* (2008).

Joni Lovenduski is Anniversary Professor of Politics at Birkbeck College, University of London, and a Fellow of the British Academy. She is author of *Women and European Politics* (1986) and *Feminizing Politics* (2005) and coauthor of *Contemporary Feminist Politics* (1993), *Political Recruitment* (1995), *High Time or High Tide for Labour Women* (1998), *Gender and Political Participation* (2004), and *The Hansard Report on Women at the Top* (2005). She is editor of *Feminism and Politics* (2000) and coeditor of *The Politics of the Second Electorate* (1981), *The New Politics of Abortion* (1986), *Gender and Party Politics* (1993), and *State Feminism and Political Representation* (2005).

Joyce Outshoorn is Professor of Women's Studies at the Joke Smit Institute for Research in Women's Studies at Leiden University and co-convenor of the Research Network on Gender Politics and the State. She is editor of *The Politics of Prostitution* (2004) and coeditor of *A Creative Tension* (1984), *The New Politics of Abortion* (1986), and *Changing State Feminism* (2007). She is also a contributor to *Abortion Politics, Women's Movements, and the Democratic State*, edited by Dorothy McBride Stetson (2001), and a co-contributor to *Gendering the State in the Age of Globalization*, edited by Melissa Haussman and Birgit Sauer (2007).

Birgit Sauer is Professor of Political Science at the University of Vienna. She is author of "What Happened to the Model Student?" in *Changing State Feminism*, edited by Joyce Outshoorn and Johanna Kantola (2007), and "Bringing the State Back In," in *Civil Society and Gender Justice*, edited by Karen Hagemann, Sonya Michel, and Gunilla Budde (2008), and coauthor of "Tu Felix Austria?" in *Social Politics* (2008), and "Headscarf Regimes in Europe," in *Comparative European Politics* (2009).

Marila Guadagnini is Professor of Political Science at the University of Turin. She is author of *Il sistema politico italiano* (1997), *La stagione del disincanto?* (2001), and *Da elettrici a elette* (2003); coauthor of *Un soffitto di cristallo?* (1999); and coeditor of *State Feminism and Political Representation* (2005). She has contributed numerous essays to collections in English, including *Comparative State Feminism*, edited by Dorothy McBride Stetson and Amy Mazur (1995); *State Feminism, Women's Movement, and Job Training*, edited by Amy Mazur (2001); *Gendering the State in the Age of Globalization*, edited by Melissa Haussman and Birgit Sauer (2007); and, as co-contributor, *Changing State Feminism*, edited by Joyce Outshoorn and Johanna Kantola (2007).